Challenges and Solutions of Using Quantum Security Frameworks for IoT Devices

Imdad Ali Shah
FEST, Iqra University, Pakistan

Noor Zaman Jhanjhi
https://orcid.org/0000-0001-8116-4733
Sunway University, Malaysia

IGI Global
Scientific Publishing
Publishing Tomorrow's Research Today

Vice President of Editorial Melissa Wagner
Director of Acquisitions Mikaela Felty
Director of Book Development Jocelynn Hessler
Production Manager Mike Brehm
Cover Design Jose Rosado

Published in the United States of America by
IGI Global Scientific Publishing
701 East Chocolate Avenue
Hershey, PA, 17033, USA
Tel: 717-533-8845 | Fax: 717-533-7115
Website: https://www.igi-global.com E-mail: cust@igi-global.com

Library of Congress Cataloging-in-Publication Data

LCCN: 2025022188 (CIP Data Pending)
ISBN13: 979-8-3373-3857-6
Isbn13Softcover: 979-8-3373-3858-3
EISBN13: 979-8-3373-3859-0
British Cataloguing in Publication Data
A Cataloguing in Publication record for this book is available from the British Library.

Table of Contents

Detailed Table of Contents

As the internet becomes essential for growth in the current times, ensuring network security and reliability stand as the biggest challenge for contemporary researchers. This chapter analyses two critical threats to any network, Distributed Denial of Service (DDoS) attacks and Flash Events(FE). The purpose of the denial-of-service attack is to bombard the target machine with more traffic than its capacity, which causes the server to become unavailable. Flash events are seemingly like DDoS attacks in high traffic, but legitimate users instead of attackers produce that volumetric traffic. In other words, Flash Events are generated organically whenever e-commerce platforms organise big sales, and Sometimes the system gets bogged down because of their incapability to manage high load. This is called a Flash Event. Given the underlying difference between the intent of DDoS attacks and Flash Events, it is very important to segregate DDoS attack traffic, Flash Event traffic and Normal/legitimate traffic so that corrective measures can be taken.

In light of the good outcomes of IoT architecture in all researched fields, we offer an intelligent, smart, and energy-efficient street road lighting system built on an IoT framework. It is made up of an LED light controller and a smart electric pole with an Internet of Things sensor base. We also achieve considerable energy savings by replacing conventional metal halide lamps with LED bulbs that have a mesophic design based on human eye sensitivity and complex decision-making modules employ PWM dimming systems to calculate intensity levels that produce pulses of varying widths based on information from sensor units that evaluate traffic movement and passenger presence or absence. Through DALI controllers housed within LED light controllers, these pulses subsequently activate LED power switches. To make effective use of sustainable energy resources, we use sustainable power systems, which are composed of PV solar panel units, battery storage systems, and smart electric power grids.

The proliferation of Internet of Things (IoT) devices has heightened concerns about data security, particularly in resource-constrained environments vulnerable to quantum-enabled attacks. This chapter proposes an AI-driven adaptive framework for lightweight, quantum-safe security protocols tailored to low-power IoT systems. By integrating post-quantum cryptography with artificial intelligence, the framework dynamically adjusts encryption strength, resource allocation, and threat response. The design emphasizes energy efficiency, scalability, and resilience against emerging quantum-era vulnerabilities. Through conceptual modeling, experimental validation, and case studies, the chapter demonstrates how adaptive, intelligent security mechanisms can ensure sustainable, secure IoT deployment in critical sectors such as healthcare, logistics, and smart infrastructure.

The convergence of quantum computing and metaverse technologies offers transformative opportunities for secure, scalable, and intelligent communication infrastructures. As metaverse platforms become more immersive and decentralized, supporting real-time voice, video, and biometric data, classical cryptography and computation encounter limitations in privacy, scalability, and trust. This chapter explores how quantum computing and communication techniques can overcome these constraints by enabling unbreakable encryption, quantum-safe identity verification, and high-efficiency processing for multi-user virtual environments. Foundational principles of quantum computing and communication are reviewed, followed by an analysis of quantum algorithms' implications for traditional cryptography. Key areas include post-quantum cryptography, quantum key distribution, and quantum secure direct communication adapted to metaverse infrastructure. Special focus is given to avatar authentication, secure asset transfers, and quantum-enabled decentralized identity systems.

The integration of quantum computing into financial systems marks a transformative leap in risk management, security, and market operations. Unlike classical computing, quantum algorithms can process vast datasets and complex models at unprecedented speeds, enabling real-time risk analytics, rapid fraud detection, and optimized trading strategies. This study explores the emerging field of quantum-driven finance, focusing on its potential to enhance predictive accuracy, reduce systemic vulnerabilities, and accelerate decision-making in volatile markets. Applications such as quantum-enhanced Monte Carlo simulations, quantum machine learning for anomaly detection, and optimization in algorithmic trading are examined alongside challenges in scalability, cybersecurity, and regulatory adaptation. By evaluating current advancements and future prospects, this research highlights quantum computing's role in shaping a secure, intelligent, and high-velocity global financial ecosystem.

Generative AI and its role in developing deepfake technologies are of great concern due to the threats to digital authenticity, privacy and information security caused by the rapid growth of deepfake technology. Classical detection systems have also advanced to detect manipulated content, but with the advent of quantum computing, new vulnerabilities are created along with new opportunities to defend against the vulnerabilities. In this chapter, quantum technologies are discussed in terms of how they intersect with deepfake detection systems and examine some of the risks associated with quantum-enhanced deepfake production as well as cryptographic breakage and manipulation of the training data. In response, it explores quantum secure paradigms such as QML, QKD and PQC algorithms. Quantum resistant protocols and hybrid classical-quantum detection models are argued to be the possible way of the future.

The integration of Artificial Intelligence (AI) and the Internet of Things (IoT) is transforming digital ecosystems, offering automation, predictive intelligence, and real-time decision-making. However, increasing interconnectivity raises serious concerns about data security, privacy, and trust. This chapter introduces the AI-IoT Security Integration Framework (AISIF), a multi-layered architecture combining AI-based analytics, blockchain-led trust management, and quantum-secure encryption to build resilient and privacy-preserving systems. The framework employs federated learning for secure data collaboration, Quantum Key Distribution (QKD) for encryption, and explainable AI for transparent decision-making. Through two case studies smart healthcare and smart grid systems the framework demonstrates improvements in anomaly detection accuracy, latency reduction, and intrusion response efficiency. The findings highlight that integrating AI intelligence with quantum security ensures sustainable, trustworthy, and adaptive IoT infrastructures for future intelligent environments.

As swarm robotics evolves into a paradigm-shifting approach for distributed autonomous systems, communication vulnerabilities pose risks in hostile environments. Conventional cryptography is limited by decentralized nature, energy constraints, and node density, while quantum computing threatens public-key encryption via Shor's algorithm. This chapter explores Quantum Key Distribution (QKD) and entanglement-based networking for information-theoretic security. We examine mobile quantum networks, highlighting drone-based relays and satellite links. Beyond security, quantum principles like superposition and entanglement can enhance swarm intelligence, task allocation, and coordination. Despite promising validations, hurdles remain: SWaP constraints, atmospheric interference, and mobility-induced decoherence. Through case studies in aerial, maritime, space, and disaster domains,

Preface

INTRODUCTION

The rapid evolution of digital technologies has transformed the modern world into an interconnected ecosystem driven by the Internet of Things (IoT), Artificial Intelligence (AI), cloud computing, blockchain, and emerging quantum technologies. While these innovations have accelerated automation, intelligence, and efficiency across industries, they have simultaneously introduced unprecedented security challenges. As quantum computing advances toward practical realization, the cryptographic foundations that currently secure digital infrastructures face significant risks. Conventional encryption schemes, which have long protected sensitive communications and data exchanges, are increasingly vulnerable to quantum-enabled attacks. Consequently, organizations, researchers, and policymakers must prepare for a future in which quantum-resistant security mechanisms become essential rather than optional.

The Internet of Things represents one of the most critical domains affected by this transition. Billions of connected devices operate within healthcare systems, smart cities, industrial automation, transportation networks, financial ecosystems, and consumer applications. Many of these devices possess limited computational resources, making the implementation of robust security mechanisms particularly challenging. The emergence of quantum computing compounds these concerns, necessitating the development of innovative frameworks that balance security, scalability, efficiency, and adaptability. Addressing these challenges requires multidisciplinary approaches that integrate post-quantum cryptography, quantum communication technologies, artificial intelligence, blockchain systems, and advanced network architectures.

This edited volume, *Challenges and Solutions of Using Quantum Security Frameworks for IoT Devices*, brings together contributions from distinguished researchers and practitioners across multiple countries and disciplines. The chapters collectively examine the opportunities, challenges, and future directions associated with securing next-generation digital ecosystems against quantum-era threats. The contributors present theoretical foundations, practical frameworks, implementation strategies, and application-oriented case studies that demonstrate how quantum technologies can enhance resilience across diverse sectors.

The primary objective of this book is to provide a comprehensive reference for researchers, academicians, cybersecurity professionals, engineers, policymakers, and graduate students interested in understanding the evolving relationship between quantum computing and IoT security. By exploring both technical innovations and implementation challenges, this volume aims to facilitate meaningful discussions and inspire future research toward building secure, trustworthy, and sustainable digital infrastructures capable of thriving in the post-quantum era.

OVERVIEW OF THE CHAPTERS

Chapter 1, *A Quantum-Safe Security Framework for IoT - Integrating PQC, QKD, and AI for Resilient Post-Quantum Environments*, establishes the foundation of the book by introducing a comprehensive security framework that combines Post-Quantum Cryptography (PQC), Quantum Key Distribution (QKD), and Artificial Intelligence (AI). The chapter addresses vulnerabilities of traditional cryptographic systems and proposes adaptive mechanisms to secure resource-constrained IoT environments against future quantum threats.

Chapter 2, *AI and the Internet of Things (IoT) Security: Protecting Connected Devices in an Autonomous Era*, explores the transformative role of artificial intelligence in securing IoT ecosystems. The author discusses machine learning, deep learning, and federated learning techniques for intrusion detection, anomaly identification, and proactive threat mitigation, while also examining practical challenges and future developments.

Chapter 3, *Blockchain and AI Convergence for Securing IoT Networks*, investigates the integration of blockchain technology and AI to create decentralized, intelligent, and trustworthy IoT security architectures. The chapter highlights identity management, tamper-proof auditing, predictive threat analytics, and governance mechanisms enabled through this convergence.

Chapter 4, *Challenges and Barriers to Implementing Quantum Security Frameworks in Healthcare Systems*, focuses on one of the most sensitive application domains of IoT. The chapter examines technical, organizational, and operational obstacles associated with deploying quantum-resistant security solutions within healthcare infrastructures while emphasizing the protection of patient data and medical devices.

Chapter 5, *Flash Events and DDoS Attacks: Understanding Network Overload and Cybersecurity Threats*, presents an analytical discussion of two major causes of network disruption. The authors examine methods for distinguishing between malicious DDoS attacks and legitimate traffic surges generated by flash events, thereby contributing to improved network resilience and incident response strategies.

Chapter 6, *Hybrid Quantum-Classical Computing for Future Network Optimization in Smart City*, introduces innovative approaches for optimizing smart city infrastructures through hybrid computing paradigms. The chapter highlights energy-efficient IoT-enabled street lighting systems and demonstrates how intelligent resource management can support sustainable urban development.

Chapter 7, *Lightweight Quantum-Safe Security Protocols for Resource-Constrained IoT Devices: An AI-Driven Adaptive Framework*, addresses the practical limitations of low-power IoT devices by proposing adaptive quantum-safe security mechanisms that dynamically balance security requirements with resource consumption.

Chapter 8, *Quantum Computing for Secure and Scalable Metaverse Communications*, explores the intersection of quantum technologies and emerging metaverse ecosystems. The chapter examines secure identity management, privacy-preserving communication, asset protection, and quantum-enhanced cryptographic solutions for immersive virtual environments.

Chapter 9, *Quantum Driven Finance Revolution Shaping the Future of Risk Intelligence, Security and Market Speed*, investigates the transformative impact of quantum computing on financial systems. The authors discuss applications in fraud detection, risk modeling, algorithmic trading, and financial security while highlighting challenges associated with adoption and governance.

Chapter 10, *Quantum-Resilient Deepfake Detection: Securing AI-Generated Media in the Post-Quantum Era*, addresses the growing threat of synthetic media and misinformation. The chapter evaluates how quantum technologies may both amplify and mitigate deepfake risks through advanced detection frameworks and quantum-secure verification mechanisms.

Chapter 11, *Quantum-Secured AI-IoT Frameworks: Building Trusted, Adaptive, and Privacy-Preserving Ecosystems*, presents a comprehensive architecture that integrates AI analytics, blockchain-enabled trust management, federated learning, and quantum-secure encryption. Through practical case studies, the chapter demonstrates how these technologies can strengthen resilience and trustworthiness in intelligent systems.

Chapter 12, *Securing Swarm Robotics Communication Using Quantum*, examines the unique communication challenges associated with autonomous robotic swarms. The authors propose quantum-enhanced architectures leveraging QKD, entanglement-based networking, and hybrid trust models to support mission-critical operations across diverse environments.

Finally, Chapter 13, *Transforming Healthcare Through Quantum Computing Innovations*, concludes the technical discussions by highlighting the transformative potential of quantum computing in healthcare. The chapter explores applications ranging from drug discovery and precision medicine to medical imaging and data analytics, demonstrating how quantum technologies may revolutionize future healthcare systems.

CONCLUSION

The transition toward the quantum era represents both a significant challenge and an extraordinary opportunity for the cybersecurity community. While quantum computing threatens many of the cryptographic mechanisms that currently safeguard digital infrastructures, it also offers powerful tools for building more secure, intelligent, and resilient systems. The contributions presented in this volume collectively illustrate that the path toward quantum-secure IoT ecosystems requires collaboration across disciplines, industries, and geographical boundaries.

A recurring theme throughout the chapters is the importance of integrating multiple technologies rather than relying on isolated solutions. Post-quantum cryptography, quantum key distribution, artificial intelligence, blockchain, federated learning, and hybrid computing architectures each contribute unique capabilities that strengthen security, privacy, and operational resilience. Together, these technologies form the foundation of future digital ecosystems capable of addressing evolving cyber threats while supporting large-scale connectivity and automation.

The diverse application domains discussed in this book—including healthcare, smart cities, finance, metaverse platforms, swarm robotics, and industrial IoT—demonstrate the widespread implications of quantum security research. These sectors are increasingly dependent on interconnected devices and data-driven decision-making processes, making the development of quantum-resilient infrastructures a strategic necessity. The insights presented by the contributing authors offer valuable guidance for researchers and practitioners seeking to navigate this complex technological transition.

As editors, we hope this volume serves as a meaningful resource for advancing knowledge, fostering innovation, and stimulating future research in quantum-safe security frameworks. We extend our sincere appreciation to all contributing authors, reviewers, and academic institutions whose expertise and dedication made this publication possible. It is our expectation that the ideas presented in this book will contribute to the development of secure, trustworthy, and sustainable digital ecosystems capable of meeting the demands of an increasingly connected and quantum-enabled world.

Imdad Ali Shah
Iqra University, Pakistan

Noor Zaman Jhanjhi
Sunway University, Malaysia

Chapter 1

A Quantum-Safe Security Framework for IoT: Integrating PQC, QKD, and AI for Resilient Post-Quantum Environments

R. N. Ravikumar
http://orcid.org/0009-0009-3705-1681
Marwadi University, Rajkot, India

S. Aarthi
http://orcid.org/0009-0006-9064-2091
Marwadi University, Rajkot, India

Azamat Abduraxmanov
Termez University of Economics and Service, Termez, Uzbekistan

Ruzmetova Gulira'no Atabekovna
Mamun University, Khiva, Uzbekistan

Khayrulla Urozboev
Alfraganus University, Tashkent, Uzbekistan

S. Kavitha Bharathi
http://orcid.org/0000-0002-5630-7963
Kongu Engineering College, Erode, India

ABSTRACT

The rapid advancement of quantum computing threatens the foundations of classical cryptography, creating severe risks for resource-constrained IoT systems widely used in healthcare, autonomous vehicles, and industrial automation. Conventional algorithms like RSA and ECC are vulnerable to Shor's and Grover's algorithms, exposing IoT to passive and active quantum-based attacks. This manuscript proposes a quantum-safe framework integrating Post-Quantum Cryptography (PQC), Quantum Key Distribution (QKD), and Artificial Intelligence (AI) to ensure confidentiality, integrity, and resilience. The framework leverages lattice, hash, and code-based PQC, lightweight cryptographic protocols, hybrid security models, and efficient

DOI: 10.4018/979-8-3373-3857-6.ch001

key management to protect IoT communications. By combining PQC, QKD, and AI-driven adaptive security, the framework offers scalable, sustainable, and future-proof protection in the post-quantum era.

1. INTRODUCTION

The accelerated rate of Quantum Computing (QC) developments generates the transformation opportunity, and the safety of dubious cyber security, mostly in the case of the IoT. The importance of proper security measures cannot be overestimated since the modern infrastructure such as smart houses, necessary healthcare and industrial automations systems has become a ubiquitous implementation of IoT devices. The IIOT devices, unlike the traditional computing systems, have a higher probability of working in highly constrained environments with regards to memory, constraint of processing and energy capacity. Such limitations expose them to more and more quantum-based attacks at an outrageous rate. The modern digital security is based on RSA and ECC classic cryptography protocols that will become outdated by quantum algorithms such as the Shor algorithm which is becoming a reality (Kumari et al., 2022). The risk of quantum decryption is impending and the planet earth relocation of the center table to Post Quantum Cryptographic (PQC) solutions will be a requirement to get the integrity, secrecy and authenticity of information in a post-quantum world. The chapter deals with the most urgent problem of the development and implementation of quantum resilient security frameworks of IoT. It proposes simple post-quantum strategies (Lightweight Cryptography, Quantum Key Distribution (QKD) and AI-based adaptive security systems that will help to design secure and sustainable IoT ecologies in the post-quantum environment (Kumari et al., 2022). (Peng et al., 2024).

1.1 Overview of QC Advancements

QC, along with, a monumental advance in the service of the capacity to commit computations in line with the quantum statutes, including superposition and entanglement. Quantum computers are the opposite of classic computers that are capable of processing bits only, i.e. 0 or 1, because qubits in quantum computers can be concurrently in any of a number of states. It means that quantum systems will resolve particular complicated issues exponentially quicker than the traditional ones. The discoveries of the past few years were characterized by the discoveries of IBM, Google and start-ups in the field of qubit stability, error correction and quantum volume. As these developments are occurring the world is even getting close to the quantum supremacy level where the quantum computer is able to do the things that the classical computer is incapable of doing. Even in its childish form, nonetheless, QC is developing rapidly enough to be a major challenge even in such fields as cryptography, optimization and simulation.

1.2 The Growing Threat to Cybersecurity, Particularly in IoT Environments

QC upsurge can threaten the very pillars of the modern cyber security. Such algorithms as Shor can break standard systems that are deployed, including RSA that is employed in communication, financial transaction and authentication as public key cryptographic systems that extensively employs Elliptic Curve Cryptography (ECC). Particularly, IoT environments are susceptible due to flaws incorporated into the design. These devices tend to operate on the scarcity of resources, lack of good update systems and in most cases operate on outdated or minimal encryption (Aarthi et al., 2025). Further, their extensive use in exposed and mostly unsecured environments including smart cities, healthcare facilities, and critical infrastructure make them very profitable to quantum-enabled attacks. The limited hardware coupled to enormous data transfer is a recipe for passive surveillance and active tampering of IoT ecosystems once QC is within easy reach (Guitouni et al., 2024).

1.3 Importance of Transitioning from Traditional to Post-Quantum Security Frameworks

With QC at hand, choosing for post-quantum security framework is no longer a choice, but a necessity. Traditional cryptographic algorithms are not quantum resistant and have to be replaced one day. To avoid such situation, known as the "harvest now, decrypt later" Trojan Horse, this transition needs to begin long before quantum computers are fully functional. The Post Quantum Cryptography (PQC) provides the new cryptographic techniques, that are resistant to the quantum as well as classical attacks (Pandit et al., 2025). These are lattice-based, hash based, code-based, and multivariate polynomial cryptosystems. Lightweight and efficient PQC schemes should be adopted in the IoT systems because of the constraint in power and bandwidth. Besides algorithmic changes, the entire infrastructure on security in organizations should be reconsidered with key distribution, authentication, and system resilience to allow organizations to shift to the post-quantum era (Andrae, 2025).

2. QUANTUM VULNERABILITIES IN IOT

Internet of Things (IoT) has revolutionized the contemporary lifestyle with the introduction of intelligence and connection into the mainstream of any item of our life, household appliances and wearable devices, critical infrastructure and industrial systems. However, with the increase in the number of devices utilized in IoT, it implies that with improved risks, more attention should be paid to QC progress. There is a general tendency of IoT devices to operate in resource-poor environments that have limited memory, processing capabilities, and energy storage. Because of this, they are likely to rely on those that are lightweight and outdated and protocol that place emphasis on speed and simplicity rather than on robustness. These are conventional protocols such as RSA and ECC that are highly susceptible to cracking with quantum algorithms. For instance, the Shor's algorithm makes it easy for a quantum computer to factor large integer and also be able to solve discrete logarithms hence breaking RSA. Also, it solves ECC with ease. This would be compromising not only encrypted data, but also mechanisms of authentication, IoT communication integrity. Also, most IoT devices do not have secure update capabilities, and it is hard to update vulnerabilities once installed. These "set-and-forget" devices can turn out to be liabilities for long-term in a post-quantum world. Their omnipresence in un/ public networks increases the threat, the adversaries possessing the quantum capabilities become able to conduct both passive attacks (listening to the communications) and active ones (data/ device manipulation). And the other one is long term secret of the sensitive data (Ravikumar & Aarthi, 2025). Data transmitted today encrypted by a weak algorithm might be stolen and stored by bad people, with the intention of decrypting it in the future when quantum computing is accessible: so-called harvest now, decrypt later. The cumulative impact of these weaknesses is that the existing situation of the IoT systems is such that they are not ready to withstand the disruptive capability of QC. It is important to implement a proactive move towards quantum resilient security measure to prevent systemic weakness throughout industries to critical infrastructures (Abomhara et al., 2015). The figure 1 illustrates how quantum threats impact vulnerable IoT devices, leading to security risks, and highlights possible cryptographic mitigations.

Figure 1. IoT Quantum Threat Model

2.1 Characteristics of IoT Devices (Limited Computation, Memory, Energy)

The purpose of IoT devices is to work with minimal resource consumption, yet there is a heavy price to such a design. The majority of appliances operate based on low-power microcontrollers that have low computing power, and it is challenging to provide a high level of cryptographic keys. They also have limited memory, storage capabilities and have very little RAM and limited space hence cannot run heavy security measures (Ravikumar et al., 2025). Moreover, several IoT gadgets are based on batteries or energy-gathering frameworks and, thus, require great energy effectiveness and limit their opportunities to execute resource-sensitive security measures. Such restriction forces developers to consider lightweight security systems that concentrate more on performance over security, hence leaving the device more vulnerable especially with the anticipated increased threats of Quantum Computing (QC) in the foreseeable future (Istiaque Ahmed et al., 2021). The figure 2 highlights the key characteristics of IoT devices limited computational power, restricted memory and storage, and low energy availability that drive the need for lightweight and efficient operations.

Figure 2. Key Features of IoT Devices

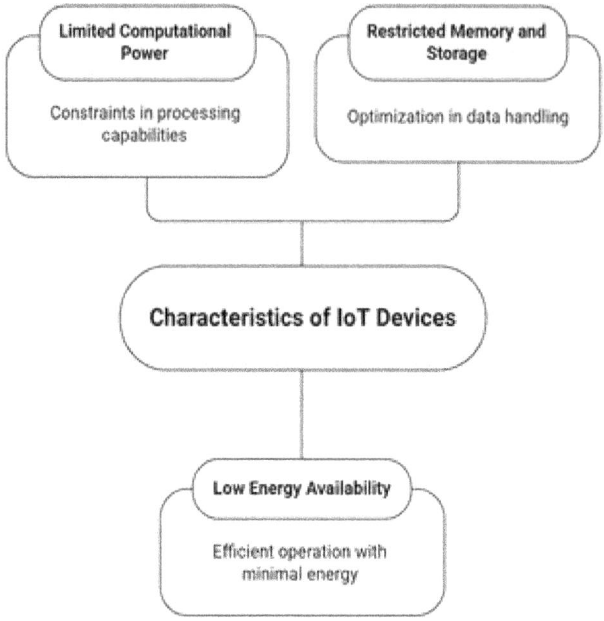

2.2 Risks from Active and Passive Quantum-Based Attacks

As Quantum Computing (QC) continues to develop, two significant types of attacks can be posed to the IoT systems: passive and active quantum-based threats. In passive attacks, attackers have the power to intercept the encrypted communications sent by the IoT devices and archive them to be used later. Although this data can be kept safe nowadays, as quantum computers are invented, the algorithms such as the Shor can break through and allow the decryption of the information, which can be collected now and decrypted later. Active attacks on the other hand are attacks by malicious actors who take advantage of some vulnerabilities in the existing cryptographic schemes to impersonate authorized devices, take control, inject malicious commands, or maliciously disrupt the services by cracking the digital signatures and authentication keys (Ashirova et al., 2026). Both passive and active attacks have been shown to be much more possible and serious due to the huge computational power of quantum systems and can be critically dangerous at both device and network levels of IoT infrastructures (Awasthi, 2025). The table 1 compares passive and active quantum-based attacks on IoT systems, their mechanisms, algorithms used, and resulting security impacts.

Table 1. Quantum-Based Attack Types on IoT Devices

Attack Type	Description	Example Quantum Algorithm Used	Impact on IoT Systems
Passive Attack	Intercepts and stores encrypted data for future decryption	Shor's	Loss of confidentiality
Active Attack	Tampering or impersonating devices using cracked keys	Shor's, Grover's	Device hijacking, false commands

2.3 Limitations of Current Cryptographic Protocols

Existing IoT security is strongly based on the public-key cryptographic modes like RSA and Elliptic Curve Cryptography (ECC). RSA is founded on the mathematical complexity of breaking down the prime numbers, where the ECC is founded on the complexity of solving the discrete logarithmic problem on elliptic curves. These are said to be very resistant to classical computers, but extremely susceptible to quantum computing. The Algorithm suggested by Shor is the most dangerous threat as it is efficient to break both RSA and ECC in the time of polyonomies, technically invalidating any security the algorithms could offer. Likewise, the Algorithm of Grover is not so devastating but capable of giving a significant boost to searches by brutality of symmetric encryption keys, meaning that very strong keys are required to ensure sufficient security. Since many of the IoT devices are likely based on such standards and cannot typically be updated with cryptographic updates in time, the rise of quantum computing poses a grave threat in the long run to IoT infrastructures (Hadi et al., 2023).

3. POST-QUANTUM CRYPTOGRAPHY (PQC)

Post-Quantum Cryptography may also be described as a new type of cryptographic algorithm that is not vulnerable to classical as well as quantum attacks. Unlike the conventional algorithms, e.g., RSA and ECC which have a mathematical problem, e.g., prime factorization and discrete logarithms, computationally feasible using the Shor Algorithm, PQC is built on mathematical assumptions, which are believed to be unsolvable by quantum computation. They are difficult challenges of lattice-based cryptography, code-based cryptography, hash-based encryptions and multivariate polygraph cryptography. PQC ensures the confidentiality and integrity of long-term data even with a quantum computer of scale by basing on quantum-resistant primitives. PQC offers a feasible channel that can be employed to defend the future communication systems against quantum-enabled attacks as the IoT devices are highly vulnerable (Sreerangapuri, 2024).

3.1 Need for PQC in IoT Environments

The fast development of Quantum Computing (QC) can prove to be a critical threat to the sphere of IoT, since the current cryptographic protocols will be out of the game in the nearest future. The IoT environments are made up of millions of remotely deployed and networked devices that are highly susceptible as a result of the lack of regular firmware updates, the long lifespan of the devices as well as their dependence on preinstalled cryptographic protocol. All these aspects put it so hard to migrate to more secure solutions in time. To offer a proactive security layer, Post-Quantum Cryptography (PQC) proposed quantum-resistant algorithms that guarantee the data confidentiality, device authentication, and system integrity of the whole lifecycle of IoT devices. PQC deployment to the IoT environment is hence essential in ensuring that future proof security is achieved against emerging quantum-based threats (Rafique et al., 2024).

3.2 Applications of PQC

The Post-Quantum Cryptography (PQC) ensures high protection in diverse areas against quantum age threats. It enables safe email banking, conversation and web traffic since it is capable of preventing quantum-based eavesdropping. PQC is a substitute of RSA and ECC to secure key exchange, certificate authorities and digital signatures in Public-Key Infrastructure (PKI). It enables quantum resistant digital signature to check documents and transactions and encryption schemes to protect sensitive data in the banking, healthcare and government industries. PQC too secures blockchain and crypto-based systems, ensures quantum-safe cloud-computing, and the internet of things-based communications are not vulnerable to vulnerabilities. In addition, PQC increases the integrity, privacy and trust of the electronic democratic procedures (Bounmy & Sisavath, 2023). This table outlines the key applications of Post-Quantum Cryptography (PQC) across domains such as communication, PKI, IoT, and cloud computing. It emphasizes PQC's role in ensuring data confidentiality, authenticity, and resilience against quantum threats.

Table 2. Applications of Post-Quantum Cryptography (PQC) Across Domains

Application Area	Description	Impact
Secure Communication	Protects emails, messaging systems, and web traffic from quantum-based eavesdropping	Ensures confidentiality of transmitted data
Public-Key Infrastructure	Replaces RSA/ECC with PQC algorithms for key exchange, digital signatures, and certificate authority	Provides quantum-safe PKI and authentication
Digital Signatures	Offers quantum-resistant verification of documents and transactions	Strengthens authenticity and trust
Encryption	Supports secure data protection against quantum assaults in sensitive sectors	Secures banking, healthcare, and government information
Blockchain & Cryptocurrencies	Ensures integrity and security of blockchain transactions and crypto systems	Protects decentralized finance and digital assets
Quantum-Safe Cloud Computing	Safeguards cloud storage and data processing from quantum threats	Maintains confidentiality and resilience of cloud infrastructures
Internet of Things (IoT)	Protects IoT communications and device data from quantum vulnerabilities	Enhances security of interconnected devices
Secure Voting Systems	Provides quantum-resistant mechanisms for electronic voting	Ensures privacy, integrity, and reliability of democratic processes

3.3 Types of Post-Quantum Algorithms

Post-quantum Cryptography (PQC) is a collection of several families of algorithms that are not yet standardized or tested by such bodies as the NIST. Lattice-Based Cryptography, which is built on the hard problem of Learning with Errors (LWE) and Ring-LWE), and provides implementation of such algorithms as CRYSTALS-Kyber (encryption) and CRYSTALS-Dilithium (digital signatures) is the most promising of them. The case of Hash-Based Cryptography is the SPHINCS which is secure provided that the hash functions are secure but requires larger signatures and can be slow. Code-Based Cryptography: This is the type of cryptography that is proven to be secure with long-lasting time, but the key size is very large, such as Classic McEliece. Lastly, Multivariate Polynomial Cryptography that is denoted by Rainbow utilizes quadratic equations, and offers resource-efficiency in the signatures. The two methods possess a speed, key size, energy consumption, and memory footprint trade-offs which is necessary in adopting the IoT (Sun, 2024). The table 3 summarizes the major types of Post-Quantum Cryptography (PQC) algorithms, highlighting examples, strengths, and weaknesses. It illustrates the trade-offs between efficiency, security, key sizes, and implementation suitability for IoT systems.

Table 3. Comparison of Classical and Post-Quantum Cryptographic Algorithms

Algorithm Type	Example	Strengths	Weaknesses
Lattice-Based	CRYSTALS-Kyber, Dilithium	Efficient, strong quantum resistance	Larger key sizes
Hash-Based	SPHINCS+	Very secure, mature cryptographic base	Slow, large signatures
Code-Based	Classic McEliece	Long-standing security proofs	Extremely large key sizes
Multivariate Polynomial	Rainbow	Resource-efficient for signatures	Less mature, implementation concerns

3.4 Challenges in PQC Implementation for IoT

Post- Quantum Cryptography (PQC) is resistant to quantum attacks, and has tremendous implementation issues in the IoT. Another key factor that should not be overlooked is the enlarged key sizes as most PQC algorithms require significantly larger keys that are not only two-three times larger but are also very heavy to the memory and communication bandwidth of limited devices. The other challenge is the computational cost since IoT devices typically possess a limited processing power and challenging cryptographic tasks are challenging to execute without affecting the performance or power consumption. Even the lack of standard finalisation is a barrier; organizations and industries may hold back until NIST and other organisations can issue fully standardised standards before they can switch to some PQC algorithms (Gitonga, 2025). These challenges explain why the implementation of PQC in constrained IoT ecosystems is challenging. The figure 4 highlights the key challenges of implementing PQC in IoT systems, namely increased key sizes, computational overhead, and lack of standardization. Table 4 outlines the main challenges of implementing PQC in IoT, including large key sizes, computational overhead, standardization delays, and compatibility issues.

Figure 3. Challenges in PQC

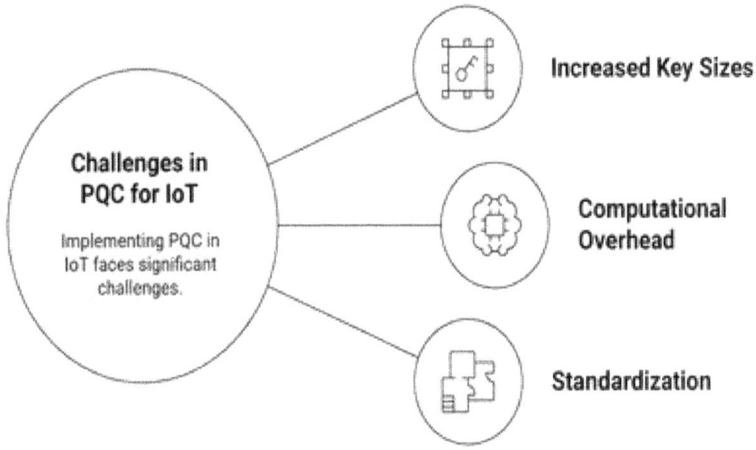

Table 4. Challenges in Implementing PQC in IoT

Challenge	Explanation
Key Size Overhead	PQC keys are larger, requiring more memory and bandwidth
Computational Overhead	PQC algorithms demand more processing than lightweight devices can offer
Standardization Delays	Full adoption pending NIST's finalized PQC recommendations
Compatibility	Difficult to retrofit PQC into legacy IoT systems

3.5 Security of PQC

There are numerous challenges that Post-Quantum Cryptography (PQC) is experiencing, and its implementation requires mitigation. PQC algorithms have to be quantum resistant to challenges of the Shor algorithm and Grover algorithm and also classical resistant to remain safe until quantum computers of large scale can become a reality. The key size is being a significant factor affecting efficiency and performance, which is particularly important in resource-constrained IoT. PQC systems that are hybridized with classical methods are advised at the transition stage. The post-quantum security needs to be analyzed continuously to detect the vulnerability like side channel attacks. In addition, NIST standardization is needed to be global, whereas interoperability and performance optimization are needed to introduce PQC into the existing infrastructures in a smooth way that would provide long-term protection (R. Liu et al., 2022).

4. QUANTUM KEY DISTRIBUTION (QKD)

QKD is a quantum cryptology technique of using quantum mechanics' concepts for two individuals to securely share cryptographic keys. Whereas has come in the traditional forms of the key sharing but has since been changed by the use of the quantum bits (qubits) that are under the regulations of quantum physics hence if any person is intercepting the message in any way will be detected. QKD bases itself on the behaviour of particles of quantum nature, i.e. photons, they can exist in superposition states and they can have quantum entanglement (Ravikumar et al., 2026). QKD is secure because eavesdropping can be detected using the knowledge that the measurement process of a quantum system will influence it. Typical QKD protocols are the most famous protocol BB84 (created by Charles Bennett and Gilles Brassard in 1984) and E91, that is based on quantum entanglement (invented by Artur Ekert in 1991) (Fernandez-Carames, 2020a).

4.1 Basic Principles of QKD

`The quantum communication utilizes the peculiarities of the physical laws to ensure the safe exchange of information. Quantum superposition The qubits may be prepared in a large number of states simultaneously and information may be encoded in such a way that it will collapse to a quantum state, which is measurable, when measured (Fernandez-Carames, 2020). Quantum entanglement relates particles in a manner that when a system alters the state of one another, the other will instantly alter regardless of the distance and it is a secure process of key exchange between the parties. Moreover, the Uncertainty Principle of Heisenberg is the principle which ensures that the act of measuring or intercepting a quantum system disrupts its state and therefore can be observed. Together with these principles, it leads to the creation of quantum-safe and unbreakable communication systems.

4.2 Key QKD Protocols

Two of the best-known Quantum Key Distribution (QKD) protocols are BB84 and E91, both of which make use of the quantum principles in order to communicate with security. The BB84 protocol entails Alice encoding random bits (0 and 1) in qubits either along the rectilinear basis of the form + or along the diagonal basis of the form X. Bob makes such qubit measurements without information about the basis that Alice used. Once transmitted, Alice and Bob match their bases using a classical channel and the results that match constitute the secret key that they share. In contrast, E91 protocol makes use of pairs of entangled photons, each being received by Alice and Bob. The polarization states are what define the key and since entanglement is nonlocal then any interception of it is bound to ruin the correlation and all it takes is to easily find out security is compromised (Senekane et al., 2015).

4.3 Security of QKD

Quantum Key Distribution (QKD) security is grounded in the laws of quantum mechanics and not the computational complexity of mathematical problems, in classical cryptography. One of its unique features is the detection of eavesdropping because any activity of an eavesdropper (Eve) to measure qubits will lead to a modification in the quantum states, which will subsequently lead to some errors to be identified in the shared key. The No-Cloning Theorem is another pillar and it explains that it is impossible to perfectly copy a quantum state, and Eve cannot perfectly copy the qubits without being exposed. Moreover, QKD has been shown to offer information-theoretic security, i.e. its protection is not based upon the complexity of the algorithm, but rather on physical law. Therefore, the privacy and integrity guaranteed by QKD cannot be violated even in case of an unlimited source of computational power (Fedorov et al., 2018).

4.4 Applications of QKD

Quantum Key Distribution (QKD) has become a backbone of the next-generation secure communication and it can be used to protect the most sensitive information, including financial, military, and personal data. QKD takes advantage of the concept of quantum to make sure that any interception is detected instantly, thus it can be heavily relied on by mission critical systems. In addition to single connections, QKD is the main concentration in quantum networks, which are expected to be the groundwork of the future quantum internet that can transfer and distribute ultra-secure information over long distances. Although QKD may be implemented as a complete cryptographic system on its own, it is often observed that it is used with classical cryptography like RSA or AES to strengthen the key exchange protocols. This is an efficient compromise between the classical efficiency and the quantum-level security, which will guarantee bountifulness in the face of threats as they evolve (Dere & Ülkü, 2023).

4.5 Challenges and Limitations

Quantum Key Distribution (QKD) has a set of limitations and limitations, even though it has a promise, which prevent its large-scale implementation. The main problem lies in the distance limitation because quantum information can be destroyed at a long distance because of the optically fibre loss or the free space loss of photons. As a way of reducing this, sophisticated technologies such as quantum repeaters and satellite-based QKD systems are being developed but they are still in experimental phases. The second important issue is the complexity of the implementation, as quantum states control as necessary in QKD systems design and maintenance is expensive and complex equipment. There is also the significant obstacle of scalability; although QKD has been demonstrated in short-range applications successfully, there is still research and development of its implementation in large-scale networks. These obstacles have to be overcome to become global (A. Liu et al., 2024).

5. AI AND MACHINE LEARNING INTEGRATION

The threat detection, prevention, and response are well-presented as AI and ML are used in the process of cybersecurity. Algorithms of atomic intelligence analyze large volumes of data, at any given time and detects trends and abnormalities that can be indicators of cyberattack (including, phishing, malware, or ransomware). ML models keep on learning about their past threats and as time goes on, they keep gaining more and more investigative and responding capabilities. To develop dynamic adaptive security systems that develop defense to the changing threats, they are employed to these technologies (Shreha et al., 2025). To illustrate, AI controlled systems are in a position to automatically update firewalls or intrusion detection system whenever new vulnerabilities are exposed. In addition, predictive analytics as an aspect of AI and ML predicts future risks relying on the trend in the pattern of cyber-attacks. Through AI and ML companies would be able to act instead of reacting to any security strategy, which would result not only in a higher detection rate but also more precise threat detection and distribution of resources. This sort of integration strengthens the cybersecurity as a whole which is a robust defence against the present and future attacks (Tychola et al., 2023).

5.1 Real-Time Threat Analysis and Adaptive Security Protocols

Machine Learning (ML) and Artificial Intelligence (AI) are changing the understanding of cybersecurity with the insight that it can offer real-time information regarding threats along with designing and building dynamic security controls. The

AI algorithms are able to trace the traffic on the networks and detect deviant patterns and find the threats in real time. In this regard, such systems are better than the detection accuracy and speed together with learning after viewing the threats of the past during the application of ML. In an example, the ML models will be capable of identifying novel malwares and abnormalities that can present an attack such as ransomware or phishing attack. Real time responses to dynamic threats and dynamically adjust security protocols are some of the capabilities of AI driven systems with the combination of adaptive security protocols and real time analysis. Such a flexibility is critical to the fight against increasingly sophisticated cyberattacks since the system will be capable of changing its defensive strategies with new strategies. Threat analysis using AI-controlled protocols in real time allows the adoption of proactive over reactive response in regards to cyber security, and it can therefore be resilient to the current and future cybersecurity challenges (Al-Garadi et al., 2020).

5.2 Role of Predictive Analytics in Anticipating Quantum-Based Threats

Algorithms supporting AI and ML, positively contribute to the detection of quantum threats before. Conventional cryptosystems can fall prey to the quantum algorithms (like those of Shor), because QC will be widespread and can be easily broken, particularly the most popular schemes of encryption of information flows. In predictive analytics, big data is used to model future threats based on quantum leaps so that organizations would be ready to the impact of QC to security. The AI algorithm can identify the emergence of new methods of attacks based on systems using quantum technologies, and determine when the latter will be used in practice through analyzing the tendencies in the field of quantum research and development. This would allow cyber security mechanism to pre-empt their defensive mechanisms and transition to quantum proof cryptography much earlier on. Due to this foresight, predictive analytics can enable organizations to secure its data and communications against future threats of quantum attacks, i.e. a smooth transition into the post-quantum world of cryptography with a minimal exposure in the here and now (Al-Mohammed et al., 2021).

6. LIGHTWEIGHT CRYPTOGRAPHIC PROTOCOLS

Cryptographic protocols with light weight have been reported to offer secure encryption and authentication and have no cost in terms of computational resources hence fit well in resource constrained environments. They are used especially with IoT devices, mobile devices, and embedded systems because they have limited processing power, memory and bandwidth. Lightweight cryptography is the one that ensures security at the resources limited by these devices without overloading this device. Protocols such as LEA or Speck are examples of light-weight cryptographic applications which offer strong security guarantees in a trade-off for being as efficient as possible. Traditionally, these protocols have used simpler algorithms that are faster and less resource hungry than say, AES, or RSA. However, they still provide core security services; encryption, decryption, authentication, and data integrity checks. The basic idea of lightweight cryptographic protocols is to achieve the balance between performance and security so that even devices with limited CPU capabilities will be able to operate securely without decreasing the overall performance of the system (Kong, 2022).

6.1 Need for Energy-Efficient and Low-Latency Protocols

Efficiency in energy consumption and low-latency protocols are important in energy limited systems, i.e. IoT devices, embedded systems within these environments render the system performance to be efficient. These devices are normally battery operated and therefore, energy consumption is a major issue of concern. Computational overheads and communications can be high and the waste of battery life can be high leading to the running time of the device being consumed very quickly. Cryptographic protocols involving energy saving methods are therefore regarded as fundamental in prolonging the battery life of the device without having to reduce on the security. It is also significant in these real time applications as autonomous cars or industrial automation where the delays can be highly detrimental. The cryptographic protocols are made lightweight and such that the energy consumption and the time spent in communication is reduced to the bare minimum so as to support timely response and work in such time hard environments. This concerns optimization of these processes that require least energy and least time to run the respective operation; the protocols enable these IoT devices to operate safely because they do not influence efficiency and therefore has a greater lifetime and enhanced reliability (Namrita Gummadi et al., 2024).

6.2 Ensuring Real-Time Performance on Resource-Limited IoT Devices

The rules of cryptography for IoT devices, which are frequently incorporated into restricted performance conditions, should be able to ensure real-time performance despite a limited number of resources. These devices require low processing power, small memory capacity, and limited communication bandwidth, this complicating the implementation of standard cryptographic algorithms. Real-time performance is guaranteed if there are lightweight cryptographic solutions that offer fast encryption/decryption, without creating delays that could interfere with how the system operates. For example, smart sensors, wearable health devices, and industrial controllers that can be deployed in the IoT require speedy data processing and safe communication. Real time performance is important in enabling devices to respond to external stimuli immediately and to send secure data without delay. Lightweight protocols that are accelerated for speed and efficiency take on this need with fast encryption and decryption cycles, low drain on resources, and low latency that enable IoT devices to continue their smooth real time operations while continuing to provide strong security guarantees (Shams et al., 2023).

7. PROPOSED QUANTUM-SAFE FRAMEWORK FOR IOT

As the threat of Quantum Computing (QC) against classical cryptographic protocols continues to grow, particularly in resource-limited contexts, such as resource-constrained Internet of Things, it is necessary to develop a quantum-safe system that can be used to guarantee security of devices over the long run. The suggested structure assimilates quantum-resistant cryptography algorithms like lattice-based encryption, hash signature, and code-based techniques instead of RSA and ECC. The lightweight cryptography will offer the energy-efficient and low latency operations to overcome the scarcity of resources. A hybrid security model will be a combination of classical and quantum-safe security model to ensure backward compatibility. The framework also focuses on effective key management to manage the challenges of PQC so that key distribution and storage in the IoT networks is secure. Lastly, security of real-time communication will be ensured by means of optimized algorithms that will facilitate timely encryption/decryption of applications as in autonomous systems and smart cities. Such a combination method improves resiliency, operational efficiency, and quantum-resistance (de Assis et al., 2020). The figure 5 illustrates the key components of a quantum-safe IoT framework, integrating quantum-resistant algorithms, lightweight cryptography, hybrid security, key management, and real-time communication security.

Figure 4. Quantum-Safe Framework for IoT

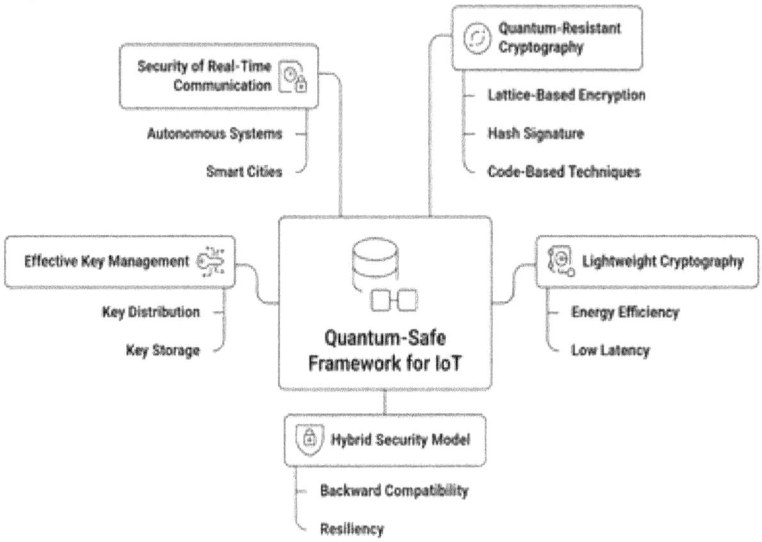

7.1 Integration of PQC, QKD, and AI

Combining PQC, QKD, and AI offers a future-proof security framework for IoT devices. PQC secure against quantum threats replaces classical cryptographic algorithms with quantum-safe algorithms. QKD, based on quantum mechanics, assures secure key exchange such that IoT devices agree upon encryption keys secure against quantum threats. AI-enhanced security enables real-time detection and response to new threats, anticipates vulnerabilities, and optimizes cryptographic usage in resource-constrained environments. AI systems monitor evolving attack patterns and learn from those threats to improve future defense. By integrating PQC for quantum-resistance, QKD for secure key-exchange, and AI-based intelligent monitoring and optimization, IoT networks can be highly secure without a performance impact. This hybrid approach ensures that IoT devices will stay safe against all present and future threats, including those considering QC (Kim & Seo, 2023). Table 4 shows Post-Quantum Cryptography (PQC), Quantum Key Distribution (QKD) and Artificial Intelligence (AI) Machine Learning (ML) work together in an IoT security framework. Every part of the three-part system has its own task PQC safeguards encryption and authentication, QKD offers unbreakable keys and can detect attempts to spy on communications and AI or ML supports detecting and reacting to security incidents as fast as possible. These combined technologies greatly improve the IoT's ability to withstand both traditional and future quantum cyber threats table 5 as follows.

Table 5. Integration of PQC, QKD, and AI in IoT Security

Component	Function in Framework	Benefit to IoT Security
PQC	Quantum-resistant encryption and authentication	Prevents decryption by quantum computers
QKD	Secure key exchange based on quantum mechanics	Detects eavesdropping, provides unbreakable keys
AI/ML	Real-time threat detection and adaptive security	Predicts threats, enables proactive defence

7.2 Scalability and Sustainability Across Various IoT Environments

The main challenges that one can identify when trying to implement a quantum-safe architecture, under various IoT environments, would be scalability and sustainability. IoT networks are mostly big and highly distributed, with devices ranging from plain sensors to fairly complex smart systems. The framework should be scalable in nature, so it should be able to handle thousands to millions of IoT devices and keep secure without overloading the system's CPU or memory resources. The framework must support different IoT environments such as a smart city, industrial IoT, or healthcare application, each with its own operational requirements concerning data transmission speeds, processing power, and energy consumption (Marisamy et al., 2025). By leveraging lightweight cryptographic protocols, PQC algorithms, and optimized AI techniques, the framework is designed to adapt to the demands of each IoT environment. Sustainability comes next, for often these devices are deemed suitable for use in an IoT network for a very long time, albeit with limited hardware. Consequently, quantum-safe frameworks must maintain efficient cryptographic operations whose implications on the environment are minimal while still maintaining a robust level of security. Combining scalable protocols, quantum-safe methods, and AI-assisted optimization makes the framework viable in terms of sustainability across various IoT environments (Rubia et al., 2024).

8. CASE STUDIES AND APPLICATIONS

The quantum-safe framework proposed here has great utility in the real world across several domains. In smart health systems, quantum-resistant cryptographic systems provide patient data confidentiality, as well as integrity, while streaming out from wearables and sensors-the AI in turn uses that data for real-time threat detection. In the case of autonomous vehicles, secure V2V and V2I communications guarantee attacks are prevented during key exchanges through QKD, while AI carries out situational threat analysis. Machine-to-machine communication in industrial automation and smart manufacturing is secured through PQC and QKD systems, masking intellectual properties, while reducing operational disruptions. AI reiterates the productivity of security by identifying anomalies and mounting a prompt response to threats. These case studies show the interworking of PQC, QKD, and AI to achieve an ultra-resilient and heavily secure, scalable infrastructure for the IoT ecosystems vulnerable to quantum threats. The framework encourages proactive security and continues to guarantee operational trust in critical sectors while simultaneously gearing infrastructures towards the future. This figure illustrates the key components of a quantum-safe IoT framework, integrating quantum-resistant algorithms, lightweight cryptography, hybrid security, key management, and real-time communication security (Hadi et al., 2023).

Table 6. Use Cases of Quantum-Safe Framework

Application Domain	Quantum-Safe Technologies Used	Benefits Achieved
Smart Healthcare	PQC, QKD, AI	Secure PHI, prevent ransomware in medical IoT
Autonomous Vehicles	QKD, AI	Secure V2V/V2I communication, detect attacks
Industrial Automation	PQC, QKD, AI	Protect IP, monitor threats in real-time

8.1 Smart Healthcare Systems

In smart healthcare systems, the foundation of connected devices includes wearables, sensors, and remote monitoring devices. These devices are connected to provide real-time health data, tracking patients, and dispatch alerts during emergencies. To enhance the security and privacy of sensitive medical data, including Personalized Health Information (PHI) and patient medical data from wearables, PQC and QKD should be integrated and utilized. AI has also played an essential role in smart healthcare, as real-time threat analysis may help to discover threats to data while being transmitted, such as the risk of cyberattacks not just on patient information, but also critical healthcare infrastructure, during the predictive stage of a risk analysis. Smart, quantum-safe frameworks will secure patient health data collected by wearables and maintain that the transmitted data is securely received before moving it to an analyzed distributed cloud-based system all while ensuring the data is encrypted and not at risk of being compromised during quantum computer-based analysis(Shams et al., 2023). Th figure 6 shows the components of smart healthcare systems, highlighting connected devices, AI integration, data security, and quantum-safe frameworks for secure medical operations.

Figure 5. Smart Healthcare Systems

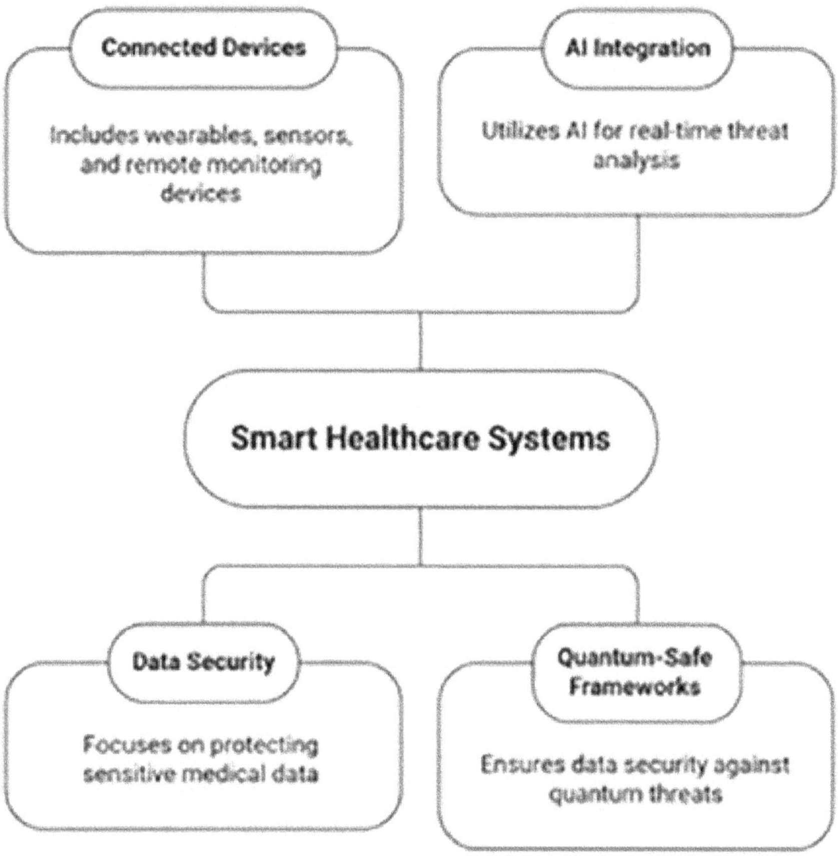

8.2 Autonomous Vehicles

Autonomous Vehicles (AVs) rely extensively on IoT devices and secure communication protocols to communicate between vehicles, infrastructure, and Cloud-based systems. In order to safely operate, AVs must have secure processing, and protect data comprising vehicle location data, vehicle status information, and surrounding environmental conditions that might weigh on their likelihood of safe movement. Quantum-safe cryptography can complement AI-enabled threat monitoring in real-time to securely enable Vehicle-To-Vehicle (V2V) and Vehicle-To-Infrastructure (V2I) communications, while securely safeguarding these critical V2V and V2I systems and communications from possible quantum-based attacks (Bounmy & Sisavath, 2023). QKD is a possible means use between vehicles, and vehicles and infrastructure to ensure that key exchanges take place with the confidence that any form of tampering is eliminated. AI-based technologies may be used to optimize the secure communication of vehicles by recognizing the patterns that indicate a potential threat in real-time, providing an opportunity for a quick response to any cyber threats or attacks (An & Seo, 2020). The figure 7 illustrates key components of autonomous vehicle security, including IoT devices, quantum-safe cryptography, secure communications, AI-enabled threat monitoring, and vehicle-to-vehicle/ infrastructure connectivity.

Figure 6. Enhancing Autonomous Vehicle Security

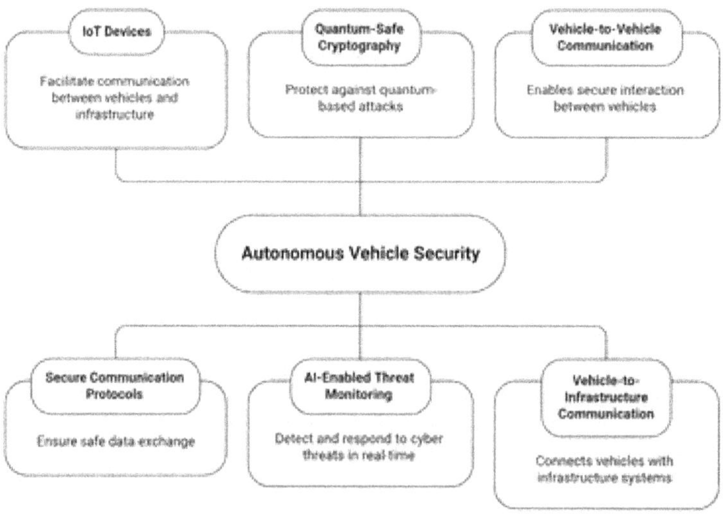

8.3 Industrial Automation and Smart Manufacturing

In industrial automation and smart manufacturing, IoT devices can control and monitor devices from production lines to supply chains. Security in these environments is extremely important because breaches can result in large financial losses, damages to equipment, or safety hazards. If manufacturers can combine PQC with QKD, manufacturing plants can assist in providing security for communication between machines, sensors, and control systems while also protecting against future attacks based on quantum technology that could compromise operationally acceptable safe practices, or intellectual property (Meziane & Ouerdi, 2023). AI is also demonstrated as a crucial safety tool for analyzing operational data from machines, and using ML to detect anomalies or intrusions, and assist humans with real time threat responses. This is a quantum-safe framework that allows manufacturers to continue innovating and expanding their automation capabilities and to do so with assurance that quantum technology does not threaten the safety of its operations, the financial viability of its methods, or the integrity of its intellectual property (Adnan et al., 2022). The figure 8 demonstrates how IoT devices, PQC and QKD, and quantum-safe frameworks strengthen industrial automation and smart manufacturing through secure communication, risk mitigation, and AI-driven anomaly detection.

Figure 7. Enhancing Industrial Security with Quantum Technology

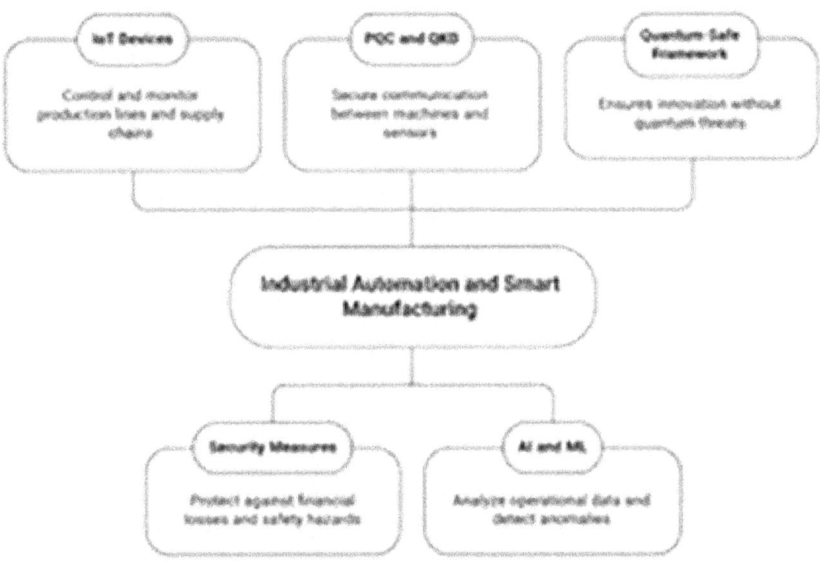

9. FUTURE RESEARCH DIRECTIONS

The emergence of quantum computing presents the challenge of an urgent need to the IoT ecosystem that requires future-oriented solutions. The future research ought to be based on the creation of lightweight, scalable, and adaptable quantum-safe systems which can be deployed in resource-constrained settings. A combination of PQC, QKD, and AI-based adaptive security systems will play an important role in providing real-time protection at the same time remaining efficient. Additionally, the development of international standardization processes and inter-industry partnership can contribute to the rapid adoption and guarantee interoperability (Al Attar & Mohammed, 2025). The investigation of hybrid cryptographic models, improved key management, and cloud-based solutions will also be the issues of priority to ensure that IoT infrastructures are resistant to post-quantum attacks.

9.1 Hybrid Security and Integration Approaches

The emergence of the hybrid security models, which include classical cryptography as well as PQC and QKD in the transition phase, is one of the main future directions. The diversity of the IoT devices is very high so these models should be able to be backward-compatible and should eventually overhaul the weak algorithms such as RSA and ECC. AI and ML should also be integrated into cryptographic systems to offer dynamic threat detection and predictive defense systems. Using the data of attacks in the past, AI has the potential to increase detection and continuously change the protocols. Also, studies on lightweight PQC algorithms that are optimized to run on the constrained IoT resource will be required. This intermediary integration will also offer a moderate solution that enhances resilience to both classical and quantum-enabled cyber threats in intricate IoT networks. (Aguilera et al., 2023)

9.2 Standardization, Scalability, and Global Collaboration

The other crucial guideline is to set up international standards and scalable solutions of quantum-safe IoT security. Today, numerous institutions await the completion of NIST recommendations, and this delays the adoption. Studies should be made on developing interoperable frameworks that will enable easy integration of PQC into the existing infrastructures without affecting the operations. Scalability also plays an important role because IoT environments can contain millions of devices in healthcare, autonomous automobiles, and industrial environments (Biswas et al., 2024). Efficiency of key management systems, quantum repeaters and satellite based QKD of long-distance communication will also improve security in large networks. Lastly, the world needs to work together to close the digital divide, whereby the developing economies can also get access to secure, sustainable and future-proof IoT systems in the post-quantum times.

10. CONCLUSION

The fast development of the Quantum Computing (QC) has created the concern of the security of the IoT objects, particularly in one-to-many interactions. IoTs are usually resource-constrained, yet they also apply the classical cryptography algorithms such as RSA and ECC that can easily be broken by quantum algorithms such as Shor algorithm. This makes IoT devices that are implemented in industries which are critical to critical quantum threats, i.e. smart healthcare, autonomous vehicles and industrial automation. The quantum-safe framework, including the combination of Post-Quantum Cryptography (PQC), Quantum Key Distribution (QKD), and the Artificial Intelligence (AI), should be implemented to reduce the risks. Lattice-based, hash-based and code-based cryptography are such PQC-based methods, which provide high quantum resistance and are intended to run on small IoT-based devices, and they can protect data integrity without any impact on performance. Based on the principles of quantum mechanics, QKD offers resistant key distribution, under which the eavesdropping is detected to enhance the security of the IoT ecosystem communications. AI and ML also contribute to the further amplification of the framework since they enable the detection and the provision of predictive analytics and adaptive updates in countering new attack vectors with quantum capabilities.

These lightweight cryptographic protocols are also provided in addition to, and lower the processing overheads and latency, and power consumption, which makes them appropriate to the performance limitations of the IoT. The framework is also devoted to the Cloud-based Secure Realizations (CSR) of scalability of the heterogeneous networks of the IoT that ensure the resilience of the mission-critical applications. Commercially, this framework ensures confidentiality and integrity of healthcare data, autonomous navigation and manufacturing processes both in the industry and flexibility to scale to small networks to complex ecosystems. However, the problems of resources limitation, regulations, and global standardization are still there. It is also necessary to bridge the digital divide between the economies to offer equal access to safe IoT spaces. Lastly, the proposed framework provides a future-proof, scalable, and flexible quantum-safe framework that conditions the IoT systems to a post-quantum environment where quantum attacks will become inevitable in the near future.

REFERENCES

Aarthi, S., Aravinthan, K., Ravikumar, R. N., Sivakumar, N., & Wanglen, S. (2025). Cryptography securing data in motion within Blockchain, internet of everything, and Federated Learning. In *Convergence of Blockchain, Internet of Everything, and Federated Learning for Security* (pp. 39–78). IGI Global., DOI: 10.4018/979-8-3373-1424-2.ch002

Abomhara, M., Department of Information and Communication Technology Norway, U. of A., K ien, G. M., & Department of Information and Communication Technology Norway, U. of A. (2015). Cyber security and the internet of things: Vulnerabilities, threats, intruders and attacks. *Journal of Cyber Security and Mobility*, *4*(1), 65–88. DOI: 10.13052/jcsm2245-1439.414

Adnan, M. H., Ahmad Zukarnain, Z., & Harun, N. Z. (2022). Quantum key distribution for 5G networks: A review, state of art and future directions. *Future Internet*, *14*(3), 73. DOI: 10.3390/fi14030073

Aguilera, A. C., Clemente, X. A., Lawo, D. C., Monroy, I. T., & Olmos, J. J. V. (2023). First end-to-end PQC protected DPU-to-DPU communications. *Electronics Letters*, *59*(17), e12901. Advance online publication. DOI: 10.1049/ell2.12901

Al Attar, T. N. A., & Mohammed, R. N. (2025). Optimization of lattice-based cryptographic key generation using genetic algorithms for post-quantum security. *UHD Journal of Science and Technology*, *9*(1), 93–105. DOI: 10.21928/uhdjst.v9n1y2025.pp93-105

Al-Garadi, M. A., Mohamed, A., Al-Ali, A. K., Du, X., Ali, I., & Guizani, M. (2020). A survey of machine and deep learning methods for internet of things (IoT) security. *IEEE Communications Surveys and Tutorials*, *22*(3), 1646–1685. DOI: 10.1109/COMST.2020.2988293

Al-Mohammed, H. A., Al-Ali, A., Yaacoub, E., Qidwai, U., Abualsaud, K., Rzewuski, S., & Flizikowski, A. (2021). Machine learning techniques for detecting attackers during quantum key distribution in IoT networks with application to railway scenarios. *IEEE Access : Practical Innovations, Open Solutions*, *9*, 136994–137004. DOI: 10.1109/ACCESS.2021.3117405

An, S., & Seo, S. C. (2020). Efficient parallel implementations of LWE-based Post-quantum cryptosystems on graphics processing units. *Mathematics*, *8*(10), 1781. DOI: 10.3390/math8101781

Andrae, S. (2025). Post-quantum cryptography in the age of quantum computing. In *Advances in Computational Intelligence and Robotics* (pp. 197–216). IGI Global. DOI: 10.4018/979-8-3693-9919-4.ch011

Ashirova, A., Bobamuratov, U., Aarthi, S., & Ravikumar, R. N. (2026). Adversarial Machine Learning in Intrusion Detection Systems. In *Advances in Computational Intelligence and Robotics* (pp. 135–164). IGI Global Scientific Publishing. DOI: 10.4018/979-8-3373-5223-7.ch005

Awasthi, A. (2025). Quantum-resistant security for IoT systems: Challenges and implementation strategies. *International Journal of Scientific Research in Computer Science. Engineering and Information Technology*, *11*(1), 671–678. DOI: 10.32628/CSEIT25111260

Biswas, S., Goswami, R. S., Hemant Kumar Reddy, K., Mohanty, S. N., & Ahmed, M. A. (2024). Exploring the fusion of lattice-based quantum key distribution for secure Internet of Things communications. *IET Quantum Communication*, *5*(4), 322–339. Advance online publication. DOI: 10.1049/qtc2.12105

Bounmy, S., & Sisavath, K. (2023). Securing Internet of Things (IoT) ecosystems: A quantum cryptography approach. *Algorithm Asynchronous*, *1*(1), 1–7. DOI: 10.61963/jaa.v1i1.45

de Assis, M. V. O., Carvalho, L. F., Rodrigues, J. J. P. C., Lloret, J., & Proença, M. L.Jr. (2020). Near real-time security system applied to SDN environments in IoT networks using convolutional neural network. *Computers & Electrical Engineering*, *86*(106738), 106738. DOI: 10.1016/j.compeleceng.2020.106738

Dere, N., & Ülkü, E. E. (2023). QUANTUM KEY DISTRIBUTION IN SMART HOME SYSTEMS. *Kahramanmaraş Sütçü İmam Üniversitesi Mühendislik Bilimleri Dergisi*, *26*(4), 932–942. DOI: 10.17780/ksujes.1325805

Fedorov, A. K., Kiktenko, E. O., & Lvovsky, A. I. (2018). Quantum computers put blockchain security at risk. *Nature*, *563*(7732), 465–467. DOI: 10.1038/d41586-018-07449-z PMID: 30451981

Fernandez-Carames, T. M. (2020). From pre-quantum to post-quantum IoT security: A survey on quantum-resistant cryptosystems for the internet of things. *IEEE Internet of Things Journal*, *7*(7), 6457–6480. DOI: 10.1109/JIOT.2019.2958788

Gitonga, C. K. (2025). The impact of quantum computing on cryptographic systems: Urgency of quantum-resistant algorithms and practical applications in cryptography. *European Journal of Information Technologies and Computer Science*, *5*(1), 1–10. DOI: 10.24018/compute.2025.5.1.146

Guitouni, Z., Maize, S., Zrigui, M., & Machhout, M. (2024). Advanced error correction method for quantum key distribution in IoT systems. *Physica Scripta*, *99*(10), 105106. DOI: 10.1088/1402-4896/ad7423

Hadi, R. H., Hady, H. N., Hasan, A. M., Al-Jodah, A., & Humaidi, A. J. (2023). Improved fault classification for predictive maintenance in industrial IoT based on AutoML: A case study of ball-bearing faults. *Processes (Basel, Switzerland)*, *11*(5), 1507. DOI: 10.3390/pr11051507

Istiaque Ahmed, K., Tahir, M., Hadi Habaebi, M., Lun Lau, S., & Ahad, A. (2021). Machine learning for authentication and authorization in IoT: Taxonomy, challenges and future research direction. *Sensors (Basel)*, *21*(15), 5122. DOI: 10.3390/s21155122 PMID: 34372360

Kim, Y., & Seo, S. C. (2023). Signature split method for a PQC-DSA compliant with V2V communication standards. *Applied Sciences (Basel, Switzerland)*, *13*(10), 5874. DOI: 10.3390/app13105874

Kong, P.-Y. (2022). A review of quantum key distribution protocols in the perspective of smart grid communication security. *IEEE Systems Journal*, *16*(1), 41–54. DOI: 10.1109/JSYST.2020.3024956

Kumari, S., Singh, M., Singh, R., & Tewari, H. (2022). Post-quantum cryptography techniques for secure communication in resource-constrained Internet of Things devices: A comprehensive survey. *Software, Practice & Experience*, *52*(10), 2047–2076. DOI: 10.1002/spe.3121

Liu, A., Zhang, Q., Xu, S., Feng, H., Chen, X.-B., & Liu, W. (2024). QBIoT: A quantum blockchain framework for IoT with an improved proof-of-authority consensus algorithm and a public-key quantum signature. *Computers, Materials & Continua*, *80*(1), 1727–1751. DOI: 10.32604/cmc.2024.051233

Liu, R., Rozenman, G. G., Kundu, N. K., Chandra, D., & De, D. (2022). Towards the industrialisation of quantum key distribution in communication networks: A short survey. *IET Quantum Communication*, *3*(3), 151–163. DOI: 10.1049/qtc2.12044

Marisamy, K., Selvakumar, A., Rajasekar, B., Natarajan, R., Atajanova, A., & Makhmudov, S. (2025). Smart logistics integrating AI, IoT, blockchain, and Robotics for a sustainable Future. In *Emerging Trends in Smart Logistics Technologies* (pp. 73–104). IGI Global Scientific Publishing., DOI: 10.4018/979-8-3373-2434-0.ch003

Meziane, H., & Ouerdi, N. (2023). A survey on performance evaluation of artificial intelligence algorithms for improving IoT security systems. *Scientific Reports*, *13*(1), 21255. DOI: 10.1038/s41598-023-46640-9 PMID: 38040952

Namrita Gummadi, A., Napier, J. C., & Abdallah, M. (2024). XAI-IoT: An explainable AI framework for enhancing anomaly detection in IoT systems. *IEEE Access : Practical Innovations, Open Solutions, 12*, 71024–71054. DOI: 10.1109/ACCESS.2024.3402446

Pandit, S., Ravikumar, R. N., Pandit, S., Joshi, N., Kishore, S., & Aarthi, S. (2025). Explainable Federated Learning for secure and transparent wireless edge networks. In *Advances in Computational Intelligence and Robotics* (pp. 127–168). IGI Global Scientific Publishing. DOI: 10.4018/979-8-3373-3576-6.ch004

Peng, D., Dong, W., Chen, X., Peng, L., Chen, K., Long, J., & Yan, B. (2024). A study of quantum-secret communication technology and its application in industrial IoT. In *Frontiers in Artificial Intelligence and Applications*. IOS Press., DOI: 10.3233/FAIA241105

Rafique, S. H., Abdallah, A., Musa, N. S., & Murugan, T. (2024). Machine learning and deep learning techniques for Internet of Things network anomaly detection-current research trends. *Sensors (Basel), 24*(6), 1968. Advance online publication. DOI: 10.3390/s24061968 PMID: 38544231

Ravikumar, A. S., Jumaev, N., Mamadiyarov, Z., Kumari, N., & Sharvanthika. (2026). Quantum-Powered Hyperautomation. In *Advances in Computational Intelligence and Robotics* (pp. 1–32). IGI Global Scientific Publishing. DOI: 10.4018/979-8-3373-4347-1.ch001

Ravikumar, R. N., & Aarthi, S. (2025). Real-time threat detection and anomaly monitoring using AI-enhanced IoT drones on blockchain networks. In *Enhancing Surveillance With Blockchain and IoT Drone Technology* (pp. 273–298). IGI Global Scientific Publishing., DOI: 10.4018/979-8-3373-4277-1.ch009

Ravikumar, R. N., Aarthi, S., Singh, A., Sivakumar, N., Kavitha Bharathi, S., & Sujitha, S. (2025). Transfer Learning for IoT applications. In *Advances in Computational Intelligence and Robotics* (pp. 55–84). IGI Global Scientific Publishing. DOI: 10.4018/979-8-3373-3146-1.ch003

Rubia, J., Lincy, B., Nithila, E. E., Shibi, S., & Rosi. (2024). A survey about Post Quantum Cryptography methods. *EAI Endorsed Transactions on Internet of Things, 10*. DOI: 10.4108/eetiot.5099

Senekane, M., Mafu, M., & Petruccione, F. (2015). Six-state symmetric quantum key distribution protocol. *Journal of Quantum Information Science, 05*(02), 33–40. DOI: 10.4236/jqis.2015.52005

Shams, M., Choudhari, J., Reyes, K., Prentzas, S., Gapizov, A., Shehryar, A., Affaf, M., Grezenko, H., Gasim, R. W., Mohsin, S. N., Rehman, A., & Rehman, S. (2023). The quantum-medical nexus: Understanding the impact of quantum technologies on healthcare. *Cureus*, *15*(10), e48077. DOI: 10.7759/cureus.48077 PMID: 38046499

Shreha, S. A., Ravikumar, R. N., & Aarthi, S. (2025). Neuro-symbolic AI and Behavioral Intelligence. In *Advances in Computational Intelligence and Robotics* (pp. 121–152). IGI Global Scientific Publishing. DOI: 10.4018/979-8-3373-5012-7.ch005

Sreerangapuri, A. (2024). Post-quantum cryptography for AI-driven cloud security solutions. *International Journal For Multidisciplinary Research*, *6*(5), 29032. Advance online publication. DOI: 10.36948/ijfmr.2024.v06i05.29032

Sun, Y. (2024). Securing the future: Shifting to Post-Quantum Cryptography amidst quantum threats. *Applied and Computational Engineering*, *110*(1), 154–160. DOI: 10.54254/2755-2721/110/2024MELB0120

Tychola, K. A., Kalampokas, T., & Papakostas, G. A. (2023). Quantum machine learning—An overview. *Electronics (Basel)*, *12*(11), 2379. DOI: 10.3390/electronics12112379

KEY TERMS AND DEFINITIONS

Hybrid Security Model: Combination of classical and quantum-safe cryptography to ensure secure transition.

IoT (Internet of Things): Network of connected smart devices like sensors, vehicles, and wearables.

Lightweight Cryptography: Security algorithms designed for devices with limited power, memory, and processing.

PQC (Post-Quantum Cryptography): Algorithms resistant to attacks from both classical and quantum computers.

QKD (Quantum Key Distribution): Method of securely sharing encryption keys using quantum mechanics.

Quantum Computing (QC): Advanced computing using qubits that can break classical encryption.

Standardization: Creating common rules and protocols (e.g., by NIST) for global adoption of PQC.

Chapter 2
AI and the Internet of Things (IoT) Security:
Protecting Connected Devices in an Autonomous Era

V. Dankan Gowda
http://orcid.org/0000-0003-0724-0333
B.M.S. Institute of Technology and Management, India

ABSTRACT

In this chapter, the role of AI and IoT and threats, as well as new techniques in the direction of securing devices in an AI propelled era, are discussed. That is why, the number of threats growing with each year, and including data leaks, unauthorized access, and others. This chapter focuses on how AI implemented in IoT can improve the IoT security, and it presents the machine learning, deep learning and federated learning techniques to detect intrusion and anomalies and to mitigate them in real time. Also, the chapters point to the impact of AI, the studies, cases and the current applications of AI in the IoT security system. The lessons, such as lack of funds, and threats, which are threats to the AI models, are as well discussed. Last of all, the chapter discusses the future trend of AI in protecting the IoT network, being an indication that more enhancements are being made to protect the growing list of connected devices.

INTRODUCTION

The Internet of Things (IoT) and Artificial Intelligence (AI) as two modern trends have become the long-awaited breakthroughs in various sectors and the human life. It stands for 'internet of things' The IoT is the assemblage of physical entities,

DOI: 10.4018/979-8-3373-3857-6.ch002

digital and electronic gadgets which are unique and connected (Joel et al., 2023), communicating and sharing information with the least outside interferes. Thus, these devices include sensors in appliances such as air conditioners, refrigerators, washing machines, and even in the large manufacturing industries (Prabavathy & Supriya, 2021). IoT has seen tremendous growth for the last two decades because of several technologies such as wireless communication, cloud service, and business analytics, and has become a part of our daily life in many fields such as healthcare, transport, smart home, and industrial automation (Lavanya et al., 2022). For instance, Internet of Things has been used to monitor patient's health through wearables in the healthcare sector while use of smart home sector has other features like lights, heating, and security. Likewise (Chanal & Kakkasageri, 2019), IoT in has also changed transportation through self-driving cars and streamlining of logistics to become safer.

In the same line, artificial intelligence, especially machine learning (ML) and deep learning (DL), have taken the central stage for automating operations, making predictions, and robust decision-making. Artificial intelligence basically employed on the capacity to analyze extent data (Shandilya & Reddy, 2024), to determine correlation among data and can without being programmed; make decisions. Such capabilities make AI suitable as a tool that can supplement IoT systems and enhance the levels of intelligently-controlled and self-governed IoT networks (D & Kawale, 2023). With AI implemented into IoT system, the devices in use have become intelligent and highly capable of acquiring knowledge by themselves so as to enhance the efficiency, resources management and effectiveness of the systems and however delivering better output to the users (Mahindrakar & Chandel, 2023).

As powerful technologies, IoT and AI present opportunities, their extensive use came with unique threats to security. Thanks to a high number of connected devices, and with the constant development of AI, more and more various opportunities for possible attacks appear. It is for this reason that it is said that as the different IoT networks increase in adoption across the globe, there is need to secure the different IoT networks in place to avoid compromise by malicious parties (Manivasagam & Prasad, 2024). If secure their implementation is not done, such networks remain prone to certain risks such as unauthorized access, illicit break-ins and other form of cyber-crimes. The application of AI is underpinning the IoT security since it enables the identification of patterns and the determination of their normalcy or otherwise. In this chapter, the main focus is to look at the security issues arising from IoT devices, opportunity of using AI in resisting some of these threats and the prospects of AI IoT security solutions.

Security Challenges in IoT

The ever-increasing number of IoT devices link the world and create an IoT network, while these movements also have certain security risks. The first issue can be considered to be vast numbers and heterogeneity of IoT devices. Due to its decentralized nature, IoT networks are made up of a large number of connected devices that have a number of differences in performance, security needs, and energy availability. Most of the IoT devices are resource-limited and cannot afford to implement complex and secure algorithms as most of them lack a satisfactory processing power (Satish et al., 2024). This issue is especially acute if we talk about low-cost IoT devices meaning devices that are claimed to be affordable and produced in large quantities where aggressive cost reduction is frequently complimented by unreliable security. Therefore, most of the IoT devices lack secure firmware, outdated firmware, possess hardcoded passwords, and limited to no encryption standards.

The last security problem relating to IoT devices is the increased connection ratio for IoT devices. These devices from day to day entail the collection, transmission, and storage of data, hence accumulating an abundance of personal data that makes them prone to data breaches by hackers. Malicious access to IoT networks can be detrimental through the stealing of individuals' personal data, personal and business financial information, as well as intellectual property. Also, IoT system is a system of connected devices which is highly vulnerable; once one device is attacked, then all other connected devices may be affected. For instance, intrusion on a smart home system can give wrongdoers, access to sensitive data or lead to physical security vulnerabilities while in the industrial IoT platform means disruptions that are essential in the supplies chain.

It has been observed that Internet is full of threats and the emergence of self-driving cars and industrial robots have only added to the security risks of IoT. These are machines with a number of algorithms that work with artificial intelligence to make decisions without the interference of a human being. Although these systems have great advantages, as they exclude a human factor in the process of work, they can be easily used in unlawful ways, if there are no special security measures. For example, an adversary can tamper with the AI models that are used in self-driving cars, and these can result to car crashes or congestion (Miettinen & Sadeghi, 2018). Likewise, the AI-driven industrial systems could be manipulated to act out of normal and this may pose risk to the lives of people as well as disrupt business activities.

Further, a significant increase of data produced by IoT devices requires its own solution. An IoT network collects a huge amount of data that is often personal and confidential in its nature. Unlike most data which is used for normal company operations, the protection of this data's confidentiality, integrity, and availability is a major concern. Most of the IoT devices are said to lack sufficient encryption and safe storage space for the exchanged information, which makes it easier for the attackers to intercept or modify the data. In addition, due to the development of the IoT networks this makes it even harder to manage and secure these networks. The heuristic solutions of security like firewalls and IDSs are unable to protect IoT networks due to the large volumes and the diversity of IoT architectures. As a result, better and more complex methods of security strategies are called for by these challenges.

Importance of AI in Enhancing IoT Security

In IoT systems, there is a large number of interconnected devices and huge amount of data being exchanged between them, thus relying solely on traditional security solutions is not enough. It is at this point that AI comes into consideration as a tool that is capable to carry out the above functions. Cybersecurity is a critical issue of current debates within the IoT networks, and with the advanced technology such as machine learning and deep learning, AI is capable of offering many perquisites to rectify it. AI has a significant benefit over human-intervention based solutions since it can process the huge amount of data within a short time hence helping detect security threats that would easily go unnoticed in traditional systems. For instance, through machine learning, automated patterns learned from the network traffic, user activities, and device communication can be supervised allowing algorithms to pick out an abnormality that can be presumed to symbolize a security threat.

It also enables the various domains of IoT security like intrusions, anomalies, and even predictive threat intelligence. Because more of these applications are connected to the IoT network, the machine learning models can learn from the new data accumulated and improve on their accuracy to detect new and different threats. For instance, it can search for intrusion signs in a network such as attempts at unauthorized access, high traffic of data as well as communication between devices that are not conventional. They can also evoked some actions like quarantining the device or inform the security team to minimize the effects of the threat.

Machine learning that employs the use of artificial neural network is commonly referred to as deep learning is very appropriate in handling large data and identifying obscure patterns that are not easily recognizable by non- intelligent systems. For instance, deep learning approaches in can be applied for processing all the data coming from the IoT sensors, and pin point out anomalous situations suggesting a security breach. Further, AI for security can be used to improve the methods of checking identity, for example using biometric identification and continuing confirmation of users' identity controlling the access of IoT devices and systems.

Federated learning, one of the paradigms to carry out the training of models in a distributed manner without compromising the data, is another promising approach toward IoT security. Here, the AI models are created on the user devices in the IoT network with no raw data collected from the devices being sent to a centralized server. This helps improve the security of data especially when it comes to data leakage during the training process since the data remains on the local machine. Specifically, it can be used in applications, where IoT devices are placed at remote or are highly portable and, thus, their interaction with the cloud might be limited.

In addition, it can be used to predict potential risks and threats to security heading to the future. Using historical data analysis, specific trends that threaten IoT networks can be determined in advance, and precautions can be made towards them. This capability is particularly significant when used in the context that has been described above, that is new risks and strategies are emerging and existing security solutions may be unsuitable.

In conclusion one can ascertain that advanced tools supported by the AI capabilities play a vital role where security of IoT systems is the end goal. This is expected to be the case given evolving networks in IoT and corresponding increase in IoT security risks that can be adequately addressed by AI security solutions.

BACKGROUND

The IoT has become an extensive security threat since the network involves unending numbers of peculiar devices that connect to the web in consumer and industrial settings. The size of IoT networks poses problems with protecting the devices; some of these devices are often placed at quite isolated areas with possibly restricted connectivity to a network. This leads to having the devices with limited computing capability, low power usage, and inexpensive components that compromise Security features at times. There are now certain risks that have been deemed to be crucial in IoT security and they range from weak authentication mechanisms, data privacy, insecure communication, and the lack of an update to IoT devices' system. These vulnerabilities pose a significant threat to the IoT networks security as they might put at risk important data, integrity of devices, and operations.

The major problem that still persists in the IoT network is the Weak Authentication. For instance, multiple IoT devices do not even use complex credentials, but possess simple universally accepted usernames and passwords that hackers can easily crack. Some users do not update the default password or apply complex passwords on the devices, or some devices have no password policies at all. Another vulnerability enables intruders to get access to some important information or sequences the device (Rizvi, 2021). This is a serious concern especially in consumer IoT devices such as smart cameras, door locks and home assistants as the attacker can then get physical or virtual access to one's home or personal details respectively. For IIoT systems, which used in manufacturing processes or critical national infrastructure, the failure of authentication may end up with manipulation of industrial processes, data leakage or industrial sabotage.

Data Privacy Concerns also rank high among IoT security challenges. Since IoT technologies are used to gather and directly share voluminous data of underlying personal, health, and geographical information, their privacy is a significant issue. Most IoT devices do not encrypt data properly or even secure it from the cloud storage, thereby create a vulnerability where the attackers can easily intercept the data in transit as well as incidentally access stored data. Moreover, data may be transferred between the gadgets, third-party contractors, and the cloud interfaces, and this happens with little regard to the consent of users. Regarding data capture the matter arises often time many users have no clue on the extent and how the collected data is being used or processed or even shared. That is why this lack of transparency, with low privacy standards, can lead to the abuse and unauthorized control of the user's information, as well as identity theft.

Another specific type of weakness in the IoT networks is the Insecure Communication Protocols. Most of the IoT devices interact using standard protocols such as HTTP, MQTT, Bluetooth, among others which are in most cases not secure. IoT devices frequently send data through unencrypted networks or utilize narrow and easier to guess encryption standards that make it easier for the attackers to eavesdrop and establish a man in the middle attack. Also, some of the protocols employed in IoT systems lack updates or were established without concerning security issues, therefore, vulnerable to attacks. For instance, the some of the devices may support the now End-of-life SSL/TLS versions with their data transmissions at the risk of interception or manipulation. The insecure communication channel, apart from compromising the contents of the transmitted data, puts the IoT systems to several types of threats such as eavesdropping and unauthorized command over the connected devices.

The failure to frequently update the software is tight as one of the key reasons behind increased vulnerabilities within the IoT devices. While typical computing systems update their software as and when vulnerabilities are found and then subscribed to patched, the IoT systems, to date, are not patched frequently, or they are rarely patchable by the end-users. Many times, manufacturers release devices with software or firmware that can not be changed, and sometimes bugs that are present in old versions of the software may never be fixed. This makes it even worse especially because most IoT devices have long life cycle, and the manufacturers don't offer updates after a few years. This is because these unfavorable vulnerabilities are not patched, hence become a denominator to the attacker to attack the devices or networks. It remains to explain that new vulnerabilities are also never patched, which makes devices targeted exposed to attacks for rather a long time.

AI'S ROLE IN IOT SECURITY

AI is being viewed as a useful asset in comprehending the security threat posed by IoT devices. When networks and digitized assets are being expanded in large scales and are in different types, then streamlining of the data that is being generated could simply inadequate or the protection from the new real-time threats common in the vast IoT networks. Machine learning and, in particular, deep learning can be a significant asset in improving the IoT system security since it allows for self-learning and real-time threat detection and identification of anomalous behavior in the system.

This is due to its capability of perusing through most data relayed by IoT gizmos and subsequently identifying most security threats in real-time. The technology used in it is able to analyze the traffic on a network, logs on devices and sensors to determine the typical behavior and track any changes which could be signs of an attack. For instance, with the historical data of device usages and behaviours of a network, an algorithm of machine learning can understand what normal usage of that particular device looks like and hence can identify any deviant usage that could be a sign of a breach. Such increased agility in detecting anomalies makes it easier to identify potential threats like: unauthorized access attempts, data leaks, or an entrance of a virus (Francisti et al., 2023). The following benefits of AI are evident in the IoT systems whereby; Thus, an AI system detects anomalies at first instance to mitigate the harm and enhance the security of the IoT systems.

AI is being viewed as a useful asset in comprehending the security threat posed by IoT devices. When networks and digitized assets are being expanded in large scales and are in different types, then streamlining of the data that is being generated could simply inadequate or the protection from the new real-time threats common in the vast IoT networks. Machine learning and, in particular, deep learning can be a significant asset in improving the IoT system security since it allows for self-learning and real-time threat detection and identification of anomalous behavior in the system.

This is due to its capability of perusing through most data relayed by IoT gizmos and subsequently identifying most security threats in real-time. It is the capability that enables the identification of normal patterns in the network traffic, device logs, or sensor information to detect any signs of an attack. For instance, with the historical data of device usages and behaviours of a network, an algorithm of machine learning can understand what normal usage of that particular device looks like and hence can identify any deviant usage that could be a sign of a breach. Such increased agility in detecting anomalies makes it easier to identify potential threats like: unauthorized access attempts, data leaks, or an entrance of a virus. The following benefits of AI are evident in the IoT systems whereby; Thus, an AI system detects anomalies at first instance to mitigate the harm and enhance the security of the IoT systems.AI's ability to Another benefit of the proposed approach is that it allows to predict future security breaches and prevent them from happening in case of IoT security. AI makes it possible to predict various threats that might likely affect the IoT devices based on data and trends generated in the past. As an example, the uses of predictive models can be used to predict when devices are at risk of exposure to new threats based on such parameters as traffic patterns in a network or the behavior of the devices. This type of protection provides a chance for IoT systems to constantly develop and become more shielded without an attack happening first. AI's analytical function can be applied when the system identifies potential vulnerabilities of IoT devices and the network so that network administrators can take action to prevent attacks as a proactive measure.

Moreover, the AI based security can enhance the other general forms of security like encryption and authentication. For instance, AI can strengthen the identification process through the use of biometric identification, behavioral identification, or continuous identification, so as to guarantee that only legal users have access to IoT devices and networks. This offers a further defense in against all forms of Users Attack such as credential stuffing or identity theft. Similarly, it can improve the aspects of encryption by identifying the current defects or holes of current encryption strategies.

It is therefore accurately revealing that AI assumes a growing special point in enhancing the security of IoT networks. Since it provides a means of analyzing large volumes of data, identifying abnormal patterns and informative markers, and automatically provide security measures and recommendations for potential threats, it is a critically important tool for addressing the issues with IoT devices. As the convergence of the Internet realizes a state so advanced expanding a more prominent number of IoT networks embrace of AI networks in the IoT security frameworks that make the fabricated gadgets secure in an all the more multi-connections and self-guided world.

LITERATURE SURVEY

The increase in the usage of IoT and its devices has led to remarkable issues of securing the IoT networks. More IoT devices are being developed and are already being introduced into homes and industries and hence there is need to protect them. Some of the traditional approaches that have been used in the security area of IoT are encryption, firewalls and intrusion detection systems; however, such methods have shown their ineffectiveness especially due to the enormous and growing heterogeneity of IoT networks.

Previous Research on IoT Security

Encryption and firewalls have been conventional ways of securing IoT devices; however, these methods entail certain difficulties. Encryption is one of the effective ways of maintaining the security of data especially when passing through the IoT devices and the central system. However, IoT devices especially low computational ones have a challenge of implementing good encryption standards and this make them less secure (Rajawat, 2022). For example, while IoT devices' security is highly important, many of them employ no encryption at all or use a lightweight encryption algorithm. Firewalls are one more traditional method, which has been successfully implemented to regulate the access of IoT devices to other networks. But the firewalls themselves are not enough to guard IoT networks because of the absence of large amounts and differences of IoT devices (Altayaran & Elmedany, 2021). In classical IT networks firewalls are able to check the traffic list by specific IP addresses while most of IoT devices act in wireless environment, where new devices may appear and disappear frequently. Besides, firewalls do not detect the behavior of various IoT devices and potential incipient sophisticated intrusion techniques that can potentially breach the filtering mechanism.

Intrusion detection systems (IDS) have also implemented to IoT security, especially in terms of detect patterns of network traffic. It is evident that using traditional IDS systems including the signature based which works on the basis of known attack patterns presents a challenge in IoT scenarios. Due to the nature of IoT comprising of millions of devices (Rahman & Shah, 2016), many of which do not communicate in the same terms and operate on different OS, great difficulty is experienced in analyzing and developing generalized macrosignatures. In addition, they observe that IDS systems are incapable of detecting new threats at a time when the IoT networks are characterized by high frequency and variability of threats. Even to date there is still heightened insecurity within IoT networks, despite the laid down traditional security frameworks. Due to the growing interconnectivity of IoT networks, it is necessary to use fresh and more effective ways of IoT networks protection. AI has proved its worth in countering the existing threats and can be considered as a viable solution for the improvement of IoT protection methods.

AI in IoT Security

The development of new technologies has enabled AI to be introduced into the system specifically to enhance the security of the IoT networks. The use of AI, especially ML, and DL allow for a faster identification and counteraction of attacks and threats concerning IoT devices and networks since the field is continuously evolving.

Machine Learning Models for Detecting Anomalous Behavior and Intrusion

Machine learning has been widely used in IoT security area, especially in the field of detecting intrusion and unusual behavior. Machine learning can be used on big amount of data produced by IoT devices to identify the so-called 'normal' behaviour patterns and detect any suspicious activities that may signal a breach. This method of machine learning is particularly suitable for applying in IoT settings since unsupervised learning does not rely on input data labeled by a human. For instance, an ML model could identify abnormal activity in the communication of IoT devices through an attempt of a botnet with an aim of marshaling devices for DDoS attacks.

AI-Powered Threat Intelligence Systems

It is also noteworthy that threat intelligence systems which are based on AI technologies are widely used to improve the IoT systems security. These systems work in such a way that data collected from different sources is retrieved, processed and analyzed using artificial intelligence and activeness of the network and device logs and threat feeds (Ogawa & Hamamoto, 2023). It aims at being on the lookout and pinpoint potential threats early before they become full-fledged incidents and pass on the intelligence to the security teams. Since the AI-based systems can analyse the vast amount of information and reveal tendencies of attacks, these sorts of systems can be extremely efficient to foresee potential threats and manage risks in shorter periods. Employing such systems that integrate data from different sources, and having AI-driven analytics, can point to connections between incidents that are not easily recognizable with other forms of security analysis.

AI for Continuous Monitoring of IoT Networks

Monitoring is another key in protection of IoT networks because most IoT are developing and ever changing hence, it may not always be easy to know the status of devices or traffic flow within the network. Using AI, it is possible to make the continuous monitoring process faster and more efficient as it would involve analyzing the traffic on the network and the interactions of the connected devices in real time (Nakagawa & Shimojo, 2017). AI-based system can learn about the status of the IoT devices and every now and then diagnose whose activity or lack of it is peculiar and could be a sign of an intrusion. This means that the threat detection and response time are faster as opposed to when an organization is handling various issues as they arise.

AI-Based Access Control Mechanisms

AI is also being used in improving the security measures used in the IoT systems by improving the access control. In general, applications of IoT devices require access control mechanisms stronger than passwords and PINs because IoT devices are often accessed by many different users or in remote areas. This will enable the implementing of advanced techniques such as biometric identification, behavior-oriented verifications, as well as perpetual verifications (Anupriya & Muthumanikandan, 2023). For instance, machine-aided facial recognition mechanisms keep on observing the user actions and device activity to identify user especially, by analyzing the behavioral characteristics of typing speed, mouse cursor movements and geographical location. This type of authentication allows the continuous authentication of the user while trying to access IoT devices and networks since even if the credentials are stolen, the user cannot access the IoT devices.

Challenges in AI-Driven IoT Security

Nevertheless, there are some challenges associated with the AI use in the IoT security enhancement. Another problem is that it is quite difficult to train the AI models for various IoT settings. Most of the IoT devices differ in their capabilities, both in terms of hardware and software components as well as the communication protocols they implement making the creation of models that can detect threats in the IoT devices challenging for all types of devices. To train an AI model, one needs to bring together extensive data and acquiring data from various IoT devices is challenging as well as a time-consuming process (Visoottiviseth et al., 2020). An issue that might be particularly acute in the case of IoT devices is the limited computational capabilities of some of them may not facilitate the execution of AI algorithms. Most of the IoT devices are low-cost devices, and to make them low power consumption devices, the incorporation of complex AI algorithms would likely reduce the performance or deplete the battery power. A few of these issues can be dealt with using edge computing, a paradigm where further processing occurs locally instead of on the cloud IOT device.

Another factor is that AI models are quite vulnerable to adversarial attacks from their users. With the integration of AI in IoT security, AI themselves are often became the targeted system of the attackers. It is one of the strategies of making the machine learning models give out a wrong predictions or classifications of results from a given input data (Saini et al., 2022). With reference to IoT security the adversarial attacks could be acts of deceiving IoT device data or even changing the inputs of the sensors to avoid being detected by AI security mechanisms. Preserving the stability of such models and their insensitivity to such attacks can be considered as a significant problem that should be solved in order to guarantee the effectiveness of the AI-based security systems.

Case Studies

In several cases, people have shown that AI can be effectively applied in IoT networks as will be discussed below. In smart homes, it is used in security of IoT objects including cameras, locks, and thermostats among others. Such systems employ patterns of sophisticated algorithms of machine learning that have potential of identifying unprecedented trends within the behaviour of the devices, especially identifying any unauthorized access or increased activity, and are programmed to execute necessary operational reactions such as closing of doors and or sending alerts to the homeowners. Likewise, in healthcare, artificial intelligence is applied to protect IoT health systems including wearable health equipment, and remote patient monitoring apparatus. Automated approaches incorporate conclusions about patients' conditions made in real time, and suggest various security threats, including unauthorized access to the patient's records or alteration of settings on any given device. In the case of self-driving cars, artificial intelligence is used in deciding on communication protocols between vehicle controller, vehicle control systems and the external environment. By this, safety measures in the identified communication channel are checked against the risks of attack like spoofing or denial-of-service (DoS) attacks for instance on the vehicle systems. The following cases will demonstrate the possible application of AI in the protection of IoT networks in multiple connections. AI is likely to have the potential of being utilized more and more widely when it comes to improving the IoT security given the increasing use of this technology for providing more intelligent, flexible, and better security for IoT devices and networks.

AI TECHNIQUES FOR IOT SECURITY

As the number of connected devices grows rapidly in the IoT world, the problem of security steadily becomes a much bigger issue. Conventional security measures that include encryption and firewalls have been found unable to address todays' complex security issues in IoT networks. Due to the large number of IoT devices, their high variety and variability of devices' interactions, it is challenging to use traditional models of protection. In this paper, ML, DL, FL, and AI authentication system are shown to be some of the powerful technologies that can be used to improve the security of IoT networks. They make the capability of detecting intrusion, monitoring for any irregularities and check and ensure only permitted users make an attempt to control the IOT devices.

Machine Learning for Intrusion Detection

There are several reasons why ML algorithm is used for the detection of intrusion attacks in IoT networks, including the capability to process big data and the overall property of analyzing and detecting trends and patterns of typical and anomalous behavior. IoT networks have a lot of devices and all of them might be of different types hence it is very difficult to distinguish between the real and an intruder hence the importance of intrusion detection. IDS have the ability to analyze the information in the network traffic, log data and sensor data to detect an unauthorized connection, an abnormal behavior of the device, or certainly attack like DoS, data leakage and commands injection. Supervised and unsupervised approaches of Machine learning are often used in detecting intrusions in IoT systems. In supervised learning, there are labeled datasets used where the kinds of attack are already known as well as the normal network traffic. These models intend to categorize network activities into known categories like normal and abnormal, and the former are the focus of these diagrams. Some of the most frequently used algorithms developed for classification of intrusion patterns are the decision tree algorithm, the support vector machine (SVM) algorithm, and the random forest algorithm. These models work well in case the patterns of attacks are well understood and there are labels to the data available for the models to classify new events.

On the other hand, unsupervised learning do not need the labels of the data and are more advantageous in new and unknown attacks. In unsupervised learning models, there is no prior knowledge of what kind of attack patterns in the IoT devices and networks will be encountered. These models help identify difference from normal flow of packets in the network, which can be a sign of intrusion. Some of the clustering, which is categorized under unsupervised learning methods, include k-means and dimensionality reduction involves methods like, principal component analysis. These models are effective in detecting the new forms of attacks that may not have a record and are therefore referred to as zero-day attacks.

Deep Learning for Anomaly Detection

Neural networks with many layers- called deep learning (DL) has been considered very appropriate for detecting various complex threats and patterns of large data stream in the IoT. Deep learning is the most suitable solution for IoT devices because of its ability to handle large amount of and complex data. While the conventional approaches in the field of machine learning mainly require the features to be defined in advance, the deep learning networks are able to extract features from the raw data and, therefore, are capable of identifying the tiny patterns and peculiarities that refer to the potential security threats. Neural networks is one of the most popular methods in deep learning to carry out the anomaly detection. Specifically, these models are similar to the neuronal structures in the human brain and are very efficient in detecting patterns and relations in the information. DNN and RNN are particularly used in IoT security, to handle time-series data resulting from IoT devices. These networks are capable of learning the normal operational patterns of devices and can easily identify instances which may lead to an act of attack or intrusion.

The second type of deep learning architecture used in anomaly detection is the convolutional neural networks (CNN) particularly when the input data is represented in a grid form such as images or multidimensional sensor data. CNNs can be trained to find spatial hierarchies in the data and are especially utilized in identifying glitches in sensor information and other mishances that might signify a security infringement in a system. Due to the capability of deep learning models to handle large number of data from different IoT devices in unstructured format, the models can be used to detect and respond to malicious activities in real time. The first benefit of applying deep learning in IoT networks for anomaly detection is the identification of unknown and intricate threats. As opposed to the classical machine learning approaches, where features for the model and attack signatures are known beforehand, the deep learning models are not constrained by it. This makes deep learning a valuable approach to the ever-complicated threats that IoT networks are exposed in the present ever-changing cyber threat environment.

Federated Learning in IoT Security

Federated learning is a relatively new method of training machine learning models on distributed data sources which is useful in the sphere of IoT security. In conventional techniques of machine learning the data are to be stored and processed in a cloud server which is not favorable in terms of security and communication cost. These challenges are solved in federated learning because IoT devices are trained locally to work on their data without having to report their data to the central server. In federated learning, all the IoT devices contribute to the training to the model, while data remains at their end. The devices just upload only the features or weights they have learned to a central server in order to contribute to enhance the model of all. This makes a decentralized approach less worrying in terms of data sharing and use as well as cuts down the excessive demands on network bandwidth. Also, it enables an ongoing and non-intrusive updating of AI models while the data, on the various devices, remain secure.

The use of federated learning is ideal for securing IoT since it retains client confidentiality of submitted big data, for example, personal and health information from medical devices or information from private homes through IoT devices while allowing for Artificial intelligence for threat detection and anomality." Moreover, it is suitable where devices are geographically dispersed and cannot reach a central server frequently through a network connection. These devices are capable of functioning independently through federated learning by training and updating their models locally while being very secure and private. The main problem of FL in IoT security is to control the quality of the updates received from different IoT devices differing in the computational capabilities. Another important challenge is to prevent mesmerizing devices to inject wrong updates into the system which would, inturn, jeopardize the model's credibility and security. Nonetheless, federated learning is still the most effective approach towards adopting artificial intelligence security systems in large-scale IoT networks.

AI-Based Authentication Systems

Identification and authentication is one of the key challenges of IoT security because the IoT network can only be accessed by the authorized persons and things. It is also important to overcome the limitations associated with the use of passwords or personal identification numbers (PINs) in the IoT devices where several users have access to the devices and password protection can be easily cracked by hacking, etc. AI-based authentication systems provide more modern and secure approaches using machine learning algorithms for the check of users' identities and constant search for intruders. Biometric recognition, particularly, fingerprint scanning, facial and voice recognition are among the widely used techniques in the field of AI for authentication. Biometric systems that are based on artificial intelligence can study invariants of a person's physiological features and compare them with the templates of the person to identify them. These are secure systems because they are not easy to forge or hack into but are rather advanced. The examples include facial recognition where the system makes use of deep learning algorithm to identify the facial features and compare them with the data base of recognized users. In the same way, voice recognition can be based on deep neural networks that analyze patterns of a human voice for the purpose of authorization for IoT devices, which is safer and more convenient than many other possibilities.

Anomaly-based authentication is yet another usage of AI, which focuses on user behavior alert and checking for abnormalities that only authorized parties have access to. This kind of process does not just rely on verifying the name and password but assesses the dynamic behavior of typing, device's usage, and geographical location and checks whether the current session falls within normal usage in case of intrusion. If any corrective event occurs, it is possible to switch to a backup authenticate process or notify the system administrators about the unwanted intruder. This is showing to the fact that the PC-PMOA continually monitors the user's behavior in order to Figure 1 Additional Security Layer Added identify when the access credentials have been compromised especially in changing environment. Lastly, continuous authentication employs the use of AI to perform further verification while a user is active on the devices rather than just at the time of getting connected. Continuous authentication guarantees that even in case the attacker gets a user's credentials he cannot remain in the system unabated to cause further damage because the system will detect his compromise and kick him out of the system. Computer programs, for instance, can recognize shocks such as input from the keyboard, the movements of a mouse, and so on, in order to determine if the person using the device currently is the same as the one who logged in the device. It also plays an important role in providing real-time monitoring over the IoT devices in order to reduce the security threat such as unauthorized access. To summarise, there are numerous AI techniques such as machine learning, deep learning, federated learning, and AI-based authentication system which present a great improvement in the security of IoT networks. With the realization of AI, the IoT networks will be capable of adjusting, analyzing and defending against Security threats in future. With the ever increasing number of IoT devices in the market, these AI driven techniques will be very useful in ensuring the security of the networked systems.

RESULTS AND DISCUSSIONS

It is for this reasons that AI-based IoT security solutions have been shown to hold a lot of promise in handling security issues in IoT networks. Its applicability is useful for real-time intrusion detection, identifying deviant behavior and threats, which are necessary for building a secure environment for the developing network of IoT devices. Here you will find details of the above discussions by illustrating the effectiveness of using AI in securing IoT networks from real simulation and experimental examples, comparing the efficacy of AI-based solutions with traditional security models, measuring performance metrics and analyzing the pros and challenges of using AI in IoT.

AI-Powered IoT Security Solutions in Action

Some of the case studies and simulation results have been presented that show the efficacy of AI in IoT network security. The results of the performance analysis of three supervised learning algorithms, namely Decision Trees, SVMs, and Random Forests for intrusion detection in an IoT network are presented in figure 1. From the simulation results of these algorithms, it is found that the efficiency of these AI algorithms is superior to transmission methods, especially, as the number of sample training figures increase so does the algorithms detection rate. For example, when the sample dataset was trained with 1000 samples, Decision Tree recorded a 90% detection accuracy, which showed how the technology could efficiently detect difficult patterns and enhance security in the IoT network. Also, Figure. 2 summarizes the performance of the other categories of algorithms, that is, unsupervised algorithms such as K-means, PCA, and DBSCAN in the detection of the anomalies in IoT networks. These models achieved better F1 scores as compared to IDS, which are commonly based on a particular attack pattern. The unbeknownst ability to pick out new threat types which have not been seen before is made possible using unsupervised learning without requiring a training dataset is a testament to differentiation, cognitive and elastic nature of AI security solutions. Based on the simulation data it can be concluded that AI can be effectively applied in real-time anomaly detection in IoT networks that are characterized by high dynamics of threat activity. Deep learning models used for anomaly detection are illustrated in Figure 3 below where CNNs, RNNs, LSTMs were used to noted anomalies in big IoT data flow. It was noted that deep learning models were able to predict with reasonable accuracy with huge volumes of unstructured data which brings in idea of deep learning models successfully flagging what might be well-hidden sophisticated threats to the traditional methods of detection. The performance of the deep learning models increased in subsequent epochs also making it possible to train them for more epochs in the future.

Comparison of AI-Based IoT Security Solutions vs. Traditional Methods

It has also been found that the accuracy rate of detection is much higher as compared with the traditional ways, and there is also ease of scalability and real time detection and handling of threats. Traditional security methods including confidentiality, identity and access, firewalls, and signature-based IDSs provide little or no solution to address the security problem present in IoT networks. These methods also do not work well with the new or advanced type of attacks. In comparison, ML-based systems and others, such as deep learning and federated learning, can identify known and unknown threats since they learn from new data. This adaptability to network changes makes AI-based security systems far more useful when it comes to IoT security threats. Figure 4 presents an evaluation of threat intelligence system based on the concept of AI in which the AI models like supervised learning and deep learning have been compared based on the threat detection rate and response time. The case of AI systems showed the effectiveness of the innovation as compared to the traditional security solutions where it highlighted the percentage level of threats that were identified by the AI systems and the time taken to do it. Previous systems, based on the concepts of use signatures for detection, provided less accuracy and more time delay during detecting threats which are not included in the program's database.

Figure 1. Intrusion Detection Performance Using Supervised Learning

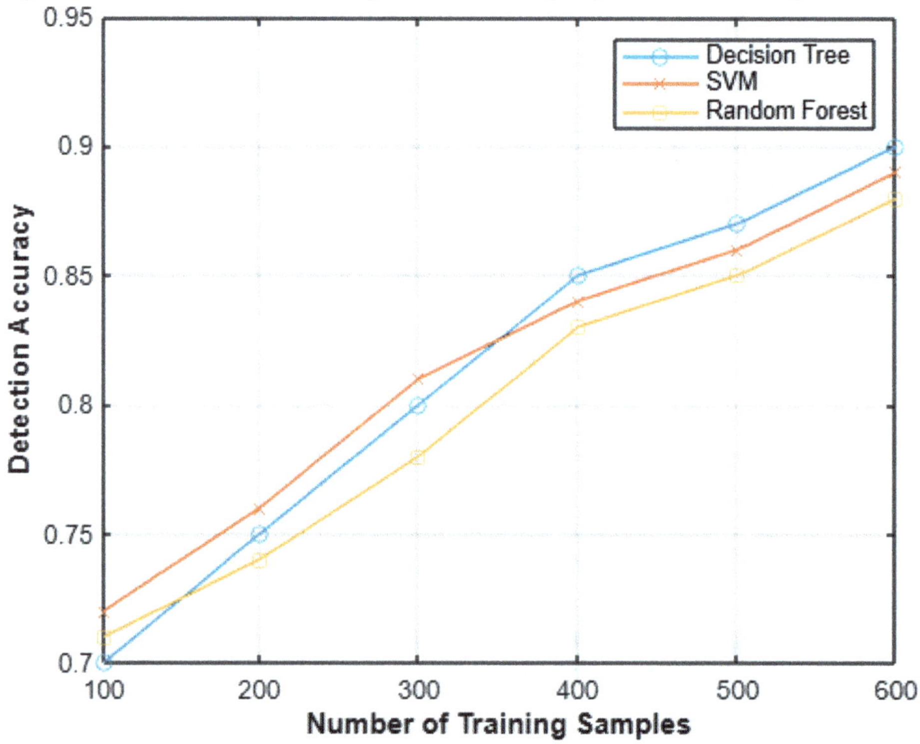

Figure 2. Anomaly Detection Using Unsupervised Learning

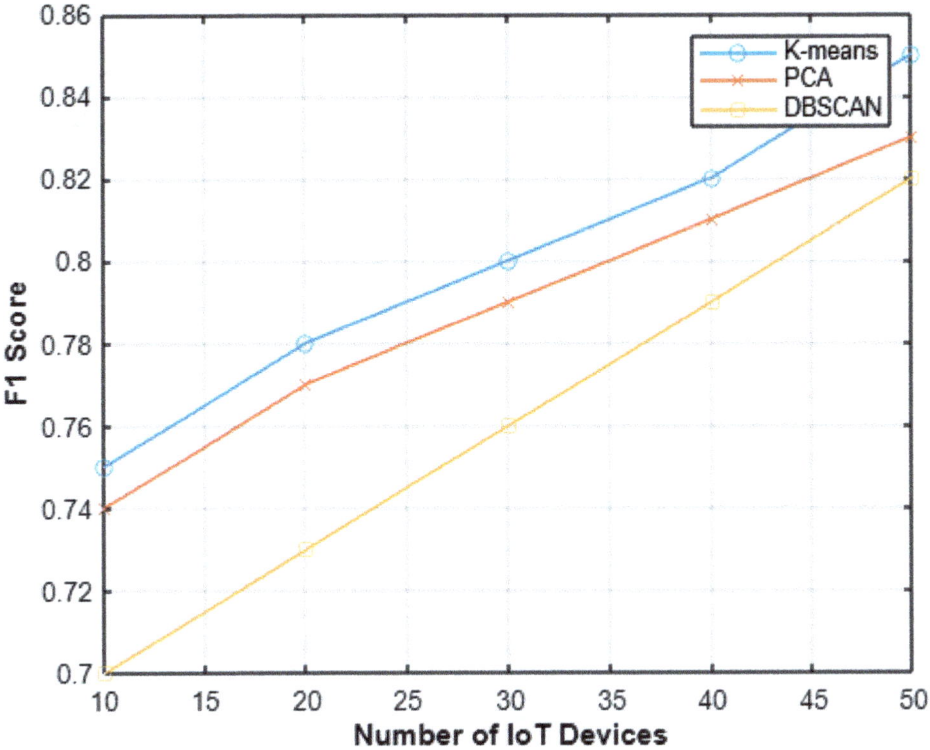

Figure 3. Deep Learning Model for Anomaly Detection

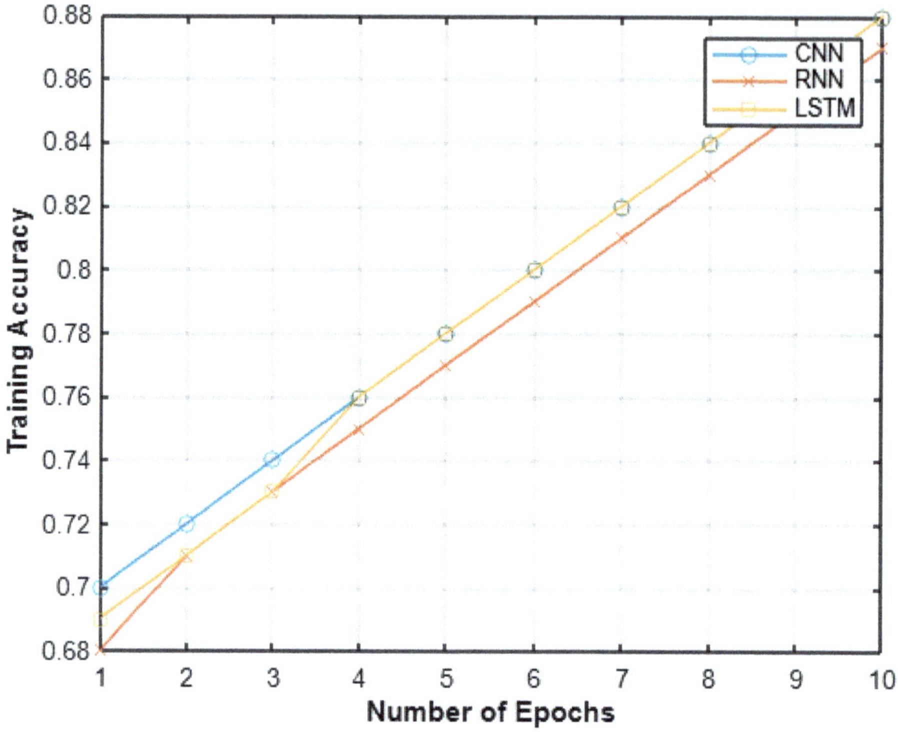

Figure 4. AI-Powered Threat Intelligence System

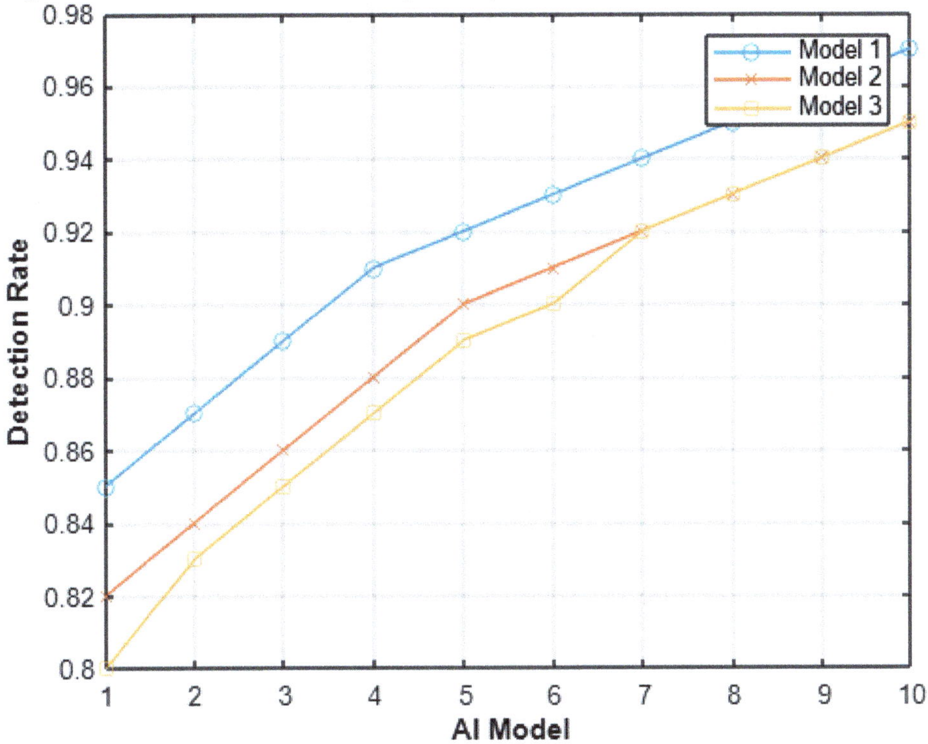

Figure 5. IoT Network Traffic with Anomalous Behavior

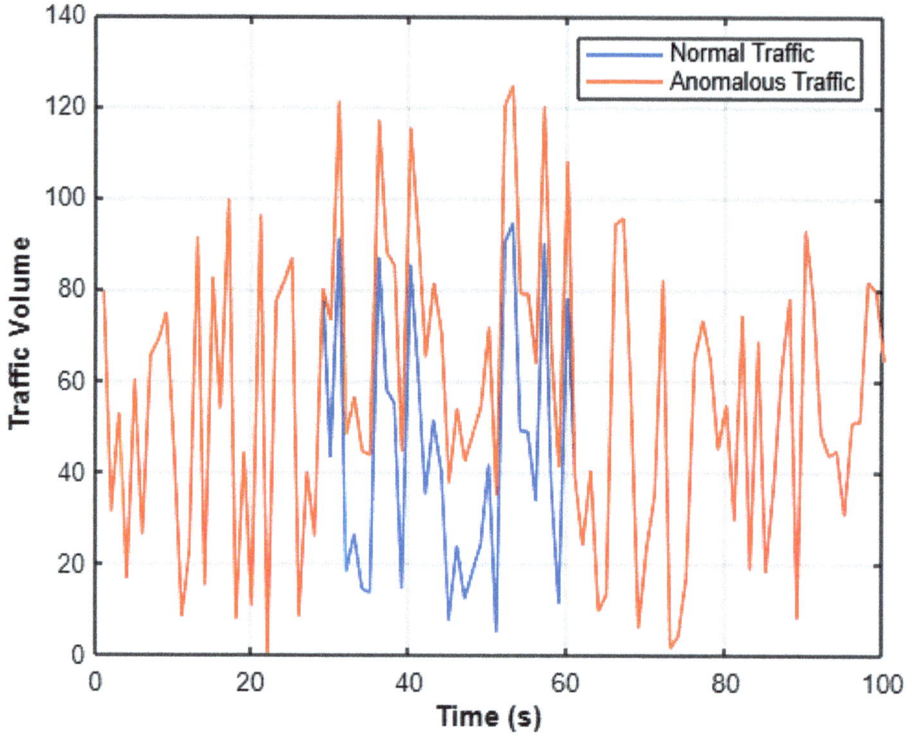

Figure 6. Federated Learning Model for IoT Security

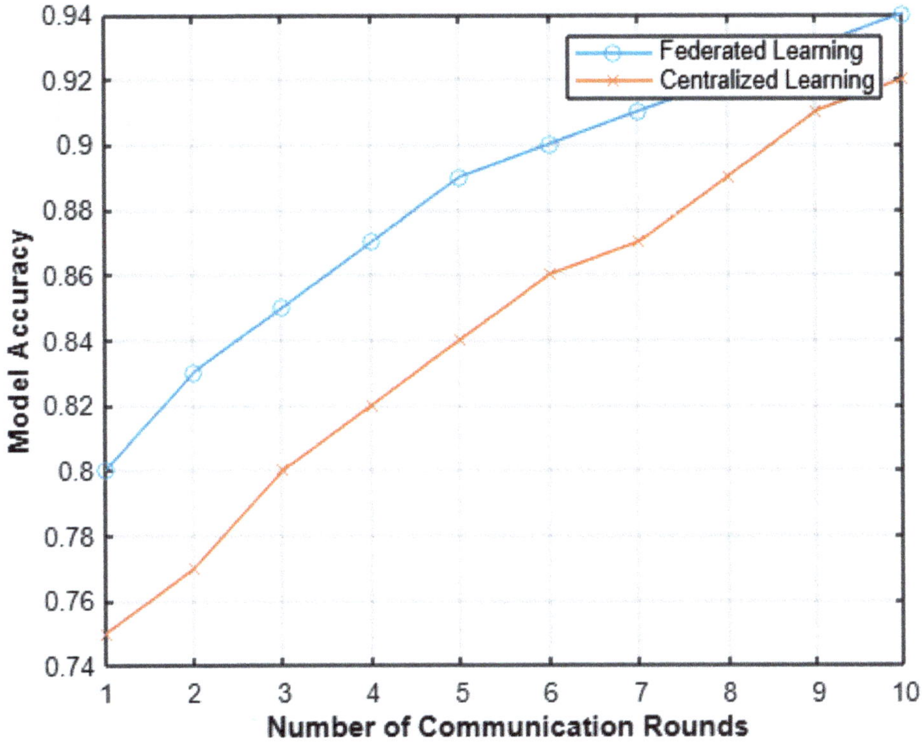

Figure 7. AI-Based Authentication System Performance

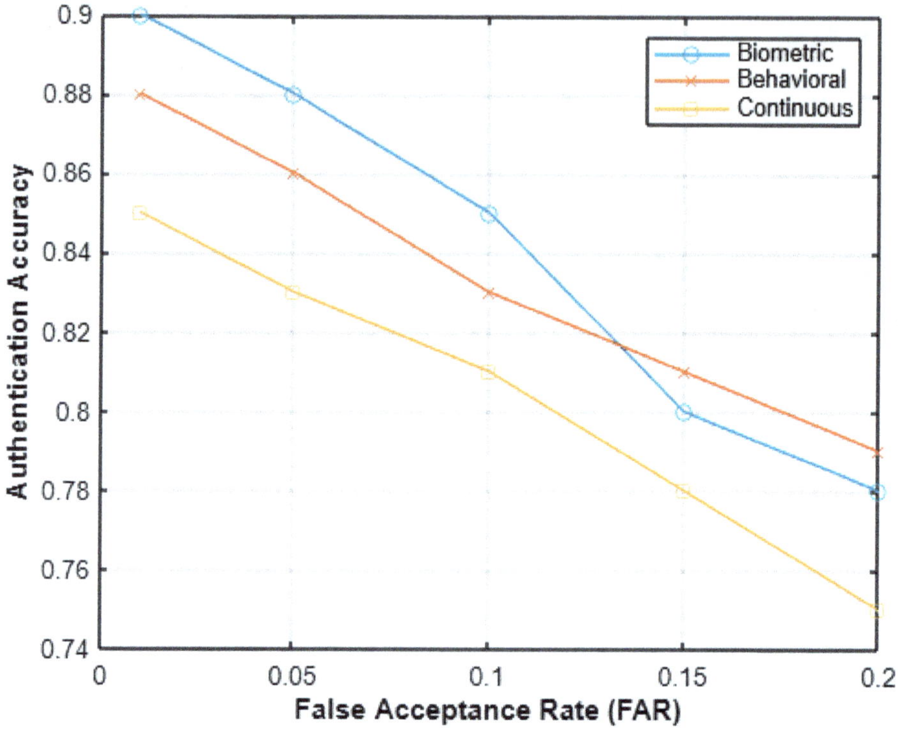

Figure 8. AI-Based Intrusion Detection and Prevention in IoT Networks

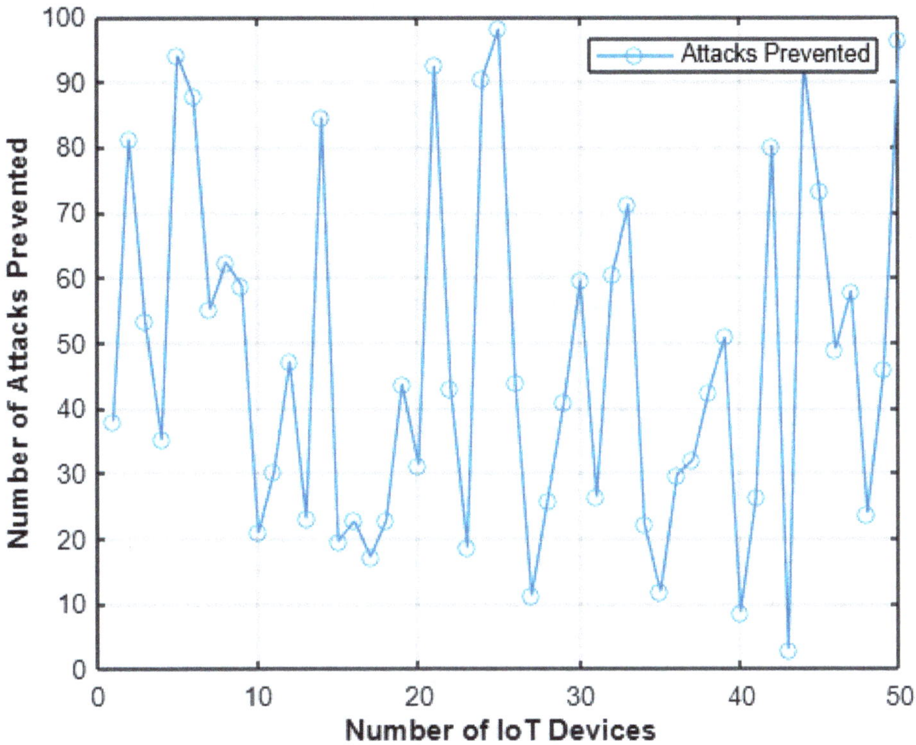

Metrics Evaluation

Performance indicators like detection rate, true positive/negative values, reaction time and IOT capability were used to measure AI solutions for IoT security. Referring to the Figure 5, the percentage of false positive and false negative was the lowest for AI- driven models comparing with the traditional ones. These characteristics made these algorithms transparent and mostly useful because the ability of learning from the data and learning from the new attack patterns enabled them to detect the attacks with better accuracy and less number of false alarms. However, it can be stated that conventional security approaches were much less efficient when it came to false positives, especially in the contexts of intricate attack patterns or fluctuations in traffic. The response time of AI-based solutions was also measured in the Figure 6 and 7, where federated learning as well as, the AI-based authentication systems were implemented. It was again evidenced by the result that the AI models were able to process the data in an efficient way and with greater speed thus enabling threat perception and prevention. This is particularly important in the IoT network since it has to be very responsive to any form of attack in order to minimize or even prevent the effect of the attack. The fourth assessment criterion for determining the efficiency of AI-based IoT security solutions was scalability. Traditional methods are a big challenge when the number of devices in the IoT network increases, and the networks become complicated. However, the machine learning models at particular, the federated learning (Figure 6), proved their efficiency in terms of scalability without burdening the network with too many requests or demands more computational power. Federated learning enabled local training on multiple IoT devices with low network usage and while maintaining a high security standard that does not slow down the device.

Challenges and Limitations

Despite the above advantages by integrating AI in the IoT security solutions, there are still some challenges that arise in the integration process. There are mainly two important aspects: 1) On the structural layer, there are many design choices that are possible but limited by computational resources of IoT devices. However, most of IoT devices are deployed in environments that could be considered resource-constrained and thus, such devices are not powerful enough to handle complex AI algorithms. Because of this limitation, AI cannot be directly applied onto IoT devices, typical operations may require edge computing or cloud processing. Another challenge is a data requests require to train the big amount of machine learning and deep learning. AI models, in order to be highly accurate, need a large amount of labeled data and collecting such data in IoT environments may demand time and costs. When the distribution of the data is not enough or not balanced, it creates poor-fit models especially when it is applied to identify the newer or rare kind of attack that is not present in the data set. IDPS thru AI-based systems performance is shown in figure 8 in identifying and preventing intrusions against IoT networking. This plot further portrays the effectiveness of the AI-based solutions in terms of the number of attacks that could be prevented with growth in the IoT devices in the network. It also proves that the AI-based IDPS has the potentiality to scale along with the IoT networks and that it enhances protection in better ways while maintaining efficiency. As the number of IoT devices is increasing, the AI model successfully saves a portion of attacks and proves the system's capacity to cope with vast and intricate IoT networks. Also, it remains vulnerable to adversarial attacks in which the attacker tries to manipulate the input data to mislead the model. This is especially the case in IoT security as the adversarial machine learning attacks can circumvent AI based IoT detection systems. Preventing such attacks on AI models and maintaining the reliability and stability of the models is still an open problem of active research and development.

Future Trends in AI and IoT Security

The use of AI in the protection of IoT is still new but has numerous possibilities for development and improvement in the future. One of them can be identified as the trend towards AI-based security systems that would be autonomous. These systems will not only be able to identify the threats and find ways on how to counteract them but it also will be able to intercept and forestall an invasion. Relatively using artificial intelligence, intelligent security systems will automatically and repetitively analyze emergent threats, and make IoT networks more independent. One more trend is oriented toward adopting edge computing for more effective AI operation. With growing intelligence of the devices and the increasing amount of data generated by IoT devices, edge computing will make AI models to be processed locally without much required help from the cloud to reduce latency. This will be highly useful in detecting threats in real time and would be specially useful in applications where time is of essence such as machine controlled automobiles and manufacturing industries. Last but not the least, the AI models to detect zero-day vulnerabilities shall be important in guarding IoT networks. Most of the conventional security systems evolved have a signature or pattern that a security analyst looks for in order to determine presence of threats. Nevertheless, machine learning models for AI can be designed to search for vulnerabilities and threats, of which were unknown earlier, thus making IoT networks less susceptible to malicious activities. This will be critical as new ways to attack these connective and complex devices are always on the horizon with introduction of new IoT devices on the market. Overall, it can be deduced that IoT security that is powered by the help of artificial intelligence is the only way to effectively combat the constantly emerging threats in the context of IoT networks. Despite this, the progress in the aforementioned technologies has continued to grow, mostly ensuring more secure IoT networks that are efficient, scalable, and effective. With the advancement in AI technology, its implementation in IoT security is set to be a key factor that will help in the protection and safety of the devices in the autonomous world.

CONCLUSION

AI can be employed to enhance the IoT security by overcoming various different issues arising from the growth of connected devices. The ability of applying machine learning and deep learning algorithms in particular provides a much better capability of identifying threats in real-time and scale and adapt the security measures for IoT environment. Such as AI-based IDS, AD models, and AI-TIS, depending on developing new strategies to secure networks as well as devices, outperformed the traditional security approaches like signature detection and firewalls. AI-learning algorithms enable the faster response to new threats and newer attacks' patterns enabling the IoT safety by ensuring confidentiality, integrity, and availability of IoT networks.

There is a need for more research and innovation in the area of machine learning especially in the labeling or designing of the model to detect threats in real-time especially in settings where resources are scarce. Integrating block chain technology with artificial intelligence can even improve the IoT devices security by providing a secure model of storing data and decentralized trust management. Some of these include improving on the security standards and features of the IoT devices based on artificial intelligence since there is also a high propensity to risks and developing new ways to achieve the same reliability in the IoT networks. Studies on the adversarial machine learning attacks and its countermeasures will also be essential to protect the AI models from the attacks. With the growth of self-organized IoT networks, people with actual AI and IoT knowledge, as well as cybersecurity professionals, should unite to design steadily improving IoT security. This shall go hand in hand in making sure that IoT devices are safe in the ever smart and connected world.

REFERENCES

Altayaran, S., & Elmedany, W. (2021). "Security threats of application programming interface (API's) in internet of things (IoT) communications," 4th Smart Cities Symposium (SCS 2021), Online Conference, Bahrain, 2021, pp. 552-557.

Anupriya, S. R., & Muthumanikandan, V. (2023). "A Survey on Exploring the Effectiveness of IOT Based Home Security Systems," *2023 International Conference on Computer Communication and Informatics (ICCCI)*, Coimbatore, India, 2023, pp. 1-10. DOI: 10.1109/ICCCI56745.2023.10128178

Chanal, P. M., & Kakkasageri, M. S. (2019). "Hybrid Algorithm for Data Confidentiality in Internet of Things," 2019 10th International Conference on Computing, Communication and Networking Technologies (ICCCNT), Kanpur, India, 2019, pp. 1-5. DOI: 10.1109/ICCCNT45670.2019.8944565

D, S., & Kawale, S. R. (2023). "Cloud-Based Multi-Layer Security Framework for Protecting E-Health Records," 2023 International Conference on Artificial Intelligence for Innovations in Healthcare Industries (ICAIIHI), Raipur, India, 2023, pp. 1-7.

Francisti, J., Balogh, Z., Molnár, G., József, K., Gergely, S., & Nagy, E. (2023). "Methods for Verifying the Security of Available IoT Devices," 2023 IEEE 21st Jubilee International Symposium on Intelligent Systems and Informatics (SISY), Pula, Croatia, 2023, pp. 000595-000600. DOI: 10.1109/SISY60376.2023.10417920

Joel, M. R., Manikandan, G., & Bhuvaneswari, G. (2023). "An Analysis of Security Challenges in Internet of Things (IoT) based Smart Homes," *2023 Second International Conference on Electronics and Renewable Systems (ICEARS)*, Tuticorin, India, 2023, pp. 490-497. DOI: 10.1109/ICEARS56392.2023.10085106

Lavanya, P., Subbareddy, I. V., & Selvakumar, V. (2022). "Internet of Things enabled Block Level Security Mechanism to Big Data Environment using Cipher Security Policies," *2022 International Conference on Advances in Computing, Communication and Applied Informatics (ACCAI)*, Chennai, India, 2022, pp. 1-6. DOI: 10.1109/ACCAI53970.2022.9752603

Mahindrakar, R. P., & Chandel, S. (2023). "Advanced IoT-Enabled Warehouse Air Quality Monitoring and Live Security System for Medical Applications," *2023 International Conference on Artificial Intelligence for Innovations in Healthcare Industries (ICAIIHI)*, Raipur, India, 2023, pp. 1-6.

Manivasagam, G., & Prasad, K. D. V. (2024). Novel approaches to biometric security using enhanced session keys and elliptic curve cryptography. *Journal of Discrete Mathematical Sciences and Cryptography, 27*(2-A), 477–488. DOI: 10.47974/JDMSC-1884

Miettinen, M., & Sadeghi, A.-R. (2018). "Keynote: Internet of Things or Threats? On Building Trust in IoT," 2018 International Conference on Hardware/Software Codesign and System Synthesis (CODES+ISSS), Turin, Italy, 2018, pp. 1-9. DOI: 10.1109/CODESISSS.2018.8525931

Nakagawa, I., & Shimojo, S. (2017). "IoT Agent Platform Mechanism with Transparent Cloud Computing Framework for Improving IoT Security," 2017 IEEE 41st Annual Computer Software and Applications Conference (COMPSAC), Turin, Italy, 2017, pp. 684-689. DOI: 10.1109/COMPSAC.2017.156

Ogawa, K., & Hamamoto, N. (2023). "Proposal of Low-Cost Automated Security Diagnosis System for IoT Devices," *2023 IEEE International Conference on Consumer Electronics (ICCE)*, Las Vegas, NV, USA, 2023, pp. 1-3. DOI: 10.1109/ICCE56470.2023.10043424

Prabavathy, S., & Supriya, V. (2021). "SDN based Cognitive Security System for Large-Scale Internet of Things using Fog Computing," *2021 International Conference on Emerging Techniques in Computational Intelligence (ICETCI)*, Hyderabad, India, 2021, pp. 129-134. DOI: 10.1109/ICETCI51973.2021.9574051

Rahman, R. A., & Shah, B. (2016). "Security analysis of IoT protocols: A focus in CoAP," 2016 3rd MEC International Conference on Big Data and Smart City (ICBDSC), Muscat, Oman, 2016, pp. 1-7. DOI: 10.1109/ICBDSC.2016.7460363

Rajawat, A. S., ... (2022). "Security Analysis for Threats to Patient Data in the Medical Internet of Things," 2022 11th International Conference on System Modeling & Advancement in Research Trends (SMART), Moradabad, India, 2022, pp. 248-253. DOI: 10.1109/SMART55829.2022.10047322

Rizvi, S.. (2021). "The Future for a Secure Internet of Things," *2021 International Conference on Software Security and Assurance (ICSSA)*, Altoona, PA, USA, 2021, pp. 56-63. DOI: 10.1109/ICSSA53632.2021.00019

Saini, K. R., Jigajinni, V., & Dofe, J. (2022). "Performance Comparison of Cryptosystems in Context to Internet of Things," 2022 4th International Conference on Data Intelligence and Security (ICDIS), Shenzhen, China, 2022, pp. 82-87. DOI: 10.1109/ICDIS55630.2022.00020

Satish, T. (2024). Cryptographic image-based data security strategies in wireless sensor networks. *Journal of Discrete Mathematical Sciences and Cryptography, 27*(2-A), 293–304. DOI: 10.47974/JDMSC-1883

Shandilya, S., & Reddy, N. S. (2024). "AI-Enhanced Cloud Security Framework for IoT Networks Using a Predictive Analytics Approach," 2024 3rd International Conference for Advancement in Technology (ICONAT), Goa, India, 2024, pp. 1-8.

Visoottiviseth, V., Chutaporn, G., Kungvanruttana, S., & Paisarnduangjan, J. (2020). "PITI: Protecting Internet of Things via Intrusion Detection System on Raspberry Pi," 2020 International Conference on Information and Communication Technology Convergence (ICTC), Jeju, Korea (South), 2020, pp. 75-80. DOI: 10.1109/ICTC49870.2020.9289311

Chapter 3
Blockchain and AI Convergence for Securing IoT Networks

Yosuf Mohamed Ismail Ahmed Hassan
http://orcid.org/0009-0005-3582-2594
Taylor's University, Malaysia

ABSTRACT

The rapid development of the Internet of Things (IoT) in healthcare, industry, smart cities, and supply chains have meant that the connection and automation have become more widespread but also more complex in terms of security and privacy issues arising from having something more homogeneous, widespread, and multifaceted by governance. Conventional centralized models of security are also incapable of providing scalable identity management, real time threat detection, data integrity and cross domain trust. The chapter is an exploration of blockchain and artificial intelligence (AI) convergence as a security by design frameworks of IoT. Decentralized identity, tamper-evident logging, auditability and programmable governance using smart contracts are provided by blockchain, adaptive intrusion detection, anomaly analytics and predictive risk assessment are provided by AI. It provides a layered architecture of device layer, blockchain layer, AI layer, applications, implementation issues, regulatory issues and future research directions in resilient IoT security.

DOI: 10.4018/979-8-3373-3857-6.ch003

1. INTRODUCTION

1.1 Overview of IoT Security Challenges

Internet of Things (IoT) is a paradigm shift in the field of computing and communication, which is potential to create a seamless interconnectedness of physical objects, sensors, actuators and digital services. By using intelligence and connectivity to fill the environment that we live, work and play in, IoT systems provide for a bevy of possible applications including smart homes, healthcare monitoring, industrial automation, intelligent transportation, and large-scale urban infrastructure. Early foundational studies define IoT as a very heterogeneous and large-scale network ecosystem which will bring the physical and virtual entities together by sensing, communicating and calculating the capacities (Atzori et al., 2010). While this paradigm promises a level of efficiency and automation which has never been seen before, deep security and privacy issues are also created.

A defining characteristic for IoT systems is that they are heterogeneous. IoT devices are highly variable in terms of hardware capabilities, operating systems, communication protocols and hardware deployment environments. This diversity makes it difficult to design homogenous security mechanisms, and are often the reason for inconsistent or weak security across devices. In addition, the IoT systems work in a massive scale and possibly millions of devices are involved creating a stream of data so the attack surface is much larger than in the case of the traditional networks (Atzori et al., 2010) and (Roman et al., 2013).

Security threats to IoT environments include device impersonation, unauthorised access to the environment, data manipulation, man-in-the-middle attacks, distributed denial-of-service (DDoS) attacks and the creation of large-scale botnets. The distributed nature of IoT deployments and the fact that often many devices are unattended, physical tampering and firmware manipulation can be very difficult to prevent or detect. In addition, IoT data often comprises sensitive information as it relates to personal health, location, or industrial processes, and raises questions of great privacy concern (Roman et al., 2013). These difficulties are complicated by the fact that many IoT devices are deployed with very little built-in security, and operate for long life-cycles without regular updates or patching.

Comprehensive surveys on IoT security highlight the following: The combination of constrained devices, pervasive connectivity and data-driven services means that IoT presents a threat landscape that cannot be effectively addressed by traditional security assumptions (Sicari et al., 2015) As IoT systems continue to proliferate in safety-critical and regulated domains, the need to ensure confidentiality, integrity, availability and accountability is becoming a basic requirement and not an option.

1.2 Limitations of Traditional Security Models in IoT Environments

Conventional security models have been developed mainly for enterprise IT systems and cloud-centric architectures, in which devices are relatively homogeneous and capable of processing (high-tech devices) and centrally managed. These models usually use perimeter-based defence s, centralised authentication servers and static access control policies. However, such approaches are unsuitable in IoT environments because of fundamental mismatches in their architecture.

One of the largest limitations is a trust on centralised authorities. Centralized identity management and authentication servers add single points of failure & performance bottleneck particularly in large scale IoT deployment. If a central authority becomes compromised, or becomes unavailable, a significant part of the IoT network could be made insecure or become inoperable. Studies consistently bring out the situation where centralized trust models ruin resilience in distributed IoT systems (Lin et al., 2017).

Another challenge is the limitation of resources for IoT devices. Many of the IoT endpoints have limited processing power, memory, and energy reserves, so it is not practical to implement heavyweight cryptographic protocols or continuous security monitoring agents on them. Traditional security solutions tend to assume that sufficient computational resources are available to perform the security algorithms, which is not true for battery-powered or embedded IoT devices (Alaba et al., 2017). As a result, security mechanisms are often simplified or even omitted altogether and become more vulnerable.

Further, traditional security architectures are challenging to work with given the dynamic and multi-domain nature of IoT ecosystems. Devices can join and leave networks dynamically, migrate between administrative domains or communicate with the services of other organizations. Static access control lists and manually configured policies are hard to maintain in such environments and are misconfigured easily. Research shows that trust relationships in IoT are fluid and context dependent and adaptive and decentralized security mechanisms are needed instead of static centralized control (Sicari et al., 2015) and (Lin et al., 2017).

These limitations show that adding extensions to existing security models is not enough. Instead, IoT requires security architectures that are both distributed and scalable and capable of running in partial trust and limited resources.

1.3 Need for Distributed Trust and Intelligent Threat Mitigation

Given the limitations on centralized approaches to security, the need for distributed mechanisms of trust in IoT systems, which eliminate the need for a central point of authority, is increasing, while strong guarantees of integrity and accountability are retained. Distributed trust means that more than one stakeholder can be involved in security governance, such as device manufacturers, service providers, operators and regulators, without the need to trust each other fully. This is particularly important in industrial and smart city deployments, for which infrastructure is shared across organizational boundaries (Sicari et al., 2015).

In parallel, the scale and complexity of IoT networks implies the use of intelligent threat mitigation mechanisms. Traditional signature-based intrusion detection systems are useless for novel/evolving attacks, which is the case in IoT environments. Instead, security solutions must be able to continuously analyze the behavior of devices, the communication patterns, and the states of the systems and detect anomalies and predict emerging threats. Machine learning techniques have been extensively studied to be applied for this purpose, since they can learn complex patterns from a substantial amount of data and adapt over time (Buczak & Guven, 2016).

However, intelligent security analytics is not enough without trusted sources of data and verifiable decision processes. IoT security systems need to ensure that telemetry that is used for threat detection has not been tampered with and that security decisions can be audited after the fact. This combination of distributed trust and smart analytics becomes the conceptual basis for integrating the decentralized ledger technologies with AI powered security models.

1.4 Motivation for the Convergence of Blockchain and Artificial Intelligence

Blockchain and Artificial Intelligence have been introduced as two transformative technologies that solve complementary aspects of IoT security. Blockchain offers a decentralized and tamper-evident ledger to securely coordinate, maintain data integrity and accountability with no central control. Due to the use of its cryptographic foundations and consensus mechanisms, it is ideal for a world of partial trust and multi-stakeholder governance (Nakamoto, 2008), (Zheng et al., 2017) and (Yaga et al., 2018).

AI on the other hand, is especially good at extracting knowledge from data and making an adaptive decision. In the field of cybersecurity, AI-based methods have been used for intrusion detection, malware classification and anomaly detection, and it is shown that such methods perform better than the traditional rule-based methods in many cases (Buczak & Guven, 2016). These capabilities are further improved with deep learning techniques, which model complex temporal and spatial patterns of network traffic (Sommer & Paxson, 2010).

The motivation for convergence is the fact that blockchain can be used to make AI more trustworthy, and on the other hand AI can be used to make blockchain enabled systems more efficient and intelligent. Blockchain can be used for verifiable data provenance for AI training and inference to reduce the risks of data poisoning, and unauthorized model manipulation. On the contrary, AI can also be used to optimize the operations of the blockchain by detecting malicious behavior, predicting network congestion, and also in the adaptive policy enforcement.

In IoT applications where data is generated at the edge and trust levels are low, the convergence of blockchain and AI provides a realization of a common data sharing and intelligent monitoring and enforcement framework. This type of convergence is becoming more and more accepted as a promising direction for next-generation IoT security architectures (Dorri et al., 2017), (Christidis & Devetsikiotis, 2016), (Reyna et al., 2018) and (Casino et al., 2019). The heterogeneous and distributed nature of IoT systems considerably increases the attack surface at the different device, network, edge, and cloud layers of the IoT systems as shown in Fig. 1 where some common threats, including device spoofing, data tampering, and distributed denial-of-service attacks are mapped to different architectural layers.

Figure 1. IoT security threat surface at device, network, edge, cloud, and data layer which represent heterogeneous attack vector at distributed environment.

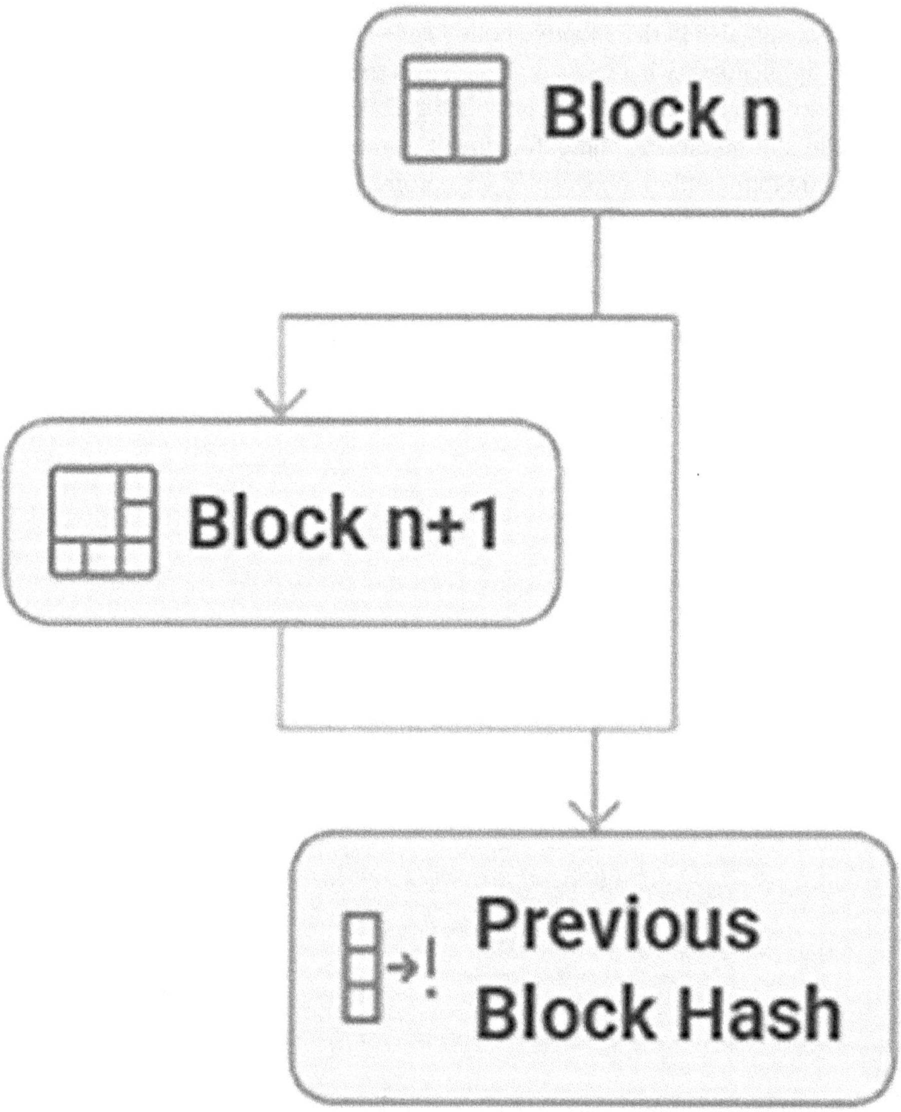

1.5 Chapter Contributions and Scope

This chapter provides a comprehensive and structured examination of blockchain–AI convergence for securing IoT networks. The primary contributions of the chapter are as follows:

1. **Systematic analysis of IoT security challenges,** emphasizing the limitations of centralized and static security models in large-scale, heterogeneous environments.
2. **Conceptual foundations** of blockchain and AI technologies as applied to cybersecurity, highlighting their individual strengths and limitations.
3. **An integrated perspective** on how blockchain and AI can be combined to provide decentralized trust, intelligent threat detection, and accountable security governance.
4. **Architectural insights and application scenarios** demonstrating how the proposed convergence can be realized in domains such as healthcare, industrial IoT, smart cities, and supply chains.

The chapter is also conceptual and architectural in nature; it concentrates on design principles and frameworks together with deployment aspects but not experimental analysis. The argument is also based on the existing surveys and background studies to make it relevant and rigorous.

1.6 Chapter Organization

The rest of this chapter has this arrangement. Section 2 has portions of the background notions in Block Chain and AI based cyber security. Section 3 addresses the requirements of security of the IoT and the gaps available. Part 4 and 5 consider security mechanisms relying on blockchain and AI respectively. It is under section 6 that the synergistic integration of them is discussed. Section 7 depicts a reference architecture and uses cases are depicted in Section 8. Section 9 and 10 have talked about implementation consideration and challenges. Section 11-13 discuss security and privacy analysis, regulatory issues and future research directions. Finally, the chapter ends on a good note with Section 14 providing some valuable insights and recommendations.

2. BACKGROUND CONCEPTS

The convergence of Block Chain and Artificial Intelligence (AI) to secure the Internet of Things (IoT) networks is an area that derives off two separate, yet complementary technological foundations. The idea of blockchain brings decentralized trust, integrity and accountability by the form of cryptography and consensus and AI brings adaptive intelligence, which has the capacity to learn, predict and make autonomous decisions. In order to best enjoy the motivation and design of integrated AI-Blockchain-IoT security architectures, one should be aware of the basic concepts that underlie such technologies and its accepted role in cybersecurity. This part offers the background that is needed, starting by taking a glimpse of the foundations of blockchain, and then discussing the methods in AI to implement cybersecurity.

2.1 Blockchain Fundamentals

2.1.1 Distributed Ledger Technology Overview

A system of this type in which a common ledger of information is being maintained within a network of distributed nodes as opposed to being operated by a central authority is called Distributed Ledger Technology (DLT). Every network user is provided with a replica of the ledger and validity of updates is agreed upon as a whole based on a set of predetermined consensus rules. The emergence of blockchain systems has proved that trust, consistency and integrity in distributed systems is possible, and can be demonstrated in environments where the participants may not absolutely trust each other.

Early work done on blockchain inspired systems have focused on the disruptive potential of decentralized ledgers and how they could be used to replace centralized intermediaries for financial and transaction purposes. On the back of this, subsequent research had widened these ideas to extra common areas, for example, cybersecurity, data sharing, and scattered government. In the context of cybersecurity, blockchain is increasingly seen a mechanism to enforce trust and accountability in environments where heterogeneity, partial trust and dynamic membership are the norms and characteristics that can be seen as matching very closely with IoT ecosystems (Sommer & Paxson, 2010).

A distributed ledger means that once a transaction gets recorded and agreed on it is very difficult to change retroactively. This immutability is ensured with the help of cryptographic methods disbursed validation which makes DLT enticing for applications that require auditability and non-repudiation. In IoT security, the following: - distributed ledgers can help to record device identities, access events, firmware updates and policy changes and enable transparent and verifiable management of security across organizational boundaries.

2.1.2 Blocks, Hashing, and Consensus Algorithms

At the heart of DLT based on blockchain is the concept of the block that packs a set of transactions or records within a unit that is structured as a block. Due to each block containing a cryptographic hash of the preceding block form a chain of blocks preserving the integrity of the history. Cryptographic hash functions play a central role as the means of generating fixed-length outputs that are computationally infeasible to invert or hash to (and so ensure that even a minor change in stored data is instantly recognisable).

Consensus algorithms regulate the agreement of the validity and sequence of blocks between the nodes of the distributed network. The oldest and most well-known consensus mechanism is Proof of Work or PoW that uses computational puzzles to control bad behaviour. However, PoW is expensive on the computational and energy levels, which means that it cannot be used in cases where the resources are constrained, such as IoT. Consequently, alternative consensus mechanisms have been proposed and analyzed including Proof of Stake (PoS), Byzantine Fault Tolerant (BFT) and hybrid approaches.

Comprehensive overviews of blockchain architectures are focused on the fact that the choice of consensus has a direct impact on the system scalability, latency, security guarantees (Jamalipour & Murali, 2021). In permissioned environments where deployments are in enterprise and IoT scenarios, more often than not, market vectors are performed using BFT based consensus protocols and authority-based validation models since they provide deterministic finality and reduce overhead. These mechanisms are what allow blockchains to exist in a relatively efficient manner in organization whose validator identities are known and already corresponding to organizational agreements.

From a security point of view, consensus algorithms are the backbone of the enforcement of trust. They make it impossible for malicious nodes to unilaterally change the ledger and for the system state to represent the agreement of the participating entities. Instead, in IoT ecosystems, where the devices and the stakeholders may reside in different administrative domains, consensus mechanisms help to implement security enforcement in a coordinated fashion, without centralised control. The basic structure of a blockchain ledger consists of cryptographically linked blocks whereby each block is referenced to the hash value of its predecessor to make it immutable as illustrated in Fig. 2.

Figure 2. Blockchain data structure showing block composition and cryptographic hash chaining that ensures immutability.

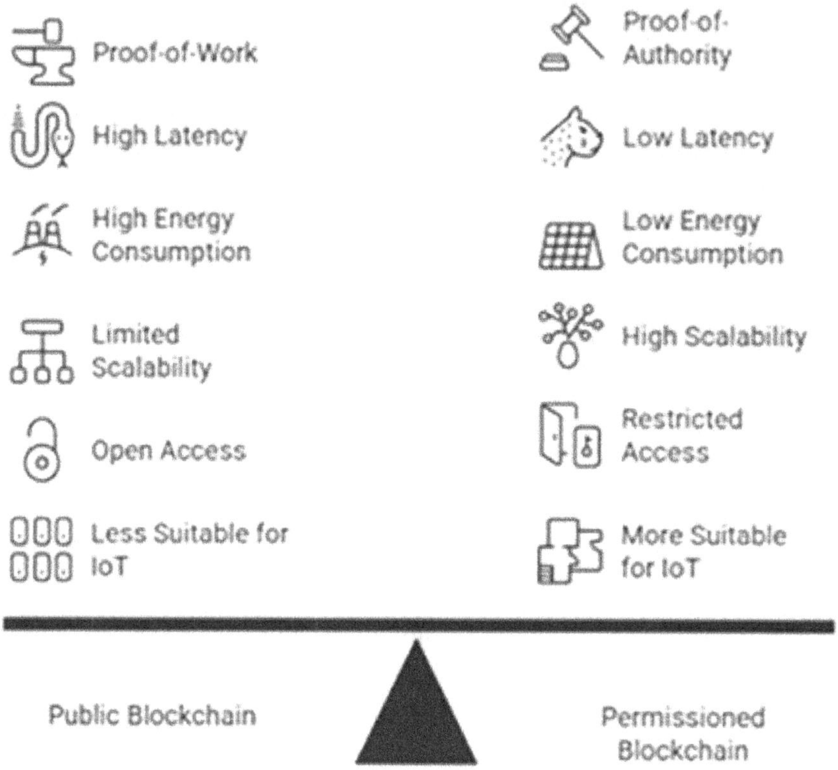

2.1.3 Public versus Private Blockchains

Blockchain platforms are typically divided into public, private and consortium blockchains based on openness and other trade-offs between openness, performance and governance. Public blockchains are open to all participants who can go on the network, send transactions and join the consensus. While this openness has its advantages for more decentralization and resistance to censorship, it comes with challenges to the IoT application in terms of scalability and latency, which is a problem if you are dealing with time-sensitive IoT applications.

Private blockchains are restricted in terms of who can take part in them and are typically restricted to one organization or a group of trusted organizations known as a consortium. Consortium Blockchains are a type of blockchain which is a hybrid system whereby the network as a whole is under the administrative control of multiple organizations. These permissioned models are especially appropriate in an

IoT environment, as they can have controlled membership, predictable performance and compliance with regulatory requirements.

Studies into blockchain integration have also noted that the most popular type of blockchain security application is a private or consortium blockchain due to its capability to balance between decentralization and efficacy and administration (Shone et al., 2018). Under such systems, the validators may be the device manufacturers, service providers, operators or regulators so that no one party may have monopoly in the system. This form of government is in line with the multi-stakeholder nature of big IoT implementations e.g. industrial automation and smart cities.

Also, permissioned blockchains can customize consumer and consent paths, implying that rules on safety can be quite easily developed in connection with the requirements of applications. These properties will make private and consortium blockchains a workable foundation for a secure IoT infrastructure.

A comparative analysis between public and permissioned Blockchain models with trade-offs in terms of Scalability, Latency, Governance and applicability to IoT deployments is provided in Fig. 3.

Figure 3. Comparison of public and permissioned blockchain models with their performance, governance, and suitability in the IoT.

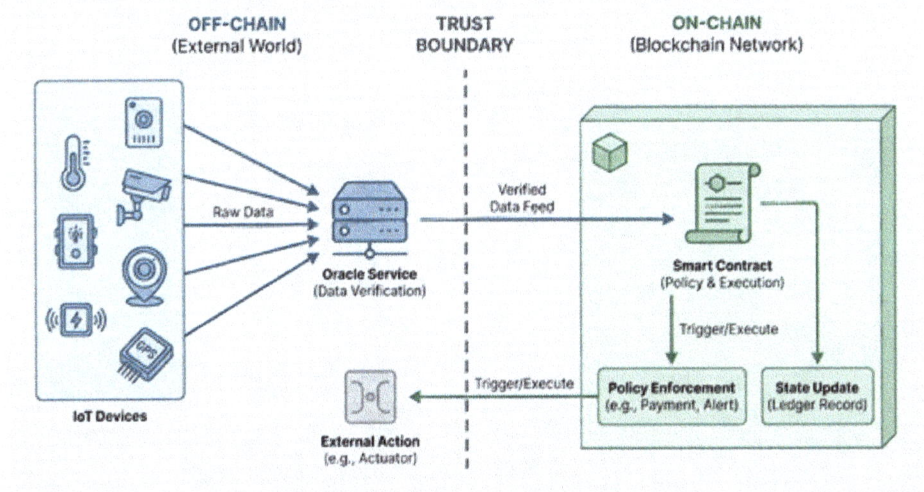

2.1.4 Smart Contracts and Oracles

Smart contracts are programmable contracts (Scripts) and programs that are deployed on a Blockchain and they perform automatically pre-set actions once certain conditions are satisfied. In opposition to the traditional contracts which are enforceable under law, smart contracts have legal enforcement by the blockchain protocol which provides them so they are deterministic and tamper resistant. Smart contracts are an important aspect of security architectures within a blockchain framework as automated access control, policy enforcement and compliance checking can be implemented through smart contracts.

In the area of IoT security, smart contracts can be used to write rules for device authentication, permissions for data access, permission for firmware updates and incident response procedures. For example, a smart contract can be used to automatically revoke access privileges of a device if some anomalous behavior is detected and recorded on the ledger. Such automation makes the system independent of manual intervention efficient and responds faster in a large-scale deployment.

Oracles make smart contracts to work together with the off-chain data sources like IoT sensors, external databases and A.I analytics engines. Since blockchains are not able to directly access any external data, oracles serve as trusted bridges to attest to the outside world to feed real data into smart contracts. However, oracle design reveals certain supplementary trust issues because untrustworthy or malicious oracles have the potential to compromise on-chain decisions.

Figure 4. Smart contract execution with oracle-mediated ingestion of off-chain IoT data and defined trust boundaries.

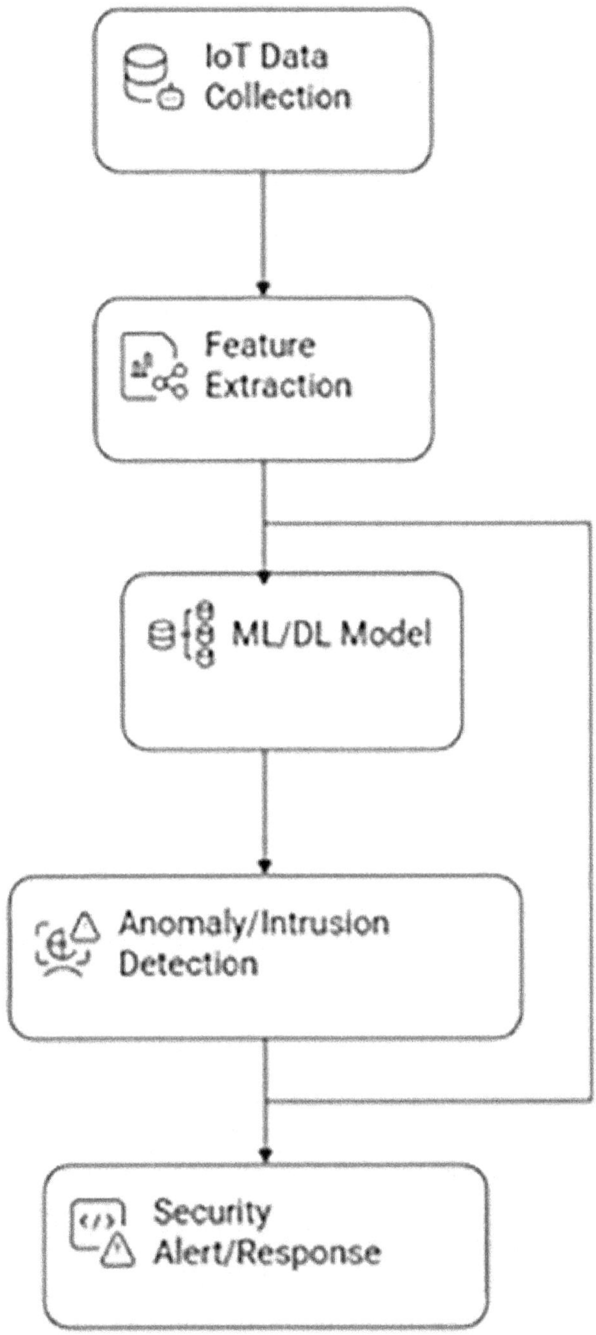

The interaction of off chain IoT data sources and on-chain Constract execution via Oracle mechanisms together with associated trust boundaries is shown in Fig. 4. Extensive studies on blockchain-IoT integration come to highlight the significance of Smart Contracts and Oracles which do pose promise and challenges at the same time or, at least, with respect to the scalability, security and trust management (Khan et al., 2019). When integrating blockchain and AI in security analytics, the existence of reliable oracle mechanisms is really powerful because about - decisions can directly affect the operation of devices and the safety of systems.

2.2 AI for Cybersecurity

2.2.1 AI Techniques: Machine Learning, Deep Learning, and Reinforcement Learning

Artificial Intelligence is a general field of computational methods that allow systems to act with intelligence such as learning from data, reasoning in the face of uncertainty and adaptability to changing environments. In cybersecurity, AI techniques are also increasingly being used to handle the automatic detection, classification and response efforts that are impractical to manage manually in the same way at scale.

Machine Learning (ML) techniques are the basis for AI-based security analytics. Supervised learning algorithms are applied to applying the training data to classify network traffic or system behavior as benign or malicious. Unsupervised learning techniques such as clustering and density estimation are used when labeled data are not abundant, and allow discovering anomalies, that is, the deviations of normal behavior.

Deep Learning (DL) which is a branch of ML relies on making use of multi-layer neural networks when modelling complex and non-linear relationships within data. DL techniques have proved to be better at extracting hierarchical features from high-dimensional inputs that represent, for example, packet traces and temporal traffic patterns. Surveys on deep learning for intrusion detection note the positive use of deep learning in the identification of advanced attack activity that beats traditional detection mechanisms (Salah et al., 2019).

A different paradigm provided by Reinforcement Learning (RL) is introduced, in which an agent learns how to act optimally from interacting with an environment. In cybersecurity, for example RL has been investigated in adaptive defence strategies (so-called) such as dynamic resource allocation, response to intrusions and automated policy tuning. By learning constantly from feedback, RL-based systems are able to adjust for changing security controls to threats or conditions of operation. The general AI-based security analytics pipeline for IoT at the level of data collection, feature extraction, inferring model, and alert generation is summarized in Fig. 5.

Figure 5. AI-driven security analytics pipeline for IoT, illustrating data processing, learning, and threat detection stages.

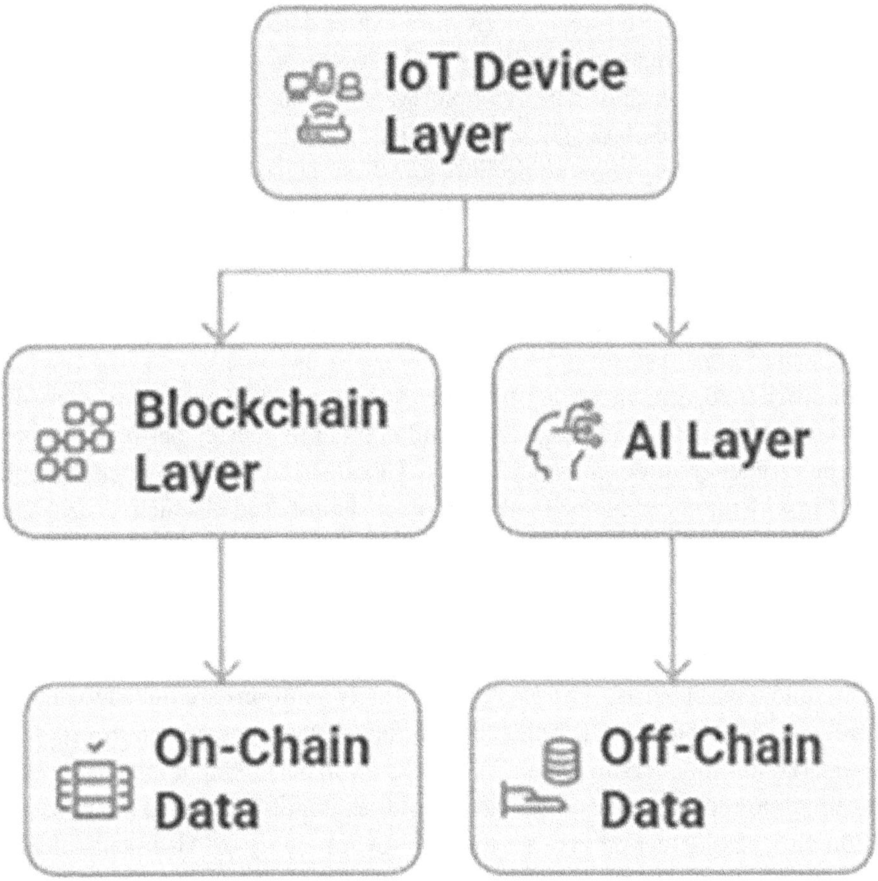

2.2.2 AI-Driven Threat Detection, Classification, and Prediction

AI driven threat detection has become one of cornerstones of modern cybersecurity, especially with environments experiencing high data volume and changing standards of attack. ML-based intrusion detection systems: These are systems that can analyze network traffic, system logs, and device telemetry to analyze the network traffic for suspicious activity in real-time. Compared to the rule-based systems, the AI-driven systems are more flexible and resistant to the zero-day attacks.

Deep learning architectures, e.g. convolutional neural networks and recurrent neural networks are implemented widely for the modelling of the spatial and temporal features of network data. These models are able to learn complex representations of normal and malicious behavior, and allow for more accurate classification and lower false-positive rates. Empirical studies have substantiated that intrusion detection systems based on DL technology has a better detection effect than traditional methods, and is more adaptive (Zhang et al., 2020).

Beyond detection and classification, AI also makes it possible to carry out predictive security analytics, in which models are used to predict which attack or system failure is likely about to occur before it happens. Predictive capabilities are of particular value in an IoT environments, where it is often possible to predict, and then stop cascading failures from rolling out between interconnected devices. By processing past trends and by taking their context into consideration, models of artificial intelligence have the potential to support, risk-aware decision-making and resource-prioritisation.

In distributed systems for IoT has often spread-out AI driven security analytics with layers that are meeting edge and cloud in order to balance between the latency and the efficiency of computations tasks. This distributed deployment model fits nicely in with the coordination method of blockchain-based in which security events and predictions are logged and verified across the board.

2.2.3 AI Limitations and Risks

Despite their benefits, AI-based cybersecurity solutions are linked to new challenges and risks which need to be handled correctly. One biggest concern representing adversarial machine learning, here in, attacks try to design input manually that will be enough to fool the AI models. Adversarial examples can cause the misclassification or bypass detection in order to avoid the reliability of AI-driven defence s.

Data poisoning attacks - this is one more possible threat of interested models, specifically when training the data model. By catering them with erroneous or biased data in the training data sets then the behavior of such model can be compromised, although it may be slight. This raises a particularly relevant threat in IoT applications, in which data is gathered from distributed and maybe untrusted sources.

Explain to an unqualified user is also an important issue. Many deep learning models represent "black boxes" - it is hard to understand or justify the decisions they make. In safety-critical IoT applications mandate e g. healthcare and industrial controlling failures of explainability can hinder trust, regulatory compliance and analysis of incidents.

Furthermore, AI models are prone to concept drift, in which changes in the behavior or environment of the system over time lead to a decrease in model accuracy. Continuous monitoring, retraining and governance is necessary to be effective. Recent studies has focused on the fact that strong AI security has to overcome these shortcomings using explainable AI models, secure AI training pipelines and adaptive learning strategies (Li et al., 2018).

2.2.4 AI in the Broader IoT Security Landscape

Intelligent and autonomous systems are a trend of which the implementation of AI in the IoT security systems is a subset. Accordingly, the IoT security survey also integrates elements with regard to AI in a regular note as an essential enabler of scalable monitoring, automated reaction and resiliency to the emerging threats (Shi & Dustdar, 2016). However, while AI is powerful, and is needed to solve and address complex problems, by itself, it cannot address fundamental issues of trust and accountability, especially in a multi-stakeholder environment.

Recent work heavily emphasizes on the importance of architectural approaches incorporating combination of AI and other complementary technologies such as edge computing and decentralized coordination mechanisms (Pan & McElhannon, 2018). Federated learning has been introduced as an interesting approach to train the AI Models in distributed IoT environments and without the challenge of centralizing the data referring to privacy and regulatory issues (Nguyen et al., 2021).

From the industrial standpoint, cloud based manufacturing and Industrial IoT architectures are now more reliant on the optimization and security of AI enabled analytics, giving rise to additional importance of good AI foundations (Lu & Xu, 2019). In healthcare and other areas of operation that are sensitive, AI-based monitoring will have to be coupled with robust governance and auditing mechanisms in order to build trust and compliance (Yue et al., 2016), (Islam et al., 2015).

Smart city deployments & supply chain systems are also good examples of the complexity of IoT security at scale, where AI-driven analytics in the supply chain have to work across heterogeneous infrastructures and organizational boundaries (Lee et al., 2015), (Zanella et al., 2014), and (Kshetri, 2018). These considerations are a good incentive for integrated frameworks to fulfil the needs for both adaptive intelligence that AI can fulfil and the decentralized trust that blockchain can provide.

This section laid the fundamentals which can be used with the blockchain and AI in cybersecurity. Blockchain provides decentralized trust, immutability as well as programmable enforcement in the form of smart contracts and consensus mechanisms which makes it favourable in IoT environments where heterogeneity and partial trust prevail. AI is an added source of adaptive intelligence for threat detection, classification, and prediction, but comes with a new range of emerging threats of adversarial manipulation, explainability, and governance. To analyze the synergistic integration of blockchain and AI in IoT network security, which is discussed in the following sections, it is fundamental to understand the following background concepts.

3. IoT SECURITY REQUIREMENTS AND GAPS

Internet of Things (IoT) systems impose security challenges unique to these systems due to their scale and heterogeneity and to the fact that they are deployed in resource-constrained and often unattended environments. Many IoT devices have limited processing power, memory, and energy capability and struggle to use traditional heavyweight security mechanisms. This presents an important need for light but effective security solutions, particularly for large-scale deployment in supply chain and logistics systems (Kshetri, 2018).

Another important requirement of IoT networks is secure communication. Lightweight protocols such as MQMT and CoAP are widely used for solving the constrained environment but, due to the improper configuration, poor key management, these protocols are vulnerable to eavesdropping, replay and message tampering attacks. Deep cryptographic primitives are needed to protect such communications, but the issue of the scalability of the key distribution has been left as an open question in practice (Diffie & Hellman, 1976).

These are the identity management and authentication which are the significant gaps in the current IoT security architectures. New in the limelight modus operandi: "Old-fashioned, centralized identity models are quite ill adapted to IoT ecosystem where the devices of multiple vendors must communicate with one another." Though cryptographic principles are good building blocks of theory to ensure security of identity, their application in the world of IoT is minimal (Goldreich, 2009).

The key to early identification of emergent and new threats in the IoT networks is real-time anomaly detection. But scale and privacy concerns were raised with centralized solutions to monitoring despite the fact that decentralized solutions are yet to be developed (Zyskind et al., 2015). Lastly, the integrity and non-repudiation of the data should also be provided, which is essential in accountability and compliance. Homomorphic encryption and zero-knowledge proofs are more advanced forms of cryptography that can be used to implement glaring solutions at a value of their price of pre-computational to limit large-scale deployment of constrained IoT infrastructure (Gentry, 2009), (Ben-Sasson et al., 2014).

4. BLOCKCHAIN FOR IoT SECURITY

Blockchain technology has been a strong contributing factor to the solution of some of the basic security restrictions in Internet of Things (IoTs). By means of having mechanisms for decentralized trust capabilities, immutability and verifiable accountability, blockchain directly address some of the gaps that are found in traditional IoT security models. This section discusses the role of blockchain in terms of decentralized identity management, tamper proof logging of communications, trustless consensus in multi-vender environments, secure firmware update mechanisms and gives an experience of the applicability through a smart grid case study.

4.1 Decentralized Identity (DID) Management

Identity Management is one of the most critical challenges on IoT security because of the heterogeneity of devices, their long-life cycle, and multi-stakeholder ownership. Traditional centralized identity authorities have the drawback of introducing single points of failure and are not inherently scalable. Blocking chain guarantees decentralized identity (DID) through devices and the stakeholders manage cryptographic identities which are anchored on a distributed ledger.

Decentralized identity frameworks by making use of public-key cryptography and verifiable credentials, it makes sure that device identities can be authenticated without the need for any central authority. Blockchain acts as an identity trust system for integrity and availability of identity records in a way that allows the secure onboarding, authentication, and revocation of identity record across organizational boundaries. Privacy preserving identity models further improve on this approach by permitting selective disclosure of credentials, so that unnecessary exposure of sensitive information is minimized (Ben-Sasson et al., 2014).

Such decentralized mechanisms of identity are especially useful in mass IoT deployments, in which devices built by and operated on by different entities must interoperate without fully trusting one another in a secure manner.

4.2 Tamper-Proof Logs for Device Communication

The consequences are a continuous flow of telemetry, control commands and security events and IoT systems. To ensure integrity and auditability of this information, it is critical towards accountability, compliance and forensics. This is because blockchain is a mechanism that cannot be tampered with to keep records of the events, which are recorded.

Rather than recording IoT data, which would be inefficient and expensive to do so, as it is, on-chain, most architectures store cryptographic hashes, or other form of metadata, in the form of representations of communication events and system actions. Any attempt to change historical records is immediately detected as a result of cryptographic chaining. This property is specifically important in forensic investigations, in which reliable evidence is needed in the wake of security events.

Blockchain-based logging is a good fit with regulatory requirements for traceability and auditability requirements, particularly in domain sectors experiencing regulation such as healthcare, energy, transportation that we have discussed in earlier posts (European Union, 2018). By storing logs across a plurality of nodes, blockchain does not depend on centralized log servers that suffer from a situation where they are susceptible to insider threats and single points of failure.

4.3 Thrustless Consensus in Multi-Vendor IoT Environments

Modern IoT ecosystems most of the time involve multiple vendors, operators and service providers, each with varied trust assumptions/incentives. Establishing a common trust framework in such environments is difficult using centralized security models. Blockchain makes it possible to have trustless consensus where participants can agree on system state and security issues without establishing mutual trust.

Permissioned blockchain networks are especially suitable for multi-vendor IoT scenarios, which can be tailored according to a controlled participation process and custom consensus. Validators can represent various stakeholder interests, which ensure fair governance and that there is a minimum risk of one-party control. This decentralised consensus model results in higher resilience and transparency, which is challenging in particular for the deployment of critical infrastructure.

Research on blockchain-based security architectures identifies improved coordination and accountability in distributed systems as a major potential benefit of trustless consensus (U.S. Department of Health and Human Services, 2013), such as in IoT-related networks which act across organizational boundaries. By incorporating security rules and governance policies in smart contracts, blockchain allows consistent enforcement of all the participants.

4.4 Secure Firmware Updates and Auditing

Firmware vulnerabilities are considered to be one of the most used IoT device weaknesses. Lack of confidence in updating mechanisms may leave room to the attackers to either introduce some malicious codes, cause the devices to fail or provide the attackers with some permanent back doors. Blockchain guarantees a robust provision of secure firmware updates, auditing.

The firmware updates meta-data (such as version identifies, cryptography hashes and approval traces) can be in an immutable form stored on the ledger using this block-chain. The enforcement of policy relative to updates can be performed with the help of smart contract to ensure that only legitimate versions of firmware are deployed and the preparation of update allow many trusted entities. Gadgets can be able to authenticate the authenticity of the firmware by matching a locally created value to blockchain anchored values.

This will not only contribute to security, but this will accrue better transparency and accountability risk during the lifecycle of the devices. Auditable update histories come in most particularly when there is compliance verification involved, and incident response. Studies emphasize that firmware management using blockchain reduces the dependency on centralized update servers and reduces the large-scale compromise issues (IEEE, 2019).

4.5 Case Study: Blockchain in Smart Grids

Smart grids are a notable example of large-scale IoT systems where security, reliability and transparency are the key. These systems combine smart meters, sensors, distributed energy resources and control platform for optimizing energy generation and distribution. Due to their criticality, smart grids are attractive targets for cyber-attacks.

Blockchain has been investigated as a smart grid security-promoting technology by providing the transparency and tamper resistance of energy data management. Distributed ledgers are able to record the meter reading, energy transactions and control commands in an immutable way, which prevents the data from being manipulated and allows for real-time audits. Smart Contracts also help in automated energy trading, demand response and compliance enforcement

Research has shown that smart grid architectures built on a blockchain increase the trust between the utilities, consumers and regulators as they have a shared, provable source of truth (National Institute of Standards and Technology, 2020). In addition, blockchain can facilitate secure peer-to-peer trading of energy and facilitate the coordination of micro-grids, resulting in the move away from heavily relying on centralized control infrastructures.

Beyond the energy management applications, there are lessons worth learning from the smart grid implementations that can apply to the IoT as a whole. They provide us with an example on how to apply decentralized trust, on-immutable logging and forced automation in safety critical systems. These can be utilized in other fields of the IoT like industrial automation, transport and smart cities (Floridi et al., 2018), (Aggarwal et al., 2018), (Bernstein & Lange, 2017), (Buterin, 2014), (Wood, 2014) and (Khan & Salah, 2018).

To address all the significant IoT security challenges, blockchain enables decentralized identity, tamper proof logging, trustless consensus and secure lifecycle management. The blockchain enhances more accountability and ease in multi-vender type of IoT settings through programmable smart contracts and distributed governance. Among the instances of utilizing Blockchain in the practical implementation of securing large-scale, mission-critical, IoT infrastructures, the smart grid case study can be mentioned. These capabilities render blockchain a construction block of next generation internet of things security architecture, particularly when it is possessed along with intelligent analytics and vibrant control procedures that are explained in the subsequent sections.

5. AI FOR ENHANCING IoT SECURITY

Artificial Intelligence (AI) entered the sphere of IoT security architecture as an essential component of the security structure due to its ability to analyse big data and massive amounts of different data types and adapt to the changing threat landscape. Traditional methods of security, such as rule-based and signature-based, are not sufficient for IoT environments where often, the attacks are new, distributed and subtle. AI driven techniques are intelligence required to detect, classify and mitigate such threats in timely and scalable manner.

5.1 Intrusion Detection Using Machine Learning and Deep Learning

Intrusion detection is one of the most popular research areas of AI in IoT security. Machine learning based intrusion detection systems (IDS) scan network traffic and telemetry from the systems and devices connected to the network in order to identify patterns of normal and abnormal behaviour. Surveys related to IoT security focus on the fact ML-based IDS are significantly better than traditional approaches for the detection of complex and zero-day attacks (Khan & Salah, 2018).

Deep learning methods are also used for furtherance of intrusion detection by learning hierarchical and temporal features from the raw data. Convolutional Neural Networks (CNNs) and Long Short-Term Memory (LSTMs) are both popular types of neural networks with CNNs being good for capturing the spatial information in traffic features and LSTMs being good for capturing the temporal information in sequential data. These models are especially suited for IoT networks, where attack behaviors may be able to change with time. Recent research show that deep learning based IDS architectures are more accurate and offer lower false positive rate, compared to conventional ML method (Saravana et al., 2026).

5.2 Adaptive Authentication Systems

AI is also making it possible to use adaptive authentication, in which access control decisions are made dynamically based on contextual risk factors instead of static credentials. In the IoT environment, authentication can be supplemented by constantly evaluating the behavior of devices, communication patterns, as well as the surrounding environment in order to improve authentication. AI models prove to level the risk and set up stronger authentication mechanisms when any anomalous behavior is detected.

These adaptive systems are specifically relevant in multi-vendor IoT ecosystems which have device and user trust assumptions that are performed in IoT devices. Through knowledge of the normal access patterns, AI-based authentication systems assist in lessening the reliance and fixity of credentials and reinstate authentication systems in a manner that is less susceptible to impersonation and credential compromise. The strategy concurs well with the decentralized security architectures, which require flexible and context-free access control (Lu, 2020).

5.3 Network Traffic Anomaly Detection

Anomaly detection: Anomaly detection is a basic functionality of IoT security that is based on AI technology. Unlike signature-based detection, an anomaly detection identifies the deviations from the established baselines which means the discovery of previously unseen attacks. Unsupervised and semi-supervised learning methods are particularly applicable to IoT application scenarios, where it is impractical to obtain a significant portion of labeled data of the attack.

AI-based network traffic anomaly detection uses statistics of network flows, packet timing, and protocol usage to determine whether there are any patterns of suspicious traffic. These methods work against distributed denial of service attacks, botnet activity and protocol abuse. Research highlights that anomaly detection is critical when it comes to maintaining situational awareness in large-scale IoT deployment where manpower monitoring isn't an option (Zhang et al., 2019).

5.4 Behavior Profiling of IoT Devices

IoT devices can have predictable and repetitive behavior, making them a good candidate for behavior profiling. AI models learn normal patterns of operation for individual devices or classes of devices and identify any deviations from those norms which may point to compromise, malfunction or misconfiguration of the device. Behavior profiling helps to continue monitoring and detect stealthy attacks at the earliest.

Through correlation of behavior across devices, coordinated attacks and lateral movement in IoT networks can also be identified by AI systems. This ability is of particular interest in industrial and smart city applications, where cascading failures can have great operational impact (Ge et al., 2019).

5.5 Federated Learning for Privacy-Preserving Analytics

While AI is used to increase security concerns, it also involves privacy concerns because of the need to have a large amount of data. The problem of training machine learning models and the need to centralize raw data is overcome by federated learning (FL), which allows for collaborative model training to take place without centralizing raw data. In FL, it is the case that models are trained on devices or edge nodes, and only model updates are shared.

Federated learning is very well suited for IoT security analytics because it allows for data privacy preservation while facilitating collective intelligence on distributed environments. In recent research, FL has been pointed out as a promising solution for scalable and privacy-preserving IoT security, especially in combination with decentralized governance mechanisms (Viriyasitavat & Hoonsopon, 2019).

AI Enhances IoT Security Smart intrusion detection, smart authentication, smart anomaly detection, behavior profiling, and privacy-preserving analytics are some of the ways in which IoT security is enhanced by AI. These capabilities overcome some of the limitations of traditional security mechanisms, and is the basis for autonomous and resilient IoT defence systems. When combined with decentralized trust technology, AI-driven security mechanisms have an important role to play in securing next-generation IoT networks.

6. SYNERGISTIC INTEGRATION OF BLOCKCHAIN AND AI

The combination of BlockChain and Artificial Intelligence (AI) have become a more popular topic around the increasing potential of this combination as a paradigm to solve complex security problems in Internet of Things (IoT) ecosystems. Individually both technologies have very powerful capabilities; however, their convergence allows for security properties that are hard to attain when either technology is used in isolation. This section covers the motivation of convergence, the discussion of what AI can do to optimize the work of blockchain systems, and what blockchain can do to ensure the security of AI workflows, and an example of integrated frameworks for IoT security.

6.1 Why Convergence? Complementary Strengths

Blockchain has a decentralized trust, immutability and transparency which is designed to be useful in establishing integrity and accountability for distributed environments. However, blockchain systems are static and reactive and have no capabilities of interpreting complex patterns and adapt to evolving threats. AI, on the other hand, is better at learning, prediction and adaptive decision making, which helps in proactive and intelligent security response. Studies on the characteristics of blockchain emphasize that even though blockchain is in charge of ensuring trust, it does not necessarily provide the intelligence and context awareness (Viriyasitavat & Hoonsopon, 2019).

On the other hand, security systems based on AI are very dependent on the quality of the data, integrity of model and trust in the decision results. Without robust guarantees of data origin and responsibility, abuses and misdeeds with AI systems are liable to occur. Surveys on the topic of security and privacy concerning blockchain has shown that blockchain can provide an anchor of trust for data driven systems by providing verifiable data lineage and tamper resistance (Zhang et al., 2019). The combination of blockchain and AI thus brings together trust without central authority and intelligence without manual intervention, which has special value in IoT environments with their scale, heterogeneity and partial trust.

6.2 AI for Optimizing Blockchain Systems

The performance, security, and manageability of blockchains can be improved by AI immensely. A notable area where this phenomenon can be used is in adaptive consensus optimization where AI models are used to collect the network conditions, transaction load, and the behavior of nodes so adjusting the consensus parameters dynamically. This adaptation can minimize the latency and enhance the throughput and not compromise security (Wang et al., 2022).

The analysis and verification of smart contracts are also becoming the use of AI with growing application. Techniques of machine learning are able to identify vulnerabilities, abnormal execution patterns and potential exploits in smart contracts prior to their deployment or run-time execution. This capability is highly valuable since the imperfections of smart contracts are usually irreversible after they have been implemented. The studies on intelligent IoT systems are aimed at the role of AI-based automation in regulating the complex infrastructures in a large scale that are decentralized (Aouedi et al., 2024).

In addition, AI can be applied to detect malicious nodes or unproductive nodes in the blockchain network by learning and recognizing the behavioural pattern and detecting the deviation. This assists in the development of resilience to insider attack and coordinated manipulation, particularly the permissioned IoT blockchains where validators are multiple stakeholders.

6.3 Blockchain for Securing AI Workflows

While AI is able to optimize blockchain, blockchain also plays a critical role to secure the AI workflows. One of the most significant and largest contributions is that of data provenance. By hashing the data used for training and the inputs used for inference and storing them on the blockchain, AI systems can verify that AI models are trained and executed using real and genuine data and inputs. This ensures the reduction of the risks associated with data poisoning and unauthorised modification of data (Yang et al., 2017).

Blockchain also can provide integrity of the model and governance of lifecycle. Model versions, updates and deployment events can be immutably written down allowing for auditability and accountability. This is an especially important factor in IoT systems where decisions made by AI may have an impact on physical processes. IoT Forensics Research Identifies the Need for Tamper-Evident Records in Post-Incident Analysis A need that Blockchain-based logging can provide well.

In addition, access control mechanisms based on blockchain can be used to control who has the right to train, update or invoke AI models in order to reduce the risk of unauthorised manipulation.

6.4 Example Framework: Blockchain-Enabled AI-Based Threat Detection for IoT

An integrated operation of an AI - Blockchain IoT security operation can work like this. IoT devices create telemetry which are collected at edge nodes where AI models are applied to perform real-time intrusion detection and behavior analysis. Security events and summaries of anomalies are then recorded on a permissioned blockchain acting as a step to ensure the integrity and cross-domain visibility (Dorri et al., 2020).

Smart contracts support the automated policy response, such as isolating any compromised device or changing access permissions. Blockchain-based governance ensures that all the actions are auditable and agreed upon by the stakeholders. Edge computing and delay-aware offloading schemes aid in the low-latency AI inference for time-sensitive (Zhang et al., 2017) applications. Architectural taxonomies of blockchain-based systems help to choose suitable ledger designs and consensus models for such systems (Xu et al., 2019).

Regarding system level, the IoT security survey is based on the statement that to address the complexity of the current IoT ecosystem, integrated architectures to combine decentralized trust and intelligent analytics are needed (Kouicem et al., 2018). Extensive studies on cybersecurity domain also enhance the fact that IoT security needs systemic solutions instead of mechanisms (Abomhara & Køien, 2015).

The combination of blockchain and AI integration is introducing a strong paradigm of security to the IoT systems through the combination of decentralized trust and adaptive intelligence. AI renders blockchain more efficient and robust whereas blockchain renders AI data, models and decisions secure. They are used together to provide a foundation of scalable, transparent and robust IoT security architectures which can operate in a multi-stakeholder and heterogeneous environment.

7. REFERENCE ARCHITECTURE

The safe implementation of the action of Blockchain and Artificial Intelligence (AI) in the Internet of Things (IoT) systems requires a clear architectural design to balance between scalability, latency, trust and intelligence. Due to the heterogeneous and distributed characteristics of the IoT environments, the layered reference architecture provides an organised way of co-ordinating the operations of the devices level, decentralised trusted mechanisms and smart security analytics. This part is a reference architecture of connecting IoT devices, blockchain architecture, and artificial intelligence-based security services.

7.1 Layered Architecture Overview

The proposed reference architecture will consist of three broad layers, these include: Device Layer, Blockchain Layer and AI Layer. Such isolation of concerns enables the layers to deal with certain areas of functionality and security needs and enables the possibility of communication between the layers.

The Device Layer comprises of IoT sensors, actuators, embedded controllers and gateways, and is deployed on the network edge. These devices create the information known as telemetry and processes control orders and communicates with local gateways. Due to the constraints on resources devices typically have light weight security mechanisms such as simple encryption, secure boot and device authentication. Continuous monitoring is done at this layer that produces the raw data for higher level security analytics.

The Blockchain Layer serves as a backbone of decentralized trust of the architecture. It keeps unalterable records of security-related events, such as device registration, access control decisions, firmware updates approvals and anomaly alerts. Permissioned deployments of the blockchains are usually preferred since they provide for controlled participation and predictable performance. Blockchain governance ensures no unilateral control by one stakeholder: it makes the system more resilient and transparent.

The AI Layer offers intelligent security type of services such as intrusion detection, anomaly detection, behavior profiling and adaptive policy learning. The deployment of components of AI may be at edge and cloud level depending upon the latency and the resource needs. Together, these layers make it possible to achieve the holistic security architecture of trust, intelligence, and autonomy. The layered integration of IoT devices, trust services based on blockchain technologies and AI-based security analytics is shown in Fig. 6, which describes the data flows, on-chain commitments and off-chain intelligence components in a unified architecture.

Figure 6. Layered reference architecture integrating IoT devices, blockchain-based trust services, and AI-driven security analytics.

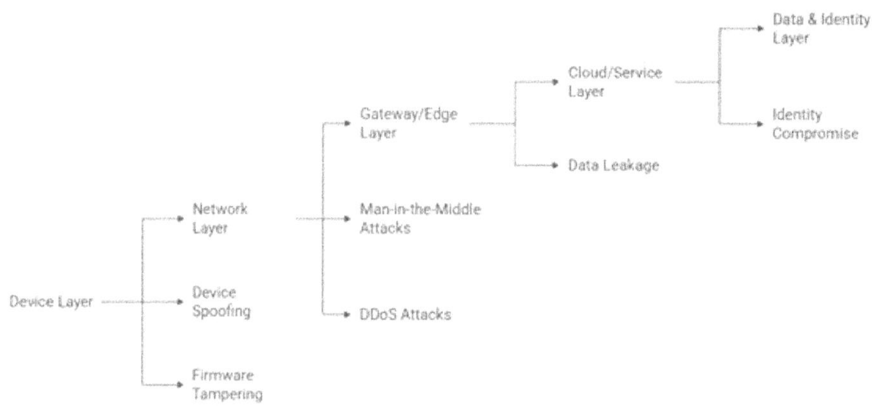

7.2 Data Flow and Component Interaction

In the proposed architecture, data flow starts at the Device Layer where data (telemetry and operational data) is generated by the IoT devices. Edge gateways preprocess this data and send it to AI modules for relevant features to analyze the data in real-time. AI models analyze patterns, behavior patterns, and contextual data of traffic and devices for any anomaly or security threat.

When an important security event is found, a summarized note in the form of an alert, risk score or policy update is recorded on the Blockchain Layer. This makes tampering of the logs evident, and also makes it possible to have cross-domain visibility into security incidents. Smart contracts can be used to automatically trigger response action such as revoking access to the device or firmware audit.

This pattern of interaction is one which promotes coordination decentralization with minimum storage overhead on the blockchain. Importantly, blockchain is not used to replace real-time control paths, but to control the policy enforcement, auditing and trust management.

7.3 Decentralized Access Control with AI-Based Policy Learning

Access control is a significant task in IoT security architectures. Traditional static policies are not enough in a dynamic environment where devices and threat conditions keep on changing. AI-based policy learning provides the adaptive access control based on the idea of learning of normal access pattern and finding the risky behavior.

Blockchain helps to improve this process, since it offers a trusted environment for the execution and audit of access control policies. Policy updates learned by AI models can be validated, approved, and immutably stored on the blockchain, making it accountable and impossible to change it in an unauthorized way. Explainable AI research stresses the importance of transparency and robustness in decision-making in security, particularly when automated actions have a critical effect (Wu et al., 2024).

7.4 Role of Decentralized and Edge Intelligence

Federated and decentralized learning paradigms play an important role in the scalability of AI-based security analytics in IoT environments. Decentralized federated learning overcomes the privacy and communication issues of centralized federated learning by allowing collaborative training of models without centralizing raw data (Yuan et al., 2024). This approach fits well with the idea of governance using blockchain technologies, the updates of models and reputation can be coordinated in a trustless way.

Edge intelligence further increases the architecture by making inference close to devices low latency. Research about edge intelligence shows the importance of edge intelligence in addressing the real-time constraints and eliminating the cloud connectivity dependency (Zhou et al., 2019). Adaptive learning and control mechanisms at the edge can be used to react quickly to threats while ensuring the stability of the system (Wang et al., 2019).

7.5 Architectural Benefits and Standardization Considerations

The proposed reference architecture has a number of advantages including scalability using distributed processing; resilience using decentralized trust, and adaptability using intelligence, AI-driven. However, without calibration to security standards and frameworks, effective deployment is impossible because of lack of interoperability and non-compliance. IoT security standards reviews stress the importance of harmonization of architectures that will bring together the technical controls and governance and risk management practices (Karie et al., 2021).

This reference architecture demonstrates how Blockchain and AI can be integrated, in a systematic way, to ensure IoT system security. By creating a layered design, decentralized trust, intelligent analytics and edge centric processing integration, the architecture helps to create a scalable and resilient base for next generation IoT security solutions.

8. USE CASES AND APPLICATIONS

The combination of Blockchain and Artificial Intelligence (AI) into the Internet of Things (IoT) security has real value that can be analysis through the different spheres of application in the real life. The implementation of IoTs in technology in fields like healthcare, industrial systems, smart cities and supply chains, has had noteworthy similarities, in terms of trust, scalability, privacy and security governance. This paper discusses representative use-cases that explain how convergence of Blockchain and AI can address such issues and enhance security, reliability and accountability considerations in IoT ecosystems.

8.1 Smart Healthcare

Smart healthcare systems are very much dependant on IoT devices such as wearable sensors, remote patient monitoring devices and smart medical infrastructure. These devices are continuously gathering sensitive physical and contextual data and healthcare IoT is one of the privacy-sensitive application areas. Security breaches in this context, can result not only in data leakage, but also in direct risks for the patient safety.

Blockchain helps to strengthen the IoT for healthcare by providing a decentralized and unchangeable structure for access and sharing medical data. Blockchain based gateways for healthcare data enable the data access events to be securely recorded and prevent data access by unauthorized users by enforcing fine-grained access control policies using smart contracts. This ensures that only authorized individuals, such as clinicians, hospitals, or insurance providers, can access certain patient data, while all attempts to access the data are also auditable [26]. Such mechanisms are especially useful in environments where different healthcare providers are at work, and there is a cross-organizational data exchange.

AI is a complementary technology to blockchain, which can be implemented for health anomaly detection in real-time and predictive analytics. Machine learning algorithms are being applied to continuous data coming from sensors and identifying the onset of medical conditions, such as irregular heart beat or respiratory difficulty. Integrating the alerting systems based on artificial intelligence with audit trails based on block chain helps to make the decision making and interventions in diagnosis in a transparent and verifiable manner. Additionally, healthcare regulatory compliance for compliance HIPAA to comply with are demanding in terms of accountability and traceability, which is easy to achieve with blockchain-based logging (U.S. Department of Health and Human Services, 2013). Together, block chain and AI form a reliable and smart healthcare IoT security framework.

8.2 Industrial IoT (IIoT)

Industrial IoT Systems: Industrial IoT systems provide the basis for modern manufacturing, energy generation and critical infrastructure operations. These environments are based on availability, security and reliability and security incidents can result in serious economic losses or physical damage. IIoT Systems So far, IIoT systems include sensors, programmable logic controllers, robotic systems, and supervisory control platforms running on heterogeneous networks.

Blockchain helps in IIoT security as it allows tamper-evident logging of operational data, maintenance data and control actions. This is especially important in Industry 4.0 environments where several vendors and service providers interact in shared industrial ecosystems (Lee et al., 2015). Blockchain-based methods of identity and access control help to alleviate reliance on centralized control systems and increase resilience to insider threats.

AI is an important element of IIoT security, including predictive maintenance, intrusion detection, and behavior analysis. By learning normal operational patterns, AI models are able to identify any deviation that might signify something is wrong with the equipment or the system, such as cyber intrusion. When coupled with the blockchain, then AI-generated alerts and decisions can be immutably recorded and ensure accountability and provide for post-incident forensics. Cloud based manufacturing architectures gain even more from this integration, as it is possible to obtain a secure coordination between edge devices, cloud analytics and decentralized governance (Lu & Xu, 2019).

8.3 Smart Cities

Smart Cities make use of IoT technologies to manage city infrastructure such as traffic systems, public transport, environmental monitoring, energy distribution, etc. These deployments are large-sized heterogeneous devices, as well as multi-stakeholder and public and private operations. Security and governance are therefore very specific in regards to smart cities.

Blockchain provides a common trusted infrastructure that will make governance among the city authorities, service providers and citizens transparent and secure. Smart contracts can be used to control who has access to the data of IoT devices within the public network and enforce a level of service SLC agreements and immutable logs can be used to establish accountability for the infrastructure's operations. Research on smart city IoT architectures focuses on the need for scalable and interoperable security frameworks that are able to manage such complexity (Zanella et al., 2014).

AI enhances the IoT security of smart cities to provide real-time analytics for optimizing traffic, pollution, and threat detection. AI based anomalous detection can detect suspicious behavior of sensors, being swished devices or coordinated attacks on urban infrastructure. When coupled with blockchain these analytics can potentially have an added layer of trust and auditability that can ensure that automated decisions with public service implications are transparent and auditable.

8.4 Supply Chain IoT

The supply chain systems have become more dependent on the IoT devices, including RFI devices, GPS trackers, and environmental sensors, to monitor the location and status of goods. These systems should guarantee the authenticity and traceability of data in a geographically distributed level of participants within the system as well as participants which are organizationally diverse.

Many have identified blockchain as a beneficial supply chain traceability and a fraud prevention tool. Blockchain provides end-to-end visibility by storing the hashes of sensor data, transaction events and custody transfers on a distributed ledger system to avoid unauthorized manipulation of other data (Kshetri, 2018). It is particularly handy in the context of such use cases like cold chain logistics, in which the quality and safety of products are directly impacted by the integrity of data.

AI is the counterpart of blockchain with regard to supply chain IoT and it will detect the anomalies like route deviation, inconsistent readings on sensors or suspicious method of transaction. Predictive analytics and behavior profiling are useful in the proactive management of risks which minimizes losses and improves efficiency of operations. The impossibility to change provenance provided by the blockchain and intelligence analytics provided by the AI makes it an effective security system that will enable the supply chain stakeholders to trust each other.

Convergence of blockchain and AI is the core of the IoT security issues of trust, intelligence and governance which are basic in healthcare, industrial systems, smart cities and supply chains. Blockchain can provide decentralized identity and immutable audit logs and straightforward execution of policies and AI can make threat detectors adaptive, predictive analytics and autonomous processing possible. These use-cases can be seen as proof that blockchain - AI integration is not something that is only a theory for the industry but brings user-friendly, scalable solutions to ensure secure real-world IoT deployments.

9. IMPLEMENTATION CONSIDERATIONS

While the confluence of Blockchain and Artificial Intelligence (AI) presents great potential for the security of Internet of Things (IoT) ecosystems, careful consideration of their technical, operational and architectural constraints must be made for practical deployment. IoT environments are extremely heterogeneous and resource-constrained environments, such that naive integration of blockchain and AI is infeasible. This section presents some of the key implementation considerations that impact the effectiveness, scalability and sustainability of integrated blockchain-AI IoT security systems.

9.1 Computational and Energy Overhead on IoT Devices

One of the most important challenges in the implementation of the blockchain - AI solutions is the low computational and energy capacity of the IoT devices. Blockchain operations such as cryptographic hashing, verifying signatures and participating in consensus are computationally expensive. Similarly, AI models, especially deep learning models, are very processing power and memory intensive.

To try to overcome this, most practical implementations take a hierarchical deployment strategy, in which constrained devices carry out minimal security operations (e.g. secure boot, simple encryption) while computationally expensive operations are offloaded to edge gateways or cloud platforms. Edge computing plays an important role by enabling low-latency AI inference near to devices, and reducing the levels of energy consumption and network bandwidth usage. This design choice is necessary for real-time security monitoring and reaction in latency sensitive IoT applications.

9.2 Interoperability Between AI Models and Blockchain Protocols

Another important issue is that of interoperability. Blockchain platforms look very different in terms of the consensus mechanism, model of transaction and smart contract languages while AI frameworks look very different in terms of model architectures, training pipelines and deployment environments. Making such interaction between these components seamless is not a trivial task.

Sometimes the different levels of standardised interfaces and middlewares are required to connect AI analytics engines and blockchain infrastructure. For example, the security alerts that emanate from AI have to be converted into blockchain transactions that can be validated and recorded in an efficient manner. Without careful designing such interactions can cause latency, synchronization problems and data consistency problems. Specifically of importance to interoperability are multi-vendor IoT ecosystems where the connected devices and services are from different manufacturers and service providers.

9.3 Lightweight Consensus Mechanisms

Consensus mechanisms are one of the major features of performance and scalability with blockchain. Traditional proof of work consensus cannot be utilized in case of IoT due to high energy consumption and latency. Instead, lightweight consensus mechanisms like Proof-of-Authority, Byzantine Fault Tolerant variants and Directed Acyclic Graph (DAG) based ledger are more suitable.

A consensus mechanism that meets the security, performance and governance requirements is a choice that must be made. Permissioned blockchains may have more popularity in IoT scenarios, since they have deterministic finality, less overhead and restricted participation. However, consensus design must account for fault tolerance and insider threats (especially when it comes to critical infrastructure applications).

9.4 Integration with Edge and Cloud Computing

Effective blockchain-AI IoT security architectures make a lot of use of edge and cloud computing integration. Edge nodes are an intermediary between constrained devices and the cloud service, which gives the capacity for aggregating data locally, running AI inference and making preliminary decisions. Cloud platforms in turn makes it easy to conduct the training of AI models at scale, analytics throughout the system, and storing the data long term.

This distributed model of computing allows the scalability and the resilience of the system, but cause coordination problems. Secure communication, consistent enforcing of policies and synchronization of updates at the edge and the cloud layers have to be carefully managed. Blockchain provides a unity of trust, a sort of orchestra of these distributed parts through enforcing policies and unerasable records of actions taken by the system.

9.5 Deployment and Maintenance Considerations

Then, the deployment and the lifecycle management is important for the long term reliability of the system. IoT devices are also running for many years and therefore they require to be securely on boarded, their firmware's to be updated and eventually decommissioned. Blockchain identity and update management in order to enable traceability and accountability through device lifecycle and Artificial intelligence based monitoring to identify degradation, compromise or mere configuration in time

System designers also have to accept the upgradeability in addition to the governance. AI models may have to be retrained on an ongoing basis to adapt to concept drift, and blockchain protocols may have to be altered in order to adapt to unforeseen threats or regulatory requirements. It is critical to the sustainable deployment, to design the systems to encourage controlled upgrades with no down-time.

To achieve this, special consideration to such resource constraints, interoperability, and consensus design and distributed computing integration is implemented in the IoT environments using the blockchain -AI security solutions. Edge-centric architectures, light consensus mechanism and standardized interface are important enablers towards real world deployment. These considerations to assure theoretical merits of blockchain-AI convergence can be accomplished in the IoT systems in reality.

10. CHALLENGES AND LIMITATIONS

Despite the huge potential of utilizing BlockChain and Artificial Intelligence (AI) in the future of Internet of Things (IoT) security, there are some technical, operational and conceptual challenges. These limitations have to be carefully considered to ensure that they are not deployed unrealistically, overengineered and that point the way for future research directions.

10.1 Scalability in High-Volume IoT Environments

One of the most prominent problems is the problem of scalability. IoT networks are the source of a huge amount of data at high speed, and blockchains systems especially those that provide strong guarantees of high consistency and immutability have low transaction throughput and storage capacity. Even in the case of permissions blockchains, it is not practical to be able to record every IoT event on chain, due to the latency and storage overheads.

As a result of that, the majority of architectures are based on off-chain storage with on-chain commitments (e.g. hash). This is a hybrid approach making the data synchronization and also managing the trust system more complex in return of improving the scalability. Poorly designed off-chain mechanisms can derail guarantees of security which can lead to discrepancies between the aspects of security in theory and practice.

10.2 Latency Constraints in Real-Time Applications

Many IoT application such as industrial control systems, healthcare monitoring, smart transportation have high requirement on the response time and cannot wait for long time. Conflict between Blockchain Consensus processes and transaction confirmation delay is the possible conflict that these latency constraints will have. Although, the light consensus mechanisms, but there could be a trade off between decentralization or fault tolerance.

Likewise, AI-based security analytics - in particular deep learning models - also can cause delays in inference, if they are not carefully optimized and deployed at the end. Balancing between the security robustness and the real time responsiveness is one of the huge design challenges, especially in safety critical environments.

10.3 Explainability and Trust in AI Decisions

AI-powered security measures are based on often obscure models. In IoT scenarios where the automated decisions can have a real impact on any physical process or the safety of the people, explainability becomes essential. Black-box AI models make it hard for operators, auditors and regulators to understand the reasons behind certain security actions.

This failure of interpretability can lead to lack of trust and difficulty related to the compliance of the regulatory and ethical frameworks. While explainable AI techniques are advancing, the challenge of seamlessly integrating AI explainability techniques into IoT security pipelines, without losing any significance in accuracy and performance, is still to be addressed.

10.4 Model Drift and Blockchain Immutability

AI models rolled out in IoT environments are affected by such issues as concept drift, in which gradually changing behavior of devices, network conditions or use conditions makes models less accurate over time. Continuous retraining and updating the models is therefore needed. However, because of blockchain's immutability, while it is great for auditability, when used with model lifecycle management, this can create a problem if not designed carefully.

This has to be reconciled with the need for flexible AI models with immutable records of them in blockchain using complex governance mechanisms. Poorly managed updates may result in outdated models being trusted indefinitely or too many records being added on the blockchain which decreases the efficiency of the system.

10.5 Data Privacy and Regulatory Compliance

Finally, data privacy and regulatory compliance is a complicated issue. IoT data tend to have some personal or sensitive information attached to them bound by some strict regulations. While blockchain is useful in terms of increasing traceability and accountability the immutability principle of blockchain is in conflict with the erasure and modification requirements of data of regulatory regimes in some jurisdictions.

AI analytics bring about privacy issue on a much larger scale with the aggregation of large-scale data within which it is easier to commit inference attacks and unintentional data disclosure. Privacy preserving techniques partially reduce some of the threats but are usually accompanied with extra computational overhead, which makes it difficult to implement in resource constrained IoT environments.

In a nutshell though blockchain and AI convergence can provide a powerful framework in IoT security it is necessary to overcome the challenges such as scalability, latency, explainability model management and privacy. Such limitations make it important to carefully design such architecture, make room for threat modelling and to achieve a balance between security, performance and compliance. Solving these issues would be basic in the process of moving from the conceptual frameworks to broadly deployable IoT security solutions.

11. SECURITY AND PRIVACY ANALYSIS

A proper security and privacy analysis is necessary to assess the effectiveness of Blockchain-Artificial Intelligence (AI) enabled Internet of Things (IoT) security architectures. Given the distributed, heterogeneous and adversarial nature of IoT environments, the security needs to be assessed holistically across device, network, data and governance layers. This section outlines a threat-oriented analysis of integrated blockchain - AI - IoT systems and looks at how key security and privacy objectives are addressed.

11.1 Threat Model for Integrated AI–Blockchain–IoT Systems

The threat mode for IoT systems, include many different adversaries such as external threat, malicious insider, compromised device, and colluding adversary. Common attack vectors include device spoofing, unauthorized access, data tampering, distributed denial of service (DDoS) attack and manipulation of security log. In systems enabled with AI, there are more threats data poisoning, adversarial examples, and unauthorized model updates.

In the case of a blockchain - AI - IoT architecture, threats can be on a layer-by-layer basis, or through interaction between layers. For example, the use of compromised IoT devices to inject false data into AI analytics data pipelines, or by malicious actors in a blockchain which attempt to manipulate the consensus or execution of smart contracts. A comprehensive threat model must therefore take into consideration cyber and cyber physical attack and cross layer dependencies.

11.2 Protection Against Spoofing, Tampering, and DDoS

Blockchain-based identity and authentication fundamentals support security to resist attacks of device spoofing and unauthorised access by locking cryptographic identities and credentials in a tamper-evident ledger. This decentralized approach to identities means that there has been less reliance on centralized authentication servers, and there are less single points of failure.

Data tampering is solved by immutability offered by block chain and that means that the security relevant events or commitments of data once recorded cannot be changed without being noticed. AI-based monitoring goes further to provide added protection by detecting abnormal communication patterns that is indicative of a tampering or replay attack.

DDoS attack continues to be a major threat on IoT infrastructures, particularly on the gateways and cloud end points. AI-driven traffic analysis helps in identifying abnormal traffic surges and orchestrated attack behavior and mitigate them using strategies such as rate limiting or traffic isolation. Blockchain based logging of attack events to support coordination of response and accountability of post-incident incident.

11.3 Data Lifecycle Protection and Privacy Preservation

IoT data lifecycle management from data generation, transmission, storage and analysis leads to significant privacy issues. Blockchain is also beneficial in improving data governance with transparent and auditable data access, sharing and modification record. Rather than storing raw data on-chain, most architectures exist using off-chain storage with blockchain-based integrity proofs with a view to balancing the privacy and accountability trade-off.

Inference and aggregation AI analytics as powerful as creating a higher risk of leaking privacy. Privacy churches such as federated learning reduce the exposure of not feeding raw data to global and fostered get to work on models together. Combined with blockchain based governance, these techniques are used to enable verifiable compliance to access and usage policies.

11.4 Advanced Cryptographic Enhancements

There are advanced cryptographic mechanisms to further increase security and privacy guarantees in integrated systems. Zero-knowledge proof techniques allow for verification of claims while preserving privacy over data bases - for example, zero-knowledge proofs can be combined with privacy-preserving techniques of authentication and claim compliance check. Homomorphic encryption provides the opportunity to develop breakthroughs in limited computation or computation of encrypted data, and consequently the ability to safely perform analytics on encrypted data without decrypting encrypted data.

While these techniques provide an improvement in the level of privacy, the computation overhead makes them unsuitable for direct implementation on constrained IoT devices. As a result, they typically have an application at edge or cloud layers, which are coordinated by blockchain-based policy enforcement and audit mechanisms.

11.5 Accountability, Forensics, and Auditability

Accountability as well as forensic readiness is important to response to incidents and compliance with regulations. Blockchain's unchangeable logs produce credible proof of security occurrences and access and system action thus offering traceability through the life-cycle of IoT. Computers that use AI-driven analytics as helpers, suggest the association of events and to draw out the exact causes in the course of looking for legal forensics.

The combination of BlockChain and AI therefore provides support not only for prevention and detection, but also post incident analysis and recovery of the scenarios which has often been neglected in the traditional IoT security designs.

Integration of Blockchain and AI provides IoT security huge boost by overcoming the identity, integrity, availability and privacy threats. Blockchain brings tamper-evident trust and accountability and AI makes smart: Enables the AI in a solution to recognize and adjust for problems which have arisen. Even though there are associated overheads associated with the application of cryptography and privacy guaranteeing mechanisms, selective application of these mechanisms in a layered architecture enables balanced levels of security and privacy protection in IoT systems.

12. REGULATORY, ETHICAL, AND STANDARDIZATION ISSUES

The implementation of Blockchain AI resulted in IoT security systems which is a complex environment of regulation, ethics and new standards. With IoT being introduced in more important and sensitive areas, compliance and responsible governance will become as important as technical robustness.

12.1 Regulatory Considerations

IoT systems are prone to processing personal, sensitive or mission-critical data, which means that they are subjected to strict data protection and cybersecurity regulations. The various regulations like GDPR, sector specific frameworks etc have various requirements in respect of data minimization, access control, auditability and accountability. Blockchain technologies for use in logging and identity management can help drive compliance, by having access to transparent and verifiable data, in addition to enforcing policy. However, the immutability of blockchains might be incompatible with the regulations on data modification or erasure that might apply depending on the state and might require careful architecture decisions such as off-chain storage and on-chain integrity proofs.

AI-powered security analytics makes the task of compliance with the regulations that much more difficult. Automated decision-making systems must be fair, transparent and explainable - in particular, if the decisions affect significantly on individuals or important operations. Regulatory scrutiny which requires AI systems to can be auditable and decision processes to be justifiable ever more often.

12.2 Ethical Implications

Ethical Considerations With the autonomous and pervasive nature of IoT security with AI, there are ethical considerations. Continuous monitoring and profiling of behaviours is a potential privacy violation if not carefully governed. Ethical AI frameworks be proportions, openness and supervision by humans, taking into consideration misuse and determined an unwitting harm.

Blockchain can be used to support ethical governance, since it can help with the transparent enforcement of policies and the immutability of accountability records. However, such ethical challenges are also raised due to decentralization in itself, e.g. ambiguity of responsibility and resolution of dispute within decentralized systems. Establish clarity and enforceability in accountability mechanisms - is much needed for ethically deploying.

12.3 Standardization and Interoperability

Standardization is an essential part of interoperability and broad-spread adoption of blockchain machine learning IoT security solutions. Existing IoT security standards and frameworks offer input into risk management, device security and system governance. However, standards relating specifically to the integration of blockchain and AI are in the early stages.

Harmonized standards are required that will define interfaces between IoT devices, the AI analytics engine and the blockchain infrastructures. Such standardization would lower the complexity of integration, increase interoperability between vendors, and provide for regulatory compliance. Continued cooperation between industry consortia's, standards bodies and research communities needed to determine best practices.

13. FUTURE DIRECTIONS

The combination of Blockchain and AI in the field of IoT security is a developing field of study with great potential in the future. It is assumed that a number of promising trends will influence the next-generation IoT security designs.

13.1 Quantum-Resistant and Long-Term Security

With the development of quantum computing, the current cryptographic primitives can be compromised. A quantum-resistant cryptographic scheme will be required in future blockchain-enabled AI IoT systems to provide long-term security or infrastructure with long lifespan.

13.2 Self-Healing and Autonomous Security Systems

The combination of AI-based analytics and blockchain-based governance will allow realizing the image of self-healing IoT networks. These systems would be able to autonomously identify threats, organize responses, and recover attacks and keep auditable records of all activities. The ability will be based on feedback loops between AI models and blockchain policies.

13.3 Web3, Decentralized Governance, and DAOs

New paradigms in the field of IoT governance can be presented by the emerging Web3 and decentralized autonomous organizations (DAOs). Distributed, open and responsive management of large scale IoT ecosystems may be facilitated by blockchain based governance and AI based decision support.

13.4 Trust-Aware Federated Learning

It is anticipated that future studies will be based on trust-aware federated learning, in which blockchain is used to aid in managing reputation, incentive, and validation of model updates. This technique can be used to make organizations collaborate and maintain privacy and trust.

14. CONCLUSION

This chapter discussed the intersection of Blockchain and Artificial Intelligence as a revolution in the process of protecting networks of the Internet of Things. IoT ecosystems are susceptible to basic security issues due to scale, non-homogeneity, resource limitation, and frail trust. The conventional centralized security models are becoming more and more ineffective in tackling these issues.

Decentralized trust, immutability, and transparent governance are some of the benefits of blockchain that allow securing identity management, creating tamper-proof logs, and implementing accountable policy enforcement. The AI assists people that have smart threat identification, an anomaly detection, smart authentication, and predictive security analytics. The reason for the fact that blockchain and AI are of mutual benefit to each other is because they create a new type of paradigm of security when used together.

This chapter has been able to demonstrate how the convergence of blockchain and AI could be used to bring resiliency, trust, and autonomy to IoT systems by analyzing the background, architectural design, use cases, and security survey of theorems. Although issues to do with scalability, latency, explainability and regulatory compliance still exist, thoughtful system design and new standards provide ways to proceed.

To sum up, integration of blockchain with AI is a very important step on the way to creating the secure, trustworthy and future proof IoT ecosystems. The future of this paradigm will require the continued interdisciplinary research and co-operation between academia, industry and policy makers to realise the full potential of this paradigm.

REFERENCES

Abomhara, M., & Køien, G. M. (2015). Cyber security and the Internet of Things. *Future Generation Computer Systems, 56*, 442–452.

Aggarwal, D., Brennen, B., Lee, T., Santha, M., & Tomamichel, M. (2018). Quantum attacks on Bitcoin. *Ledger, 3*, 68–90. DOI: 10.5195/ledger.2018.127

Alaba, F. A., Othman, M., Hashem, I. A. T., & Alotaibi, F. (2017). Internet of Things security: A survey. *Journal of Network and Computer Applications, 88*, 10–28. DOI: 10.1016/j.jnca.2017.04.002

Aouedi, O., Vu, T. H., Sacco, A., Nguyen, D. C., Piamrat, K., Marchetto, G., & Pham, Q. V. (2024). A survey on intelligent Internet of Things: Applications, security, privacy, and future directions. *IEEE Communications Surveys and Tutorials.*

Atzori, L., Iera, A., & Morabito, G. (2010). The Internet of Things: A survey. *Computer Networks, 54*(15), 2787–2805. DOI: 10.1016/j.comnet.2010.05.010

Ben-Sasson, E.. (2014). Zerocash: Decentralized anonymous payments from Bitcoin. In *Proceedings of the IEEE Symposium on Security and Privacy* (pp. 459–474).

Bernstein, D. J., & Lange, T. (2017). Post-quantum cryptography. *Nature, 549*(7671), 188–194. DOI: 10.1038/nature23461 PMID: 28905891

Buczak, A. L., & Guven, E. (2016). A survey of data mining and machine learning methods for cybersecurity intrusion detection. *IEEE Communications Surveys and Tutorials, 18*(2), 1153–1176. DOI: 10.1109/COMST.2015.2494502

Buterin, V. (2014). *A next-generation smart contract and decentralized application platform.*

Casino, F., Dasaklis, T. K., & Patsakis, C. (2019). A systematic literature review of blockchain-based applications. *Telematics and Informatics, 36*, 55–81. DOI: 10.1016/j.tele.2018.11.006

Christidis, K., & Devetsikiotis, M. (2016). Blockchains and smart contracts for the Internet of Things. *IEEE Access : Practical Innovations, Open Solutions, 4*, 2292–2303. DOI: 10.1109/ACCESS.2016.2566339

Diffie, W., & Hellman, M. (1976). New directions in cryptography. *IEEE Transactions on Information Theory, 22*(6), 644–654. DOI: 10.1109/TIT.1976.1055638

Dorri, A., Kanhere, S. S., & Jurdak, R. (2017). Blockchain in Internet of Things: Challenges and solutions. In *Proceedings of the IEEE PerCom Workshops* (pp. 273–278).

Dorri, A., Steger, M., Kanhere, S. S., & Jurdak, R. (2020). Blockchain: A distributed solution to automotive security. *IEEE Communications Magazine*, *55*(12), 119–125. DOI: 10.1109/MCOM.2017.1700879

European Union. (2018). *General Data Protection Regulation (GDPR).*

Floridi, L.. (2018). AI4People—An ethical framework for a good AI society. *Nature Machine Intelligence*, *1*(1), 389–399. PMID: 30930541

Ge, M., Fu, X., Syed, N., Baig, Z., Teo, G., & Robles-Kelly, A. (2019). Deep learning-based intrusion detection for IoT networks. In *Proceedings of the IEEE 24th International Conference on Parallel and Distributed Systems (PRDC)* (pp. 256–260). IEEE. DOI: 10.1109/PRDC47002.2019.00056

Gentry, C. (2009). Fully homomorphic encryption using ideal lattices. In *Proceedings of the ACM Symposium on Theory of Computing (STOC)* (pp. 169–178).

Goldreich, O. (2009). *Foundations of cryptography*. Cambridge University Press.

. IEEE. (2019). *IEEE P7000 series: Ethical considerations in AI systems.*

Islam, S. M. R., Kwak, D., Kabir, M. H., Hossain, M., & Kwak, K. S. (2015). The Internet of Things for health care: A comprehensive survey. *IEEE Access : Practical Innovations, Open Solutions*, *3*, 678–708. DOI: 10.1109/ACCESS.2015.2437951

Jamalipour, A., & Murali, S. (2021). A taxonomy of machine-learning-based intrusion detection systems for the Internet of Things: A survey. *IEEE Internet of Things Journal*, *9*(12), 9444–9466. DOI: 10.1109/JIOT.2021.3126811

Karie, N. M., Sahri, N. M., Yang, W., Valli, C., & Kebande, V. R. (2021). A review of security standards and frameworks for IoT-based smart environments. *IEEE Access : Practical Innovations, Open Solutions*, *9*, 121975–121995. DOI: 10.1109/ACCESS.2021.3109886

Khan, M. A., Karim, M., & Kim, Y. (2019). A scalable and hybrid intrusion detection system based on deep learning. *IEEE Access : Practical Innovations, Open Solutions*, *7*, 177352–177366.

Khan, M. A., & Salah, K. (2018). IoT security: Review, challenges, and solutions. *Future Generation Computer Systems*, *82*, 395–411. DOI: 10.1016/j.future.2017.11.022

Kouicem, D. E., Bouabdallah, A., & Lakhlef, H. (2018). Internet of Things security: A top-down survey. *Computer Networks*, *141*, 199–221. DOI: 10.1016/j.comnet.2018.03.012

Kshetri, N. (2018). Blockchain's roles in meeting key supply chain management objectives. *International Journal of Information Management*, *39*, 80–89. DOI: 10.1016/j.ijinfomgt.2017.12.005

Lee, J., Bagheri, B., & Kao, H. A. (2015). A cyber-physical systems architecture for Industry 4.0-based manufacturing systems. *Manufacturing Letters*, *3*, 18–23. DOI: 10.1016/j.mfglet.2014.12.001

Li, W., Sforzin, A., Fedorov, S., & Karame, G. O. (2018). Towards scalable and private industrial blockchains. In *Proceedings of the ACM Conference on Computer and Communications Security (CCS)* (pp. 1817–1832).

Lin, J., Yu, W., Zhang, N., Yang, X., Zhang, H., & Zhao, W. (2017). A survey on Internet of Things security. *IEEE Communications Surveys and Tutorials*, *19*(3), 1762–1780.

Lu, Y. (2020). Blockchain and IoT integration: A review. *Journal of Industrial Information Integration*, *20*, 100174.

Lu, Y., & Xu, X. (2019). Cloud-based manufacturing and Industrial IoT. *Journal of Manufacturing Systems*, *49*, 87–97.

Nakamoto, S. (2008). *Bitcoin: A peer-to-peer electronic cash system.*

National Institute of Standards and Technology. (2020). *Artificial Intelligence Risk Management Framework.*

Nguyen, D. C., Ding, M., Pathirana, P. N., Seneviratne, A., Li, J., & Vincent Poor, H. (2021). Federated learning for Internet of Things: A comprehensive survey. *IEEE Communications Surveys and Tutorials*, *23*(3), 1622–1658. DOI: 10.1109/COMST.2021.3075439

Pan, J., & McElhannon, J. (2018). Future edge cloud and edge computing for IoT applications. *IEEE Cloud Computing*, *5*(1), 6–12.

Reyna, A., Martín, C., Chen, J., Soler, E., & Díaz, M. (2018). On blockchain and its integration with IoT: Challenges and opportunities. *Future Generation Computer Systems*, *88*, 173–190. DOI: 10.1016/j.future.2018.05.046

Roman, R., Zhou, J., & Lopez, J. (2013). On the features and challenges of security and privacy in distributed Internet of Things. *Computer Networks*, *57*(10), 2266–2279. DOI: 10.1016/j.comnet.2012.12.018

Salah, K., Rehman, M. H. U., Nizamuddin, N., & Al-Fuqaha, A. (2019). Blockchain for AI: Review and open research challenges. *IEEE Access : Practical Innovations, Open Solutions*, *7*, 10227–10249. DOI: 10.1109/ACCESS.2018.2890507

Saravana, M. K., Roopa, M. S., Arunalatha, J. S., & Venugopal, K. R. (2026). Transformers for multivariate time series forecasting: Comprehensive analysis, challenges, research opportunities and future prospects. *IEEE Access : Practical Innovations, Open Solutions*, *14*, 11424–11457. DOI: 10.1109/ACCESS.2026.3654408

Shi, W., & Dustdar, S. (2016). The promise of edge computing. *Computer*, *49*(5), 78–81. DOI: 10.1109/MC.2016.145

Shone, N., Ngoc, T. N., Phai, V. D., & Shi, Q. (2018). A deep learning approach to network intrusion detection. *IEEE Transactions on Emerging Topics in Computational Intelligence*, *2*(1), 41–50. DOI: 10.1109/TETCI.2017.2772792

Sicari, S., Rizzardi, A., Grieco, L. A., & Coen-Porisini, A. (2015). Security, privacy and trust in Internet of Things: The road ahead. *Computer Networks*, *76*, 146–164. DOI: 10.1016/j.comnet.2014.11.008

Sommer, R., & Paxson, V. (2010). Outside the closed world: On using machine learning for network intrusion detection. In *Proceedings of the IEEE Symposium on Security and Privacy* (pp. 305–316). DOI: 10.1109/SP.2010.25

U.S. Department of Health and Human Services. (2013). *HIPAA Security Rule.*

Viriyasitavat, W., & Hoonsopon, D. (2019). Blockchain characteristics and consensus. *Journal of Industrial Information Integration*, *15*, 100–109.

Wang, S.. (2019). When edge meets learning: Adaptive control. *IEEE Communications Magazine*, *56*(8), 63–69.

Wang, Z., Qing, S., Wan, X., Fan, Z., Xu, Y., & Duo, B. (2022). Secrecy rate maximization algorithm for IRS assisted NOMA-UAV networks. *IEEE Communications Letters*, *45*(3), 1–8.

Wood, G. (2014). *Ethereum: A secure decentralized generalized transaction ledger.*

Wu, T., Cui, C., Xian, X., Qiao, S., Wang, C., Yuan, L., & Yu, S. (2024). Explainable AI security: Exploring robustness of graph neural networks to adversarial attacks. *arXiv*. https://arxiv.org/abs/2406.13920

Xu, X.. (2019). A taxonomy of blockchain-based systems for architecture design. *ACM Computing Surveys*, *52*(5).

Yaga, D., Mell, P., Roby, N., & Scarfone, K. (2018). *Blockchain technology overview* (NIST Internal Report No. 8202). National Institute of Standards and Technology.

Yang, Y., Wu, L., Yin, G., Li, L., & Zhao, H. (2017). A survey on security and privacy issues in IoT. *IEEE Internet of Things Journal*, *4*(5), 1250–1258. DOI: 10.1109/JIOT.2017.2694844

Yuan, L., Wang, Z., Sun, L., Yu, P. S., & Brinton, C. G. (2024). Decentralized federated learning: A survey and perspective. *IEEE Internet of Things Journal*, *11*(21), 34617–34638. DOI: 10.1109/JIOT.2024.3407584

Yue, X., Wang, H., Jin, D., Li, M., & Jiang, W. (2016). Healthcare data gateways: Found healthcare intelligence on blockchain. *Journal of Medical Systems*, *40*(10), 218. DOI: 10.1007/s10916-016-0574-6 PMID: 27565509

Zanella, A., Bui, N., Castellani, A., Vangelista, L., & Zorzi, M. (2014). Internet of Things for smart cities. *IEEE Internet of Things Journal*, *1*(1), 22–32. DOI: 10.1109/JIOT.2014.2306328

Zhang, K., Mao, Y., Leng, S., Vinel, A., & Zhang, Y. (2017). Delay-constrained offloading for mobile edge computing. *IEEE Access : Practical Innovations, Open Solutions*, *5*, 20914–20928.

Zhang, R., Xue, R., & Liu, L. (2019). Security and privacy on blockchain. *ACM Computing Surveys*, *52*(3), 1–34. DOI: 10.1145/3316481

Zheng, Z., Xie, S., Dai, H., Chen, X., & Wang, H. (2017). An overview of blockchain technology: Architecture, consensus, and future trends. In *Proceedings of the IEEE Big Data Congress* (pp. 557–564). DOI: 10.1109/BigDataCongress.2017.85

Zhou, Z.. (2019). Edge intelligence: Paving the last mile of AI with edge computing. *Proceedings of the IEEE*, *107*(8), 1738–1762. DOI: 10.1109/JPROC.2019.2918951

Zyskind, G., Nathan, O., & Pentland, A. (2015). Decentralizing privacy using blockchain. In *Proceedings of the IEEE Security and Privacy Workshops* (pp. 180–184).

Chapter 4

Challenges and Barriers to Implementing Quantum Security Frameworks in Healthcare Systems

Imdad Ali Shah
http://orcid.org/0000-0003-2015-1028
FEST, Iqra University, Pakistan

Quartul Ain Sial
Independent Researcher, Pakistan

ABSTRACT

In the rapidly emerging digital age, sensitive information has been transformed through medical devices in the healthcare industry and network-connected, leading to an increase in multiple security issues and challenges. Conventional techniques are facing vulnerabilities due to advances in computing, making quantum-resistant solutions critical for protecting sensitive patient data, medical devices, and healthcare networks. However, executing a quantum security framework in a healthcare situation presents challenges. These Conventional cryptographic techniques are significantly vulnerable to the development of quantum computing capabilities, which requires a transition toward a quantum security framework.

DOI: 10.4018/979-8-3373-3857-6.ch004

1. INTRODUCTION

In the modern era, IoT technologies played a key role in healthcare and the use of medical devices for connectivity, such as managing data and patient care. Furthermore, it extends the role of wearable sensors to a remote monitoring system, increasing daily operation, such as maintaining patient data, institutions' sensitive data and these devices are interconnected for communication with each other, while the current studies show that interconnected devices are increasing in healthcare, and they need new standards of security threats and risks (Shen et al., 2021). To identify these challenges and issues regarding the quantum security frameworks, focus on a comment defense mechanism for secure healthcare information in IoT ecosystems. These frameworks impact quantum-resistant algorithms and cryptographic techniques designed to secure quantum computers and protect them from cyberattacks (Gupta et al., 2024; Rosa et al., 2023; Saxena et al., 2023). Adopting the advanced security models within healthcare IoT environments presents particular difficulties and issues, such as limited device processing power. Figure 1 Quantum Security Frameworks: Issues and Challenges (2020–2024).

Figure 1. Quantum Security Frameworks: Issues and Challenges (2020–2024) adopted from studies

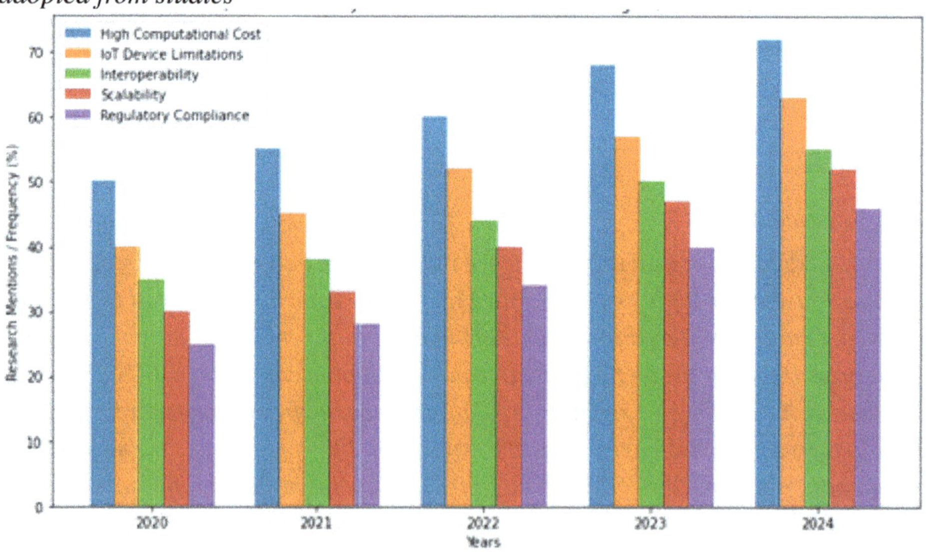

Healthcare institutions have been moving their information and assembling data from various medical IoT devices and sensors over the cloud platform (Pan et all., 2023; Shah et al., 2024). Cloud service platforms are implemented for digital health systems to enable the digital retrieval of patient information and significant clinical data, such as quality management, transnational research and healthcare administration (Fan et al., 2023; Coulter et al., 2020). The acceptance of the digital framework in healthcare organizations can bring various advantages, such as healthcare services, doctors and patients. However, concerns regarding the security issues and challenges of consumer information are a major issue in several healthcare institutions (Gupta et al., 2024; Mishra & Gupta, 2024). The healthcare institutes need to engage with multiple stakeholders, such as academia, researchers, patients, doctors and regulatory bodies (Mishra & Mishra, 2022; Hou et all., 2024). The stakeholders are sharing the sensitive information in a digital framework, which is required for medical expansions, but it is risky and susceptible to security threats and data breaches. While the healthcare breaches have increased in the last four years (Zhao et al., 2021; Abd Elaziz et al., 2021). Furthermore, there is a comprehensive study focused on the security issues and challenges concerning the Electronic Health Records (Abd EL-Latif et al., 2020; Abdulhussien et al., 2023). The unforeseen encounter of essential medical information with an illegal party can promote direct financial loss and damage the reputation of any organization and its overall expansion. The results of the data breach are impactful in a wide range of. It is a big challenge in sharing cloud environments and needs to be handled properly (Fateh et al., 2024).

Our contribution

1. This research has provided a comprehensive Literature Review of Quantum Security Issues and Challenges.
2. This Research has focused on Healthcare and Quantum Computing
3. This research has focused on Quantum Computing Applications in Healthcare
4. This research has provided a detailed discussion on challenges for applying Quantum Security Frameworks
5. This research has provided recommendations and future work

2. LITERATURE REVIEW

Current studies draw attention to the fact that IoT-enabled healthcare systems are significantly prone to cyberattacks in view of the distributed framework and sensitive information change (Acar & Yilmaz, 2021). Numerous studies have been presented on healthcare information security issues and challenges, and prediction approaches (Ahmadi et al,2021; Alharbi et al.,2022). Studies have presented a practical and scalable solution to identify the problem of keeping a privacy dataset in connection through the concept of a prototype (Biamonte et al.,2017).The data leakage prevention (DLP) model limits data access to users through a simple piece-wise linear function for model learning (Castle et al., 2021; Cedillo-Hernandez, 2020). In the remote medical field, implantable devices play an important role, but they have suspects of data breach and spoofing. While information reveals pose threats and risks to information security (Chen et al., 2023; Cheplygina et al., 2019). The proposed model supports several participants in sharing their information securely; further, it involves several unreliable parties through encryption and machine learning approaches (Choudhuri & Halder, 2023; Alokeparna et al., 2022). The proposed model analysis the security performance in the complex healthcare environment using CNN, and in this model, parameters have been reduced (Darwish et al., 2023; Shah et al., 2024). Figure 2 Overview of the healthcare data management framework adopted by Gupta, K.

Figure 2. Overview of the healthcare data management framework adopted by Gupta, K.

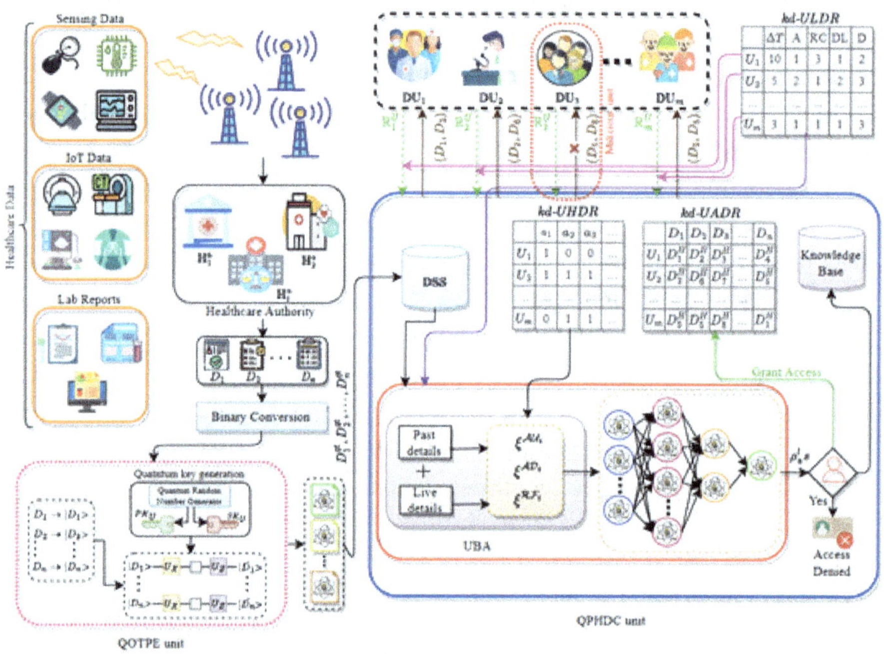

In the digital age, security remains a critical concern in modern healthcare, including the security of cloud-based patient data systems and storing and managing vast volumes of private medical, financial data and personal (Das et al., 2018), these systems have given scalability, accessibility, and cost efficiency, but the vulnerabilities have been exploited, and hackers' activities have been conducted through these systems. The growing advancement of cyber threats and risk, concerns about the efficacy of conventional encryption methods, in rapid advancements in quantum computing. (Deshmukh et al., 2023; Dhall & Gupta, 2021) these developments require a shift toward quantum-resistant encryption to ensure the long-term save patient information, specifically, current cryptographic techniques are becoming susceptible to compromise. The increasing environment of quantum computing risks and threats has motivated essential investment in quantum-resistant cryptographic solutions (Di et al., 2017).

3. HEALTHCARE AND QUANTUM COMPUTING

In the age of technological innovation, the environment of healthcare is undergoing a significant change from the conventional use of paper writing techniques to devices to interconnected devices for maintaining health records, and these need protections of their sensitive data, patients' records, etc. In order to reduce the security risk in healthcare institutions, we need to take the required measures to meet user demands. The current studies identified that the use of quantum-resistant encryption numbers has grown in most health institutes. Several studies have been identified that healthcare services and changes to cloud-based records of patients and information systems mostly focus on security risks and continuously remain complexity. According to the Shah, I. A.,2025,Elhadad, A.2021,Ezugwu AE,2022, the adoption of the cloud has grown by about 86% in 2024, which is an increase (cloud) in the healthcare institutions requiring data safety to reduce the data breaches and threats. In view of these findings, healthcare institutions rely on cloud computing (Fateh et al.,2025).

3.1 Quantum Computing Application in Healthcare

Quantum Computing Applications (QCA) supports improving the reconstruction in terms of speed and accuracy of images, and increased pattern recognition to address complex diseases in enormous datasets such as MRIs. QC models can affect imaging modalities for enhancing data security. Figure 3 Overview of QC application in healthcare data collected by the study.

Figure 3. Overview of QC application in healthcare data collected by study

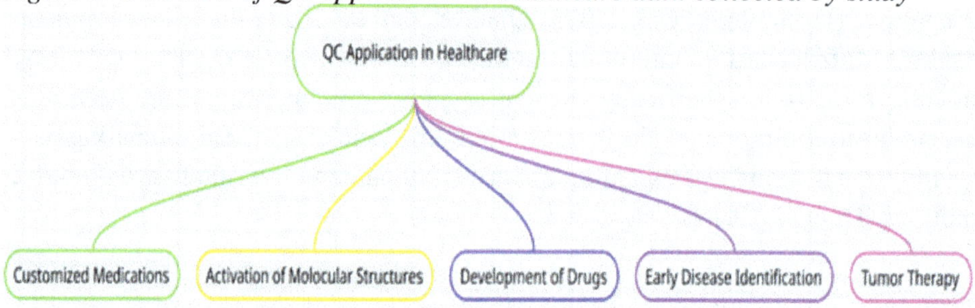

3.2 Customized Medications (PM)

PM provides a medical model that divides people into groups for medical decisions and specifically focuses on modifying drugs to meet of the individual patients. This treatment is based on the genetic and health conditions.

3.3 Activation of Molecular Structures (AMS)

AMS refers to the process by which a molecule becomes more reactive and prone to experience a chemical reaction, either by using heat to increase its energy, through a more focused interaction, including the use of enzymes and catalysts or electrical excitation. This activated state is frequently an unstable, high-energy "transition state" that can give rise to a novel chemical process.

3.4 Development of Drugs (DD)

DD, a basic scientific discovery, is turned into a new medication for patients through the difficult, time-consuming and costly process of drug development, which includes discovery, preclinical testing, several stages of human clinical trials, regulatory review by organisations such as the FDA, and continuous post-market surveillance. To guarantee that a new medication is safe, effective, and accessible to the general public, a multidisciplinary effort involving scientists, doctors, regulators, and patients is necessary.

3.5 Early Disease Identification (EDI)

Through the EDI process, we know the illness in advance. Several studies presented a model to detect diseases, but still need to improve results. These types of models have been designed based on a mathematical framework (Ganjefar & Tofighi, 2018). The models give more focus to the researchers to give attention to understanding the mechanisms of the spread of the disease and the development of predictive control strategics.

3.6 Tumor Therapy (TT)

Quantum computing gives an excellent chance to transform tumour treatment by reshaping drug discovery and personalized plans. Furthermore, improving the diagnosis using data analysis and imaging in advanced (Sial & Jhanjhi, 2025).

4. QUANTUM METHODS FOR MEDICAL IMAGE PROCESSING (QMMIP)

QMMIP are developing approaches that implement the principles of QM and improve the speed and accuracy of analysing complex medical images, such as MRI and CT, such as superposition and quantum parallelism. Furthermore, its techniques can process high-dimensional data efficiently and perform image segmentation.

5. CHALLENGES OF APPLYING QUANTUM SECURITY FRAMEWORKS

Quantum Security Frameworks (QSF) show exceptional challenges in the Healthcare Industry. QSFs are difficult for health institutions due to their high cost, particularly in emerging regions, to accept these advanced QSFs. Scalability challenges arise when taking steps to secure electronic health records that are part of connected healthcare networks, such as telemedicine platforms and medical IoT devices. Figure 4 overview of the QSF challenges for the healthcare.

Figure 4. overview of the QSF challenges for the healthcare

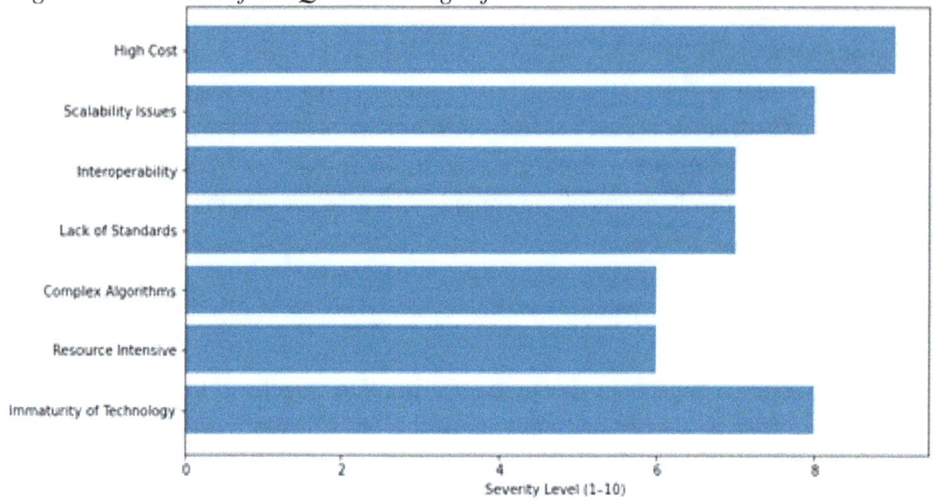

Interoperability with Classical Security Systems (ICSS) is another boundary, as most healthcare institutions still rely on traditional encryption techniques, which are difficult to match well with applying a quantum-based solution. Furthermore, the lack of regulatory guidelines in the healthcare Industry (HI) and the risk of adoption for the industry and the complexity of quantum algorithms require unique expertise that is unusual in the IT workforce. Finally, the immaturity of quantum technology raises concerns about reliability, stability, and trustworthiness in life-critical healthcare applications.

6. CONCLUSION

This chapter proposes to give highlights on the security issues and challenges in protecting healthcare data by applying the quantum security framework for healthcare. In the studies, we find that IoT technologies are used in healthcare, including the use of medical devices for connectivity, such as managing data and patient care. Additionally, it expands the use of wearable sensors to a remote monitoring system, enhancing everyday operations like protecting patient information and sensitive institutional data. These devices are connected to communicate with one another, and recent research indicates that the number of interconnected healthcare devices is growing, necessitating new security standards and risks. Focus on a comment defence mechanism for secure healthcare information in IoT ecosystems in order to discover these difficulties and problems with quantum security frameworks. These frameworks have an impact on cryptographic methods and quantum-resistant algorithms intended to safeguard quantum computers against cyberattacks. Limited device processing capacity is one of the unique challenges and problems associated with implementing enhanced security models in healthcare IoT systems.Healthcare organisations have been using cloud platforms to transfer and compile data from a variety of medical IoT devices and sensors. Security is still a major concern in modern healthcare in the digital age, particularly protecting cloud-based patient data systems and storing and handling enormous amounts of private financial, medical, and personal data.

7. FUTURE WORK

Our studies addressing the challenges of applying QSF for healthcare institutions need to focus on developing and implementing a scalable and practical quantum safe algorithm that can work seamlessly integrated into existing IT frameworks and IoT-enabled medical devices. The study would need to highlight hybrid approaches to combine classical cryptography with post-quantum techniques to ensure smooth transitions during the quantum era.

REFERENCES

Abd EL-Latif, A. A., Abd-El-Atty, B., Abou-Nassar, E. M., & Venegas-Andraca, S. E.Abd EL-Latif. (2020). Controlled alternate quantum walks based privacy-preserving healthcare images in Internet of Things. *Optics & Laser Technology, 124*, 105942. DOI: 10.1016/j.optlastec.2019.105942

Abd Elaziz, M., Mohammadi, D., Oliva, D., & Salimifard, K. (2021). Quantum marine predators algorithm for addressing multilevel image segmentation. *Applied Soft Computing, 110*, 107598. DOI: 10.1016/j.asoc.2021.107598

Abdulhussien, A. A., Nasrudin, M. F., Darwish, S. M., & Alyasseri, Z. A. A. (2023). Feature selection method based on quantum-inspired genetic algorithm for Arabic signature verification. *Journal of King Saud University. Computer and Information Sciences, 35*(3), 141–156. DOI: 10.1016/j.jksuci.2023.02.005

Acar, E., & Yilmaz, I. (2021). COVID-19 detection on IBM quantum computer with classical-quantum transfer learning. *Turkish Journal of Electrical Engineering and Computer Sciences, 29*(1), 46–61. DOI: 10.3906/elk-2006-94

Ahmadi, M., Sharifi, A., Hassantabar, S., & Enayati, S. (2021). QAIS-DSNN: Tumor area segmentation of MRI image with optimized quantum matched-filter technique and deep spiking neural network. *BioMed Research International, 2021*(1), 6653879. DOI: 10.1155/2021/6653879 PMID: 33542920

Alharbi, A. R., Ahmad, J., Jamal, S. S., Masood, F., Ghadi, Y. Y., Pitropakis, N., & Buchanan, W. J.. (2022). A new multistage encryption scheme using linear feedback register and chaos-based quantum map. *Complexity, 2022*(1), 1–15. DOI: 10.1155/2022/7047282

Alokeparna, C., Sourav, S., Sanjoy, P., & Oishila, B. (2022). Multilevel segmentation of hippocampus images using global steered quantum-inspired firefly algorithm. *Applied Intelligence, 52*(7), 7339–7372. DOI: 10.1007/s10489-021-02688-6

Biamonte, J., Wittek, P., Pancotti, N., Rebentrost, P., Wiebe, N., & Lloyd, S. (2017). Quantum machine learning. *Nature, 549*(7671), 195–202. DOI: 10.1038/nature23474 PMID: 28905917

Castle, P. E., Einstein, M. H., & Sahasrabuddhe, V. V. (2021). Cervical cancer prevention and control in women living with human immunodeficiency virus. *CA: a Cancer Journal for Clinicians, 71*(6), 505–526. DOI: 10.3322/caac.21696 PMID: 34499351

Cedillo-Hernandez, M., Cedillo-Hernandez, A., Nakano-Miyatake, M., & Perez-Meana, H. (2020). Improving the management of medical imaging by using robust and secure dual watermarking. *Biomedical Signal Processing and Control, 56*, 101695. DOI: 10.1016/j.bspc.2019.101695

Chen, Z., Liu, Y., Zhang, Y., & Li, Q. (2023). Orthogonal latent space learning with feature weighting and graph learning for multimodal Alzheimer's disease diagnosis. *Medical Image Analysis, 84*, 102698. DOI: 10.1016/j.media.2022.102698 PMID: 36462372

Cheplygina, V., de Bruijne, M., & Pluim, J. P. W. (2019). Not-so-supervised: A survey of semi-supervised, multi-instance, and transfer learning in medical image analysis. *Medical Image Analysis, 54*, 280–296. DOI: 10.1016/j.media.2019.03.009 PMID: 30959445

Choudhuri, R., & Halder, A. (2023). Brain MRI tumour classification using quantum classical convolutional neural net architecture. *Neural Computing & Applications, 35*(6), 4467–4478. DOI: 10.1007/s00521-022-07939-2

Coulter, R., Han, Q.-L., Pan, L., Zhang, J., & Xiang, Y. (2020). Data-driven cyber security in perspective—Intelligent traffic analysis. *IEEE Transactions on Cybernetics, 50*(7), 3081–3093. DOI: 10.1109/TCYB.2019.2940940 PMID: 31634146

Darwish, S. M., Abu Shaheen, L. J., & Elzoghabi, A. A. (2023). A new medical analytical framework for automated detection of MRI brain tumor using evolutionary quantum-inspired level set technique. *Bioengineering (Basel, Switzerland), 10*(7), 819. DOI: 10.3390/bioengineering10070819 PMID: 37508846

Das, S., De, S., Bhattacharyya, S., & Hassanien, A. E. (2018). Color MRI image segmentation using quantum-inspired modified genetic algorithm-based FCM. In *Recent trends in signal and image processing: ISSIP 2017* (pp. 151–164). Springer.

Deshmukh, S., Behera, B. K., Mulay, P., Ahmed, E. A., Al-Kuwari, S., Tiwari, P., & Farouk, A. (2023). Explainable quantum clustering method to model medical data. *Knowledge-Based Systems, 267*, 110413. DOI: 10.1016/j.knosys.2023.110413

Dhall, S., & Gupta, S. (2021). Multilayered highly secure authentic watermarking mechanism for medical applications. *Multimedia Tools and Applications, 80*(12), 18069–18105. DOI: 10.1007/s11042-021-10531-w

Di, X., Li, J., Qi, H., Cong, L., & Yang, H. (2017). A semi-symmetric image encryption scheme based on the function projective synchronization of two hyperchaotic systems. *PLoS One, 12*(9), e0184586. DOI: 10.1371/journal.pone.0184586 PMID: 28910349

Elhadad, A., Ghareeb, A., & Abbas, S. (2021). A blind and high-capacity data hiding of DICOM medical images based on fuzzification concepts. *Alexandria Engineering Journal*, *60*(2), 2471–2482. DOI: 10.1016/j.aej.2020.12.050

Ezugwu, A. E., Ikotun, A. M., Oyelade, O. O., Abualigah, L., Agushaka, J. O., Eke, C. I., & Akinyelu, A. A. (2022). A comprehensive survey of clustering algorithms: State-of-the-art machine learning applications, taxonomy, challenges, and future research prospects. *Engineering Applications of Artificial Intelligence*, *110*, 104743. DOI: 10.1016/j.engappai.2022.104743

Fan, Q., He, D., Chen, J., Peng, C., & Wang, L. (2023). ISOGA: An isogeny-based quantum-resist searchable encryption scheme against keyword guessing attacks. *IEEE Systems Journal*, *17*(2), 2101–2112. DOI: 10.1109/JSYST.2022.3182788

Fateh, S., Shah, I. A., Sial, Q., & Jhanjhi, N. Z. (2025). Deep learning applications for healthcare risk assessment. In *Generative AI techniques for sustainability in healthcare security* (pp. 59–76). IGI Global Scientific Publishing.

Fateh, S., Sial, Q., Dar, S. H., Shah, I. A., & Rani, A. (2024). Smart healthcare system in Industry 4.0. In *Advances in computational intelligence for the healthcare industry 4.0* (pp. 297–311). IGI Global Scientific Publishing. DOI: 10.4018/979-8-3693-2333-5.ch016

Ganjefar, S., & Tofighi, M. (2018). Optimization of quantum-inspired neural network using memetic algorithm for function approximation and chaotic time series prediction. *Neurocomputing*, *291*, 175–186. DOI: 10.1016/j.neucom.2018.02.074

Gupta, K., & Kush, A. (2020). A learning-oriented DLP system based on classification model. *INFOCOMP Journal of Computer Science*, *19*(2), 98–108.

Gupta, K., Saxena, D., Gupta, R., Kumar, J., & Singh, A. K. (2024). FedMUP: Federated learning driven malicious user prediction model for secure data distribution in cloud environments. *Applied Soft Computing*, *157*, 111519. DOI: 10.1016/j.asoc.2024.111519

Gupta, K., Saxena, D., Gupta, R., & Singh, A. K. (2024). MAIDS: Malicious agent identification-based data security model for cloud environments. *Cluster Computing*, *27*(5), 6167–6184. DOI: 10.1007/s10586-023-04263-9

Gupta, K., Saxena, D., Rani, P., Kumar, J., Makkar, A., Singh, A. K., & Lee, C. N. (2024). An intelligent quantum cyber-security framework for healthcare data management. *IEEE Transactions on Automation Science and Engineering*.

Hou, C., Zhou, C., Wu, C.-G., Cong, R., & Li, K. (2024). Optimization of cloud-based multi-agent system for trade-off between trustworthiness of data and cost of data usage. *IEEE Transactions on Automation Science and Engineering*, *21*(1), 106–122. DOI: 10.1109/TASE.2022.3224984

Mishra, V., Gupta, K., Saxena, D., & Singh, A. K. (2024). A global medical data security and privacy preserving standards identification framework for electronic healthcare consumers. *IEEE Transactions on Consumer Electronics*, *70*(1), 4379–4387. DOI: 10.1109/TCE.2024.3373912

Mishra, V., & Mishra, M. (2022). Privacy and security concerns with electronic health records: Shreds of evidence from India. *IMI Konnect*, *11*(3), 41–54.

Pan, S., Zhang, Y., & Wang, S. (2023). A secure aggregate authentication scheme with efficient revocation for IoT-based primary healthcare service. *IEEE Systems Journal*, *17*(4), 6480–6491. DOI: 10.1109/JSYST.2023.3310485

Rosa, B. M. G., Anastasova, S., & Yang, G. Z. (2023). NFC-powered implantable device for on-body parameters monitoring with secure data exchange link to a medical blockchain-type network. *IEEE Transactions on Cybernetics*, *53*(1), 31–43. DOI: 10.1109/TCYB.2021.3088711 PMID: 34197334

Saxena, D., Gupta, R., Singh, A. K., & Vasilakos, A. V. (2023). Emerging VM threat prediction and dynamic workload estimation for secure resource management in industrial clouds. *IEEE Transactions on Automation Science and Engineering*, •••, 1–15.

Shah, I. A., Jhanjhi, N. Z., & Brohi, S. N. (2024). IoT smart healthcare security challenges and solutions. In *Advances in computational intelligence for the healthcare industry 4.0* (pp. 234–247). IGI Global Scientific Publishing. DOI: 10.4018/979-8-3693-2333-5.ch012

Shah, I. A., & Sial, Q. (Eds.). (2024). *Advances in computational intelligence for the healthcare industry 4.0*. IGI Global. DOI: 10.4018/979-8-3693-2333-5

Shah, I. A., Sial, Q., & Jhanjhi, N. Z. (2025). Internet of Things cyber-physical systems in smart healthcare. In *Generative AI techniques for sustainability in healthcare security* (pp. 279–300). IGI Global Scientific Publishing.

Shen, B., Xie, W., & Kong, Z. J. (2021). Clustered discriminant regression for high-dimensional data feature extraction and its applications in health care and additive manufacturing. *IEEE Transactions on Automation Science and Engineering*, *18*(4), 1998–2010. DOI: 10.1109/TASE.2020.3029028

Sial, Q., Shah, I. A., & Jhanjhi, N. Z. (2025). Generative AI applications for enhancing medical training. In *Generative AI techniques for sustainability in healthcare security* (pp. 161–174). IGI Global Scientific Publishing.

Zhao, Z., Huang, Y., Zhen, Z., & Li, Y. (2021). Data-driven false data injection attack design and detection in cyber-physical systems. *IEEE Transactions on Cybernetics*, *51*(12), 6179–6187. DOI: 10.1109/TCYB.2020.2969320 PMID: 32086230

Chapter 5
Flash Events and DDoS Attacks:
Understanding Network Overload and Cybersecurity Threats

Shaveta Gupta
http://orcid.org/0009-0008-3776-8247
Post Graduate Government College, India

Jimmy Singla
http://orcid.org/0000-0003-2077-1622
Lovely Professional University, India

ABSTRACT

As the internet becomes essential for growth in the current times, ensuring network security and reliability stand as the biggest challenge for contemporary researchers. This chapter analyses two critical threats to any network, Distributed Denial of Service (DDoS) attacks and Flash Events(FE). The purpose of the denial-of-service attack is to bombard the target machine with more traffic than its capacity, which causes the server to become unavailable. Flash events are seemingly like DDoS attacks in high traffic, but legitimate users instead of attackers produce that volumetric traffic. In other words, Flash Events are generated organically whenever e-commerce platforms organise big sales, and Sometimes the system gets bogged down because of their incapability to manage high load. This is called a Flash Event. Given the underlying difference between the intent of DDoS attacks and Flash Events, it is very important to segregate DDoS attack traffic, Flash Event traffic and Normal/legitimate traffic so that corrective measures can be taken.

DOI: 10.4018/979-8-3373-3857-6.ch005

1 INTRODUCTION

In recent years, DDoS attacks have resulted in significant financial, security, as well as credibility losses for victims. For a long time, the cyber community, the government, service providers and users have been troubled by this vexing issue. Despite extensive study in this sector, a feasible answer has so far eluded us, and the complexity is only increasing (Gupta et al.,2018). According to this research, the fundamental reason for the illusion of an efficient solution is a striking match between the features of DDoS attacks and those of FEs in legitimate traffic. As a result, this research effort has sought to develop a solution by clearly distinguishing among regular traffic, DDoS attacks, and FEs (Gupta et al., 2018).

When a hacker overwhelms a server with traffic, it renders the server unable to handle the load, halting all services. This phenomenon is known as a DDoS attack (Gupta et al., 2021). On the other hand, a Flash Crowd resembles a DDoS attack, but legitimate users rather than attackers generate the volumetric traffic (Gera et al.,2018). For example, a highly anticipated multi-billion-dollar mega sale on an e-commerce website commences, and several customers worldwide are connected to products at reduced prices. However, traffic suddenly increases, and the network infrastructure cannot keep up. The website is expected to have a positive response and has all the settings, but it feels powerless due to the sudden flood of data requests. The web server may also be unavailable due to the overload of legitimate traffic from many bona fide customers. This type of situation is called a Flash Event (FE). In the case of a Flash Event, traffic is generated by real consumers instead of bots.

Much research has been conducted to detect attacks and Flash Events, but no foolproof solution exists to date. Attackers tried to mimic the behavior pattern of genuine users. So, it can be challenging to discriminate FE from DDoS attacks. The approaches proposed by different researchers (Behal et al., 2018; Bhandari et al., 2021; Zekri et al., 2018) have highlighted detection approaches for this complex issue, but have not fully resolved it.

There have been numerous incidents reported in past, as shown in Table 1, that clearly highlight the need to study these events in depth and to develop reliable detection and differentiation techniques to handle them effectively.

Table 1. Flash Events and DDoS Attacks

S No	Category	Date	Server	Description	Impact
1	Flash Events	2024-04-10	Shopify	During the big sale, an unexpected surge in users caused several online shopping sites to experience temporary outages.	Many merchants reported that their websites went down, and customers experienced checkout issues.
2		2024-09-12	Binance	A sudden change in the market sharply increased trading activity, causing short outages and slower system response.	Traders and account holders noticed delays when executing trades or accessing their accounts.
3		2022-12-10	Blizzard Entertainment	Launching a widespread expansion led to server overload, causing login queues and game disconnects.	Many players were unable to access the game for several hours.
4.	DDoS attacks	2024-03-12	Asian Hosting Provider	A massive 2 Tbsp attack hit an Asian hosting provider, making it one of the most significant incidents reported in 2024.	A DDoS attack at the network layer disrupted services, highlighting the strength of botnets such as Mirai.
5.		2024-04-10	Sweden	After joining NATO, Sweden experienced a 466% increase in DDoS attacks.	This attack targeted HTTP services, disrupting critical systems and is thought to have a political motive.
6.		2024-03-31	Global (Cloudflare mitigations)	Cloudflare mitigated 4.5 million DDoS attacks during the first quarter, totalling roughly 59 petabytes of traffic.	Network-layer attacks have risen worldwide, affecting several services across different regions.

2. CLASSIFICATION OF FLASH EVENTS AND DDOS ATTACKS

This segment proposes a comprehensive classification of FE and DDoS attacks, based on an in-depth evaluation of various attacks (Chawla et al.,2016), as shown in Figures 1 and 2. These events can be classified based on specific parameters, as shown below:

2.1 Flash Events Categorization

Figure 1. Classification of Flash Events

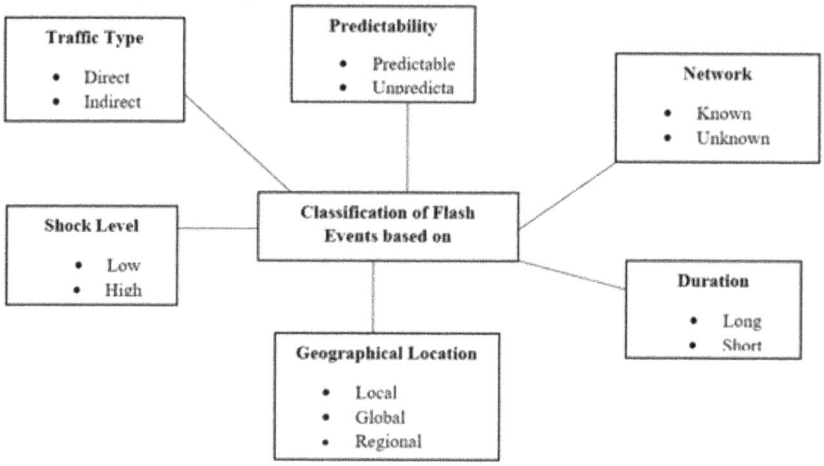

- Predictability: The first factor that can classify the FEs is "Predictability". Two situations can arise. First, when an increase in traffic load is expected, e.g., when a university releases results of a well-known course, election results on a specific website, or bumper sales on a famous e-commerce website like Black Friday. Second, when traffic from legitimate users is unpredictable, e.g., information about the demise of a renowned personality, the load on the specific web engine increases as the news spreads; sudden stock or cryptocurrency price movements cause trading platforms to experience overload, etc. (Behal et al., 2017).
- Network Known/ Unknown: The second factor that can classify FEs is whether the source network that bombards the traffic on the web server is known or unknown. Traffic originating from established and identifiable sources, such as specific user accounts, organizations, or previously registered devices, is known as known networks. Companies hosting webinars can generally estimate how many employees will attend, and streaming services can anticipate viewership on planned release dates. Traffic from unexpected or unfamiliar sources that leads to sudden spikes is called unknown network traffic. A sudden surge in traffic to a website due to a trending social media topic that was not previously anticipated, or to News articles or announcements that unexpectedly attract large audiences, leading to server strain. (Sachdeva et

al.,2011). This differentiation is needed to provide a better defense strategy in case of an attack.

- Traffic Type: The third factor that helps to categorize the FEs is whether the traffic generated is direct or indirect. In "Direct Traffic," a rush of legitimate clients is generated towards a particular website. For example, users try to buy products from popular e-commerce websites such as Flipkart and PayPal. However, when small websites are linked to popular websites, a sudden surge in small websites can indirectly affect famous websites.
- Duration: The fourth categorization factor is "Duration". Sometimes, the traffic lasts on the web server for a short duration, e.g., the outcome of a particular event, such as cricket match results. In contrast, legitimate rush on the website lasts longer. For example, on 03–04 September 2014, the DDA (Delhi Development Authority) website was heavily impacted by a flood of online requests attempting to apply for published flats.
- Shock Level: Another classification considers "Shock Level," where the power of Flash Events is measured based on the increase in traffic following an event. The higher the news shock level, the higher the network traffic load. For instance, the death of a celebrity or a popular leader can trigger this traffic.
- Geographical Location: Another factor to be considered is the geographical location of clients, such as local, regional, or global. It is assumed that network access will usually be located in the same geographical unit. For example, if a specific product is launched on Flipkart, most of the traffic should come from India; any rush from foreign countries should trigger an alarm for suspicious activity.

2.2 DDoS Attack Categorization

The following criteria can classify DDoS attacks:

Figure 2.Classification of DDoS attacks

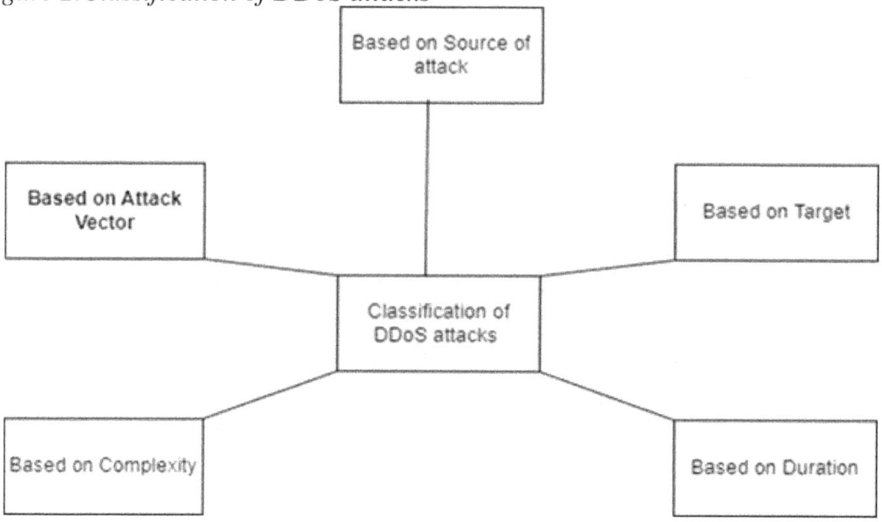

- **Based on Attack Vector**

1. Volumetric Attacks: Under this attack, the attacker sends high-volume traffic to the target to consume all its available bandwidth. As a result, genuine users will not be able to use the services. Examples include UDP Flood, ICMP Flood, etc.
2. Protocol Attacks: Under this, attackers target the network protocols and infrastructure resources like firewalls, routers, etc. Attackers are well aware of protocol weaknesses, so their main aim is to exhaust server resources or network equipment. Examples include SYN floods and the Ping of Death.
3. Application-layer: Under this, attackers target the applications running on the servers instead of flooding the network bandwidth to disrupt their normal functioning. This happens when many login or search page requests come in; it appears genuine, but it can crash the website. This attack is very hard to detect. Examples include HTTP GET and HTTP POST floods (Gupta et al.,2021)

- **Based on the Source of the Attack**

1. Botnet-Based Attacks: Under this, attackers create an army of bots through which massive traffic is generated at the same time. This is totally controlled

by the attacker. Examples include the Mirai botnet attack and SYN Floods from multiple bots.

2. Amplification Attacks: Under this, attackers use the publicly available servers to amplify the traffic volume. In this case, a hacker sends a small request to the server, but on the server side, a big response is generated that overloads the network. Examples include DNS Amplification Attack and NTP Amplification Attack.

- **Based on Target**

1. Network-Level Attacks: Under this, attackers target network devices like routers and firewalls to disrupt their normal functioning. Examples include SYN Flood, UDP Flood, etc.
2. Service-Level Attacks: Under this, attackers target the applications or services running on the server. Examples include SQL injection, DNS Query Flood, etc.

- **Based on Duration**

1. Short-term Attacks: Under this attack, the attacker's main target is to create instant chaos, and it lasts for a few minutes to some hours. Examples include a 30-second SYN flood and a 1-minute UDP burst.
2. Long-term Attacks: This attack lasts for a long duration, like several days to even weeks, resulting in slow performance from the server side. Examples include a 48-hour DNS flood attack and a week-long HTTP-GET flood attack.

- **Based on Complexity**

1. Simple Attacks: These attacks are easy to launch, like traffic generated from a single source. These are easy to detect as well. Examples include a Simple ping flood, a single-device UDP Flood, etc.
2. Complex Attacks These attacks are advanced, multilayer, multisource and even more complex to detect. Examples include a multi-vector DDoS attack.

The above classification of DDoS attacks and Flash Events helps researchers gain a deep understanding of different attack types and flash events, enabling the development of a detection algorithm to detect and mitigate attacks and flash events accurately.

3 RATIONALE TO DIFFERENTIATE BETWEEN FES AND DDOS ATTACKS

Different Researchers develop different rationales to differentiate between Flash Events and DDoS attacks. (Behal et al.,2017) Some of them are below:

Table 2. Comparison of FEs and DDoS attacks based on rationale

S. No	Rationale	DDoS Attack	Flash Event
1	Number of requests per IP	More	Less
2	Accessing Layer	Application/Network Layer	Application Layer
3	Type of request	GET	GET/POST
4	Change in the rate of new source IPs	High in the initial stage	High
5	Page referred	Random	Hot Page Only
6	Client Legitimacy	Unknown	Mostly Known for Predictive Unknown in Un-Predictive
7	Two-Way Traffic	Low	High
8	Flow Similarity	High	Low
9	Types of Users	Bots	Real Users
10	Time interval between requests	Small	Large
11	Correlation Coefficient	Less than 1	Higher than 1
12	Distribution of Clients	Uniform	Skewed
13	Web Server Response	Low	High
14	Duration of Traffic per Client	Long	Short
15	Number of Distinct Clusters	Less and overlapped	Relatively more new clusters

The above rationale helps researchers gain a clear understanding of some parameters and their behavior under DDoS attacks and Flash events. With this knowledge, they can easily determine whether the generated traffic is genuine or harmful, so that appropriate mitigation measures to be applied.

4 MEASURES TAKEN AGAINST FLASH EVENTS AND DDOS ATTACKS

To mitigate DDoS attacks and Flash events following measures can be taken:

4.1 Preventive Measures Against Flash Events

- **Scalable Infrastructure** Organizations should use auto scaling features provided by cloud providers to manage sudden heavy traffic. During planned events such as big billion sales or exit poll results, more servers need to be added to distribute the load (Rout et al., 2023; Alharthi et al., 2024).
- **Content Delivery Networks (CDNs)** Content Delivery Networks can be used to store and deliver content across different locations. Some providers keep copies of website content on edge servers to reduce the load on the central server. This arrangement helps users access content from the nearest server, preventing sudden traffic surges (Peng et al., 2004).
- **Caching Strategies** Server-side caching should be implemented to ensure the website performs well under heavy traffic. This can be done by using in-memory databases to cache frequently accessed data, images, scripts, etc., thereby reducing server load (Lykouris et al., 2021).
- **Traffic Rate Limiting** The number of requests on a particular device should be limited to avoid congestion on that device or on the network (Serbout et al., 2023; Cappers & van Wijk, 2016). If traffic exceeds a specific limit, an alert will be generated, enabling the concerned team to respond quickly.
- **Staggered Traffic Management** User activity can be spread out over time to prevent the server from overloading. This can be done with virtual queuing, which allows users to access services in batches rather than all at once (commonly used in ticket sales) (Eicken et al., 2002).
- **Stress Testing** This testing should be conducted regularly to evaluate how the network resources perform under extreme conditions. Several tools, such as Apache JMeter, can be used to simulate high traffic volumes to test the infrastructure's ability (Ware et al., 2025).
- **Optimize Database Performance** Databases should be optimized to handle large requests efficiently. It can be done by properly indexing databases to improve query performance. Replication helps distribute read operations across multiple database servers. Also, dividing large databases into smaller ones helps optimize performance (Eicken et al., 2002).
- **Disaster Recovery and Failover Plans** A strong disaster recovery and failover plan should be in place to ensure the business can continue operations. Backup systems should be there in case the primary one fails. Traffic can be automatically redirected to secondary one when needed.
- **User Experience and Communication** Proper communication with the user should be in place in case of an adverse situation to ensure a better experience. Some messages should be redirected to them so that they can know the

situation and behave accordingly. A dedicated status page showing real-time updates is helpful in these situations (Hardre et al., 2016).

4.2 Preventive Measures Against DDoS Attacks

- **Traffic Filtering** Intrusion Prevention Systems and firewalls play an important role in identifying and blocking the harmful traffic from entering the system. These systems are programmed to detect suspicious patterns. Moreover, the number of requests that a particular device can generate should be limited (Kallepalli et al., 2021).
- **DDoS Protection Services** There are online security services, such as Cloudflare and Akamai, that can help protect websites and resources from suspicious activity, such as DDoS attacks (Vakali et al., 2003).
- **Network Redundancy** We should use load balancers to distribute incoming traffic across multiple servers to avoid congestion on one server. Geographically distributed data centers should also be used to absorb and mitigate attacks (Bourke, 2001).
- **Monitoring and Detection** Traffic analysis tools help to monitor and examine traffic patterns in real time, enabling the detection of unusual or unexpected spikes. This helps the organizations to respond quickly to potential issues (So-In et al., 2009).
- **Best Practices in Configuration** Some precautions on the user side are needed, such as disabling unnecessary services and ports. It is important to go through DNS security features (Hayes et al., 2021).
- **Engagement with ISPs** Proper collaboration with the Internet Service Provider is essential for traffic filtering and monitoring (Harris et al., 1996).

Measures for both Flash Events as well as DDoS attacks have been discussed above. Now, researchers can use this to develop algorithms that can help to mitigate these serious concerns in the field of cybersecurity. Now they know that if genuine heavy traffic is present, it should be handled differently from a DDoS attack to improve the user experience. Knowing this, researchers and network teams take the right action at the right time. Applying the correct measures keeps the network stable and prevents service interruptions during heavy traffic.

5 MAJOR OBSTACLES WHILE PROTECTING AGAINST DDOS ATTACKS AND FES

There are several obstacles to protect a system from such deadly incidents. These are as follows:

- Accurate detection of suspicious traffic.
- Discrimination of DDoS attacks from FEs.
- Separation of legitimate traffic from attack traffic with high accuracy.
- Reaction against this DDoS attack with minimum collateral damage.
- Deployment of the defense system.

The obstacles mentioned above show how challenging it is to save a network during both DDoS attacks and Flash Events. Each of them shows how difficult it is to detect and mitigate them accurately with less collateral damage. If these are not handled properly, the network might miss a real attack or sometimes block a genuine user. Therefore, understanding of these obstacles is important for building a strong defense system that can protect the system without stopping normal traffic.

SUMMARY

This chapter goes over the sudden rush created on a network by Flash Events and DDoS attacks, alongside highlighting the importance of understanding the difference between them. The classifications of both these heavy-load events explain their behaviour as well as the effect they have on a system. The segregation of genuine users from malicious traffic is outlined by the key indicators of the rationale section. In order to handle Flash Events and DDoS attacks, various measures have been highlighted, all the while bringing to light how they have different mitigation approaches. The significant obstacles faced in detection and protection are showcased by the chapter, while also outlining the essentiality of accurate identification and careful responses to avoid service disruptions. In a nutshell, researchers and network engineers are aided by the understanding of these aspects in order to build stronger and more reliable defense mechanisms.

REFERENCES

Alharthi, S., Alshamsi, A., Alseiari, A., & Alwarafy, A. (2024). Auto-scaling techniques in cloud computing: Issues and research directions. *Sensors (Basel)*, *24*(17), 5551. DOI: 10.3390/s24175551 PMID: 39275461

Behal, S., & Kumar, K. (2017). Detection of DDoS attacks and flash events using novel information theory metrics. *Computer Networks*, *116*, 96–110. DOI: 10.1016/j.comnet.2017.02.015

Behal, S., Kumar, K., & Sachdeva, M. (2018). D-FACE: An anomaly-based distributed approach for early detection of DDoS attacks and flash events. *Journal of Network and Computer Applications*, *111*, 49–63. DOI: 10.1016/j.jnca.2018.03.024

Bhandari, A., Kumar, K., Sangal, A. L., & Behal, S. (2021). An anomaly-based distributed detection system for DDoS attacks in Tier-2 ISP networks. *Journal of Ambient Intelligence and Humanized Computing*, *12*(1), 1387–1406. DOI: 10.1007/s12652-020-02208-3

Bourke, T. (2001). *Server load balancing*. O'Reilly Media, Inc.

Cappers, B. C., & van Wijk, J. J. (2016, October). Understanding the context of network traffic alerts. In *2016 IEEE Symposium on Visualization for Cyber Security (VizSec)* (pp. 1-8). IEEE. DOI: 10.1109/VIZSEC.2016.7739579

Chawla, S., Sachdeva, M., & Behal, S. (2016). Discrimination of DDoS attacks and flash events using Pearson's product-moment correlation method. *International Journal of Computer Science and Information Security*, *14*(10), 382.

Gera, J., & Battula, B. P. (2018). Detection of spoofed and non-spoofed DDoS attacks and discriminating them from flash crowds. *EURASIP Journal on Information Security*, *2018*(1), 9. DOI: 10.1186/s13635-018-0079-6

Gupta, S., & Grover, D. (2021, March). A comprehensive review of the detection of DDoS attacks using ML in the SDN environment. In *2021 International Conference on Artificial Intelligence and Smart Systems (ICAIS)* (pp. 1158–1163). IEEE. DOI: 10.1109/ICAIS50930.2021.9395987

Gupta, S., Grover, D., AlZubi, A. A., Sachdeva, N., Baig, M. W., & Singla, J. (2022). Machine Learning with Dimensionality Reduction for DDoS Attack Detection. *Computers, Materials & Continua*, *72*(2), 2665–2682. DOI: 10.32604/cmc.2022.025048

Gupta, S., Grover, D., & Bhandari, A. (2018). Vulnerability Analysis of Existing Distributed Denial of Service (DDoS) Defense Frameworks. *Asian Journal of Computer Science and Technology*, *7*(3), 62–67. DOI: 10.51983/ajcst-2018.7.3.1895

Gupta, S., Grover, D., & Singla, J. (2021, March). Characterization of Flash Events and DDoS Attacks: A Survey. In *2021 7th International Conference on Advanced Computing and Communication Systems (ICACCS)* (Vol. 1, pp. 1442–1447). IEEE. DOI: 10.1109/ICACCS51430.2021.9441793

Harris, S. J. (1996, April). Proactive service management: leveraging telecom information assets for competitive advantage. In *Proceedings of NOMS'96-IEEE Network Operations and Management Symposium* (Vol. 3, pp. 700-710). IEEE. DOI: 10.1109/NOMS.1996.539529

Hayes, W., & Langston, M. (2021). DNS. *Best Practice.*

Kallepalli, K., & Chaudhry, U. B. (2021). Intelligent security: Applying artificial intelligence to detect advanced cyber-attacks. In *Challenges in the IoT and Smart Environments: A Practitioners' Guide to Security, Ethics and Criminal Threats* (pp. 287–320). Springer International Publishing. DOI: 10.1007/978-3-030-87166-6_11

Lykouris, T., & Vassilvitskii, S. (2021). Competitive caching with machine learned advice. [JACM]. *Journal of the Association for Computing Machinery*, *68*(4), 1–25. DOI: 10.1145/3447579

Peng, G. (2004). CDN: Content distribution network. *arXiv preprint cs/0411069.*

Rout, S. K., Ravindra, J. V. R., Meda, A., Mohanty, S. N., & Kavididevi, V. (2023). A Dynamic Scalable Auto-Scaling Model as a Load Balancer in the Cloud Computing Environment. *EAI Endorsed Transactions on Scalable Information Systems, 10*(5).

Sachdeva, M., Singh, G., & Kumar, K. (2011, September). An emulation-based impact analysis of DDoS attacks on web services during flash events. In *2011 2nd International Conference on Computer and Communication Technology (ICCCT-2011)* (pp. 479–484). IEEE. DOI: 10.1109/ICCCT.2011.6075134

Serbout, S., El Malki, A., Pautasso, C., & Zdun, U. (2023, July). API Rate Limit Adoption—A pattern collection. In *Proceedings of the 28th European Conference on Pattern Languages of Programs* (pp. 1–20).

So-In, C. (2009). *A survey of network traffic monitoring and analysis tools. Cse 576m computer system analysis project.* Washington University in St. Louis.

Vakali, A., & Pallis, G. (2003). Content delivery networks: Status and trends. *IEEE Internet Computing*, *7*(6), 68–74. DOI: 10.1109/MIC.2003.1250586

Von Eicken, T., & Vogels, W. (2002). Evolution of the virtual interface architecture. *Computer, 31*(11), 61–68. DOI: 10.1109/2.730738

Ware, B., & Mercy, R. (2025). *Cloud Computing 2025 and Beyond: Trends*. Obstacles, and New Possibilities.

Yusuff, M. Improving Scalability and Performance of AI Systems in High-Traffic Environments. Conţu, C. A., Popovici, E. C., Fratu, O., & Berceanu, M. G. (2016, June). Security issues in most popular content management systems. In *2016 International Conference on Communications (COMM)* (pp. 277-280). IEEE. Hardré, P. L. (2016). When, how, and why do we trust technology too much? In *Emotions, technology, and behaviors* (pp. 85-106). Academic Press.

Zekri, M., El Kafhali, S., Aboutabit, N., & Saadi, Y. (2017, October). DDoS attack detection using machine learning techniques in cloud computing environments. In *2017, the 3rd International Conference of Cloud Computing Technologies and Applications (CloudTech)* (pp. 1-7). IEEE. DOI: 10.1109/CloudTech.2017.8284731

Chapter 6
Hybrid Quantum–Classical Computing for Future Network Optimization in Smart City

C. Balakumar
http://orcid.org/0009-0002-4655-2786
Karpagam Academy of Higher Education, India

S. Rameela
Karpagm Academy of Higher Education, India

ABSTRACT

In light of the good outcomes of IoT architecture in all researched fields, we offer an intelligent, smart, and energy-efficient street road lighting system built on an IoT framework. It is made up of an LED light controller and a smart electric pole with an Internet of Things sensor base. We also achieve considerable energy savings by replacing conventional metal halide lamps with LED bulbs that have a mesophic design based on human eye sensitivity and complex decision-making modules employ PWM dimming systems to calculate intensity levels that produce pulses of varying widths based on information from sensor units that evaluate traffic movement and passenger presence or absence. Through DALI controllers housed within LED light controllers, these pulses subsequently activate LED power switches. To make effective use of sustainable energy resources, we use sustainable power systems, which are composed of PV solar panel units, battery storage systems, and smart electric power grids.

DOI: 10.4018/979-8-3373-3857-6.ch006

INTRODUCTION

Networks of communication have grown significantly in size and significance in recent years, and they are now essential to the operation of modern society. The next generation of networks will need to be highly data-processing capable, have a lot of bandwidth, be resilient, flexible, scalable, and reliable in order to provide these application services. It is the responsibility in spite of few facilities and high demand for services.

Overcome obstacles including shortages of resources, channel difficulties, and user disagreements to raise the quality of your services. Network optimization concerns of large size, which are NP- difficult mixed-integer processing problems, are frequently employed. Even though a lot of scholars have been working on these problems, their complicated structure and abundance of integer variables make it impossible to solve them quickly on conventional computers. Thankfully, there is an acceptable replacement for these highly computational activities in the form of novel quantum technology approaches.

1.1 Quantum Approximate Optimisation Algorithm

The idea of creating computer systems that to mimic the workings of quantum physics was initially put up by Bonior and Feynman. The scientists go on to demonstrate that quantum computer systems are almost as powerful as traditional computers. Recently, variation techniques such as variation classical issues. Specifically, conventional quadratic unregulated binary optimisation (QUBO) problems such as the max-cut issue, which are challenging to answer on conventional machines, may be handled by both QAOA and quantum thermal annealing techniques.

The lack of availability and expensive expense of quantum computing have limited the uses of quantum algorithms, despite several examples showing their advantages. A significant barrier to quantum electronics remains to be the availability of quantum bits in particular. Clouds for regular and quantum computing can coexist because to this technique. Benders' decomposition strategy is one of the deconstruction strategies. The goal of the investigation is to combine network optimization with quantum computing.

Figure 1. Framework for hybrid quantum-classical computing

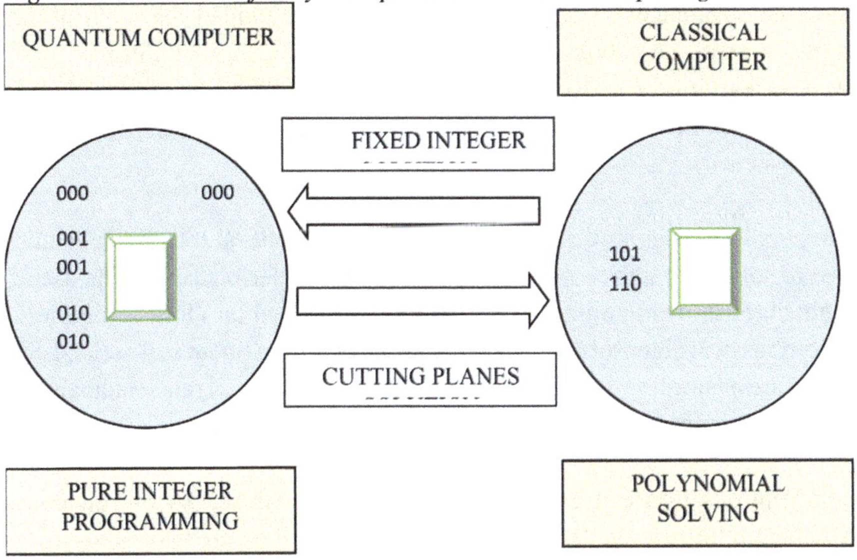

As seen in Figure. 1, we provide a general decomposition structure to accommodate large-scale integer-variable optimization problems. With this approach, One of the subdivisions is a quadratic/linear equation using just integers. Quantum computers are used to solve computational programs. The other sub problem involves polynomials, which can be addressed on a regular computer, much as linear programming issues. Solving programming component can be accomplished by applying procedures that take advantage of quantum thermodynamic techniques for computing.

According to many studies, the use of the quantum adiabatic technique performs four times better in search tasks than the classical strategy. For NP-complete integer programming problems, the classical branch-bound solution has an exponential complexity, whereas the challenges of quantum adiabatic techniques are not evident. It is important to note that the constraints and goal functionality in this pure integer sub problem might be either linear or quadratic. We must first change is to structure in order to use the aforementioned techniques.

1.2 Quantum Computing

Due to its potential and efficiency in resolving hitherto unsolvable problems, quantum computer science (QC) has become a rapidly developing field of study. Digital quantum computing are subfields of quantum computing technology. In gate-based quantum computing, preliminary processing, state getting ready, unitary modification, measurements, and post-processing are all essential stages. Quantum dynamics is used in analog quantum technology to complete computational tasks. The remarkable advantages of quantum technology have piqued the interest and capital of businesses and scholars in a variety of disciplines, including finance, chemistry, deep learning, cryptography, and machine intelligence. In addition, quantum computing has drawn interest and has been explored theoretically in relation to electrical systems.

i. Researchers looked at how quantum computing concepts and techniques may be used to solve problems and enhance power system performance. The use of quantum algorithms in power system research is divided into four categories:
ii. Variation classical eigensolver (VQE), variation quantum linear solver (VQLS), and HHL are examples of quantum linear algebra methods. Transient analysis, state estimation purposes, and power flow calculation are a few of the study areas.
iii. Quantum optimisation techniques such as quantum annealing (QA) and quantum approximate optimisation algorithm (QAOA), as well as areas of study such power system optimization planning and unit dedication
iv. Quantum machine learning (QML): QML work focuses on prediction and classification issues, such identifying and diagnosing faults and assessing the reliability of power systems. Model development and high-dimensional data processing are two areas where QML techniques have great promise.
v. Quantum parameter estimation: Compared to normal Monte Carlo simulation (MCS), the convergence rate of atomic amplitude estimation (QAE) is quicker. The application of the QAE technique and its advantages in assessing power system reliability.

Large-scale problems can only be solved by quantum algorithms using deep quantum circuits and enormous quantum bits, or qubits. The hybrid quantum-classical (HQC) algorithm is a more feasible choice given the constrained amount of qubits and short coherence time of current quantum hardware. A hybrid quantum-classical computing paradigm is presented in the reference to tackle future network resource optimization issues. Although the HQC optimisation algorithm is unlikely to achieve exponential speedup over classical algorithms in the noisy intermediate-scale quantum (NISQ) era, it does present a novel way to improve existing algorithms and skillfully combines the resource-saving benefits of both quantum and classical computing in a few practical applications.

The initial optimization problem in HQC algorithms is often divided into smaller issues using a variety of coordination and decomposition approaches. In addition to subproblems that can be effectively handled by classical computers, quantum processing units (QPU) can be assigned issues or subproblems that can be transformed into quadratic unconstrained binary optimization (QUBO) form. The multi-block alternating direction method of multipliers (ADMM) heuristics serve as the foundation for a mixed-binary optimization strategy that can handle QUBO problems utilizing VQE and QAOA. In order to improve upon current deterministic optimisation techniques, we provide an HQC-based solution to the job-shop scheduling problem that leverages QA. HQC heuristics are applied to the QUBO transaction settlement problem using this n-qubit Ising Hamiltonian as reference.

By suggesting the use of quantum computers as a scientific tool for a better understanding of quantum processes, the early recommendations on quantum computing have later propelled research into astounding advances such as superconducting quits, ion trap quits, or spin qubits. At the moment, quantum-state entanglement is regarded as the essential foundation of the vast majority of quantum technologies, which are classified into three broad categories: quantum communication, quantum sensing, and quantum computation.

1.3 Deep Learning

Through the creation of novel network architectures, the addition of regular constraints, the integration of learning, and the improvement of optimization techniques, researchers apply deep learning insights to improve GAN. The better methodologies outlined above, however, are not based on people because the GAN algorithm learns rules indirectly. Changing a trained generator's structure or input makes it more difficult to create data that fits specified requirements. Conditional generative adversarial network (CGAN) has been proposed; GAN may sample from the conditional distribution and generate data driven by conditional inputs, hence increasing the application possibilities of the GAN method.

QGAN is a technique to that combines GAN and quantum computing. The idea of QGAN was introduced, which theoretically studied the performance of three distinct QGAN frameworks and as well as the parameter gradient estimation approach used for training the network.

The researchers carried out tests to demonstrate the viability of optimising of quantum generator building. The convergence and resilience to noise of these approaches are all demonstrated utilising quantum hardware while producing PQCs as the generator and discriminator of QGAN .

LITERATURE SURVEY

Moreover, integrating various Internet of Things (IoT) nodes and devices, developing shared trust models to enable even the most basic devices, and enhancing interoperability are just a few of the numerous difficulties smart utility systems confront. If a common peer-to-peer (P2P) architecture for processing data from many devices was implemented, the costs associated with administering and sustaining digital environments would undoubtedly decrease.

2.1 Internet of Things

The Internet of Things, big data analytics, cloud computing, social media, and smart metres have all made significant contributions to smart utility innovation and deployment. The Internet of Things (IoT) is rapidly becoming an important part of communication technology. Smart nodes, which are made up of IoT devices, sensors, services, and applications, are becoming more capable of interacting and communicating in real time, making them an important component of Industry 4.0 says Ramouthar et al (2023). Smart utility ecosystems based on IoT involve new players whose primary identity is digital; as a result, stakeholders face a variety of difficulties relating to data, infrastructure, and service security. As a result, smart utilities have serious challenges about security, secrecy, and authentication .

Fu et al (2023) explains thatBlockchain is a peer-to-peer system that securely conducts and records transactions, asset registries, and enables transnational transdisciplinary spread trust through peer-to-peer contacts. Blockchain technology is likely to play an important role in providing effective security solutions for existing IoT security infrastructure Blockchain is an intriguing technology that has the potential to lessen the risk of cyber-attacks that might result in network failure. As a result, blockchain security and privacy concerns are critical from a cybersecurity standpoint.

2.2 Blockchain Systems

Based on their computing environments, blockchain systems are divided into two groups: quantum blockchain and conventional blockchain, or blockchain. For instance, Ullah, In order to achieve vehicular network security, vehicular forensics, and vehicle trust management, Md. Habib et al. (2022) introduced a novel blockchain-based architecture for safeguarding smart automobiles. A novel privacy-preserving architecture based on blockchain technology for Internet of Things information management systems was presented by Ramouthar (2023) and does not require the engagement of an impartial third. In order to enable a variety of applications over limited in resources edges, Rojo, Javier, et al. (2021) developed an innovative framework for big data sharing based on blockchain technology's features.

For industrial Internet of things applications with power restrictions, Abd El-Latif et al. (2021) created the "LightChain" blockchain technology. Furthermore, to allow blockchain technology in heterogeneous IoT devices, Ramouthar et al. (2023) suggested a blockchain approach based on appropriate algorithms and a space-structured ledger. In order to protect data, identity, use, and terminal position, Liu et al. (2021) proposed a privacy-aware fog-enhanced blockchain-assisted task scheduling that enables fog components to perform cloud activities at the network's edge. A method for assessing was developed by Liu, Wenjie, and associates in 2021. A blockchain-powered public auditing solution for massive data sets stored in cloud storage was created in 2021 by Liu, Wenjie, and associates. Salek et al (2023) also presented a distributed management system for authorization and identification rules that uses blockchain technology to keep a global view of the system's security regulations. Biswas et al. (2022) proposed a healthcare system that takes advantage of blockchain benefits to confirm the source of mHealth data. To address security vulnerabilities in smart contracts, Sushmit & Mahbubul (2023) proposed a transaction-based detection and classification approach for Ethereum smart contracts.

Liu et al. (2021) suggested a blockchain-based data storage system as a solution to the latency and volume issues. A LoRa-based dual-chained information system that leverages blockchain's tamper-resistance to provide global cross-validated security. In addition, the system's identification rules utilize blockchain technology to run a worldwide picture of its security principles. a medical facility that verifies the source of mHealth data using the network's benefits.

To address security problems, Hong et al. (2023) proposed a transaction-based detection and classification technique for Ethereum smart contracts, together with a blockchain-based data storage solution. They also offered a solution to the latency and loudness issues. A dual-chained LoRa-based information system with global cross-validated security based on blockchain tamper resistance was proven by Hong et al. in 2023. Quantum technologies might therefore pose a danger to blockchain technology. Making new blockchain components based on quantum technologies is an intriguing approach to enhance the system as it is today. Creating new blockchain frameworks based on quantum models that are resistant to assaults by quantum computers is the primary contribution of current efforts. To fend against assaults by quantum computers, Sun, Sopek, Wang, and Kulicki's (2019) "Logicontract" quantum blockchain architecture, for example, uses a digital signature technique based on quantum key distribution. The World Health Organization projects that, given that the illness affects around 24 million people worldwide and is predicted to rise every 20 years, there will be a substantial health burden from Alzheimer's disease in the years to come. Advances in DCC have already had a big impact on computer vision, especially in the realm of medical imaging. Recurrence and feedforward learning networks solved the problem of out-of-set generalization in vision for computers.

DNNs may be used to learn classification decision boundaries and find hidden patterns in data, which can save processing time and make them a competitive alternative to medical imaging modalities, according to Sood (2023).Given recent discoveries, such as those presented in for noisy intermediate-scale quantum technology, The first commercially viable and socially significant application is far more likely to be a hybrid system that combines a quantum accelerator with a conventional computer. The underlying principle is that any end-application comprises several computational kernels, each with characteristics best achieved by a particular accelerator. Examples of these accelerators include field-programmable gate arrays, graphics processing units, neural processing units (like Google's tensor processing unit), and so forth. According to Amdahl, an accelerator is a coprocessor that is connected to the main processor and has the ability to speed up overall performance by accelerating the execution of certain computationally demanding kernels. Computer architectures have advanced significantly during the last few decades. The distinction between compute logic and memory was imperceptible to the first computers. Only because of von Neumann's idea to properly separate and develop them did the famous von Neumann architecture come to be. This architecture was driven ahead by the chip's continuously increasing number of transistors, which doubled every 18 months, for a considerable amount of time. It was based on a single CPU. Around the turn of the century, single cores were quite complex and provided little discernible processing improvement.

Amos et al. (2020) explained that as a consequence, a number of cores were added. For a few years, the homogeneous multicore CPU dominated chip research, but businesses Businesses such as IBM and Intel came to recognize that heterogeneity is the most effective technique to boost computing power. Given that FPGAs and GPUs are considered to be natural extensions of computer design, a quantum accelerator would seem to be the next advancement in computer architecture.The bottom layer displays the many quantum technologies available. Second, in order for companies and other organizations to employ high-performance accelerators for specific calculations that are exclusive to the quantum device, high-level quantum logic has to be created. Companies that wish to take advantage of this path must make sustained investments in technical know-how and human resources. demonstrates the industry's commitment to including the necessary quantum logic, which can be generated utilizing the entire stack and verified and validated on a quantum simulator.

For FPGAs, these algorithms are translated into Verilog or VHDL. Often, while building a language for GPUs, one uses libraries or arithmetic and the compiler transforms it into an assembly language that can be mapped onto the GPU architecture. For FPGAs, there is no standard microarchitecture on which to run Verilog or VHDL. An architecture specific to each application that has to be accelerated is needed. The last layer is an implementation of the microarchitecture based on chips that has all the required hardware accelerate blocks. The understanding that Vaidyan et al. (2023) have of quantum computer design is discussed.

They properly emphasised the importance of studying computer engineering in order to better comprehend the similarities and differences between quantum and regular computing. As previously stated, the most basic distinction between qubits and quantum gates and CMOS technology is their significantly greater error rate. Make certain that fault-tolerant computing consumes more than 90% of total computational activity. The nearest-neighbor (NN) constraint states that two-qubit gates may be used only if the qubits are physically close to one another. The copying of quantum states is forbidden by the no-cloning theorem. The use of two-qubit gates necessitates that the two qubits be near enough to one another.

They also provide a hierarchical tiered structure, but the schema is explained in terms of various, pertinent fields and study disciplines rather than discussing those levels in terms of more computer engineering concepts. Examples include computer languages, quantum error correction (QEC) theory, and FT implementation. It will take further solutions with unknown temporal costs to construct (ideally) effective and performant FT-quantum processing. State evaporation for ancilla factories is one instance that as is the accumulation of numerous errors and flaws, which put additional stress on the microarchitecture and associated run-time supervision.

According to Syed & Garcia (2023), two more prerequisites for quantum communication to occur are the ability to transport flying qubits between specified locations and interconvert stationary and flying qubits. We can argue that given the current status of quantum processors, DiVincenzo's requirements are already met, leading to the creation of a computer with quantum technology. The number of qubits required for each feasible the application, however, remains an important unmet need. Estimates of the quantity of qubits vary from a few hundreds to several billions, contingent upon the application industry. Less importantly, the first condition states the system's size clearly, which is still a big problem when calculating accurately.

Two other requirements for quantum communication, according to Syed & Garcia (2023), are the capacity to interconvert stationary and flying qubits as well as move floating qubits between predetermined places. We can claim that DiVincenzo's prerequisites are already satisfied, resulting in the development of a computer using quantum technology, considering the state of quantum processors at the moment. However, there is still a significant unmet requirement about the quantity of qubits needed for any viable application. Quantity estimates range from a few hundred to several billions, depending on the application sector. Less significantly, the primary condition explicitly mentions the extent of the system, which is still a major issue when doing correct calculations.

In the perspective of general social science, Ghimire (2021) provides a semi-systematic evaluation of eighty publications on quantum technologies. When choosing and incorporating papers in the review, we give priority to scholarly contributions that are connected to cities. After determining which QTs are most significant for cities, we use semantic analysis of 567 abstracts of papers on smart city technology to establish a taxonomy that encompasses conventional smart city solutions. The prior stage establishes the frequency of selected terms representing various typical smart city solutions, which are then used to explore the semantic relationships between eighty publications on quantum computers.

Principal component analysis, agglomerative hierarchical clustering, and partial least squares route modeling were the methods employed by Sierra-Sosa et al. (2020) to look into the semantic connections among the eighty articles. Semantic link inquiries, while completely exploratory, might identify current and potential future research areas related to the study problem. Lastly, we carry out a qualitative topic analysis of possible applications of quantum technology inside the chosen categories of conventional smart city proposals in order to accomplish a methodological triangulation of quantitative data. Prior to exploring how the two kinds of quantum technologies may benefit a smart city, we tried to characterize the latter in an easier theoretical way. Creating a thorough taxonomy is one way to more practically describe smart city technological advancements.

We developed a taxonomy of smart city solutions based on automatic classification in place of the existing system.Blockchain ledgers and conventional payment systems may work together in the future thanks to a protocol being developed for interacting with various blockchain systems. Cross-chain transactions in this type of protocol are sent via the inter-ledger through a connector. There are two kinds of cross-chain transaction execution and trusteeship. By making donations of money, participants in one alternative ensure security for payments. In the second alternative, people follow instructions in order to make money.

SYSTEM DESIGN

The premise that different objects connected to one another wirelessly or by wires can communicate with one another over the internet is the basis of this technology. Items connected to the Internet of Things converse and share information with one another. An item's CPU, analog-to-digital converter, and wireless module are its three main components. It appears to be a worldwide network architecture of some sort. It is made up of several interconnected information-processing devices that perceive, process, and transfer data to other devices via networks. The primary technology utilized in the Internet of Things is RFID. Data is transferred via wireless transmission and a microprocessor. Wireless sensor networks are the second significant IoT technology (WSNs). WSNs get information from devices located across several locations. The Internet of Things has profited from notable advancements in RFID and wireless sensor networks.

3.1 Environmental Monitoring Services

The CoT is capable of implementing and offering a broad range of environmental monitoring services, such as noise, river, air quality, and marine monitoring. Wireless Sensor Networks (WSN) are able to assess environmental conditions and relay that information to various cloud services that collect and handle this kind of data. When cloud computing is integrated with warning systems, the latter can detect unsuitable environmental conditions by comparing present levels to permitted limits. Fog computing can prolong the lifetime and lower the energy consumption of the deployed WSN in addition to minimizing communication traffic between the cloud and the deployed WSN. Furthermore, fog computing may assist in localizing various decision-making processes to provide controls instantly and quicken response times.

3.2 Security Services

Numerous security services for smart cities might be offered by the CoT. Providing crowd control services for sizable special events, such parades, outdoor concerts, and important sporting events, is one example. Law enforcement must be able to predict and monitor crowd movements during such events in order to quickly determine the best course of action for security measures, such as increasing police presence in specific areas, closing certain roads to facilitate pedestrian flow, and creating extra parking lots. Street cameras, traffic sensors, Smartphone location monitoring, and vehicle tracking can all be used for crowd surveillance. These technologies make it possible to track and find out information about the crowd's position, focus, and movement. This data can be gathered and assessed by a range of cloud services to give a comprehensive picture of the present state of affairs, potential hazards, and feasible solutions. In general, the following steps are typically included in the best practice:

i) i) Historical data is often used to forecast energy costs, the heat load, and the power load;
ii) ii) Energy output projections are generated from many generators, with renewable energy posing the biggest uncertainty;
iii) Make a model for every cost function related to energy generation.
iv) Model the equality and inequality conditions for the optimization as well as the objective function of the operation;
v) Select the optimal optimization method to solve the model.

However, since an exact estimate of the renewable generation is needed, standard deterministic algorithms are unable to produce an ideal solution. Chance-constrained programming gives an explicit description of the uncertain variable distributions and permits system optimization. Assuming a random distribution of the uncertainty variable values, the CCP needs to be addressed by system optimization that satisfies both chance and safety requirements. This is achieved by assigning a probability level to the chance restrictions.

3.3 Mathematical Modeling and Evaluation

Using motion detection sensors connected to smart city-based equipment, the proposed approach optimizes energy efficiency. In this case, the objective function to reduce energy consumption will be energy optimization. If Equation (1) is correct, Cluster 1, which is the first in the city to have all of the SL operating and is known as Si, will be in an optimal state. This assumes that the devices in a smart city are organized into four clusters: C1, C2, C3, and C4.

$$C_1 = \sum_{i=1}^{n} t_i = \begin{cases} 1, \forall_i \; if\, all\; t_i\; are\; working \\ 0,\; else \end{cases} \quad (1)$$

Cluster two will resemble C2, the second cluster, if Equation (2) is accurate. In C2, all billboards are located on the smart city road and on the buildings that are marked as Bi and bj, respectively.

$$c_2 = \sum_{i=1}^{n} \sum_{j=1}^{n} B_i b_j = \begin{cases} 1, \forall_{i,j} \; if\, all\; B_i and\; b_j\; are\; working \\ 0, else \end{cases} \quad (2)$$

All of the Pi-designated smart parking equipment are found in C3, or the third cluster of smart cities. Assuming the validity of Equation (3), Cluster Three will be in an optimal state.

$$C_3 = \sum_{i=1}^{n} p_i = \begin{cases} 1, \forall_i \; if\, all\; p_i\; are\; working \\ 0,\; else \end{cases} \quad (3)$$

A smart house, which has several smart home devices known as ℏ1, ℏ2, ℏ3...n = 1, n = 2, n = 3, is one of the most crucial parts of a smart city. Our fourth cluster, C4, has a smart home with all of the appliances working. In the event that Equation (4) is accurate, Cluster 4 will be flawless is satisfied.

$$C_4 = \sum_{i=1}^{n} F_i = \begin{cases} 1, \forall_i \; if\, all\; F_i\; are\; working \\ 0,\; else \end{cases} \quad (4)$$

We will calculate the entropy of each cluster (E(Ci)), assuming that the appliance data in each of the four clusters (C1, C2, C3, and C4) is significant.

Node performance is also thought to be impacted by the reported events' (gi) priority. Under this technique, reporting on more important environmental issues is encouraged. Consequently, performance benefits more from the submission of events with a higher priority (performance increases linearly with the reported events' priorities). In a similar spirit, node performance is also impacted by the total amount of data delivered, expressed in bytes. Events impacting performance more strongly .

Lastly, due to the possibility of packets being sent in various configurations. The transmission reliability of the packets is determined by the particular selection of BW/CR/SF/TXP. In particular, The packet reception probability (PRR), which may be thought of as the likelihood that a packet will be received successfully, is used to weight the node performance in order to calculate the expected quantity of information that will be received successfully. From an implementation perspective, nodes can add this information to any downlink packet (like the one they send when they initially connect to the LoRaWAN network) to learn the SNR that the gateway detects. Eventually, the node performance is modeled by Eq. 2.

$$\gamma = \frac{\sum_{i=1}^{2} \rho_i^{eff} . L_i . g_i . PRR(BW, CR_i, SF_i, TXp_i}{T}$$

Furthermore, rather than relying just on λi, the effective event-generation probability is taken into account. This term takes into account the likelihood that type I events will transpire when the node is in the transmittable state. The two requirements stated in Section 4 must be fulfilled in order for an occurrence of type I to be recorded:

a. A type I event is found with probability λi.
b. The likelihood that the node will become a transmittable signal is denoted by P, the event cannot be recorded because there is not enough TDC available.

"Performance" number takes into consideration priority and the chance that the reported data will be received correctly. A node's performance is given that it generates events each of which has a discrete of happening . The total value for both types of events is what represents the node's performance. It is important to note that since λ denotes the likelihood that an event will be generated in a sensing cycle.

RESULT AND DISCUSSION

The suggested remedy is contrasted with the established, understandable rules that result from the suggested SA algorithm. In this case, consideration will be given to the following possible transmission regulations:

- Selecting parameters at random. From the list of all plausible choices, C will be chosen at random. $\omega<\omega max$ is the only requirement that must be met.
- Selecting reasonable bounds. Large PRR values are prioritized under this policy. C will be chosen with the criteria. The combination with the greatest PRR will be selected if more than one combination satisfies the qualifying requirements.
- Adaptive data rate (ADR) for LoRaWAN. To optimize packet throughput, energy consumption, and packet to area ratio (ToA), technique utilized in LoRa networks, we will consider The Things Network's, which is the largest public LoRaWAN network, in this scenario. The ADR process, operating based on a given SNR history.

4.1 Genetic Algorithm

Utilizing GPS for Reservations and Navigation Among the population-based optimization methods is the genetic algorithm. It makes use of the essential ideas of natural selection. It can be applied to contained or uncontrolled issues. Three operators are used in the approach to modify the population iteratively: crossover, mutation, and selection. The genetic algorithm chooses parent chromosomes at each stage and uses genetic operators to produce the new individuals. The genetic algorithm's general steps.

Figure 2. The Steps of Genetic Algorithm

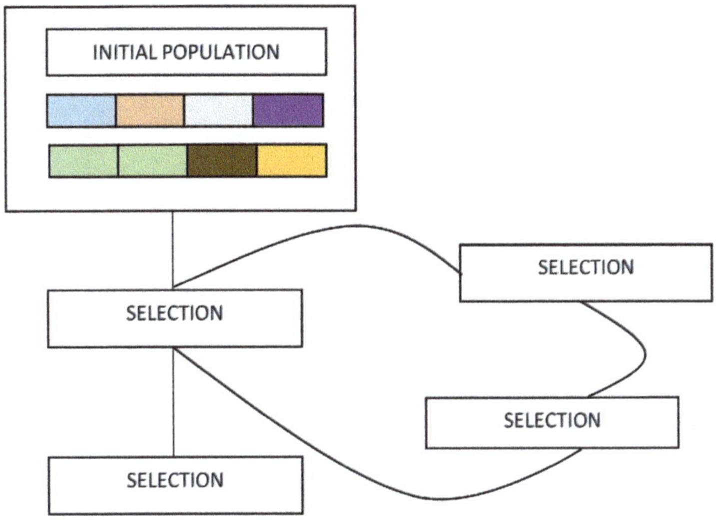

In this work, a genetic algorithm is used to find a path from our current location to the closest parking space. Several boulevards that lead to two streets in the center of Elazığ are marked as a result. There are free parking lots accessible with a minimum trip at these sites. The starting point is a fixed place that is always the position as determined by GPS. It's possible that you'll land in one of the available parking spaces. Two randomly chosen genes are changed to produce the mutation. The starting point is a fixed place that is always the position as determined by GPS. It's possible that you'll land in one of thc available parking spaces. Two randomly chosen genes are changed to produce the mutation.

Figure 3. Map Location

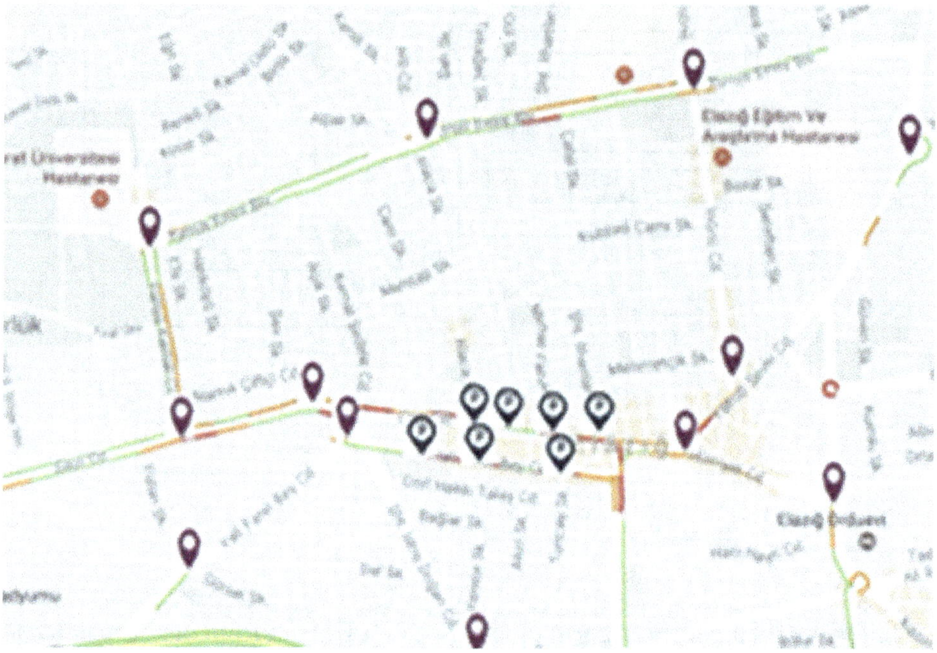

The starting point is a fixed place that is always the position as determined by GPS. It's possible that you'll land in one of the available parking spaces. Two randomly chosen genes are changed to produce the mutation. Two people in turn were subjected to a one point crossover operator. However, because of crossover, it can be passed twice from the same location. In this case, the minimum gene missing from the chromosome takes the place of the repeating gene.

Figure 4. GPS Navigation

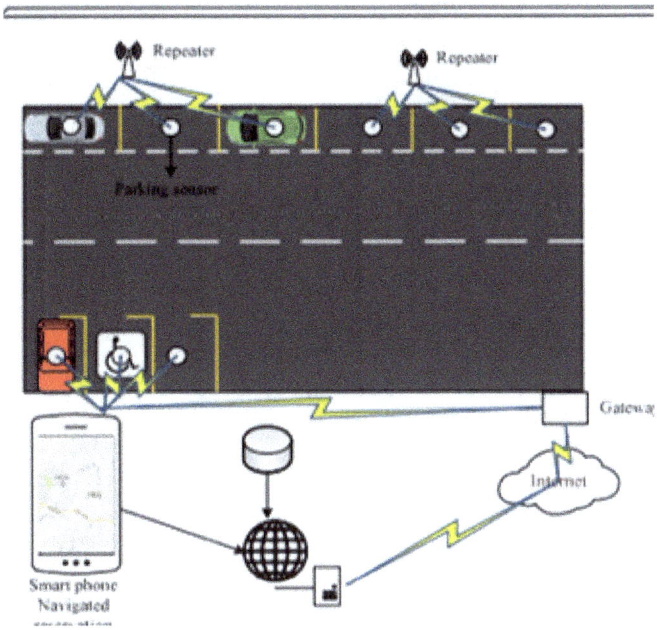

4.2 Smart Parking Module

Developing the hardware platform is the initial stage in the suggested smart parking system. Two streets located in the center of Elazig are considered in the implementation. Gazi and Vali Fahri Bey are these streets. Parking is permitted on the sides of these two streets for fifteen minutes. There is a gateway device assigned to each street. These gadgets gather information on parking lot conditions and transmit it to a web server. The parking sensor has an integrated 802.15.4 transmitter that communicates the parking state to the gateway. The GPRS module of the gateway node uses this information to send the obtained date to the internet server. It is possible to tell if a parking space is occupied or open by using a magnetic sensor.

CONCLUSION

This work presents an innovative, ideal guided reservation-based technique for finding an open parking spot in smart cities. The recommended method looks for the quickest route to the free Parkins spot. To do this, the task is presented as an optimization problem, and the closest accessible parking place is found using a genetic algorithm.The GPS on the driver's smartphone is used to determine their exact location, and a genetic algorithm finds the next open parking space. These concerns include the architectural layout of the CoT system, security, privacy, and appropriate optimization strategies tailored to the specifics of the smart city and the CoT system in use. Numerous apps have the potential to drastically cut resource usage and raise the standard of living for citizens in smart cities if the primary barriers to their use are eliminated.

REFERENCES

Abd El-Latif, A. A., Abd-El-Atty, B., Mehmood, I., Muhammad, K., Venegas-Andraca, S. E., & Peng, J. (2021). Quantum-inspired blockchain-based cybersecurity: Securing smart edge utilities in IoT-based smart cities. *Information Processing & Management, 58*(4), 102549. DOI: 10.1016/j.ipm.2021.102549

Amos, R., Georgiou, M., Kiayias, A., & Zhandry, M. (2020, June). One-shot signatures and applications to hybrid quantum/classical authentication. In *Proceedings of the 52nd Annual ACM SIGACT Symposium on Theory of Computing* (pp. 255-268). DOI: 10.1145/3357713.3384304

Biswas, C., Pal, J., & Majumder, S. (2022). An Overview of Quantum Computing Approach in the Present-Day Energy Systems. Advances in Smart Energy Systems, 39-54.

Ghimire, B., Mahmood, A., & Elleithy, K. (2021, November). Hybrid Quantum Approximate Optimization Using Enhanced Ant Colony Optimization to Solve Large-Scale Combinatorial Optimization Problems. In *2021 8th International Conference on Soft Computing & Machine Intelligence (ISCMI)* (pp. 108-113). IEEE. DOI: 10.1109/ISCMI53840.2021.9654824

Hong, Y. Y., Arce, C. J. E., & Huang, T. W. (2023). A Robust Hybrid Classical and Quantum Model for Short-Term Wind Speed Forecasting. IEEE Access.

Liu, W., Zhang, Y., Deng, Z., Zhao, J., & Tong, L. (2021). A hybrid quantum-classical conditional generative adversarial network algorithm for human-centered paradigm in cloud. *EURASIP Journal on Wireless Communications and Networking, 2021*(1), 1–17. DOI: 10.1186/s13638-021-01898-3

Ramouthar, R., & Seker, H. (2023). Hybrid Quantum-Classical Computing-A Fusion of Classical And Quantum Computational Substrates. *Energy, 284*, 129314. DOI: 10.1016/j.energy.2023.129314

Ramouthar, R., & Seker, H. (2023). A Review of Hybrid Quantum Computational Substrates-A Fusion of Classical And Quantum Computational Substrates. *ScienceOpen Preprints.*

Ramouthar, R., & Seker, H. (2023). Hybrid Quantum Algorithms and Quantum Software Development Frameworks. *ScienceOpen Preprints.*

Rojo, J., Valencia, D., Berrocal, J., Moguel, E., Garcia-Alonso, J., & Rodriguez, J. M. M. (2021). Trials and tribulations of developing hybrid quantum-classical microservices systems. *arXiv preprint arXiv:2105.04421.*

Sierra-Sosa, D., Telahun, M., & Elmaghraby, A. (2020). TensorFlow quantum: Impacts of quantum state preparation on quantum machine learning performance. *IEEE Access : Practical Innovations, Open Solutions*, *8*, 215246–215255. DOI: 10.1109/ACCESS.2020.3040798

Sood, S. K. (2023). Quantum Computing Review: A Decade of Research. *IEEE Transactions on Engineering Management.*

Sushmit, M. M., & Mahbubul, I. M. (2023). Forecasting solar irradiance with hybrid classical–quantum models: A comprehensive evaluation of deep learning and quantum-enhanced techniques. Energy Conversion and Management, 294, 117555.

Syed, M., & Garcia, P. (2023, October). A Hybrid Quantum-Classical Machine Learning Approach to Vision Sensor Data Analysis in Aerospace Applications. In *2023 IEEE/AIAA 42nd Digital Avionics Systems Conference (DASC)* (pp. 1-7). IEEE. DOI: 10.1109/DASC58513.2023.10311313

Ullah, M. H., Eskandarpour, R., Zheng, H., & Khodaei, A. (2022). Quantum computing for smart grid applications. *IET Generation, Transmission & Distribution*, *16*(21), 4239–4257. DOI: 10.1049/gtd2.12602

Vaidyan, V. M., & Rimal, B. P. (2023). Hybrid Quantum Artificial Intelligence Electromagnetic Spectrum Analysis Framework for Transportation System Security.

Chapter 7

Lightweight Quantum-Safe Security Protocols for Resource-Constrained IoT Devices: An AI-Driven Adaptive Framework

R. Vettriselvan
http://orcid.org/0009-0005-1097-0806
Academy of Maritime Education and Training (AMET), India

ABSTRACT

The proliferation of Internet of Things (IoT) devices has heightened concerns about data security, particularly in resource-constrained environments vulnerable to quantum-enabled attacks. This chapter proposes an AI-driven adaptive framework for lightweight, quantum-safe security protocols tailored to low-power IoT systems. By integrating post-quantum cryptography with artificial intelligence, the framework dynamically adjusts encryption strength, resource allocation, and threat response. The design emphasizes energy efficiency, scalability, and resilience against emerging quantum-era vulnerabilities. Through conceptual modeling, experimental validation, and case studies, the chapter demonstrates how adaptive, intelligent security mechanisms can ensure sustainable, secure IoT deployment in critical sectors such as healthcare, logistics, and smart infrastructure.

DOI: 10.4018/979-8-3373-3857-6.ch007

1.INTRODUCTION

The growth of the Internet of Things (IoT) in the last 20 years has radically transformed the paradigms of operation in healthcare, transport, logistics, energy management and smart-city infrastructure. The real time generation, processing, and exchange of sensitive data by billions of connected sensors and embedded devices now make it possible to make decisions much faster and deliver services more effectively. However, these benefits are also accompanied by unprecedented extent and heterogeneity which is a major security risk. In contrast to traditional computing platforms, most IoT nodes have tough performance limits in terms of processing power, memory and battery life; making it challenging to deploy traditional cryptographic systems which were not designed to run on such highly-constrained platforms. At the same time, the technology of quantum computing represents a direct risk to the cryptographic framework of the contemporary communication network. Algorithms, including those suggested by Shor and Grover, show that large quantum systems could break popular primitives in the public-key cryptography, including RSA, Elliptic Curve Cryptography (ECC), and Diffie-Hellman (DH) (Eren, Karaduman, and Genanco, 2025). The development of quantum-enabled adversaries poses a significant systemic risk in IoT ecosystems already challenged by the lightweight attacks because of the limited security capacity. An intrusion into IoT-based healthcare systems, smart transportation infrastructure, or automated industrial solutions would have consequences that are much more severe than a loss of data, and they can put the lives and financial sustainability of people at risk (Abbood et al., 2025). It is the combination of these converging pressures that have led to the necessity to have security mechanisms that are both lightweight and quantum-resilient. It is not enough to protect existing systems anymore, but mitigation efforts should be forward-looking in terms of the cryptographic environment of the quantum universe (Akinsanya, Bello, and Adeusi, 2023). Lightweight quantum-safe security protocols (LQSPs) are a conceptual answer to this dilemma, combining resource efficient cryptographic constructions with post-quantum based algorithms that can resist quantum-level attacks. The creation of protocols that stand to be effective in the wide field of IoT, is, however, especially tricky, since security demands differ depending on the abilities of a specific device, the conditions under which it is operated, and the risk profiles. An example medical sensor including wearables can have severe computational constraints but require a high level of confidentiality whereas a smart-traffic controller can benefit real-time urgency over strong encryption (Fazrina, 2024).

These conflicting needs require dynamic security solutions that can self-optimise dynamically. Therefore, the chapter suggests an AI-based dynamic framework where protocol parameters, including encryption strength, key length and the computational intensity, are dynamically adjusted based on the capabilities of the device, as well as the context of the threat. Artificial intelligence, especially machine learning and reinforcement learning architectures, will enable such changes and design the best trade-offs without the need to monitor them continuously by human agents (Elkhodr, 2025). The applicability of this study has a global perspective. IoT platforms are being actively deployed by many developing economies to deliver health care, monitor agriculture, and manage urban-services (Alhakami, 2024), but frequently they lack the financial resources to regularly upgrade their hardware or implement high-performance cryptography systems (Alharbi and Almazmomi, 2025). Adaptive, lightweight, quantum-safe solutions are the way ahead to the future because they propose a secure and sustainable path way forward by matching security to the resources reality of constrained environments. IoTs are also coming together with robotics, AI decision systems, and 5G/6G networks in more technologically developed economies, and this is creating a terrain where a quantum-era attack can spread rapidly through connected critical infrastructure (Bolgouras, Farao, and Xenakis, 2024). As a result, the creation of adaptive lightweight security is not only a technological requirement but also a strategic element of cyber resilience in the world. This chapter follows up this developing discipline by:

- Visualisation of the security liabilities of IoT systems in the two-fold environment of resource constraints and the new quantum threats.
- Suggestion of a conceptual architecture of lightweight quantum-safe security combining lightweight cryptography, post-quantum mechanisms and AI-based adaptivity.
- Conceptual model, experimental knowledge and domain specific scenarios of analysing protocol behaviours and performance trade-offs.
- Presenting the variants of the proposed framework such as LQSP-AI, LQSP-Chain, and LQSP-Edge and demonstrating how all three can be applied to healthcare, logistics, and smart-infrastructure systems.
- An opportunity to discuss the issues of implementation such as monetary issues, regulatory, and ethical concerns, focusing on resources-diverse setting.

The chapter lies at the crossroads between cryptography, computational intelligence, and sustainable systems design based on the principles of optimisation and the socio-technical frameworks. In practise, the discussion is based on real-life limitations by looking at representative case studies in the healthcare IoT, logistics tracking, and smart-infrastructure application. The rest of the paper elaborates the conceptual framework, theoretical background, methodology, analytical results, and conclusions in the context of resilient quantum-safe IoT security.

2. CONCEPTUAL FRAMEWORK

The theoretical framework of this chapter is a combination of three mutually reinforcing areas, including lightweight cryptography, post-quantum cryptography and AI-enabled adaptivity, which can be used to enforce secure, scalable and sustainable protection of resources-constrained IoT ecosystems (Ishtaiwi et al., 2024). Although the sizes and heterogeneity of IoT deployments are both on the rise, these have a range of devices, with simple sensing devices on one end, and complex embedded systems at the other end, both of which are limited in computing capabilities, memory, and battery size. These limitations make most traditional cryptographic designs infeasible; e.g., such algorithms as RSA or ECC take excessive computational time and energy consumption and cannot be deployed on systems that need to be power-efficient and energy-efficient (Jeyalakshmi, Balan, and Benitha, 2025). These limitations are further enhanced by the emergence of quantum computing. Quantum algorithms such as those by Shor and Grover demonstrate existential threat to common public-key primitives and is an indication that most commonly employed security protocols will become useless when quantum computers are fully operationalized (Cherukupalle & Cherukupalle, 2025). This, therefore, creates the need to develop a new breed of cryptographic architectures that can work effectively and provide long term security guarantees in the face of resource constraints and the emergence of quantum threats. The lower layer of the framework is lightweight cryptography. Its principles are based on compact implementations, less memory usage and low energy usage. Lightweight block, stream, and hash-based ciphers (PRESENT and LED, Trivium and Grain, and SPONGENT and PHOTON) make it clear that it is possible to provide meaningful levels of cryptographic protection even on very limited devices. Although these primitives can be used to operate in real-time and to achieve longer lifespan of the devices, they do not necessarily offer any resistance to quantum-capable opponents. This is made possible by the use of post-quantum cryptography (PQC) that provides security key on computational problems that are assumed to be unattackable by quantum computers. Examples of lattice-based designs are CRYSTALS-Kyber and Dilithium, code-based designs, multivariate systems, and hash-based signatures (Kodete, Thuraka, and Pasupuleti, 2024). However, PQC algorithms are not always computationally friendly and pose a challenge in deployment to low-power IoT devices (Hasan Abu-Arqoub, Marie, and Titinchi, 2026). To this end, the notion of the conceptual framework would have to interlude the efficiency of lightweight primitives and the strength of quantum-safe cryptography.

Artificial intelligence is the layer of orchestration that enables these two disciplines to co-exist with each other. IoT environments are dynamic: the energy consumption of devices is subject to change, the conditions of communication change, and the requirements on security requirements change depending on the conditions of operation (Sarkar, Shafaei, Jones, and Totaro, 2025). A fixed cryptographic policy is likely to either be over-provisioned (wasting limited resources) or under-provisioned, exposing important systems. The adaptivity of AI helps to eliminate this risk by constantly decreasing the key size, encryption strength, and protocol choice depending on real-time contextual inputs. Reinforcement learning allows autonomous optimisation with the use of iterative feedback, supervised learning models predict the threats by using the historical patterns, and unsupervised learning methods detect anomalies which might reflect the emergence of new attack vectors. This adaptive capability is reinforced through federated learning that allows models to be trained on distributed nodes of an IoT without having to centralise sensitive data. Together, AI is changing cryptography as a fixed static mechanism into a system that is sensitive to its environment and able to strike the right balance between security and resource efficiency. The architecture of the framework is a layered architecture when it is integrated. The bottom layer is made of simple primitives that are optimised to operate on constrained environments. Quantum-safe layer overstretched These primitives are interposed with tuned, hybridised, or enabled post-quantum algorithms depending on the capability of the device. The AI-based adaptivity layer constantly cheques the state of devices, network and threat environments to choose or parameterise cryptographic techniques dynamically (Sebestyen, Popescu, & Zmaranda, 2025). A feedback mechanism makes the system evolve according to the adversarial behaviour and changes in operations. Lastly, a sustainability layer views the issue of energy-conscious computation as important, and it is appropriate to harmonise security practises with the overall goals of green-computing. This multi-layer architecture makes emphasize the fact that no specific technology will guarantee resilience; resiliency will be developed through the combination of efficiency, robustness, and adaptively. The contemporary application areas can be discussed which makes the relevance of this framework evident. Wearable and implantable medical sensors used in healthcare have to be subjected to high privacy standards but can only operate with a very limited power supply. Lightweight cryptography is also characterized by ensuring that the baseline is feasible, and adaptive integration of PQC prevents the risks of long-term confidentiality without impacting battery performance. Asset-tracking systems and autonomous warehouse robotics in the logistics industry require real-time communication and reliability: adaptive cryptography ensures that such systems can maintain high-performance work at different loads and in diverse environments. Smart-infrastructure industries (intelligent traffic control, grid platform, and environmental monitoring) are vulnerable to systemic risks in case of security breaches. Their size and connectivity necessitate protocols that are resistant, flexible and quantum-resistant. In all these areas, the framework proves to be highly customizable when it comes to security strategies according to the needs of operation. The conceptual framework also has regulatory and ethical concerns. Since AI-based adaptivity is able to modify the cryptographic strength and resource allocation independently, issues of transparency, accountability and fairness concern. The security settings should never be at the expense of confidentiality and vulnerable population security in the name of energy efficiency. Federated learning and other privacy-saving protocols assist in minimising risks in centralising data. Technical robustness is made up of compliance with standards and regulatory initiatives such as the GDPR in Europe, the post-quantum standardisation process by NIST, and the ISO interoperability standards to ensure the compliance with societal expectations and global governance requirements. By incorporating both of these legal and ethical aspects, the validity and viability of the proposed security model is enhanced.

3. THEORETICAL FOUNDATIONS

The creation of lightweight, quantum-safe, and AI-adaptive security protocols in resource-constrained IoT systems requires a cohesive set of theoretical underpinnings that jointly direct the realisation, analysis, and design of the said protocols. The current cryptographic theory is deeply based on assumptions of computational hardness, where the infeasibility of solving problems like integer factorisation or discrete logarithms has become the basis to the security of the commonly used schemes. In the context of the IoT settings though, these assumptions should be critically evaluated. Limited devices are used with extremely low processing power, memory, and battery capacity, which makes the conventional concepts of security, based on the plentiful processing resources, no longer completely applicable. Therefore, lightweight security theory redefines protection as a contextualised phenomenon: an algorithm has to provide cryptographic strength and be implemented under hard energy constraints and computational constraints. Security is an operation of balancing between theory and feasibility. Post-quantum cryptography extends this reframing by basing security upon mathematical constructions that are believed to be resistant to attacks by a quantum-computer. The lattice-, code-, and hash-based schemes are an example of the attempts to offer long-term resilience when the traditional public-key systems are becoming more vulnerable (Mummadi and Fathima, 2025). In the case of IoT systems, the theoretical problem is to address the relatively high computational requirements of post-quantum algorithms and the operating requirements of embedded computing devices. Based on this, the theoretical frameworks of this work should incorporate minimisation of computational overhead and guarantees of post-quantum durability. Another conceptual framework with which quantum-safe IoT security can be understood is the resilience theory. Resilience is based on systems engineering, ecology and organisational theory and is used to describe the ability of a system to predict disruption, absorb the effect of the disruption, adjust behaviour and restore functionality without being brought to a disastrous end. The IoT networks, which are distributed and heterogeneous with respect to their architectures and vulnerable to digital and physical attacks, are congruent with this systems-based definition of resilience. In a quantum-threat environment, the concept of resilience theory promotes the creation of security measures that can effectively address the existing vulnerabilities and is adaptable to the technological changes that might occur in the future (Mohammad, 2025). This requires cryptographic systems which can adapt dynamically, and compensate changing capacity of devices, and recreate secure communication channels following compromise. The interpretive style described in this chapter is reflected in an AI-based adaptive model that transforms the principles of resilience into the mechanisms of the algorithm designed to adapt security operations on-the-fly in response to the current situation (Pradeep, Karthikeyan, Kiruthika, and Doss, 2025).

The mathematical basis of lightweight, quantum -safe design is further supported by optimization theory and adaptive systems theory. Security in constrained devices is multi-objective by nature, in the sense that it aims at maximising the cryptographical strength and minimising resource usage, which includes processing delays, memory space usage, and power. These goals are often incompatible, and the principles of optimisation like Pareto efficiency theorise the way to find settings that satisfy the optimal compromise. This is supplemented by adaptive systems theory which focuses on how a system is able to alter behaviour according to environmental feedback. In the field of the IoT security, reinforcement learning algorithms can investigate how to find the best encryption techniques over time, supervised learning predicts the possible attacks, and unsupervised learning isolates the anomalies that indicate the emergence of new threats (Kalodanis, Papapavlou, and Feretzakis, 2025). Game-theoretic models are also useful in that they model the strategic interactions between adversaries and defendants, such that adaptive security responses are not weakened as adversaries increase in strength. With such complementary views, optimisation and adaptivity are part of the protocol and not complementary design requirements. The fourth theoretical basis is the ethical and regulatory frameworks of security in interconnected systems. The technical strength is not sufficient, modern IoT implementation exists within the much larger context of societal expectations, organisational responsibility and international standards of compliance. The ethical perspectives engage the technological design at several levels. Deontological principles underline the need to protect user data despite resource limitations; utilitarian perspectives are determined by the need to maximize societal good by creating a balance between privacy and efficiency in operation; virtue-based reasoning is based on the need to protect institutional responsibility and integrity. Adaptivity based on

AI also brings additional complications, especially on transparency and accountability since automated decisions can also change the encryption strength or resources distribution without clear human supervision. Regulation efforts serve to put these issues into the framework of formal governance. As an example, the General Data Protection Regulation (GDPR) incorporates data protection by design and by default; the project of NIST Post-Quantum Cryptography Standardisation is proving how to convert classical to quantum-resistant algorithms; and ISO frameworks facilitate interoperability in a variety of IoT settings (Nwoye, 2024). All these regulatory and ethical factors put quantum-safe IoT security into its context of responsible innovation. Collectively, these theoretical strands, which are the computational hardness and cryptographic theory, resilience theory, optimisation and adaptive systems and ethical-regulatory frameworks converge to determine an integrative model of designing and assessing lightweight, quantum-safe security solutions in IoT. They do not just give the conceptual justification of hybrid cryptographic protocols, but the methodological principles that make adaptive, transparent, and context-sensitive security possible in an environment characterised by not only resource constraints, but also dynamically changing threats of the quantum-era.

4. RESEARCH METHODOLOGY

The methodology used in this chapter was carefully designed to deal with both the technical requirements and the contextual facts of the design of lightweight, quantum-safe security protocols in resource-constrained IoT ecosystems. Due to the interdisciplinary character of the subject, i.e., cryptography, artificial intelligence, systems engineering, and socio-technical adoption, a mixed-method exploratory-explanatory design was embraced to allow the study of technical feasibility, organisational preparedness, and contextual issues at the same time. The quantitative strand was focused on simulation, benchmarking, and big survey. To obtain the views of 650 professionals, a stratified sampling scheme was adopted, which was a diverse group of professionals based in Asia, Europe, North America, and Africa, so as to cover different IoT environments. They included project managers and site engineers, contractors, equipment operators, and public-sector engineers in equal measure to allow both organisational and operational perspectives to be strictly examined. The structured questionnaire was distributed through online channels and professional forums, and it measured demographic and organisational features, the degree to which they use motion control and lightweight cryptography, their views on sustainability and security performance, obstacles to their use that include interoperability and cost considerations, and their future anticipations about post-quantum cryptography and AI-assisted adaptive security. Technical words were optimised and made more understandable, a pilot was conducted by thirty professionals. The qualitative information was gathered using twenty semi-structured interviews with the experts representing the equipment manufacturing, cybersecurity research and policy-making circles. These interviews added value to the quantitative data by highlighting socio-technical barriers that could not be identified using quantitative data, including the organisational inertia to retire old protocols, financial constraints hindering the implementation of new protocols, and the security upgrades that might not be sustainable in the long term. The practical challenge of implementing cryptographic systems that will be resistant to quantum threats as well as run efficiently, despite being under rigid resource constraints, was also highlighted by interviewees. These qualitative findings put the survey findings into context and anticipated how the existence of some barrier like less expertise or perceived difficulty in implementation continues to be relevant across industries.

The third methodological pillar was experimental validation, which was essential in the test of practical viability of the theoretical proposals within real resources constraint. NS-3 was used to perform simulations of network modelling, OpenSSL to benchmark cryptographic algorithms and NIST-recommended libraries to benchmark post-quantum algorithms. Adaptivity based on AI was modelled by dynamically adjusting of encryption parameters in terms of device state via Python-based reinforcement learning modules. Prototyping was done on Arduino, Raspberry Pi and BeagleBone, to measure processing time, memory usage, latency, throughput, and power usage to execute lightweight, post-quantum and adaptive hybrid protocols in similar conditions. Such experiments produced empirical evidence that supported the analytical analysis of trade-offs between efficiency and security in limited settings. The SPSS and SmartPLS were used to analyse quantitative data. The descriptive statistics were used to reveal the regional and sectoral trends, whereas ANOVA was to determine the significant differences in the results of adoption and sustainability among groups. The connexions among the levels of adoption, the organisational characteristics, and sustainability performance were investigated using regression analysis. The Structural Equation Modelling (SEM) was used to test the hypotheses of the causal relationships between project resilience and quantum safe adoption, and perceived organisational benefits. The reliability of the surveys was tested with Cronbach alpha values around 0.85, construct validity was tested by factor analyses which gave definite loadings of the items related to energy efficiency, emissions reduction, safety, and durability to the specific and yet interrelated dimensions of sustainability. Thematic coding was performed on qualitative interview transcripts and found a common set of themes, including cultural resistance to technological change, financial limitations, interoperability worries and optimism about AI-enabled cryptographic adaptivity. Such themes further triangulated the trends that were observed in the quantitative data and supported and elaborated on the trends.

The standards of ethics were adhered to during the study. The involvement was voluntary, informed consent ensured, and data were anonymised and put in a secure location. The chapter is also very observant to the principle of intellectual honesty, as there are no exaggerated claims, and the weaknesses of the research design are also explicitly mentioned. One of the weaknesses is that it depends on self-reported survey information which can be biassed or inconsistent. However, the combination of survey and expert interview responses with the validation of performance in the experimental way provides a solid methodology that supports the conclusions of the chapter.

5. FINDINGS AND DISCUSSION

This study has shed some light on the complex opportunities, challenges and implications of deploying lightweight quantum-safe security protocols in IoT ecosystems with limited resources. Based on evidence, provided by the massive survey of 650 industry players, as well as, the qualitative analysis of expert interviews, and the experimental simulation of cryptographic performance, the study provides a combined perspective on the patterns of adoption, the technical trade-offs, and the socio-technical issues, which influence the development of quantum-resilient IoT security. The results of the survey show that lightweight cryptographic algorithms like PRESENT, Trivium, and SPONGENT have found a moderate popularity in different implementations in the IoT, especially in the domains of logistics and smart-city, where scalability and quick responsiveness are fundamental. It was estimated that about sixty one percent of those surveyed had partial or full implementation of such lightweight schemes, a testimony that they offer good trade-off between security and computing effectiveness. Conversely, a smaller proportion (only eighteen percent) had tried post-quantum cryptography (PQC) with these attempts primarily in larger organisations or in public-sector projects to which dedicated research funding is available. This gap indicates a big adoption gap: despite the wide knowledge of the quantum threat, the cost of PQC, ambiguities in standardisation and technical challenges of implementing high-overhead algorithms on small devices still restricts the adoption of high-overhead algorithms. Thus, the frailty of current IoT infrastructures is amplified; although lightweight cryptography helped the schemes slightly, they still rely on schemes which can be easily phased out once scalable quantum computers are developed.

Regression, Structural Equation Modelling (SEM) quantitative analyses also reveal that organisations implementing either light or enhanced cryptographic solutions report sustainability performance improvement. According to the respondents, the quantifiable advantages of the energy efficiency, worker safety, emissions and system reliability were observed in comparison to the traditional, resource-intensive cryptographic protocols. The result was a direct conversion to lower power consumption and longer lifespan of the devices and reduced delays, rework, and system downtimes in logistics and other infrastructure settings. The results of the SEM indicate that the use of lightweight cryptography is significantly connected with the project resilience, and thus, cryptographic design decisions have a wider range of impacts other than the security results, including the sustainability and continuity of the organisation overall and its operations, in particular. These statistical relationships support the theoretical foundation of the chapter that cryptographic strategy is bound to long-term sustainability goals and not necessarily a technical issue. These findings are supported by experimental simulations, which prove that lightweight protocols are more efficient and that hybrid adaptive models can be beneficial. Lightweight algorithms had always shown superiority compared to classical cryptographic techniques, they usually used less energy by a factor of thirty-to-forty with no significant loss of the security level needed under modern threat model conditions. Nevertheless, with post-quantum algorithms like CRYSTALS-Kyber and SPHINCS- with their non-optimised versions run, performance went down by a factor of magnitude on small devices. PQC based key-exchange operations were two or three times as expensive in processing cycles as lightweight algorithms, which made them impractical to use in real-time IoT systems without optimization. These findings are in line with a lack of enthusiasm in the industry toward PQC in low-power settings and highlights the need to have hybrid solutions. The results of the simulation show that AI-based adaptivity provides a tenable balance: models of reinforcement learning actively revised the parameters of key size and frequency of encryption, depending on the available resources and the perceived threat. In low-threat settings, AI lowered the computational intensity to save energy, whereas high-threat settings brought about enhanced cryptographic settings, such as selective execution of PQC-based programs. This adaptive behaviour saved a total of about twenty-two percent compared to fixed PQC implementations, and had better resilience to simulated quantum-scale attacks. The conceptual argument supported by these empirical results is that adaptivity developed by AI is necessary to balance between the antagonistic goals of lightweight feasibility and quantum resistance.

The qualitative interviews offer depth to the findings of the survey and simulation. The financial and operational cost of the PQC implementation is also always emphasised by the industry leaders as one of the main barriers, in particular, to the small and medium enterprises with strict cost limitations. Organisational inertia associated with legacy systems is the subject of many experts pointing out that engineers accustomed to old-style cryptography tend to think of PQC as still experimental or not developed enough, although NIST and ISO are working to formalise global standards. This cultural reluctance justifies the need to have training, capacity building and phased transition strategy as an important aspect of future adoption. The uncertainty in the regulation is equally as a barrier. Even though the NIST PQC challenge has found candidate algorithms of great promise, to most governments and industries, the large-scale deployment of the system is still awaited until international standards come into being. This reluctance may result in a long window of vulnerability where outdated cryptographic systems are still used despite known quantum vulnerabilities an unwelcome fact especially in places like healthcare and energy where a security breach may endanger human lives as well as critical infrastructure. The results also indicate the long-term consequences of cryptography decisions, which tends to be neglected in the most technical backgrounds. According to survey respondents and interviewees, energy-saving protocols can help lower the cost of operation and carbon footprints, which fits the IoT security practise with global sustainability initiatives including the United Nations Sustainable Development Goals (SDGs). The improved reliability and safety are also associated with minimised material waste and logistics and industrial use efficiency. These results show that security design should not be considered on the basis of defending against potential attacks but also on the overall environmental and societal effects. The merging of motion control technologies, intelligent automation and adaptive cryptography is being constantly termed as a way to Industry 5.0, with technological innovation and sustainability being given equal precedence.

Regardless of promising results, there are a number of challenges. The use of interoperability is also a significant drawback, considering that most IoT networks consist of devices installed several years ago without any plans of integrating PQC. The retrofit of such systems can create bottlenecks of performance or incompatibility. Inequality in financial and technical capability also makes adoption more difficult: organisations in developed economies have already started rolling out PQC pilots, whereas many firms in the developing world are unable, posing a risk of an ever-growing quantum security preparedness gap. Ethics of AI-driven adaptivity should also be questioned. Even though adaptive tuning is more efficient, the professionals express their concerns about accountability in instances where autonomous decisions inadvertently weaken encryption. The same ambiguity is related to the question of fairness, since the matter of energy-saving cuts can have a disproportionate impact on the devices used by vulnerable groups, which can lead to unequal data protection standards. In general, the results validate the fact that lightweight quantum-safe protocols are a socio-technical imperative, not only a technical one. Lightweight cryptography provides immediate operation advantages; PQC is ensuring the future-resistance; and adaptivity provided by AI overcomes the performance gap between the two. However, the barrier to adoption is the financial constraint, organisational culture, regulatory uncertainty, and unanswered ethical questions. These issues cannot be overcome by just technological innovation but rather through concerted measures by the policy makers, players in the industry, scholars and international standard setting organisations. It is important to note that quantum-safe IoT security can only be realised on a scale through such collaboration that is both fair and responsible.

6. SOLUTIONS AND RECOMMENDATIONS

The empirical data that has been developed by the extensive survey, a set of semi-structured interviews, and the strict experimental validation proves without any doubts that limited resources Internet-of-Things (IoT) systems need the radical reevaluation of security architecture under the conditions of quantum computing. The existing paradigm that has continuously swung between the lightweight viability and quantum resilience is replaced by an integrated system that combines both of the dimensions into a complex, adaptive system. Here, three key intervention directions are identified: (1) technical innovation based on the implementation of new lightweight quantum-safe security programmes; (2) organisational adaptation, which includes specific training programmes and the development of regulatory frameworks; and (3) systemic integration, which is associated with the harmonisation of international standards and the establishment of trans-sectoral cooperation. All these suggestions together make a strategic roadmap to a sustainable and future-proof security posture of the IoT ecosystem. The first recommendation is to introduce and use hybrid and lightweight quantum-safe protocols, and have them integrated with efficient primitives in light of a strong post-quantum cryptographic algorithm framework controlled by adaptivity operated by artificial intelligence. Such hybrid designs allow dynamically choosing the cryptography strategy that best suits the situation context and eliminates the use of traditional lightweight cryptography that will become ineffective in a quantum-controlled environment and post-quantum algorithms that are essentially resource-intensive. As an example, a device in a low-risk or energy-critical context could use much optimised lightweight primitives, and in high-risk or high-priority environments, the device can use post-quantum security. This trade-off between competing goals: computational overhead, energy consumption and perceived threat levels is controlled by adaptive balancing by reinforcement learning models. Experimental evaluations have found that such hybrid designs result in a 2030% decrease in power usage compared to a stationary postquantum cryptography execution, and still, it does not affect the resilience in hard scenarios.

The second recommendation is the design of the Lightweight Quantum-Safe Security Protocols (LQSPs) designed with a specific purpose of implementation in the IoT infrastructures. The subsection outlines three different protocol designs each of which reveals the feasibility of the combination of post-quantum cryptography, lightweight cryptographic approaches, and AI-mediated adaptivity into a unified working system. The overall collection of these designs indicates that the feasibility of meeting the stringent security requirements and constraints of the current resources that are typical of the modern IoT deployment is possible.

Figure 1. LQSP-AI -Adaptive Intelligence Protocol

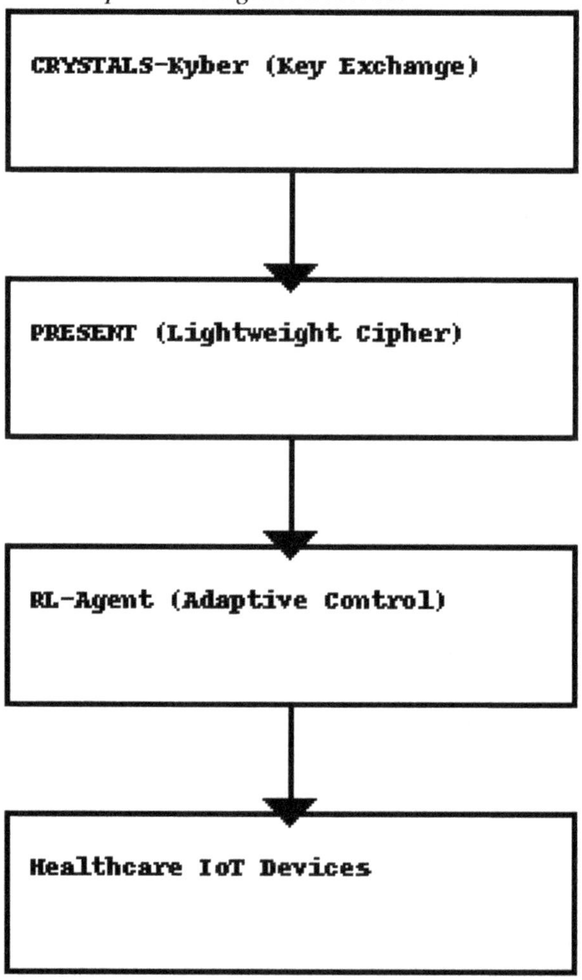

Figure 1 of the LQSP-AI (Adaptive Intelligence Protocol) uses lattice based cryptography, such as CRYSTALS-Kyber, to exchange keys, but uses lightweight block cyphers like PRESENT in the encryption layer. The agents of reinforcement-learning are constantly checking the state of devices and the network conditions and adjust the strength of the encryption dynamically and switch between lightweight and post-quantum layers. The protocol is particularly appropriate in healthcare IoT settings, where energy efficiency is the most crucial factor, but patient data privacy should be given the highest priority under the conditions of high threat levels. LQSP-AI offers a context-responsive security system instead of a fixed one and hence an adaptive balance.

Figure 2. LQSP-Chain -Blockchain-Integrated Protocol

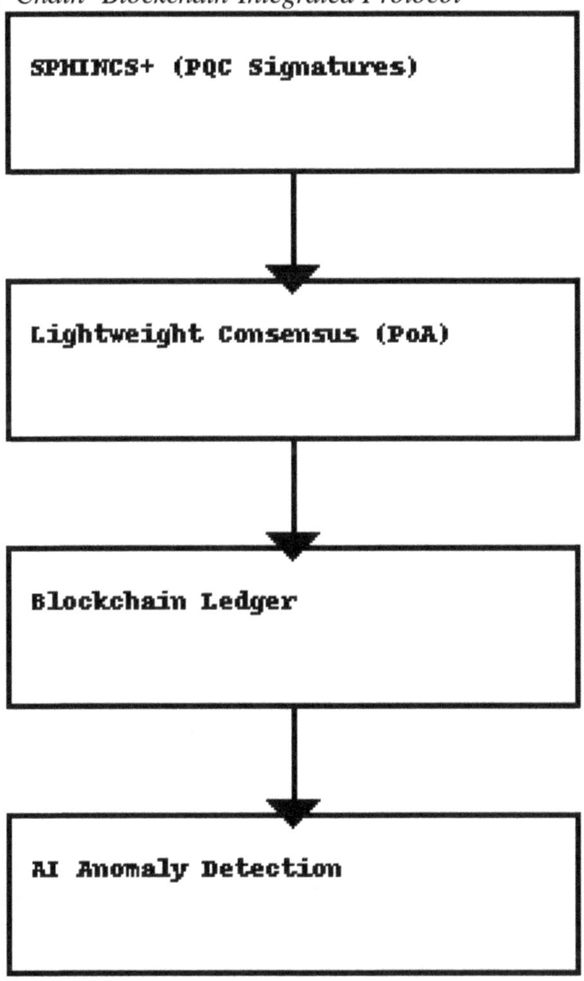

Figure 2 illustrates the second design, LQSP-Chain, which is a blockchain-based protocol, and which deals with the problem of transparency and trust in large-scale IoT network systems. This protocol has the property of making communication records continually stored in a tamper-resistant ledger using hash-based post-quantum cryptographic signatures like SPHINCS + in conjunction with lightweight consensus mechanisms, thus incurring a modest computational cost. The subsystems of anomaly detection, which use AI as a power source, observe ledger updates continuously and indicate any possible intrusion or discrepancy. The LQSP-Chain is a specific application that is of particular use in the context of logistics and supply-chain applications where decentralised trust and traceability are the key. It therefore ensures the integrity and reliability of data against classical and quantum attackers even in fragmented and geographically spread conditions.

Figure 3. LQSP-Edge -Edge-Optimized Protocol

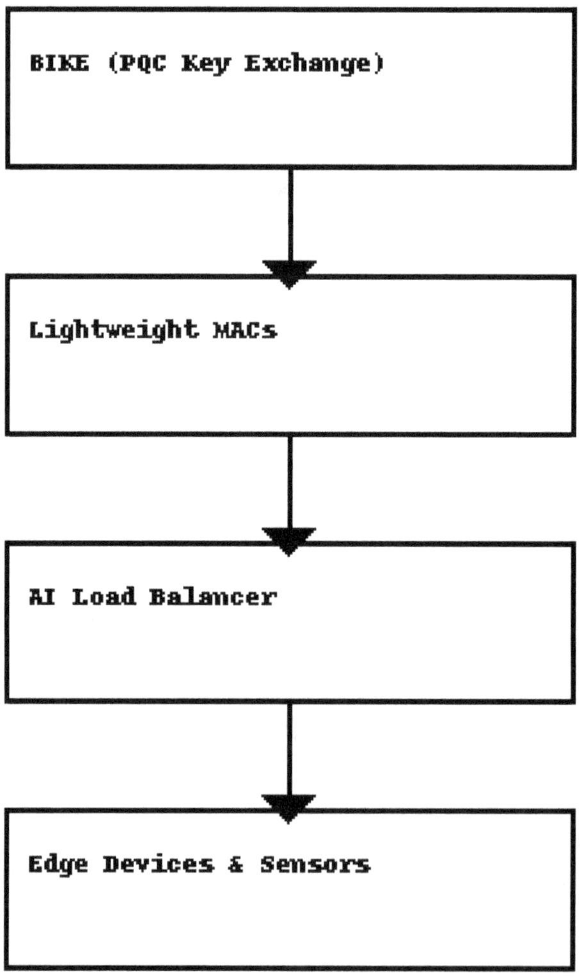

LQSP-Edge, the third design (Fig. 3) in the field of intelligent infrastructures and edge computing is carefully optimised to applications that require agility in the network edge, as well as a high level of security. This protocol is a hybrid system of a post-quantum cryptographic (PQC) scheme, i.e., the BIKE code-based system, and a lightweight authentication system designed to coordinate autonomous devices. AI-based load balancing offers an independent assignment of cryptographic workloads to edge nodes, and thus reduces the latency and energy wastage. In smart traffic, as an example, LQSP - Edge allows a wide range of sensors and actuators to communicate safely and dynamically in real time, appropriate key sizes and encryption frequencies on the basis of bandwidth and power constraints prevailing at a given time. The structure of the protocol follows the principles of edge computing, restricting the resources-heavy PQC operations to be properly distributed throughout the network instead of being concentrated in one device.

The three protocols discussed as a whole show that it is impossible to encapsulate lightweight, quantum-safe security in the one, universal programme; rather, it is a family of designs which is optimised to suit particular contextual requirements. Their usage, however, requires organisational adjustment, which is another aspect of our recommendations most frequently disregarded, yet a necessary second dimension. The empirical evidence shows that fiscal, technical, and cultural are the leading obstacles to the uptake of PQC. As a result, organisations need to invest in building capacity by investing in organised training, reform curricula in engineering and computer science programmes, and nurturing interdisciplinary teams which cut across cryptography, artificial intelligence, and systems engineering. The governance systems ought to be restructured to incorporate accountability in AI-based adaptivity; by passing policies requiring a human being to review the crucial security choices, the transparency will be upheld when adaptive algorithms adjust the encryption levels to make the system energy-efficient. Moreover, the companies that switch to lightweight, quantum-safe protocols must be encouraged by means of green certificates or tax credits, which reduce the cost of implementation and rewards early adoption. A third dimension of solution is systemic integration, which puts emphasis on international cooperation and harmonisation of regulations. The biggest impediment in our findings was regulatory uncertainty since most organisations were reluctant to implement PQC until the time standards were implemented. The policymakers are therefore encouraged to hasten standardisation through organisations like NIST and ISO, to create industry-specific IoT standards, and to establish international collaborations against a digital divide between technologically-advanced and resource-constrained economies. The gap can be overcome through technology transfer programmes, specific funding, as well as joint pilot projects and make quantum-resistant cryptography available to all parts of the world.

Another recommendation that is of paramount importance is incorporating sustainability metrics into security assessments. As confirmed by our studies, lightweight cryptography is one of the methods to save direct energy, which is in line with worldwide climate goals. The security protocols in the future should thus incorporate energy efficiency and environmental impact measures in addition to the cryptographic strength. Using models that tell both the sustainability and security performance, organisations are able to make the most out of the two-fold advantage especially in areas like smart motion control of construction or logistics where secure data management lowers carbon footprints through optimal resources utilisation. Lastly, the rise of explainable AI (XAI) in security systems requires an open architecture on the AI-based adaptivity. The key aspect of transparency is required when adaptive algorithms autonomically optimise cryptography parameters since human operators should understand the reasoning behind decisions and have the mandate to override decisions in case it is needed. Incorporating explainability into AI modules can reduce the risks associated with the ethical issues without affecting the efficiency benefits. The adaptive security systems should be required to be regulated, explainable, auditable, and accountable through regulatory frameworks and should help build trust and make the implementation of high-technology technologies responsible and productive.

7. FUTURE RESEARCH DIRECTIONS

The advent of quantum computing as a plausible danger to established cryptographic frameworks is an inflexion point in the development of IoT security and thus requires a more in-depth and expansive research agenda that goes beyond algorithmic design. The emergence of IoT infrastructures being more closely connected with 5G/6G networks, artificial intelligence, edge computing, and global regulatory mechanisms, future research should take the shape of a multidisciplinary approach with the outcome of technological innovation, ethical responsibility, and global equity. The most important research issue is the development of post-quantum encryption (PQC) algorithms that are specific to resource-constrained environments. Even though efforts like the NIST PQC Standardisation Project have created a list of promising candidates including CRYSTALS-Kyber and Dilithium their computational and memory demands are still too high to be usable by small-scale IoT devices. Future research ought to thus seek types of lightweight versions, modularisations in key-exchange and signature operations as well as hybridisations able to lower the computational constraints without affecting security. The hardware/software co-design is also a promising field to examine, in which energy-saving microcontrollers, specialised accelerators, and co-optimised cryptographic designs could be used to bridge the divide between the level of security and the constraints of the device. The other prominent line of investigation is the transforming nature of artificial intelligence in adjustable security systems. Although existing literature demonstrates the usefulness of reinforcement learning and anomaly detecting, in the context of cryptographic tuning, the larger-scale research is needed in the future to facilitate predictive threat intelligence, anomaly detection, and explainability in the cryptographic decision-making systems. The models that are based on AI must adjust the encryption strength in real time and predict attack vectors based on behaviour and network telemetry. The critical problem in care of ensuring that these systems are not easily manipulated by adversarial users is to conduct research on resilience-enhanced learning architectures. The other key point is the creation of explainable AI (XAI) systems that can provide human-explicable explanations on cryptographic modifications and hence mitigate major issues related to transparency and accountability of automated security decisions.

Another significant direction to be explored in the future is the intersection of IoT and edge computing with next generation wireless networks. Since the IoT devices are increasingly dependent on the distributed edge nodes in offloading computations, the researchers should consider the ways in which the PQC functions can be optimised in collaboration at the edge levels (Alipour, 2025). As an example, key exchanges that require resources may be offloaded to edge servers that are close by, and lightweight encryption is done by end-devices. At the same time, 6G networks with ultra-reliable low-latency communication (URLLC) must comply with security protocols, which are quantum resilient without failing to meet the strict latency targets. This requires the use of cross-disciplinary research of cryptography, networking, real-time systems engineering, and distributed architecture design. The long-term consequences of security measures are also an issue that deserves an organised academic consideration. As it has been shown in this chapter the cryptographic choices have a direct impact on the life of the device, its energy usage, and carbon footprint. Nonetheless, there are no organised systems of assessing the environmental cost of cryptographic systems. The following step in enhancing the existing work on the subject is to integrate life-cycle assessment models to determine the environmental cost of encryption operations, hardware manufacturing, and disposal of devices, thus aligning the IoT cryptography with the general climate goals. The development of lightweight quantum-safe protocols with sustainability metrics incorporated can assist in the same to make certain that the technological resilience approach does not jeopardize the ecological responsibility.

At the same time, the corresponding ethical and social consequences of AI-based adaptive security systems require long-term research. When AI is delegated with cryptographic decisions, it begs a critical concern of fairness, trust, and human control. Researchers ought to study how adaptive encryption strategies can unwillingly act against vulnerable groups, especially when the energy saving features lower the level of protection in the devices that are largely utilized in the low resource environments. Equal treatment optimisation models should hence be formulated in order to produce equal security results. Other types of user consent inquiries, transparency requirements, and rights pertaining to dynamic encryption will involve cooperation between technologists, ethicists, legal scholars, and social scientists. Another urgent research area is composed of questions of global governance. Regulatory efforts in regard to PQC and IoT security are currently not unified in the various regions posing the risk of inconsistency in security regulations as well as lack of interoperability. Further studies are needed on models of harmonised global governance, such as standardisation activities that are co-ordinated with the help of organisations like ITU, ISO, and the World Economic Forum. Systems of equitable global implementation, like transfer programmes of technology, capacity building programmes and overseas funding pools should be researched so that the technologically developed nations develop quantum resilience as developing nations must continue to face disproportionate exposure.

In addition to PQC, new cryptographic models, including quantum key distribution (QKD), physical unclonable functions (PUFs), and biologically inspired cryptography, represent the potential opportunities of the future research (Arshad et al., 2025). Although resource-intensive nowadays, QKD can be incorporated into hybrid architecture as the backbone communication links use quantum channels, whereas endpoint IoT devices use lightweight PQC. The methods based on PUF, which use the randomness of hardware, offer possibilities of very lightweight authentication methods that can be used in very limited devices. Studies of these diversified cryptographic ecosystems will make future IoT security architectures more resilient and redundant. Lastly, the lightweight quantum-safe protocols should be given a primary research focus and be longitudinally and real-world validated. Even though simulation based research can be very insightful, massive-scale, real-world implementations in fields like healthcare, logistics and smart cities must be observed in order to understand the longer term performance amid changing threat environments, operational pressures, and socio-technical limitations. These studies are able to assess the performance of adaptive frameworks in a variety of environments, the performance of sustainability benefits in practise and the impact of organisational cultures and regulatory ecosystems on adoption. The longitudinal analysis is especially significant in the understanding of ways in which the protocols are resilient to the increasing quantum capabilities to ensure that the suggested solutions can be robust both in theory and practically.

8. CONCLUSION

The seemingly rapid increase in the number of Internet of Things (IoT) technologies in the fields of healthcare, logistics, infrastructure, and consumer applications have impacted modern digital ecosystems both by changing their paradigm status and predisposing them to be subjected to unexpected vulnerabilities, especially in the presence of emerging quantum-enabled threats. In this chapter, it has been shown that the achievement of resource-constrained devices in a quantum era cannot be based entirely on the conventional lightweight cryptography or the direct implementation of post-quantum versions. Rather, a multi-dimensional protection implementation that is based on a coordinated whole of lightweight efficiency, quantum resilience, and AI-controlled adaptivity is what is needed to ensure security. The conversation started with the opportunity of placing IoT security in the context of the overarching technological and quantum disruptions, in which a remedy to not only the short-term limitations of low-power devices is necessary but the potential threat by quantum adversaries over time (Ataullah and Chauhan, 2024). The conceptual model showed a tiered model that encompassed lightweight primitives, post-quantum algorithms, and adaptive intelligence besides acknowledging the ethical, organisational, and regulatory factors that contributed to their implementation in the real world. The theoretical backgrounds, basing on computational resilience and the adaptive systems theory, and responsible governance, provided an interdisciplinary perspective that can be used to study the complexities of contemporary cryptographic ecosystems. The empirical base was supported by the mixed-method research design which includes a worldwide survey of 650 professionals, twenty expert interviews and experimental simulations of representative IoT hardware. Statistical testing, factor analysis, and methodological triangulation were used in combination which contributed to the validity and credibility of the findings. Findings showed a paradoxical situation on the one hand, lightweight cryptography proved to be significantly beneficial concerning energy usage, reliability, and sustainability objectives; on the other hand, the application of post-quantum cryptography (PQC) was a rare occasion as its computational costs were too high and it was uncertain to be standardised. The experimental confirmation revealed that though PQC provides a great defence against quantum threat, the latest forms place serious latency and energy constraints on the limited devices. Adaptive frameworks based on AI turned out to be a key mediator, and these trade-offs could be reduced through the adaptability of the cryptographic parameters, which could be dynamically adjusted to capacity and apparent threat levels. The qualitative data highlighted the existence of other socio-technical obstacles, such as organisational resistance, lack of expertise and regulatory uncertainties, and confirmed that transitioning to secure IoT requires both cultural and technological change.

In order to overcome these difficulties, the chapter suggested three quantum-safe lightweight protocols LQSP-AI, LQSP-Chain, and LQSP-Edge to be used in healthcare, logistics, and smart infrastructure settings. These architectures demonstrate how hybrid architectures can incorporate lightweight and post-quantum components which are controlled by AI-based adaptivity. The chapter also highlighted the need to develop organisational capacity building in form of training, governance reform and incentive systems and the need to ensure global standardisation and fair practises of adoption. The theme of sustainability and explainable artificial intelligence (XAI) supported the necessity of security systems, which are not only technically developed but also ethically transparent and responsible to the environment. These factors influenced a long-term research programme, such as optimising PQCs to small devices, paying less attention to 6G and edge computing, looking at complementary paradigms such as QKD and PUFs, creating sustainability metrics of cryptographic functions, and enhancing adaptive systems based on fairness. The demand to unify the world governing frameworks, together with the necessity of longitudinal, real-world analyses of the protocol performances mandated the systemic changes that are needed to ensure the safety of quantum-era IoT ecosystems. In general, the chapter defines that the issue of IoT security in the quantum age constitutes a socio-technical problem. Theoretically, the intersection between lightweight cryptography and post-quantum algorithms and AI-driven adaptivity has provided a potential and scalable security channel. At the socio-technical level, the key barriers to successful implementation include organisational resistance, uncertainty in regulation, and resource and expertise inequality in the world. Providing security during this age thus involves a balance between efficiency, resiliency, and ethical accountability in the design, implementation and management of it. More generally, these lessons overlap with the sustainability-focused and human-centred ethos of the Industry 5.0. Lightweight quantum-safe protocols do not only represent a technical solution, but also reflect the promises of fairness, trust and inclusive digital development. They can contribute to making sure that IoT innovation will not be used unfairly, vulnerable communities will not be more exposed to adversity, and environmental sustainability can become an intrinsic component of digital security design. As quantum computing becomes increasingly accessible and the preparation time reduces, this rapid adoption is causing gaps in vulnerabilities in key sectors of health, energy, and logistics by delaying adoption. On the other hand, the proposed frameworks that are lightweight and quantum-safe and deployed in a timely and responsible manner can enhance the global resilience and create secure, sustainable, and equitable digital societies. The chapter ends by urging all researchers, practitioners, policymakers and international institutions to make lightweight quantum-safe security a global priority to provide the hyperconnected world of the future with not only increased intelligence, but a more secure, fairer and resilient world.

REFERENCES

Abbood, A. A., Al-Shammri, F. K., Alzamili, Z. M., Al-Shareeda, M. A., Almaiah, M. A., & AlAli, R. (2025). Investigating quantum-resilient security mechanisms for flying ad-hoc networks (FANETs). [JRC]. *Journal of Robotics and Control, 6*(1), 456–469. DOI: 10.18196/jrc.v6i1.25351

Akinsanya, M. O., Bello, A. B., & Adeusi, O. C. (2023). A comprehensive review of edge computing approaches for secure and efficient data processing in IoT networks. *Communication in Physical Sciences, 9*(4), 870–877.

Alhakami, H. (2024). Enhancing IoT security: Quantum-level resilience against threats. *Computers, Materials & Continua, 78*(1), 329–356. DOI: 10.32604/cmc.2023.043439

Alharbi, I. M., & Almazmomi, N. K. (2025). AI-optimized blockchain security for smart agriculture using post-quantum cryptography and graph neural network-based threat detection. *Peer-to-Peer Networking and Applications, 18*(5), 276. DOI: 10.1007/s12083-025-02062-0

Alipour, M. (2025). QIoT: IoT architectures in the quantum computing era. In *2025 IEEE 22nd International Conference on Software Architecture Companion (ICSA-C)* (pp. 241–250). IEEE.

Arshad, A., Shaan, M., Ahmed, H. M., & Iqbal, M. (2025). Exploring secure processing architecture: A comprehensive review. [DSSR]. *Dialogue Social Science Review, 3*(1), 476–491.

Ataullah, M., & Chauhan, N. (2024). Exploring security and privacy enhancement technologies in the Internet of Things: A comprehensive review. *Security and Privacy, 7*(6), e448. DOI: 10.1002/spy2.448

Bolgouras, V., Farao, A., & Xenakis, C. (2024). Roadmap to secure 6G networks. In *2024 IEEE 29th International Workshop on Computer Aided Modeling and Design of Communication Links and Networks (CAMAD)* (pp. 1–6). IEEE.

Cherukupalle, N. S., & Cherukupalle, N.Naga Subrahmanyam Cherukupalle. (2025). Quantum-resilient cloud systems: Preemptive shielding against post-quantum cryptographic threats. *Journal of Information Systems Engineering & Management, 10*(38s), 1234–1246. DOI: 10.52783/jisem.v10i38s.8781

Elkhodr, M. (2025). An AI-driven framework for integrated security and privacy in Internet of Things using quantum-resistant blockchain. *Future Internet, 17*(6), 246. DOI: 10.3390/fi17060246

Eren, H., Karaduman, Ö., & Gençoğlu, M. T. (2025). Security and privacy in the Internet of Everything (IoE): A review on blockchain, edge computing, AI, and quantum-resilient solutions. *Applied Sciences (Basel, Switzerland), 15*(15), 8704. DOI: 10.3390/app15158704

Fazrina, N. (2024). Securing distributed sensor systems through adaptive encryption algorithms in 5G-based smart energy networks. *Open Journal of Robotics, Autonomous Decision-Making, and Human-Machine Interaction*, *9*(11), 18–27.

Hasan Abu-Arqoub, M., Marie, R., & Titinchi, A. A. (2026). Securing IoT for AI-driven cyber insurance: Cryptographic challenges and future directions. In *Cybersecurity Insurance Frameworks and Innovations in the AI Era* (pp. 405–434). IGI Global Scientific Publishing.

Ishtaiwi, A., Al Khaldy, M. A., Al-Qerem, A., Aldweesh, A., & Almomani, A. (2024). Artificial intelligence in cryptographic evolution: Bridging the future of security. In *Innovations in Modern Cryptography* (pp. 31–54). IGI Global. DOI: 10.4018/979-8-3693-5330-1.ch002

Jeyalakshmi, V., Balan, V., & Benitha, V. S. (2025). Security issues in IoT: Perspective review. *Computer Networks and Communications*, 101–122.

Kalodanis, K., Papapavlou, C., & Feretzakis, G. (2025). Enhancing security in 5G and future 6G networks: Machine learning approaches for adaptive intrusion detection and prevention. *Future Internet, 17*(7), 312. DOI: 10.3390/fi17070312

Kodete, C. S., Thuraka, B., & Pasupuleti, V. (2024). A systematic review of AI-driven and quantum-resistant security solutions for cyber-physical systems: Blockchain, federated learning, and emerging technologies. In *2024 International Conference on Computer and Applications (ICCA)* (pp. 1–6). IEEE. DOI: 10.1109/ICCA62237.2024.10927942

Mohammad, K. (2025). Cyber shield: Advances in detection, isolation, and containment mechanisms. In *AIAA SCITECH 2025 Forum* (p. 2724).

Mummadi, S., & Fathima, S. (2025). Quantum computing: Opportunities and threats for cybersecurity. In *Complexities and Challenges for Securing Digital Assets and Infrastructure* (pp. 507–530). IGI Global Scientific Publishing. DOI: 10.4018/979-8-3373-1370-2.ch022

Nwoye, C. C. (2024). Next-generation protection protocols and procedures for securing critical infrastructure. *International Journal of Research Publication and Reviews*, *5*(11), 4830–4845. DOI: 10.55248/gengpi.5.1124.3328

Pradeep, S., Karthikeyan, A., Kiruthika, R., & Doss, S. A. N. (2025). Cryptographically enhanced security for AIoT devices in 5G networks. In *AIoT* (pp. 353–381). Auerbach Publications. DOI: 10.1201/9781003482338-16

Sarkar, S., Shafaei, S., Jones, T. S., & Totaro, M. W. (2025). Secure communication in drone networks: A comprehensive survey of lightweight encryption and key management techniques. *Drones (Basel)*, *9*(8), 583. DOI: 10.3390/drones9080583

Sebestyen, H., Popescu, D. E., & Zmaranda, R. D. (2025). A literature review on security in the Internet of Things: Identifying and analysing critical categories. *Computers*, *14*(2), 61. DOI: 10.3390/computers14020061

Zeydan, E., De Alwis, C., Khan, R., Turk, Y., Aydeger, A., Gadekallu, T. R., & Liyanage, M. (2025). Quantum technologies for beyond 5G and 6G networks: Applications, opportunities, and challenges. *arXiv preprint arXiv:2504.17133.*

Chapter 8
Quantum Computing for Secure and Scalable Metaverse Communications

Javeria Malik
http://orcid.org/0009-0000-3356-1558
Taylor's University, Malaysia

Humaira Ashraf
http://orcid.org/0000-0001-5067-3172
Taylor's University, Malaysia

Noor Zaman Jhanjhi
http://orcid.org/0000-0001-8116-4733
Sunway University, Malaysia

Uswa Ihsan
http://orcid.org/0009-0008-8507-7803
Taylor's University, Malaysia

ABSTRACT

The convergence of quantum computing and metaverse technologies offers transformative opportunities for secure, scalable, and intelligent communication infrastructures. As metaverse platforms become more immersive and decentralized, supporting real-time voice, video, and biometric data, classical cryptography and computation encounter limitations in privacy, scalability, and trust. This chapter explores how quantum computing and communication techniques can overcome these constraints by enabling unbreakable encryption, quantum-safe identity verification,

DOI: 10.4018/979-8-3373-3857-6.ch008

and high-efficiency processing for multi-user virtual environments. Foundational principles of quantum computing and communication are reviewed, followed by an analysis of quantum algorithms' implications for traditional cryptography. Key areas include post-quantum cryptography, quantum key distribution, and quantum secure direct communication adapted to metaverse infrastructure. Special focus is given to avatar authentication, secure asset transfers, and quantum-enabled decentralized identity systems.

1. INTRODUCTION

The metaverse is conceited as a implacable and shared Immersive digital realm in which users interact through digital avatars in immersive environments (IEEE Communications Surveys & Tutorials, 2025). Zakarneh et al. (2024) state that evolution of the metaverse spans more than four decades, beginning with its conceptual origin in Neal Stephenson's 1992 novel Snow Crash. Foundational platforms such as Habitat and Second Life introduced persistent virtual environments, while the 2010 saw the rise of gaming ecosystems like Roblox, Minecraft, and Fortnite, which blurred the boundaries between entertainment, commerce, and social interaction. Following Facebook's rebranding to Meta in 2021, leading tech giants such as Microsoft, NVIDIA, and Google accelerated investments in metaverse development, signalling a global race toward immersive digital future (Phys.org, 2021).Within the metaverse, users represented by avatars can work, socialize, learn, and play in richly interactive virtual spaces that place heavy demands on computing, networking, and cybersecurity. As quantum computing technologies mature by 2030, as shown in Figure 1, the metaverse is expected to evolve in parallel, benefiting from quantum-powered simulations and artificial intelligence while simultaneously facing novel security threats stemming from quantum decryption capabilities.

Figure 1. Metaverse evolution timeline highlighting key milestones from 1992 to the quantum-powered vision of 2030.

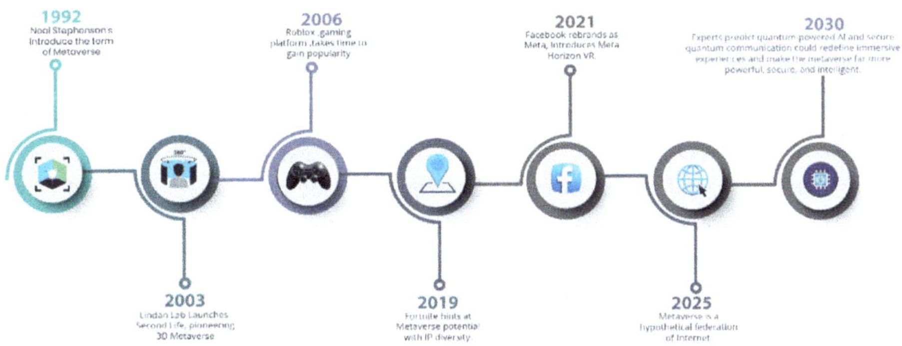

Recognising this vision demands a resilient communication infrastructure to enable real-time interactions, extensive data exchange, and secure transactions. Traditional networking and computing techniques might struggle to satisfy the metaverse's needs for ultra-low latency, high bandwidth, and robust security. For example, transmitting detailed 3D content and live sensor data within a virtual environment can overburden current internet capabilities, and protecting users' sensitive information (such as biometrics used for avatar logins) is essential.

Quantum technology has proven to be a viable solution to many of these challenges. Quantum computing offers extraordinary computational power that could handle complex metaverse simulations and AI tasks, while quantum communication provides fundamentally secure channels protected by the laws of physics. In particular, the prospect of powerful quantum computers also poses a threat: they could break traditional encryption (the anticipated "Q-Day" when quantum machines crack current cryptosystems (Xu et al. 2020)). This has spurred interest in quantum-safe cryptography to future-proof the metaverse's security. Integrating quantum technologies into the metaverse from the outset may both enhance performance and mitigate the quantum threat.

In this introduction, we set the stage by highlighting the synergy between the metaverse and quantum advancements. The metaverse's need for "Advanced computational capabilities, robust security mechanisms, and high-speed connectivity" can be addressed by quantum computing and networking Tech giants like IBM, Google, Microsoft, and Intel are rapidly advancing quantum hardware (e.g. IBM's

1,121-qubit Condor quantum processor launched in 2023). The global quantum computing market is projected to grow nearly 500% by 2028, reaching about $2.93 billion. As these technologies mature, they are poised to intersect with next-generation platforms like the metaverse. In the following sections, we delve into:

- Fundamental concepts of quantum computing.
- The architecture of metaverse communications and where quantum fits in.
- Quantum communication technologies and cryptographic methods relevant to the metaverse.
- Quantum-based identity verification and privacy solutions for virtual worlds.
- The integration of quantum techniques with blockchain in metaverse applications.
- The emerging quantum network infrastructure (quantum internet) could support a global metaverse.
- Key challenges, open research issues, and future directions towards a quantum-enabled metaverse.

By exploring each of these topics in detail, we aim to show how quantum communication in the metaverse can transform it into a more secure, efficient, and innovative environment for all users.

1.1. Fundamentals of Quantum Computing

To understand the role of quantum communication in the metaverse, one must first comprehend the fundamentals of quantum computing. Quantum computers operate on principles of quantum mechanics that are fundamentally different from those of classical computing. Below, we present key concepts and compare them to their classical equivalents in Table 1.

a. Qubits vs. Classical Bits

Classical computers use bits (0 or 1) as the basic units of information. In contrast, quantum computers use quantum bits or qubits (see Figure 2), which can exist in a superposition of the |0⟩|0\rangle|0⟩ and |1⟩|1\rangle|1⟩ states simultaneously (Rietsche et al. (2022). A normalized pure quantum state of a single qubit is expressed in Equation 1.

Equation 1. Normalized pure state of a single qubit.

$$|\psi\rangle=\alpha|0\rangle+\beta|1\rangle,\alpha,\beta\in C,|\alpha|2+|\beta|2 =1$$

where α\alphaα and β\betaβ are complex probability amplitudes, and the normalization condition ensures that the total probability equals one with complex amplitudes α and β such that |α|^2 + |β|^2 = 1. Visually, a qubit's state can be represented on the Bloch sphere, a unit sphere where the poles correspond to the basis states |0⟩ and |1⟩. The Bloch sphere highlights that unlike a bit confined to {0,1}, a qubit can be in any quantum superposition of those states (points on the sphere's surface). Figure 2 illustrates the difference: a classical bit vs. a qubit on the Bloch sphere.

Figure 2. Representation of a classical bit versus a qubit on the Bloch sphere, illustrating superposition and measurement probabilities

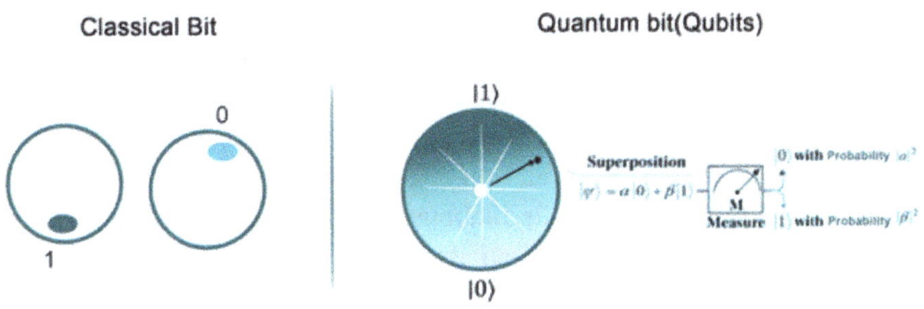

Gyongyosi & Imre, (2019) describes the principle of superposition means a qubit can hold a combination of 0 and 1 until measured. This property enables quantum computers to process a vast number of possibilities in parallel. A famous analogy is Schrödinger's cat: a thought experiment in which a cat in a box can be considered simultaneously alive and dead (a superposed state) until an observation is made. Similarly, a qubit remains in a superposition of outcomes until measurement forces it into either 0 or 1, with probabilities given by the amplitudes α and β.

b. Entanglement

Another key principle is quantum entanglement, a phenomenon where the quantum states of two or more qubits become correlated so that measuring one instantly influences the state of the other, regardless of the distance between them. Entangled qubits share a single quantum state and cannot be described separately as shown in Figure 3.

Figure 3. Entangled photon generation and detection setup

This non-classical correlation has no analogy in classical computing. Entanglement is crucial for advanced quantum communication protocols (like teleportation and certain QKD schemes) and for quantum computers to perform certain algorithms with exponential speedups (Rietsche et al.2022).

For example, in an entangled pair of qubits (say in the singlet state), if one qubit is measured to be 0, the other is immediately found to be 1, and vice versa – outcomes are perfectly anti-correlated. Entanglement underpins the concept of a future quantum internet and enables distributed quantum computing.

Table 1. Comparison between classical bits and qubits

Aspect	Classical Bits	Qubits
Value Representation	Can represent either 0 or 1.	Can represent 0, 1, or any quantum superposition of 0 and 1.
State	A bit is always in one of two definite states: 0 or 1.	A qubit can exist in a superposition of states, meaning it can be in multiple states simultaneously.
Superposition	No superposition: a bit can only be in one state at a time.	A qubit can exist in a superposition of states, allowing for multiple possibilities simultaneously.
Measurement	A bit is measured and returns either 0 or 1 with certainty.	A qubit, when measured, collapses to either 0 or 1, but until measured, it exists in a probabilistic superposition of both.
Entanglement	Bits are independent and do not exhibit entanglement.	Qubits can be entangled, meaning the state of one qubit is directly correlated with the state of another, even at a distance.
Operations	Operations are deterministic, based on classical logic gates (AND, OR, NOT, etc.).	Operations on qubits are probabilistic and involve quantum gates (e.g., Hadamard, CNOT, etc.) that manipulate their quantum state.

continued on following page

Table 1. Continued

Aspect	Classical Bits	Qubits
Parallelism	Classical bits process information sequentially.	Qubits enable quantum parallelism, allowing quantum computers to process a vast amount of data simultaneously due to superposition.
Storage	Classical bits can store one piece of information per bit.	A qubit can store a vast amount of information due to the superposition of states.

c. Quantum Parallelism and Algorithms

Thanks to superposition and entanglement, a quantum computer with n qubits can represent 2^n states simultaneously. This exponential state space allows for quantum parallelism, where certain computations are done on multiple inputs at once.

Not all problems see a speedup, but some famous quantum algorithms demonstrate dramatic advantages. Shor's Algorithm Factors large integers exponentially faster than classical algorithms, threatening RSA and ECC encryption by enabling quick key recovery. Grover's Algorithm Speeds up unstructured search with O(N) O(\sqrt{N}) O(N) complexity, effectively halving symmetric key strength, impacting AES and other key-based systems. Quantum Fourier Transform (QFT) performs Fourier analysis exponentially faster, serving as the core of Shor's and other quantum algorithms, making some classical transforms obsolete. Deutsch-Jozsa Algorithm determines if a function is constant or balanced in a single quantum step, showcasing extreme speedups for specific problems over classical checks. Quantum Phase Estimation (QPE) Efficiently finds eigenvalues of unitary operators, revolutionizing cryptography, chemistry simulations, and optimization tasks beyond classical reach. HHL Algorithm Solves certain linear systems exponentially faster, threatening classical simulation, optimisation, and machine learning methods as shown in Table 2.

These capabilities underscore why quantum computing's rise is a double-edged sword: it offers powerful tools (e.g. for simulation, AI) but also endangers current encryption. The metaverse will rely on cryptography for secure communication, identity, and asset protection – hence the urgency to deploy quantum-resistant or quantum-based cryptography before quantum computers become potent enough to crack classical encryption (the Q-Day scenario) (Markidis, 2024).

Table 2. Comparison of Key Quantum Algorithms and Their Security Threats to Classical Computing.

Quantum Algorithm	Classical Counterpart	Problem Solved	Quantum Advantage	Threat to Classical Algorithms
Shor's Algorithm	Classical factoring algorithms (e.g., RSA cryptanalysis using General Number Field Sieve)	Integer factorization	Polynomial time O((log N)^3) vs. exponential time O(e^{(1.9)(log N)^{1/3}(log log N)^{2/3}})	It can break widely used public-key cryptography (RSA, ECC) by factoring large numbers efficiently.
Grover's Algorithm	Classical brute-force search	Unstructured search	O(√N) vs. O(N)	Reduces security level of symmetric-key cryptography by halving effective key length (e.g., 128-bit AES → 64-bit security).
Quantum Fourier Transform (QFT)	Discrete Fourier Transform (DFT)	Frequency domain analysis	O(n^2) vs. O(n 2^n) for large datasets	Enables exponential speedups in algorithms like Shor's, making specific classical algorithms obsolete.
Deutsch–Jozsa Algorithm	Deterministic or randomized classical checking	Determine if a function is constant or balanced	1 quantum evaluation vs. 2^{n-1}+1 classical evaluations	Demonstrates exponential speedup, showing that some problems are trivial for quantum but hard for classical.
Quantum Phase Estimation (QPE)	Eigenvalue estimation via iterative methods	Estimating eigenvalues of unitary operators	Polynomial-time estimation vs. exponential time	Powers algorithms for quantum chemistry and cryptography, outperforming classical numerical methods.
HHL Algorithm	Classical matrix inversion algorithms	Solving linear systems	Exponential speedup for sparse systems (O(log N) vs. O(N^3))	Could disrupt classical simulation, optimisation, and machine learning methods., and machine learning methods.

d. Noise and Quantum Error Correction

Keçeci (2025) states that Present-day quantum computers are mostly NISQ (Noisy Intermediate-Scale Quantum) devices, meaning they have dozens to a few hundred error-prone qubits. Qubits are sensitive to decoherence (loss of quantum state information due to environmental noise) and gate errors. Quantum error correction is an active field aiming to stabilize quantum computations via redundancy and clever encoding of qubit states across many physical qubits (Jayashankar & Mandayam, 2023). A fault-tolerant quantum computer (FTQC) is the eventual goal – one that can operate reliably at scale. Until then, hardware limitations constrain the size of quantum computations we can run. For metaverse applications, this means near-term quantum benefits might come from quantum communication (which can be done with single photons and is relatively mature) and hybrid classical-quantum approaches, rather than full-scale quantum computing for all tasks.

2. METAVERSE COMMUNICATION ARCHITECTURE

A typical metaverse platform involves a complex architecture of client devices, network infrastructure, and servers/cloud services. Communication in the metaverse must be real-time, high-bandwidth, and resilient, often requiring decentralized operation (Ali et al. 2023). Here we describe the metaverse communication architecture in Figure 4 and identify points where quantum technologies can integrate:

Figure 4. Metaverse Communication Architecture

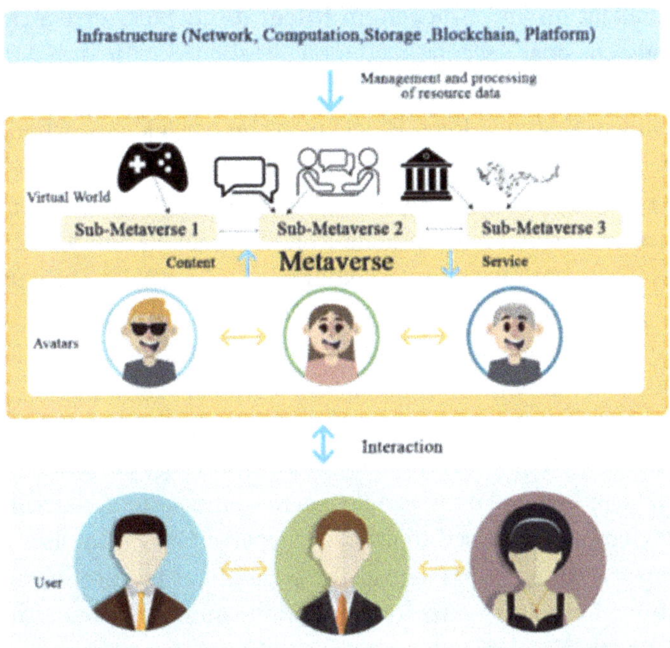

- **User Devices and Interface Layer:** This includes VR/AR headsets, haptic devices, PCs, or even future quantum personal devices. Users connect to the metaverse through these devices, which generate and consume immersive data (graphics, audio, sensor streams). In today's architecture, a user's device communicates over the classical internet to metaverse servers. In a quantum-enhanced future, a user might connect via a quantum-enabled device or through a local quantum network for certain functions. For example, one could imagine a quantum personal computer or a quantum co-processor that handles secure communications or complex computations locally before interfacing with the broader metaverse.

- **Network Layer (Connectivity):** The metaverse requires a network that supports seamless interactions without lag. This means low-latency data transfer and high throughput. The current approach leverages high-speed Fiber optics, 5G/6G wireless, edge computing, and content delivery networks. A future Quantum Internet could augment this layer by providing quantum communication channels in parallel to classical channels. In a hybrid quantum-classical network, the classical channel carries bulk data (video, game state updates, etc.) while a quantum channel carries quantum information (entangled photons or QKD qubits) for security or synchronization purposes.
- **Decentralization and Blockchain Integration:** Metaverse architectures increasingly consider decentralized models (aligned with Web 3.0 principles). Instead of all data going through centralized servers, peer-to-peer and edge networks can share the load. Blockchain can provide a backbone for ownership, transactions, and identity in a decentralized metaverse. Network architecture thus may include distributed ledger nodes. Quantum communication can enhance this by securing node-to-node channels and protecting consensus messaging with quantum cryptography, which we discuss in a later section. Moreover, decentralization means less reliance on a single authority, aligning with the quantum network vision of distributed trust (since quantum protocols inherently involve direct exchanges between peers).
- **Edge and Cloud Computing Layer:** To reduce latency, metaverse systems use edge computing – servers close to the user (e.g., in cellular base stations or local data centres) that handle some computation/rendering. Quantum edge devices are proposed to offload intensive tasks from user devices. For example, a quantum computer at the edge could perform complex physics simulations for an AR game or run optimization for many avatars' interactions faster than a classical server could. Cloud data centres could also host large quantum processors in the future to handle metaverse-wide computations. The architecture might allow dynamic offloading: certain tasks go to classical GPUs/CPUs, others to a quantum processing unit (QPU) if available, achieving a hybrid computing environment optimized for performance and cost (Keçeci, 2025).

- **Metaverse Servers and Platforms:** The core logic managing virtual world states, running physics engines, storing user data, etc. – typically runs on centralized or distributed servers. In a quantum- For reasons of integrated design, these servers might apply quantum algorithms to perform better on specific tasks (such as pathfinding via quantum search, or AI behaviour generation via quantum machine learning). Should the communications be encrypted with the help of QKD, they would also be closely intertwined with the quantum key management services as well. Quantum random number generators may be interfaced into the servers to offer higher security (providing actual random seeds used in simulations or cryptographic schemes).
- **Communication Protocols**: On protocol level, communication can bound state synchronization, events, real-time streaming (in scenario of VR). They run on top of regular internet protocols (TCP/UDP, WebRTC, etc.) now. A quantum-sensitive architecture can also bring through new protocols / layers, e.g. a quantum secure session layer, which negotiates keys using QKD before switching to the classical channels to transfer the bulk data. There may also be semantic communication standards tuned to the metaverse (sending the meaning rather than raw data) and quantum tech may help to compress or secure these in a new way (Ali *et, al.,* 2023).

To conclude, it is possible to assume that the metaverse communication architecture is a multi-layered system of the following layers: devices-network-edge/cloud-servers, complemented by blockchain to introduce decentralization. Quantum communication technologies may fit into such architecture by offering secure key exchange channels, additional quantum processing at edge/cloud, and perhaps even an all-new quantum network supplementary to the existing classical one. One practical scenario is having a user connect to a virtual world on a hybrid connection: his/her headset communicates routinely via the internet, but also uses entangled photons delivered by a satellite connection to key-establish with the game server. The outcome is a safer and more effective session, that can not be eavesdropped upon because of quantum physics.

Crucially, as metaverse standards are still evolving, now is the time to design quantum compatibility into the architecture. Retroactively fitting quantum security into an established global VR network would be far harder than planning for a quantum-ready infrastructure from the start

3. QUANTUM COMMUNICATION TECHNOLOGIES

Quantum communication technologies leverage quantum states (typically of photons) to transmit information in ways impossible to eavesdrop on without detection. In the context of the metaverse, these technologies can secure data streams, synchronize distant servers, and more. The most mature quantum communication tech today is Quantum Key Distribution (QKD), but other notable developments include quantum teleportation and quantum repeaters for long-range networks, and emerging methods like Quantum Secure Direct Communication. Below, we discuss the key quantum communication tools:

a) Quantum Key Distribution (QKD)

Cao et al. (2022) QKD is a method to generate and share encryption keys between two parties using quantum signals, with security guaranteed by quantum physics. The goal of QKD is not to send the actual message data quantumly, but to produce a secret key known only to the two endpoints as the key sharing as shown in Figure 5. Once the key is established, the users can encrypt their metaverse data (chat messages, transactions, etc.) using classical algorithms (e.g. AES), but with the peace of mind that the key was generated securely.

Figure 5. Quantum key distribution process with photon polarization, eavesdropping detection, and shared key generation between Alice and Bob.

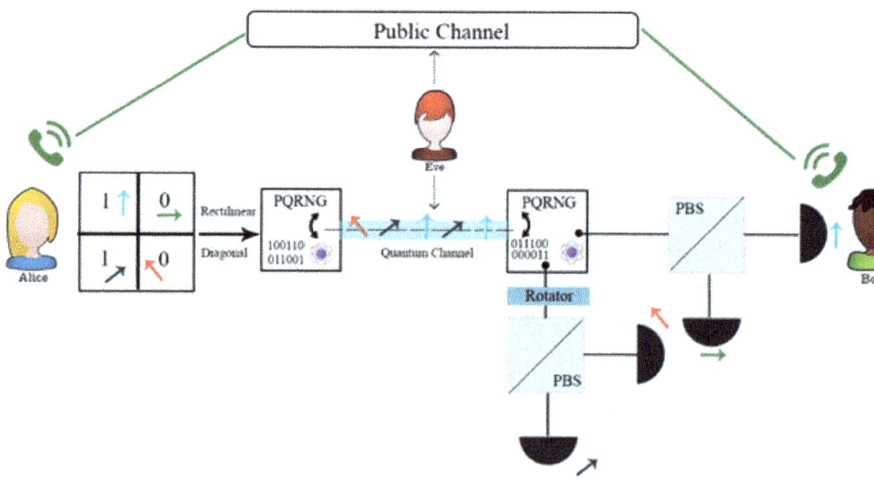

The main advantage of QKD is its ability to detect eavesdropping. Quantum signals will be disturbed by any third-party measurement because, according to the no-cloning theorem, observing quantum signals without altering them is impossible. Such disturbances can be identified by legitimate users. If eavesdropping exceeds a certain threshold, the protocol is immediately aborted, and a compromised key is never used. QKD protocols are generally classified into two main categories, as shown in Table 3 comparison: discrete-variable QKD (DV-QKD), which uses single photons and their polarization or phase (such as the well-known BB84 protocol), and continuous-variable QKD (CV-QKD), which involves quantum light states characterised by continuous parameters like the amplitudes of electromagnetic fields.

Compared to CV-QKD, DV-QKD has demonstrated the ability to operate over long distances (beyond 1,200 km using satellite links), and may, although the DV hardware needed is more costly, perform better in terms of compatibility with existing networks (e.g., employing homodyne detection and even functioning in the THz spectrum for wireless QKD over short distances). Both approaches could have applications within the metaverse: for example, satellite DV-QKD might be used to connect remote data centres or distant users, while CV-QKD over fibre or 6G networks could be utilised to secure short-range communications (such as between an AR headset and an edge server). It is important to clarify that QKD generates random secret bits (keys); it does not transmit the actual voice or video content of a metaverse call. In practice, a QKD system is deployed alongside classical communication lines. The large volumes of data and some of the coordination are transmitted via the classical channel, while the quantum channel (a dedicated fibre or free-space optical link) is solely used to send quantum states to generate keys (Kumar & Mondal, 2025).

It should be made clear that QKD does not transmit the actual voice or video signals of a metaverse session; instead, it generates random secret bits (keys). In practice, a QKD system is operated alongside classical communication channels. The bulk of the data, along with some coordination, is transmitted via the classical channel, while only a quantum state of a key is sent through the quantum channel (e.g., dedicated fibre or free-space optical link). Once a shared secret key is generated, users typically use it to encrypt information, often employing the One-Time Pad, which makes the code impossible to break as long as the key remains secret. The benefit of this synergy is that an attacker would need to breach both the quantum channel (which is generally only practical with detection) and the classical encryption (which can be secure in an information-theoretic sense, assuming OTP).

Table 3. Comparative analysis of major quantum key distribution (QKD) protocols.

Protocol	Principle	Quantum Properties Used	Key Exchange Process	Security Basis	Advantages	Limitations	Applications
BB84 (Bennett & Brassard)	Encodes bits in randomly chosen bases (rectilinear/ diagonal)	Superposition, Heisenberg uncertainty	Alice sends qubits in random bases; Bob measures; basis reconciliation & error correction	Eavesdropping causes detectable errors	Simple, proven security, easy to implement	Limited distance (~100–200 km), needs trusted relays for long distances	Secure fibre links, point-to-point encryption
E91 (Ekert)	Uses entangled photon pairs	Entanglement, Bell's theorem	Alice & Bob measure entangled photons in different bases; correlations verify security	Violation of Bell's inequalities	Strong theoretical security, no need for trust in source	Requires stable entanglement distribution	Quantum networks, government communications
B92 (Bennett)	Uses only two non-orthogonal states	Superposition, quantum no-cloning	Alice sends qubits in two states: Bob measures with chosen basis	No-cloning theorem	Simpler than BB84, fewer states	Less efficient, more error-prone	Low-complexity QKD devices
SARG04	Modified BB84 to resist photon number splitting attacks	Superposition, decoy states	Alice encodes using BB84 states but different sifting rules	Photon number splitting resistance	Better against multi-photon attacks	More complex post-processing	Commercial QKD with weak coherent pulses
DPS-QKD (Differential Phase Shift)	Encode key in the relative phase of consecutive pulses	Phase coherence	Receiver measures the phase difference between pulses	Interference & phase randomness	Resistant to certain attacks, high-speed	Sensitive to phase drift & dispersion	Long-distance QKD in fibre
CV-QKD (Continuous Variable)	Uses quadrature's of coherent states instead of discrete photons	Gaussian modulation, quantum uncertainty	Alice modulates amplitude/phase; Bob measures via homodyne/ heterodyne detection	Quantum uncertainty principle	Compatible with telecom components, high key rates	Requires complex error correction	Metropolitan QKD over standard fibre
MDI-QKD (Measurement-Device Independent)	Eliminate detector side-channel attacks	Bell state measurement, entanglement swapping	Both parties send states to an untrusted relay for Bell measurement	Device-independent security	Removes major attack vector	Requires stable interference from two sources	High-security commercial QKD

For the metaverse, a quantum network could function similarly to today's internet but would carry qubits. We might assign Quantum Local Area Networks (QLANs) within data centres or campuses, Quantum Metropolitan Area Networks (QMANs) for city-wide connections, and extend up to global networks. Several national initiatives (China, EU's EuroQCI, US DOE Quantum Internet Blueprint) are progressing to connect quantum devices via fibres and satellites. As these develop, the metaverse could utilise them to secure its backbone. In an ideal scenario, each metaverse server cluster could be quantum-entangled with others, ensuring that any communication or synchronization between them is inherently secure and managed at the quantum level.

b) Quantum Repeaters and Entangled Networks

Thanalakshmi et al. (2023) emphasize to cover large distances (beyond the ~100 km limit of QKD in Fiber due to photon loss), quantum repeaters are envisioned. These are devices that can extend quantum links by storing and re-transmitting entanglement, without measuring the quantum states (since measurement would collapse them). A chain of quantum repeater nodes could enable an entangled network spanning cities or continents – the foundation of a true Quantum Internet. Mantri, Li, and Brown (2025) state that an entanglement-based network, users share entangled qubit pairs; performing operations on these can achieve tasks like teleporting quantum states or generating keys with security against even quantum attacks).

Azuma et al. (2023) further emphasize entangled networks are more complex but enable advanced protocols. For example, distributed metaverse simulations might synchronize random number generators via entanglement correlations, or remote users might "teleport" their qubit states to a server for cloud quantum computing. The main challenges are that entanglement is fragile over distance (hence the need for repeaters and quantum error correction even in communications) and that quantum memory (to store qubits at intermediate nodes) is still an evolving technology. Environmental noise and attenuation make maintaining entanglement over long Fiber or free-space links difficult. Researchers are actively developing quantum repeater architectures using atomic ensembles, nitrogen-vacancy diamonds, etc., to eventually form a global quantum network.

For the metaverse, a quantum network could operate analogously to today's internet but carrying qubits. We might designate Quantum Local Area Networks (QLANs) for within data centres or campuses, Quantum Metropolitan Area Networks (QMANs) for city-wide links, and so on up to global scale. Several national projects (China, EU's EuroQCI, US DOE Quantum Internet Blueprint) are underway to connect quantum devices over fibres and satellites. As these mature, the metaverse could piggyback on them to secure its backbone. In a fully realized scenario, each metaverse server cluster could be quantum-entangled with others, ensuring that any communication or synchronization between them is intrinsically secure and coordinated at the quantum level.

c) Quantum Secure Direct Communication (QSDC)

Pan et al. (2024) discusses the evolution of QSDC, an emerging concept Quantum Secure Direct Communication, where the message itself is transmitted via quantum states (not just the key). In QKD, once the key is established, the actual message goes over a classical channel encrypted by that key. In QSDC, one encodes the message in quantum states such that it arrives securely without requiring a separate encryption step. Recently, a team in China proposed a Long-Distance Free-Space QSDC (LF-QSDC) protocol that allowed direct encrypted messaging without a prior key exchange, using entangled photons over long distances. This was suggested to protect Web 3.0 and metaverse communications from quantum attacks while aligning with decentralization (since it can operate without centralized key servers).

In practice, QSDC remains experimental, but it could mean that in the future, a metaverse client might send a quantum-encrypted message (such as a bank transfer or a vote in a virtual governance system) directly to the recipient. Even if intercepted, the eavesdropper would gain nothing (and could be detected). It removes the need for storing keys, which could be a vulnerability. The challenge is that QSDC protocols often require low noise, pair generation rates can be slow, and error correction is complex, especially in free space where atmospheric turbulence can disrupt photons. Nonetheless, the existence and testing of prototypes suggest that by the time the metaverse becomes widespread, QSDC might be a viable option for the most sensitive communications.

d) Other Quantum Communication Advances

Other technologies include Quantum Teleportation, which is a method to transfer a quantum state from one location to another using entanglement and a small amount of classical communication. While not a means of sending classical information faster (you still need a classical channel), teleportation is essential for connecting quantum processors in a network (so one could imagine teleporting qubits between quantum servers in the metaverse backbone). It has been demonstrated over distances of up to 1,400 km via satellites (Micius satellite experiments) (Labonté et al. 2024). Teleportation could allow, for example, one quantum avatar's state to be moved to another server seamlessly if they switch virtual worlds – though this is speculative and far-future.

Furthermore, Quantum Random Number Generators (QRNGs) deserve mention. They generate true random numbers from quantum processes. Many cryptographic tasks require randomness, and in the metaverse, features such as procedural generation of worlds or unpredictable avatar behaviours might benefit from true randomness. QRNG devices are already commercially available (often as USB devices or cloud services) and integrating them ensures no pattern or predictability (which is vital because pseudo-random numbers can be exploited if their algorithm is discovered).

In summary, quantum communication technologies centred on QKD (and its evolutions) provide the tools to make metaverse communications secure against both classical and quantum threats. They introduce new communication paradigms where any eavesdropping attempt is evident and where certain attacks become physically impossible. By investing in quantum communication infrastructure, metaverse developers can ensure that virtual experiences – whether a simple chat between friends' avatars or a complex financial transaction in a virtual marketplace – have security rooted in the laws of physics rather than just computational assumptions.

4. QUANTUM CRYPTOGRAPHY

While often used interchangeably with quantum communication, quantum cryptography is a broader term that includes any cryptographic scheme strengthened or enabled by quantum mechanics. QKD, discussed above, is one form of quantum cryptography (key establishment). Here we consider additional aspects: how cryptography needs to evolve in the quantum era, and what specific quantum cryptographic techniques can be applied to the metaverse.

1) Post-Quantum Cryptography vs. Quantum Cryptography

Dam et al. (2023) highlight key difference exists between post-quantum cryptography (PQC) and quantum cryptography. PQC involves new classical cryptographic algorithms (running on traditional computers) believed to be secure against quantum computer attacks. Examples include lattice-based cryptosystems, hash-based signatures, and others. These do not involve quantum phenomena; instead, they are mathematical schemes designed to withstand known quantum algorithms (such as Shor's and Grover's). Governments and standards organisations (like NIST and ETSI) are actively working on standardising PQC algorithms, preparing for the replacement of vulnerable schemes like RSA and ECC. PQC is especially relevant to the metaverse because it's a software solution that can be quickly deployed to secure data and blockchain systems from future quantum adversaries.

Ricci, Dobias, Malina, Hajny, and Jedlicka (2024) further emphasise on quantum cryptography that leverages quantum physics (like QKD, quantum signatures, etc.) to provide security. It often requires specialized hardware (single-photon sources, detectors, quantum channels). In an ideal scenario, both approaches complement each other: PQC can secure aspects of the metaverse where deploying quantum hardware is impractical, while quantum cryptography can secure critical links and high-value assets with ultimate security. For instance, a metaverse platform might use post-quantum digital signature algorithms to verify software updates or authenticate users (ensuring that even a quantum computer in the future couldn't forge identities) and use quantum key distribution to secure the most sensitive communication channels (like between data centres or for high-profile meetings). There is ongoing research into hybrid cryptographic protocols that combine PQC and quantum techniques for layered security.

2) Quantum-Resistant Authentication and Signatures

Authentication is crucial in the metaverse – users need to prove they are who their avatar claims to be, and systems need to verify the integrity of actions (like a transaction or a vote). Today this often relies on public-key cryptography (e.g., RSA/ECDSA signatures, which are vulnerable to quantum attacks). Transitioning to quantum-resistant authentication is thus a priority.

One approach is to adopt PQC-based signatures (like CRYSTALS-Di lithium or Falcon, which are lattice-based signature schemes selected by NIST for standardization). These can be implemented in the metaverse client and server software without needing new physics.

Another approach involves using quantum digital signatures (QDS). In QDS schemes, quantum states are employed to encode signatures that cannot be forged or repudiated. Some research has demonstrated protocols where multiple recipients can verify the origin of a message with information-theoretic security, using entangled photons or other quantum resources (Tuli et al., 2024b). For example, a quantum signature may involve sending a sequence of polarized photons that only the intended recipient can fully decipher, and any tampering would be apparent. The practicality of QDS is still limited compared to classical signatures, but they could serve niche roles in the metaverse for ultra-secure contracts or asset transfers (Thanalakshmi et al., 2023).

In general, multi-factor authentication in the metaverse could incorporate quantum elements. Imagine logging in not just with a password and 2FA code, but with a challenge-response where the server sends you a quantum state (via a QKD channel) that only your device (with the correct quantum key) can respond to correctly. This would negate phishing or replay attacks, because an attacker couldn't intercept or reuse the quantum challenge.

3) Quantum Cryptography for Privacy and Anonymity

Beyond authentication, cryptography in the metaverse must address privacy. Users may want to interact pseudonymously, proving certain rights or attributes without revealing their identity (e.g., proving you own a certain NFT or that you are an adult, without revealing who you are). Classical cryptographic constructs like Zero-Knowledge Proofs and Ring Signatures are one way to achieve this. Quantum cryptography might enhance them; for instance, quantum zero-knowledge proofs could leverage quantum information to provide assurance with less communication or fewer assumptions. There's theoretical work on quantum interactive proofs that could eventually translate to more efficient privacy protocols (Thalacker et al., 2021).

Another angle is anonymous quantum communication. Researchers have investigated protocols for sending messages where the sender and receiver can be anonymous to third parties (and even to each other to some degree) using quantum techniques. A metaverse might implement, say, an anonymous voting system for governance of a virtual community, where quantum cryptography ensures the votes are encrypted and tallied without any possibility of tracing them back to individual avatars.

4) Securing Blockchain with Quantum Techniques

Since blockchain is integral to many metaverse visions (for ownership of digital goods, currency, identity tokens, etc.), cryptography for blockchain in a quantum age is critical. We will discuss blockchain more in a dedicated section, but cryptographically speaking, two issues arise:

1. Current blockchains (Bitcoin, Ethereum, etc.) rely on elliptic curve signatures and hashing. Shor's algorithm could compromise ECDSA signatures, threatening wallet security; Grover's algorithm can brute-force hash functions more quickly (though quadratic speedup is manageable by increasing hash lengths).
2. The advent of quantum computing might enable entirely new blockchain paradigms (quantum blockchain) which incorporate quantum operations.

From a pure cryptography viewpoint, one should upgrade blockchains to post-quantum signature schemes. In fact, work is underway to propose PQC-based addresses. Also, hash-based signatures (which are quantum-safe) could be used for one-time signing of transactions (they have larger sizes, but for many metaverse uses that might be acceptable).

Quantum cryptography can also provide quantum randomness to blockchains (making certain lotteries or consensus steps truly unpredictable) and could enable quantum consensus mechanisms where, for example, entangled states are used in voting on the next block (some proposals exist using GHZ entangled states in a consensus algorithm[REMOVED HYPERLINK FIELD] (Gao et al. 2018).

Overall, quantum cryptography in the metaverse will likely manifest as a combination of:

- Deploying quantum-resistant algorithms for all critical functions now (to be safe against future quantum attacks).
- Gradually integrating quantum communication (like QKD) for high-security use cases.

- Exploring novel quantum cryptographic protocols (like QDS, quantum oblivious transfer, etc.) as they become feasible, to enhance privacy and trust.

This two-pronged approach ensures that the metaverse's security foundations remain strong both through the quantum revolution (with PQC as a stopgap) and beyond it (with native quantum cryptography for ultimate security) (Gupta, Wood, Engstrom, Pole, & Shrapnel, 2025).

5) Quantum Identity & Avatar Authentication

Yang et al. (2023) emphasises that Identity in the metaverse is represented by avatars – digital personas that user's control. Ensuring that an avatar truly belongs to a certain user (and not an imposter or AI) is crucial for trust and safety. Moreover, with potentially high-stakes interactions (business meetings, financial trades, educational credentials) happening via avatars, robust authentication is needed. Quantum techniques can fortify avatar authentication and identity management, making it extremely difficult for attackers to fake identities or steal credentials.

i. Challenges in Avatar Authentication

Today's metaverse or online game platforms typically rely on username/password logins, possibly augmented by two-factor authentication. Once logged in, an avatar can roam freely. However, several threats exist:

- Account Takeover: If credentials are stolen (via phishing, data breach, etc.), an attacker can impersonate the user's avatar, wreak havoc or steal virtual assets.
- Sybil Attacks: One person creating many fake accounts/avatars to manipulate outcomes (for example, swaying a vote in a virtual community).
- Identity Spoofing: Someone may try to mimic another user's avatar (if able to circumvent authentication) – imagine appearing as someone else to discredit them or commit fraud.
- Biometric Data Risks: Advanced metaverse devices may use biometrics (eye tracking, fingerprints, voice) for login or realism. This sensitive data, if intercepted, can be misused (Eltanbouly et al. 2025).

Traditional methods (strong passwords, 2FA, biometrics) help but have weaknesses. Quantum approaches offer some novel solutions:

6) Quantum-Assisted Multi-Factor Authentication

Tuli et al.(2024a) describes a conceptual secure metaverse authentication framework leveraging QKD is shown in research .In that scheme, whenever a user attempts to log in, the system establishes a QKD link between the user's device and the server to share a one-time pad key and uses that key to transmit the user's credentials or biometric data over the classical channel with information-theoretic security . Essentially, even if an attacker intercepts the login data packets, they cannot decrypt them without the QKD key, and any attempt to compromise the key would be noticed. This would protect login exchanges against eavesdropping or man-in-the-middle attacks by future quantum adversaries.

For example, suppose login involves scanning your fingerprint using an AR headset. Instead of sending the fingerprint data plainly (even if encrypted by traditional methods that could be broken later), the device and server perform a quick QKD session and then use the new quantum key to encrypt the fingerprint. The data remains secure both now and, in the future, (recording the ciphertext is pointless, as it cannot be decrypted without the key, which was never transmitted but only derived via quantum signals).

Furthermore, the existence of a QKD process can act as a second factor. An attacker who somehow steals your password would also need to have your quantum connection or device to complete the QKD handshake – an unlikely scenario. This links the authentication to physical hardware (quantum optics equipment in the device) in a way that's very difficult to spoof remotely.

7) Quantum Signatures for Avatar Actions

As avatars perform actions (signing documents, making transactions, etc.), quantum digital signatures (mentioned earlier) can be used to ensure non-repudiation and authenticity. A potential implementation: each user is issued a pair of quantum-safe keys or a small quantum token that can generate signatures. When an avatar "signs" an in-world contract, the system could employ a quantum proxy signature protocol where the avatar's device (proxy) signs on behalf of the user using quantum states. This might involve pre-shared entangled states with the metaverse server that ensure only the genuine user could have produced that signature string.

Research has proposed blockchain-assisted quantum signature schemes for the metaverses (Tuli et al. 2024a), which use a 7-qubit entangled state to sign a transaction and then record evidence on a blockchain. In these schemes, forging a signature is practically impossible without the quantum state that only the real user possesses, and the blockchain provides public verifiability and traceability. Such developments indicate that in the future, whenever an avatar makes a binding action, a combination of blockchain and quantum cryptography could validate it beyond any doubt.

8) Avatar Traceability and Quantum Blockchain

One interesting concept is avatar traceability: ensuring that if an avatar behaves maliciously, it can be traced to the human or entity controlling it (while still preserving privacy in normal use). A delicate balance between anonymity and accountability is needed in the metaverse. A proposed solution involves blockchain and quantum tech: for instance, an authentication framework to guarantee traceability of avatars uses a blockchain with special signatures, where each login or movement by an avatar is immutably recorded. If quantum-secured, these records cannot be tampered with by even quantum computers. In the event of disputes or cybercrime, authorized parties could decrypt the relevant quantum-protected logs to reveal the culprit's identity (like unmasking the avatar).

A concrete approach from IEEE TIFS 2023 detailed a secure login and location access control system for metaverse spaces using a quantum-blockchain network. In this, multiple authorities share some quantum-secret information and utilise a Delegated Proof-of-Stake consensus to verify new identity blocks. Users must register by providing credentials encrypted with keys transmitted via quantum channels and divided among several authorities (ensuring no single authority can compromise the identity). Only when consensus is achieved (enough authorities approve) is the avatar permitted entry, and a block is added linking the user to that avatar session. This method distributes and strengthens identities through quantum encryption. If an avatar behaves badly, the blockchain record can be examined (with proper authorisation) to identify the user behind it. The utilisation of quantum channels in registration and authentication prevents an attacker from stealing or forging credentials during transfer.

9) Protecting Biometric and Personal Data

As mentioned, metaverse devices may use biometric data for realism and authentication (face scans for avatar expressions, voice, iris scans for login, etc.). This data is extremely sensitive – leaks could enable identity theft or unwanted surveillance. Quantum encryption ensures that when this data is in transit (say from your headset to a cloud server that applies your facial expression to your avatar), it is secured even against a future quantum adversary. Additionally, systems could employ quantum-secured storage: storing hashes of biometric templates on a blockchain protected by post-quantum hashes or encrypting personal data with keys derived from QKD that are regularly refreshed.

In a fully realized quantum-enabled metaverse, one could envision continuous authentication: as you interact, your device continuously sends proof of your liveliness and identity (like heartbeat, EEG, voice tone) encrypted via quantum keys, so the system knows in real-time that the real you is still present and in control, not some replay or AI. If someone tries a man-in-the-middle (somehow injecting commands as your avatar), they will fail the continuous quantum-auth challenge.

In summary, quantum identity and avatar authentication focus on making it practically impossible to impersonate a user or tamper with identity-related data:

- QKD ensures login credentials and biometric data exchanges are secure against interception.
- Quantum-safe signatures and blockchain provide integrity and traceability for avatar actions.
- Multi-authority schemes with quantum secrets prevent single points of failure in identity verification
- Any attempt to take over an avatar or fake its identity would be detectable and thwarted by quantum cryptographic checks.

For metaverse users, this means you can trust that the person you're interacting with is genuine (if the system says it's Alice's avatar, you know it's really Alice), and in turn, your own avatar is under your exclusive control with much less risk of hijacking. This layer of trust is vital as we begin engaging in serious business, education, and social activities within virtual worlds.

5. APPLICATION AREAS OF QUANTUM COMMUNICATION IN THE METAVERSE

Tightiz et al. (2024) observe that Quantum communication and computing could enhance numerous metaverse application domains. Here we highlight key areas where a quantum-enabled metaverse could bring significant benefits, along with examples of what becomes possible as shown in Figure 6.

Figure 6. Application Areas of Metaverse

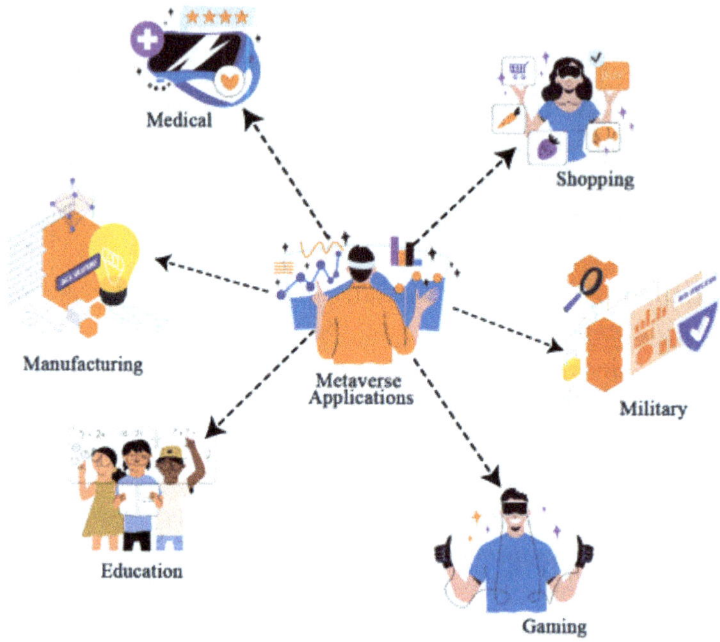

- **Healthcare and Telemedicine**: In a metaverse healthcare setting (e.g., virtual clinics, remote surgery simulations, or patient support groups in VR), privacy and data integrity are paramount. Quantum-secured communication can protect sensitive medical data being shared in real time (imagine a doctor in one city examining a patient's scans in an XR environment, with QKD ensuring the data link is secure). Moreover, quantum computing can power the medical simulations or drug molecule modelling within the metaverse. For instance, a pharmaceutical company might use a quantum computer to simulate drug interactions and then visualize the results in a metaverse lab. Quantum machine learning could also analyse patient data (genomes, MRI scans) within the metaverse to assist doctors with diagnoses, while preserving encryption in transit. The outcome: more accurate, secure, and collaborative healthcare solutions in virtual environments (Gupta et al.2025).

- **Industrial and Manufacturing:** The metaverse is used to create digital twins of factories and supply chains for planning and monitoring. Quantum optimization algorithms can greatly enhance these industrial metaverse applications by quickly solving complex scheduling, logistics, or design problems. For example, a car manufacturer might have a metaverse twin of its assembly line were engineers test adjustments. A quantum computer could rapidly find an optimal configuration that minimizes waste and energy usage, and feed that back into the digital twin. In terms of communication, factories could use quantum networks to secure telemetry data from sensors in a plant to its twin in the cloud, ensuring data integrity (important for safety). Quantum IoT security would stop attackers from spoofing or altering the data in the industrial metaverse. In short, quantum tech can make industrial simulations more powerful and secure, leading to efficiency gains in the real world.
- **Autonomous Vehicles (Transportation):** The metaverse can simulate traffic systems or provide VR environments for autonomous vehicle AI training. Quantum computing can handle the enormous state space of traffic optimization – a quantum algorithm might coordinate thousands of self-driving cars more efficiently than a classical one. In the metaverse, city planners could run quantum-powered simulations of traffic flow in a virtual city to design better routes or traffic light patterns. Communication-wise, vehicles need ultra-secure, low-latency comms to avoid accidents. Quantum communication can secure V2V (vehicle-to-vehicle) and V2X (vehicle-to-infrastructure) links against hacking. A practical example: distributing QKD keys to all cars in an area via quantum-enabled roadside units or satellites, to authenticate and encrypt their inter-vehicle communications, preventing malicious actors from sending false signals (a serious concern for smart traffic systems). So, quantum ensures trust in the data exchange in an AR/VR traffic control centre and in real vehicles.
- **Energy Systems:** The metaverse is being used to manage smart grids and energy trading in some forward-looking projects (Gupta, Wood, Engstrom, Pole, & Shrapnel, 2025). Quantum computing is very promising for optimising power grid distribution, managing loads, and improving battery technology tasks that might be visualised and controlled via a metaverse interface. Imagine a power grid operator using a metaverse control room with a digital twin of the grid: a quantum computer could crunch through load balancing calculations or predict demand spikes far better, and those insights are presented in VR for the operator to act. Also, energy transactions between prosumers (people with solar panels, etc.) might be handled through blockchain in the metaverse; integrating quantum cryptography here ensures those transactions are fraud-proof and future-proof (no one can later break the en-

cryption to alter records). Quantum sensors (not exactly communication, but related tech) could be deployed to monitor physical grid parameters with extreme precision and feed data to the metaverse – providing early warning of issues. All data from these sensors can be sent via quantum-secured channels to maintain grid security, which is a national security concern.

- **Military and Defence:** Defence organizations are exploring the metaverse for training, simulations, and mission planning. Quantum communication is of high interest to military for secure communications (quantum-secure networks cannot be eavesdropped on, which is vital for covert operations or command-and-control). In a defence metaverse scenario – say a virtual war game or a digital twin of a battlefield – secure and authenticated communications and orders in the simulation could be done with quantum key distribution among participants. Also, quantum computing can be used to simulate complex scenarios (like cryptanalysis of an adversary's code within the simulation or optimizing logistics for troop deployment). A concrete example: a NATO exercise in a virtual environment might use quantum-encrypted links between different force simulators (air, land, sea) to prevent any spying on their coordination (Krelina, 2021). The traceability feature of quantum-blockchain identity could also prevent adversaries from infiltrating the simulation as fake avatars. Additionally, quantum-enhanced sensors and navigation (e.g., quantum gyroscopes) could feed into the metaverse, providing ultra-accurate positioning for training scenarios. Defence is an area where quantum and metaverse synergy can be game-changing, but also where adoption might be carefully guarded.
- **Finance and Virtual Economy:** The metaverse includes virtual economies – people owning, trading, and selling digital goods or currencies (like NFTs, game items, crypto). Financial transactions require strong security. Quantum-secured channels can protect high-value transactions from man-in-the-middle attacks. If a virtual bank exists in the metaverse, it could communicate with clients via QKD to ensure the privacy of banking details. Quantum random numbers could be used for truly fair gambling in a virtual casino (ensuring unpredictability). Moreover, large financial institutions are looking at quantum computing for portfolio optimization and risk analysis. They could integrate those quantum-calculated results into a metaverse trading floor where traders visualize complex risk landscapes in VR. Thus, quantum computing provides the heavy analytics, and the metaverse provides the intuitive interface to act on it. Quantum-safe blockchain will be vital here too (so that crypto-assets in the metaverse aren't at risk when quantum arrives) (Naik, Jain, & Tiwari, 2025).

- **Others:** Other sectors include Education (quantum computers could personalize learning paths in a metaverse classroom by quickly analysing student performance data; quantum communications could secure student records), Entertainment (quantum-generated random events in games for unpredictability; QKD to prevent piracy or cheating by intercepting game data), Climate and Environment (using quantum simulations to model climate scenarios in a metaverse visualization, aiding understanding and policy decisions; secure sensor networks for climate data via quantum channels), and Smart Cities (digital twins of cities in the metaverse for planning – quantum optimization for utilities and traffic as discussed, quantum encryption for city data streams to prevent cyber-attacks).

Each of these application areas stands to gain either performance improvements (through faster computation or better optimization via quantum algorithms) or security/privacy enhancements (through unbreakable encryption and authentication via quantum communications). The quantum-enabled metaverse would thus be a step-change in what we can do in virtual environments, taking them beyond just immersive experiences into platforms for solving real-world problems securely and efficiently.

It's worth noting that many of these applications are prospective – active research is exploring feasibility. For example, a 2024 survey identified healthcare, industry, autonomous vehicles, energy, and defence among the primary fields where quantum computing can empower the metaverse (Xu et al. 2020). The ultimate impact will depend on progress in quantum hardware and the willingness of industries to invest in integrating these cutting-edge technologies into metaverse solutions.

6. TECHNICAL IMPLEMENTATIONS AND CASE STUDIES

After exploring concepts, this section highlights real-world implementations and prototypes that illustrate the fusion of quantum tech with communication systems, foreshadowing their application in the metaverse.

- **Quantum-Secured Communication Networks:** One landmark achievement is the satellite-assisted QKD network developed by the Chinese Academy of Sciences. Using the "Micius" quantum satellite and a network of ground stations and Fiber, researchers conducted the first-ever quantum-encrypted video call between continents (Beijing and Vienna). In this demonstration, quantum keys were distributed via satellite to both locations and then used to encrypt a 75-minute video conference in real time. This case proved that long-distance, high-bandwidth communication (like video streaming) can be secured with quantum technology outside of the laboratory. It effectively was an early *metaverse communication analogue* — a secure telepresence spanning the globe. Since then, several countries and companies have invested in quantum communication testbeds (e.g., Quantum Network in the U.S., EuroQCI in Europe). These networks are steadily increasing in length and reliability, moving toward a future quantum Internet that metaverse platforms could ride on for secure data transport.

- **Prototype Quantum Metaverse Systems:** On the quantum computing side, cloud-based quantum processors (offered by IBM, Google, etc.) have allowed researchers to experiment with integrating quantum algorithms into networking and blockchain. The MSSA framework described earlier is a prime example: its authors built a proof-of-concept quantum blockchain on IBM's Quantum Experience simulator, implementing three sequential blocks with quantum-generated proofs. This prototype validated the system's security (withstanding various simulated attacks) and measured performance metrics to show feasibility. Another case study is quantum-enhanced secure multi-user VR conferencing (conceptual prototypes where each user shares QKD keys with a server to join a fully encrypted VR room). While not publicly deployed yet, trials combining VR headsets with quantum key distribution devices have been reported in research labs, aiming to demonstrate that a group of users can share a holographic meeting where all communications (audio, video, and even haptic signals) are protected by quantum-derived encryption keys. These case studies, though early, illustrate the tangible progress in marrying quantum tech with metaverse-like applications
- **Industry and Standards Initiatives:** It's important to recognise that beyond academia, industry initiatives are advancing these technologies. Companies like Quantum Xchange and ID Quantique already offer commercial QKD services and quantum-safe network devices, which could be used to protect sensitive metaverse data streams. Standardisation organisations (ISO, ETSI) have started issuing specifications for quantum cryptography integration, and consortia are working on interoperability (ensuring, for example, that one metaverse's quantum identity token can be recognised on another platform). These efforts show that the fundamental components for quantum-safe, quantum-enabled communications are quickly developing and are on course to intersect with the expanding metaverse ecosystem.

7. QUANTUM PRIVACY IN IMMERSIVE SPACES

Sorrentino and López-Guzmán (2025) states that the metaverse promises richly immersive spaces – virtual or augmented reality environments where users socialize, work, and play. However, immersion can come at the cost of privacy: vast amounts of personal data (physical movements, biometrics, conversations) are continuously generated. Quantum communication technologies can play a pivotal role in preserving privacy in these immersive spaces by securing communications and enabling new privacy-preserving techniques.

a. End-to-End Encryption with Quantum Keys

In an immersive space like a VR conference or a virtual home, users may want assurance that their interactions are private. End-to-end encryption (E2EE) is the standard solution in messaging apps; in the metaverse context, it means that all voice chats, gestures, file transfers, etc., are encrypted such that only the intended recipients can decrypt. Quantum key distribution can strengthen E2EE by providing truly secret keys for encryption (Xu et al., 2020). With QKD, even if someone records the entire data stream of a VR meeting (which might include audio, video, haptics), they cannot decrypt it later because the key was delivered via quantum means and known only to the participants. This addresses a unique threat: in immersive spaces, an attacker might not be able to crack encryption now but could save the data hoping to break it when quantum computers arrive. QKD thwarts that by giving you keys that are safe from future quantum decryption attempts (since they were never exposed to interception without detection).

Consider a virtual reality telehealth session between a therapist and patient – extremely sensitive information is discussed. Using quantum keys to encrypt the session ensures confidentiality beyond what standard encryption can guarantee. If any network node along the way (or any third-party observing traffic) tries to eavesdrop, the QKD process would have flagged the intrusion and aborted the key exchange. Thus, the session would either not proceed or switch to a backup channel, but it would not silently compromise privacy.

b. Secure Metadata and Anonymity

Privacy isn't just about content; metadata (who you are, when and with whom you communicate) is also revealing. In immersive worlds, metadata includes your location in virtual space, your movement patterns, even where you look or what you touch (since VR systems track head and hand motions). Protecting such metadata is hard because the system needs some of it to function. However, quantum communication can help reduce metadata leakage. For example:

- Using quantum authentication, users can join a public virtual space anonymously (the system only verifies a quantum token as valid, but not the user's real identity). This can be achieved with a zero-knowledge proof scheme that is quantum-resistant or supported by quantum communication. The outcome is that you can demonstrate you're a legitimate participant (such as holding a paid ticket, being over 18, etc.) without revealing which user you are – thereby maintaining pseudonymity.
- Mix networks or rerouting can obscure who communicates with whom. Quantum networks might enable "teleportation" of qubits, aiding the implementation of mix nets at the quantum level. Alternatively, one could imagine a system where all user communications pass through a quantum-secured node that shuffles them around (like a quantum Tor network) to break profile linkage.

Quantum secure direct communication (QSDC) as mentioned, could allow sending a message without even exchanging keys in advance, which means fewer round trips and potentially less metadata (like you don't need a lengthy handshake that could be observed, you just send the encrypted payload directly).

Additionally, decentralization via blockchain for identity can allow users to control their identity data. If those blockchain transactions (for logging into a space or transferring an asset) are protected by post-quantum cryptography, users can trust that their pseudonymous identities won't be unwittingly linked or cracked by future quantum analysis.

c. Quantum Safe Spaces and Bubbles

We might see features like "quantum-secure private rooms" in the metaverse. For instance, two avatars could step into a virtual meeting room that is advertised as being quantum-encrypted. Under the hood, the environment sets up a QKD session for that room and ensures no other process can access the conversation. Even the platform administrators (if the system is properly designed) wouldn't be able to eavesdrop, because they too lack the keys. This is analogous to how some messaging apps now have encrypted rooms; the difference is the assurance that not even future tech can compromise it. Corporate metaverse applications would demand such features for discussing confidential plans.

Furthermore, recording prevention could be improved through quantum techniques. One possible idea is to apply quantum watermarking to streams so that any copy would carry a mark or be degraded if duplicated. Quantum watermarks might enable detection if someone attempts to record the output of their VR device (although this is difficult since one can always film the screen externally; however, integrated devices could enforce DRM-like protections enhanced by quantum keys).

d. Differential Privacy and Quantum Computing

Quantum computing also touches privacy from a data analysis perspective. When lots of user data is collected in the metaverse (for improving services or AI training), maintaining privacy requires techniques like differential privacy or homomorphic encryption. Quantum computers can be used to perform certain analyses on encrypted data (there's research into quantum homomorphic encryption). Or conversely, quantum algorithms might break naive anonymization, so it's crucial to adopt robust privacy frameworks. Ensuring that aggregated behavioural data from metaverse users cannot be traced back to individuals could be aided by quantum-resistant algorithms.

For example, a metaverse education platform could collect usage data to personalise teaching while protecting student identities. They might use a combination of classical differential privacy and quantum-secure multiparty computation, where sensitive calculations (such as computing an average performance metric) are performed on encrypted shares, possibly using quantum resources for efficiency. This is somewhat futuristic but illustrates the convergence of quantum computing and privacy-preserving data analysis.

e. Protecting Against New Surveillance Methods

As technology advances, there might be attempts to use quantum sensors or quantum-enhanced AI to glean information about users. For instance, could a sensitive quantum sensor pick up subtle electromagnetic emanations from VR devices to spy on usage? Or could a malicious quantum computer analyse encrypted traffic patterns to infer private info? The defence is to always assume that adversaries might have quantum capabilities and thus to design communication protocols with quantum adversary models in mind. By using information-theoretically secure schemes (like OTP with QKD, or quantum secure direct comm), you remove even a quantum computer's ability to glean information from intercepting communications. Also, by adding cover traffic or quantum noise, one could confound traffic analysis. Quantum communication can generate perfectly random padding bits to mix with real data, making it harder to analyse patterns.

In summary, quantum privacy in immersive spaces is about leveraging quantum-secure channels and computations so that:

- Conversations and interactions remain confidential, now and in the future.
- User identities and metadata have strong protection, enabling anonymous or pseudonymous participation without fear of unwarranted tracking.
- The system is resilient even against powerful adversaries with quantum computers or sensors.

Users should feel as safe having a private talk in the metaverse as they would in their living room. Achieving that level of trust will likely require quantum-grade security, given the scope of data and the looming threat of quantum computing to classical encryption. The good news is the core technologies (QKD, etc.) are maturing, and early prototypes have proven that quantum-secure communication is feasible on scales relevant to consumer applications (e.g., satellite QKD delivering keys globally. As these deploy, the metaverse can become not just a rich space but a protected one, ensuring users' digital lives remain private.

8. INTEGRATION WITH BLOCKCHAIN

Yang et al. (2023) assert that blockchain technology is expected to underpin many metaverse functions – from currency and asset ownership (think NFTs for virtual goods) to identity and access control (perhaps via self-sovereign identity tokens). However, blockchains face challenges in a quantum future: many current blockchain cryptographic primitives (like ECC signatures) are not quantum safe. Conversely, quantum tech also offers opportunities to make blockchains more secure and even more functional. In this section, we explore how quantum communication and computing integrate with blockchain in the metaverse context:

i. Quantum Threats to Blockchain

Blockchains like Bitcoin and Ethereum rely on cryptographic algorithms (ECDSA signatures, SHA-256 hashing). A sufficiently powerful quantum computer running Shor's algorithm could break ECDSA, allowing an attacker to forge transactions or steal funds by deriving private keys from public keys. This is a serious long-term threat: for example, if an avatar's wallet uses a classical public key, a quantum attacker might hijack all their assets. Additionally, Grover's algorithm could make mining (which relies on hash puzzles) easier, potentially upsetting consensus mechanisms by giving quantum miners an edge.

The metaverse, with potentially vast in-world economies, must address this by moving to quantum-resistant blockchain schemes. This is part of the broader category of post-quantum blockchain (Rietsche, Dremel, Bosch, Steinacker, Meckel, & Leimeister, 2022). Efforts are already underway to:

- Use post-quantum signature schemes (lattice-based, hash-based, etc.) for transaction signing.
- Increase hash sizes or use quantum-resistant hash functions.

Some projects have launched blockchains that implement PQC for wallets, and standards will likely develop. Metaverse platforms can either adopt these standards or upgrade their own systems. For example, a metaverse coin could switch to a signature scheme like Di lithium (from the CRYSTALS suite) to protect user accounts against quantum attacks.

In addition, quantum storage threats: one might worry that an attacker could record the entire blockchain data and if any encryption is used (some blockchains encrypt transaction details for privacy, e.g., Zcash or others), they could decrypt it later. Ensuring any encryption on blockchain (like for privacy coins or layer-2 solutions) is quantum-safe is vital.

ii. Quantum-Enabled Blockchain Concepts

Beyond just defence, there's active research into quantum blockchain – leveraging quantum principles in how a blockchain operates. Some ideas include:

- **Quantum Randomness for Consensus:** Blockchains often require randomness (for proof-of-stake lotteries, leader elections, etc.). Quantum random number generators can produce genuinely unpredictable numbers, reducing susceptibility to manipulation. Some consensus protocols may incorporate quantum-generated beacons to select validators in an unbiased manner.
- **Quantum Consensus Algorithms:** There are proposals (like Rajan et al. 2019 and Gao et al. 2020) where entanglement is used to have nodes reach consensus faster or more securely. For example, a Quantum Delegated Proof of Stake (QDPoS) has been conceptualized, where GHZ entangled states are shared among delegates to perform a kind of coin-flip that selects the next block producer, making it tamper-evident (Zakarneh, Annamalai, Alquqa, Mohamed, & Al Salhi, 2024). The idea is that any cheating in the consensus (like trying to bias the selection) would be detectable due to the properties of the entangled state.
- **Quantum Blockchains for Authentication:** The Scientific Reports 2024 article by Tuli et al. demonstrated a quantum blockchain-based authentication for metaverse spaces. In their framework (MSSA: Multiparty Space Sharing

and Authentication), each block of the blockchain contains information about user access requests, and quantum methods (quantum secret sharing and coin flipping) are used to validate these in a distributed way. Essentially, the blockchain becomes not just a ledger of transactions, but a ledger of access events, secured by quantum encryption and consensus. This ensures tamper-proof logs of who entered which space and when, solving traceability with privacy (since only hashes or encrypted info is on-chain).

- **Quantum Digital Signatures on Blockchain:** To secure transactions, one could use quantum digital signatures that are verified via quantum states. One challenge is that blockchain nodes are classical computers distributed globally – introducing quantum operations is non-trivial. But a hybrid approach might be possible where only certain nodes (say a few trusted validation nodes or oracles) have quantum capabilities and assist in verifying quantum signatures, writing confirmed results to the chain for others. Over time, as quantum networks grow, we might even see fully quantum blockchains where both data and consensus are quantum (though that is far out).

iii. Post-Quantum and Hybrid Solutions in Metaverse

A practical near-term approach for metaverse developers is a hybrid blockchain strategy:

- Immediately adopt post-quantum cryptography for wallets, identities, and asset custody. This might mean offering users new address formats with PQC keys and phasing out old ones (with notifications to users to migrate funds).
- Utilise quantum communication for vital blockchain network connections. For instance, if the metaverse operates its own blockchain nodes across data centres, connect these data centres with QKD to prevent any man-in-the-middle attack that could partition the network or inject false data. This maintains the integrity and consistency of the distributed ledger.
- Leverage quantum random beacons. There are services (like NIST's quantum random beacon project) that provide certified random bits. A metaverse blockchain could use these to seed smart contract operations or in-game procedural generation, providing fairness.
- Plan for future quantum software updates: e.g., the system might detect if a node has a quantum accelerator and then utilises it for certain tasks like faster cryptographic verification or running quantum-safe hashing if it proves to be beneficial.

iv. NFTs and Asset Security

Non-Fungible Tokens (NFTs) represent unique items (art, virtual real estate) in the metaverse. They often live on blockchains. Quantum integration ensures these remain secure and authentic. For instance, an NFT might include a quantum-generated fingerprint (some extra metadata created by a quantum process) to guarantee uniqueness in a way that's impossible to counterfeit. If someone tried to duplicate the token data and create a fake NFT, the lack of the genuine quantum fingerprint (which could be verified through a network of quantum oracles) would expose the fraud.

Additionally, trading of NFTs could use quantum-secured channels, because high-value items might attract hackers. Imagine an auction of a famous piece of metaverse art: bidders could connect via QKD to the auction house server to place bids privately (preventing spies from gleaning their strategy by intercepting communications), and the final transfer of ownership recorded on a PQC/quantum-backed blockchain so it can't be altered.

v. Bridging Real and Virtual with Quantum Blockchain

One particularly intriguing notion from Tuli et al. is bridging the real-world and the metaverse via quantum blockchain (Xu et al. 2020). This could refer to linking physical credentials to virtual ones. For example, a university degree could be a token on a blockchain; quantum verification might tie that token to a real person via biometric quantum-secure ID. The blockchain, being tamper-proof and transparent, acts as the bridge, while quantum tech ensures the link (person <-> token) is unforgeable. In the metaverse, this could allow easy verification of claims (like "I am a certified doctor" or "I purchased this physical concert ticket, so give my avatar access to the virtual concert") using a combination of blockchain records and quantum-proof authentication of the user.

In conclusion, integration with blockchain means:

- Securing blockchain: making the underlying ledgers and transactions safe from quantum attacks by moving to quantum-resistant cryptography.
- Using blockchain + quantum together: harnessing the immutability of blockchain and the security of quantum to provide new features (like advanced authentication, randomization, and trust less operations) in the metaverse.
- Quantum-enabled blockchain can be a backbone for a decentralized metaverse that is resilient to both classical and quantum threats. As one reference put it, the development of post-quantum blockchain splits into quantum-resistant (protecting against quantum) and quantum-enabled (using quantum to improve blockchain) approaches. Both are important for the metaverse.

The path forward likely involves gradually introducing these changes: first ensure quantum resistance (so the metaverse doesn't collapse when quantum computers arrive), then explore quantum advantage (to make it better than ever with faster consensus, etc.). Early experiments, like the one implementing QKD in a blockchain setting for metaverse login, show this is feasible. The role of quantum blockchain is essentially to be the trust glue between many components of the metaverse – identities, transactions, assets – in a future-proof way.

9. QUANTUM NETWORK INFRASTRUCTURE

To support all the quantum-enhanced capabilities discussed, we need a Quantum Network Infrastructure interwoven with the classical internet. This emerging "Quantum Internet" would consist of nodes (quantum processors, QKD stations, etc.) connected by quantum channels (Fiber, free-space laser, or satellite links) that carry qubits or entangled photon pairs. Here's how such infrastructure is shaping up and how it would underpin a quantum metaverse:

1. Quantum Internet Basics

Yang *et al.* (2023) describe the quantum internet (QI) is envisioned as a parallel network where information is transmitted in quantum form, enabling tasks like ultra-secure communication, distributed quantum computing, and precision time-synchronization beyond classical limits. It doesn't replace the classical internet but works alongside it (often requiring classical channels for coordination). Key elements include:

- Quantum Nodes: could be quantum computers, quantum sensors, or special devices called quantum repeaters that store and forward qubits without reading them.
- Quantum Links: typically, optical Fibers for ground connections and satellites for long distance (since photons can travel in space without losing coherence over thousands of km). Ground stations (GS) connect to satellites to uplink or downlink quantum signals.
- Quantum Protocols: e.g., QKD protocols, entanglement swapping (to extend distance by linking entangled segments), teleportation protocols, etc., which form the "network stack" of QI.

In the context of metaverse:

- Local quantum networks might connect user devices to nearby quantum servers (e.g., a home quantum router providing QKD keys to all your devices).
- Metro-scale quantum networks can link base stations or data centres in a city for secure data sync (imagine all AR/VR servers in London share entanglement for coordinated rendering or secure content distribution).
- Long-haul quantum backbones would connect major hubs (like New York <-> Tokyo) via satellites and repeater chains, ensuring even global metaverse traffic can be quantum-encrypted end-to-end.

China has already demonstrated a 2,000-km QKD fibre network (Beijing to Shanghai) combined with the Micius quantum satellite, achieving intercontinental quantum key exchange (China to Austria) (Yang et al., 2023). The EU is launching the EuroQCI initiative to build a quantum network across Europe. The US has a blueprint for a nationwide quantum internet, with testbeds achieving entanglement distribution in cities. These efforts suggest that by later 2020s or 2030s, a rudimentary quantum internet with regional coverage will exist.

2. Supporting Metaverse via Quantum Infrastructure

For the metaverse, the quantum network provides primarily security services (QKD, quantum authentication as discussed) and potentially distributed quantum computing. Consider a scenario:

- A VR user in Singapore wants to collaborate with a user in Paris on a sensitive design. The quantum internet can deliver them shared secret keys (via satellite or Fiber QKD) to set up an encrypted channel. Even if this involves multiple hops (local Fiber QKD networks in each city plus a satellite link between cities), the infrastructure manages that – much like today's internet routes packets, tomorrow's QI will route entanglement or keys.
- A network of quantum data centres could exist where intensive computations for the metaverse are carried out. If these quantum computers are entangled through QI, they can share qubits to tackle larger problems collaboratively (for example, global optimisation for a metaverse event schedule or complex physics simulations distributed across continents). This resembles cloud computing but at quantum speed; it necessitates high-fidelity entanglement between the quantum processors.

One challenge is that current quantum links are low bandwidth (in terms of qubits per second) compared to classical links in bits per second. This will improve with technology (better sources, parallelization, etc.), but initially the QI will likely be used sparingly for the most critical data (keys, authentication, maybe small qubit transfers), not for streaming bulk VR video (which will remain classical for the foreseeable future due to sheer volume).

3. Infrastructure Components

- **Quantum Repeaters**: Since direct transmission of photons suffers loss and decoherence, repeaters will extend range. They are like the "routers" or "signal boosters" of QI. A fully functional repeater performs entanglement swapping and purification between segments. The first generations are being developed (using quantum memories to temporarily hold qubits). As repeaters come online, we'll see a patchwork quantum network turn into a continuous one.
- **Satellite Constellations:** Much as SpaceX's Starlink is creating a mesh of internet satellites, one could imagine a constellation of quantum satellites providing global QKD coverage. Projects in China (Micius-2 satellite) and EU (SES/O3b plans) are exploring this. A metaverse company might even lease quantum satellite services to secure its global traffic.
- **Quantum Network Standards:** Organisations and researchers (like the Quantum Internet Research Group of the Internet Engineering Task Force, IETF) are working on protocols analogous to TCP/IP for quantum links (Chandre et al. (2024). This includes how to request entanglement, how to manage quantum connections, etc. Eventually, a metaverse application might simply call an API to get a quantum-secure channel, without needing to know the physics behind it. Standardization will ensure interoperability (so a quantum device from Company A can entangle with one from Company B, etc.).

From a timeline perspective: Right now, we have small networks (a few tens of km) and satellite demos. Over the next 5-10 years, national quantum communication networks will solidify (like Europe connecting major cities, US linking labs, China expanding its network). By the time metaverse applications have massive global penetration (say a decade or two), a quantum internet could be available in parallel. Thus, it's plausible that the metaverse could transition smoothly into using the QI as it becomes available.

4. Combining Classical and Quantum Networks

The quantum network infrastructure will be tightly integrated with classical infrastructure:

- A hybrid node will have both a classical router and a quantum repeater functionality. It might route classical packets and also facilitate quantum key exchanges for those sessions.
- Classical network operations (like session management) will often coordinate the quantum operations. For example, two nodes might use classical messaging to say, "let's establish entanglement now", then do the quantum exchange, then again classical to acknowledge receipt of keys.
- The overall reliability may rely on a classical fallback. If a quantum link is down (maybe weather disrupts a free-space link), the network could revert to using stored keys or PQC in the interim. This means early QI will augment classical networks rather than entirely replace aspects.

For metaverse providers, integrating quantum infrastructure will involve adding quantum equipment to data centres and possibly user devices (though user-end quantum devices might initially be limited to special cases; more likely, telcos or ISPs will incorporate quantum tech in their backbone and offer "quantum secured line" as a service to enterprise clients).

One can foresee Quantum-as-a-Service (QaaS) offerings: e.g., a cloud provider might offer QKD key management or on-demand access to a quantum computer over the network. A metaverse developer could use these services to secure their platform or to perform complex computations. Already, services like AWS Braket allow access to quantum processors over the internet (classically sending jobs). In the future, Braket could allow *quantum* sending of qubits for more interactive cloud quantum computing, enabled by QI.

5. Security of Quantum Infrastructure

We should note that quantum networks themselves need security. While quantum channels are immune to eavesdropping, the devices and classical control channels could be attacked (e.g., hackers might target the software coordinating QKD or try denial-of-service attacks on quantum links by blinding detectors with bright light). Thus, deploying quantum infrastructure includes robust classical cybersecurity and trust in the hardware supply chain. Organizations like banks, governments, etc., are deeply interested in QI specifically for high security. The metaverse, if built on this foundation, indirectly inherits that security rigor.

To illustrate, if a metaverse government meeting is happening, it might utilize a government quantum network that exists to connect ministries. That network uses its own Fibers, QKD, etc., to ensure no interception. The meeting's VR communication would be just another application running on that ultra-secure backbone.

In conclusion, the quantum network infrastructure is the enabler for all the quantum communication benefits in the metaverse:

- It provides the secure channels (quantum links for QKD, etc.) and possibly the computational links (for distributed quantum computing or sensing).
- It will gradually expand similarly to how the internet did, likely starting with linking key facilities, then eventually reaching end-users (maybe via quantum-enabled 6G base stations offering wireless QKD to your AR glasses).
- The metaverse, being a bandwidth-heavy application, will mostly use classical channels for bulk content, but quantum infrastructure will guard the gates and keys – ensuring that the content remains confidential and the system's integrity is maintained.

The synergy of quantum networks and metaverse could ultimately fulfil the vision of a secure, global digital reality where distance and threats are fewer limiting factors than ever before. As one report states, *"quantum internet is not only a theoretical concept but also an under-construction reality"*, highlighting that it is coming and we should be ready to integrate it (Chandre et al. (2024).

10.RESEARCH CHALLENGES AND OPEN ISSUES

While the fusion of quantum technologies and the metaverse is promising, there are several research challenges and open issues that must be addressed. These span technical hurdles, security concerns, and even socio-economic factors. We outline the major challenges below:

1. Hardware Limitations

Current quantum hardware faces limitations in qubit count, coherence time, and error rates. Noisy Intermediate-Scale Quantum (NISQ) devices can only handle short computations before errors dominate results. This presents a major challenge if we aim to use quantum computing for complex metaverse simulations or real-time services. Achieving long-term entanglement over distances is also very difficult due to environmental noise. For instance, photons transmitted through fibre experience loss; quantum memories are not yet efficient enough for widespread repeater deployment. Until these hardware issues are addressed, quantum networks will have limited reach and bandwidth, and quantum computers will need error correction to solve major problems.

Open issues include:

- Scaling up quantum processors: How to reach thousands or millions of logical qubits needed for robust, general-purpose quantum computing. Advances in qubit design, error correction codes, and manufacturing are required.
- Improving quantum memory and repeater technology: Without reliable quantum repeaters, global quantum networking relies on trust in intermediate nodes or satellites (which might not be fully QI in the ideal sense). Research into materials and protocols to extend entanglement range is critical.
- Hybrid system design: In the near term, we need efficient hybrid classical-quantum systems (middleware) that decide which tasks go to quantum hardware vs. classical, maximizing benefits despite hardware constraints.

2. System Architecture & Integration

Integrating quantum components into existing metaverse architectures presents design challenges. Many metaverse platforms are built on distributed cloud architectures with microservices – adding quantum QKD devices or quantum co-processors requires new frameworks. System redesign might be needed to handle quantum key management, quantum error probabilities, and new trust models.

Challenges:

- Middleware for Quantum-Classical Conversion: As noted earlier, we need software layers that seamlessly handle data going between classical and quantum processes. This includes APIs and standards for developers to request quantum-secure channels or quantum compute resources without deep quantum expertise.
- Network Routing and QoS: Ensuring that quantum-secured packets meet latency requirements. The metaverse is sensitive to delay (for VR, <20ms is ideal to avoid motion sickness). QKD adds some overhead (e.g., time to generate keys). Research is needed on minimizing the impact – maybe pre-fetching keys during idle times or integrating key refresh into network protocols so it doesn't add noticeable latency.
- Scalability: Quantum techniques often work well point-to-point but scaling them to thousands or millions of users (typical for a popular metaverse event) is an open issue. For instance, how to distribute QKD keys to a large audience for a broadcast securely? Possibly via tree structures or QKD networks, but these need development and testing.

3. Security Challenges

While quantum tech offers better security, it introduces new attack vectors and uncertainties:

- **Side Channels and Implementation Attacks:** QKD systems can be subject to side-channel attacks (e.g., hackers aiming bright light at a detector to saturate it, known as blinding attacks). Ensuring the real-world implementations match theoretical security assumptions is a challenge. Devices must be rigorously tested and improved (this is an active area in quantum cryptography – making QKD devices hacking-resistant).
- **Human Factor:** The age-old problem remains; users can still fall victim to social engineering. Quantum security does not address poor password habits or phishing. A secure quantum login is pointless if a user reveals their credentials to a scammer. Therefore, user education and making secure systems user-friendly are challenges. For instance, if quantum keys complicate the login experience, users might be reluctant. Consequently, researchers must ensure that quantum-secured workflows are seamless and accessible.
- **Interoperability & Standards:** Many vendors might produce quantum solutions; if they don't interoperate, the metaverse could become siloed. Security also depends on avoiding weakest links – a single non-quantum-safe component could undermine the whole system. A challenge is orchestrating an industry-wide move to quantum-safe practices, which requires coordination (standard bodies, agreements on protocols, etc.) (Abu Hilal, H. (2024).

4. Quantum-Metaverse Working Groups and Policy

The integration of these fields (quantum + XR + blockchain) crosses typical academic and industry silos. There is a need for interdisciplinary research and working groups. Right now, quantum physicists might not be thinking about VR applications, and metaverse developers might not know the latest in quantum. Bridging that gap is a challenge. Conferences, joint task forces, and collaborative projects will be needed to share knowledge and set common goals.

Additionally, policy and regulation will lag technology. Governments might need to update laws, such as export controls on quantum cryptography hardware, regulations on post-quantum encryption standards, or privacy laws to accommodate new technology. Achieving policy consensus, especially at an international level, is complex. It remains an open question how law enforcement will operate in a quantum-encrypted metaverse – existing lawful interception methods (like wiretapping) won't work if strong quantum encryption becomes widespread, which prompts debates about balancing privacy and public safety.

5. Cost and Accessibility

Quantum technologies are costly. QKD equipment, quantum computers, and similar devices currently have high expenses and are accessible only to well-funded organisations. For a metaverse intended to serve millions, deploying quantum technology widely might be financially unfeasible in the near future. Reducing costs through mass production or finding cheaper alternative technologies, such as Quantum Random Number Generators which are simpler and more affordable, presents an ongoing challenge. If quantum security remains expensive, there is a risk of creating a security disparity: only some high-end users or organisations will access the best security, leaving others with weaker protections. Research into economical implementations—like integrating basic QKD on a chip or harnessing upcoming quantum communication features in consumer devices—is essential to democratising quantum safety.

6. Future Uncertainties and Research Horizons

Finally, there are open-ended questions: The metaverse itself is evolving, and quantum technology is too. We don't fully know how people will use the metaverse ten years from now, nor what quantum breakthroughs or new algorithms will emerge. Perhaps new quantum algorithms (or quantum AI) will pose unforeseen threats — for example, a quantum algorithm that can quickly crack certain "secure" blockchain puzzles, or an AI that uses quantum computing to breach privacy in novel ways. We must stay flexible and informed. Ongoing research is essential to monitor developments – for instance, regularly assessing whether progress in quantum computing requires immediate updates to security protocols (like if someone builds a 1-million-qubit machine earlier than expected, do we need an emergency switch to post-quantum security for everything?).

Conversely, unknown opportunities could emerge, such as a breakthrough in topological qubits making scalable quantum computers a reality, thus unlocking possibilities we hadn't previously considered for the metaverse — like realistic physics simulation with quantum computation of every particle in a virtual world. Therefore, open research directions include investigating such novel applications: quantum machine learning for content creation, quantum-enhanced rendering algorithms (there are ideas of quantum algorithms for graphics, though still in their infancy), and more.

In summary, bridging quantum tech and the metaverse is a frontier area with multiple challenges:

- Technical (hardware and integration issues),
- Security (ensuring new tech is implemented correctly and widely adopted),
- Organizational (fostering collaboration and setting standards),
- Economic (cost and access).

Researchers must tackle these to achieve the vision of a reliable quantum-powered metaverse. Encouragingly, papers have started identifying these gaps; for instance, a survey highlighted hardware scalability, system design, and security standards as key issues that need to be addressed for a successful quantum-enabled metaverse. Each challenge is an opportunity for innovation – solutions will likely involve a mix of improved engineering, clever protocols, and close cooperation between the quantum and metaverse tech communities.

11. FUTURE DIRECTIONS

Looking ahead, the convergence of quantum technologies and the metaverse opens many future directions for research and development. Here we outline some promising avenues and potential milestones on the horizon (Sami et al., 2024):

Enhanced Quantum Algorithms for Metaverse Optimization

As the metaverse expands, so do its computational challenges – large numbers of users, complex virtual economies, and extensive 3D simulations. Future research will investigate specialised quantum algorithms to address these issues. For example:

- Quantum optimization algorithms for resource allocation in the metaverse. A quantum optimizer could handle things like dynamic server load balancing, network routing, or even in-world economic equilibria (like setting optimal prices dynamically for virtual goods) better than classical ones. This draws on quantum approaches to solving linear systems, combinatorial optimization (QAOA, quantum annealing), etc.
- Quantum AI and machine learning for the metaverse. Already, quantum machine learning (QML) and quantum neural networks are being studied. In the future, a metaverse AI agent (say an NPC or virtual assistant) might be trained or run on a quantum computer to achieve more human-like intelligence. This could enable more sophisticated interactions in virtual worlds – e.g., NPCs

that can understand and respond to users almost like real people, powered by quantum-accelerated learning. Hybrid quantum-classical ML might personalize experiences in real-time for each user by crunching their data faster.

- Content generation: One can imagine using quantum randomness and quantum generative algorithms to create unique environments or art in the metaverse. Every time you visit a virtual landscape it could be uniquely generated by measuring a complex quantum state, giving practically infinite variability.

Post-Quantum Transition and Standardization

In the nearer term, a significant direction is the transition to post-quantum cryptography across the internet and metaverse. As NIST and other bodies finalize PQC standards (targeted around 2024-2025), implementing those in all metaverse-related systems will be crucial. We will see:

- New authentication systems: Replacing RSA/ECDSA with lattice-based or hash-based signatures in identity verification, perhaps even in blockchain wallets in the metaverse.
- Upgraded secure communications: Protocols like TLS (which secure web traffic) will get post-quantum versions (this is already in testing). Metaverse platforms will adopt those for all client-server traffic. Expect patches and updates focusing on quantum-proofing.
- Standard APIs for quantum networks: Just as we have SSL/TLS libraries today, tomorrow we might have libraries that abstract QKD. For example, a QuantumSecureSocket library that a developer can use to get a socket which uses QKD under the hood if available, else falls back to PQC.

Interoperability will be a key focus, ensuring that a quantum key generated in one network can be used by another, or that a VR system from one vendor can interface with a quantum security device from another. This involves collaborative work on standards, possibly through organisations like IEEE, IETF, ITU, etc. The Quantum Internet also has its own evolving standards, such as an RFC (request for comments) outlining its architecture. Future directions include implementing these frameworks in real networks, possibly even test deployments during large-scale events — for example, a future Olympics where the communications infrastructure is partly quantum-secured as a demonstration.

Quantum Networking Expansion

By 2030 and beyond, we should see more of the quantum network infrastructure being deployed:

- Satellite networks providing QKD globally. Perhaps services akin to GPS – small devices that can receive quantum keys from overhead satellites. This could allow any metaverse user to partake in QKD with minimal ground infrastructure.
- Quantum repeaters demonstration: There are roadmap milestones like achieving entanglement across 1000 km with repeaters by late 2020s. Once achieved, it validates that ground fiber quantum networks can span countries without trust nodes. This would accelerate building such networks connecting data centers (benefiting metaverse backends).
- Multi-user QKD networks: Research will focus on making QKD not just point-to-point but multi-point (so-called network QKD, where any user in a network can establish keys with any other via intermediate nodes). A future direction is implementing Quantum Key Distribution for group communications – for example, setting a shared key for an entire VR conference with dozens of attendees via some quantum means. Some protocols (quantum conference key agreement) are being studied.

Quantum-Enabled Privacy and Ethics

The availability of strong privacy through quantum encryption will raise new questions and opportunities:

- Personal data vaults: Each user might have a quantum-secured personal data store (maybe on a blockchain or cloud) that only they can access/control, ensuring privacy. Research into how individuals can manage their own keys and data (perhaps with help from quantum tech to prevent any leakage) will be valuable.
- Ethical frameworks: If everything can be encrypted beyond reach, how do we handle moderation, crime prevention in the metaverse? Future policy might require some balance, like quantum-secure but *with user consent* data sharing for specific cases (maybe using techniques like secure multi-party computation).
- Decentralized governance: With quantum-safe blockchains, decentralized autonomous organizations (DAOs) in the metaverse could be more secure and reliable. One future direction is exploring quantum-resistant voting sys-

tems for governance of virtual communities. Ensuring fairness, anonymity, and verifiability of elections in DAOs using PQC or quantum protocols will be an active area.

New Metaverse Paradigms via Quantum Tech

Looking further ahead, quantum tech might enable metaverse concepts that are currently out of reach. For instance:

- Physically grounded virtual worlds: By utilising quantum simulations for physics, virtual worlds could obey the laws of physics very accurately (for specialised uses like scientific collaboration in VR or high-fidelity training). Currently, simulations simplify many aspects due to computational limits. Quantum simulation might manage chemical reactions, quantum optics, and more within a virtual lab in real time, enabling scientists to virtually experiment with materials at an atomic level.
- Real-time language translation and processing: A quantum computer could crunch natural language data faster, so maybe we get instantaneous universal translators in metaverse meetups, or real-time content moderation (scanning for harmful content) without lag, even with heavy encryption (perhaps by homomorphically analysing encrypted chat on a quantum machine).
- Quantum teleportation for avatars: This is speculative, but some futurists imagine if we had brain-computer interfaces and quantum networks, could we "teleport" a human's consciousness state (or some representation of it) securely from one device to another? It sounds sci-fi, but it's conceptually like quantum teleportation of qubits. While actual human teleportation is not feasible, the idea of transferring an avatar's state (their whole data/context) from one server to another seamlessly could borrow from quantum teleportation principles for security and continuity.

Continued Interdisciplinary Research

Finally, one clear future direction is the continued blending of disciplines: quantum information science, computer science, and immersive media. Academic curricula might start producing graduates versed in both quantum and AR/VR development. Research grants and labs might specifically target "quantum metaverse" studies, fostering innovation at the intersection.

We expect to see more experimental demonstrations, e.g., a prototype quantum-secured VR chat application in a few years, or a small-scale metaverse game that uses a quantum random number generator to drive its storyline. These proofs-of-concept will help identify unforeseen issues and refine designs.

In conclusion, the future directions point to a metaverse that is:

- More intelligent and optimised (quantum computing powering AI and decision-making),
- Highly secure and private (quantum comm ensuring confidentiality and integrity),
- Robust against future threats (with post-quantum measures and quantum-based solutions),
- Innovative in functionality (quantum algorithms enabling new experiences and capabilities).

Achieving this will require overcoming current challenges, but the trajectory is set. As one survey noted, *"numerous possibilities for investigation and invention"* exist in this field, ranging from network traffic optimization to applying QKD for one-time-pad encryption in authentication. The rapid progress in both quantum hardware and metaverse technologies gives hope that many of these futuristic ideas will become reality. The quantum-enabled metaverse might not arrive overnight, but each incremental step – a quantum key here, a post-quantum patch there, a new quantum cloud service – will pave the way to that transformative future.

12. CONCLUSION

The metaverse and quantum technologies are both advancing along transformative trajectories, and their convergence has the potential to define a new era of digital interaction. This chapter has examined in detail how quantum communication and computing can enhance the metaverse across multiple dimensions. Quantum computing offers unprecedented computational capabilities, enabling advanced simulations, optimized virtual environments, and quantum-enhanced artificial intelligence for immersive experiences. Although current hardware remains in the early stages of development, rapid progress projected to drive nearly 500% market growth by 2028 signals an imminent and significant role in metaverse infrastructure.

Quantum communication technologies, particularly quantum key distribution (QKD) and emerging quantum secure direct communication (QSDC), provide physics-backed, tamper-evident security for immersive interactions, transactions, and real-time streaming. The integration of quantum cryptography with blockchain further reinforces decentralized architectures through quantum-resistant consensus mechanisms, secure digital asset management, and robust avatar authentication. Beyond security, quantum applications extend to diverse sectors including healthcare, industry, autonomous systems, energy, defence, and finance—delivering both performance improvements and enhanced privacy protections. The early development of quantum internet infrastructure underscores the necessity of embedding quantum compatibility into metaverse standards before either ecosystem reaches full maturity.

Despite this transformative potential, several challenges persist, including qubit stability, long-distance entanglement maintenance, seamless system integration, standardization, and substantial implementation costs. Addressing these issues will require interdisciplinary collaboration, sustained research investment, and active knowledge exchange between quantum scientists and metaverse developers. Promising future directions include quantum-optimized content delivery systems, privacy-preserving identity frameworks, and globally synchronized quantum-secured events. Ultimately, the convergence of quantum and metaverse technologies should be viewed not only as a defensive measure against quantum-enabled threats but also as a strategic opportunity to design a trustworthy, high-performance digital commons. By embedding quantum readiness during this formative stage, the metaverse can evolve into a secure, scalable, and innovation-driven platform—delivering richer, safer, and more empowering virtual experiences.

REFERENCES

Abu Hilal, H. (2024). Unveiling the Quantum Internet: Potentials, Challenges, and Security Issues. *Unveiling the Quantum Internet: Potentials, Challenges, and Security Issues (December 24, 2024). OR*. Advance online publication. DOI: 10.2139/ssrn.5070407

Ali, M., Naeem, F., Kaddoum, G., & Hossain, E. (2023). Metaverse communications, networking, security, and applications: Research issues, state-of-the-art, and future directions. *IEEE Communications Surveys and Tutorials*, *26*(2), 1238–1278. DOI: 10.1109/COMST.2023.3347172

Azuma, K., Economou, S. E., Elkouss, D., Hilaire, P., Jiang, L., Lo, H. K., & Tzitrin, I. (2023). Quantum repeaters: From quantum networks to the quantum internet. *Reviews of Modern Physics*, *95*(4), 045006. DOI: 10.1103/RevModPhys.95.045006

Cao, Y., Zhao, Y., Wang, Q., Zhang, J., Ng, S. X., & Hanzo, L. (2022). The evolution of quantum key distribution networks: On the road to the q-internet. *IEEE Communications Surveys and Tutorials*, *24*(2), 839–894. DOI: 10.1109/COMST.2022.3144219

Chandre, P., Hingoliwala, H., Uttarkar, A., Shendkar, B. D., Lokare, D., & Sontakke, P. (2024, December). Post-Quantum Cryptography: Securing Critical Infrastructure Against Emerging Quantum Threats. In *2024 IEEE 4th International Conference on ICT in Business Industry & Government (ICTBIG)* (pp. 1-7). IEEE. DOI: DOI: 10.1109/ICTBIG64922.2024.10911612

. Dam, D. T., Tran, T. H., Hoang, V. P., Pham, C. K., & Hoang, T. T. *A survey of post-quantum cryptography: start of a new race. Cryptography. 2023; 7: 40.*), DOI: DOI: 10.3390/cryptography7030040

Eltanbouly, S., Halabi, O., & Qadir, J. (2025). Avatar privacy challenges in the metaverse: A comprehensive review and future directions. *International Journal of Human-Computer Interaction*, *41*(4), 1967–1984. DOI: 10.1080/10447318.2024.2374091

Gao, Y.-L., Chen, X.-B., Chen, Y.-L., Sun, Y., Niu, X.-X., & Yang, Y.-X. (2018). A secure cryptocurrency scheme based on post-quantum blockchain. *IEEE Access : Practical Innovations, Open Solutions*, *6*, 27205–27213. DOI: 10.1109/ACCESS.2018.2827203

Gupta, R. S., Wood, C. E., Engstrom, T., Pole, J. D., & Shrapnel, S. (2025). A systematic review of quantum machine learning for digital health. *npj. Digital Medicine*, *8*(1), 237. DOI: 10.1038/s41746-025-01597-z PMID: 40316703

Gyongyosi, L., & Imre, S. (2019). A survey on quantum computing technology. *Computer Science Review, 31*, 51–71. DOI: 10.1016/j.cosrev.2018.11.002

IEEE Communications Surveys & Tutorials. (2025). *What is the infrastructure of the metaverse? Metaverse Reality*. Retrieved from https://metaversereality.ieee.org/publications/articles/what-is-the-infrastructure-of-the-metaverse/#:~:text=The%20metaverse%20aims%20to%20be,unified%20and%20cohesive%20virtual%20universe

Jayashankar, A., & Mandayam, P. (2023). Quantum error correction: Noise-adapted techniques and applications. *Journal of the Indian Institute of Science, 103*(2), 497–512. DOI: 10.1007/s41745-022-00332-x

Keçeci, M. (2025). Quantum error correction codes and their impact on scalable quantum computation: Current approaches and future perspectives DOI: DOI: 10.5281/zenodo.15499657

Krelina, J. (2021). Quantum technology for military applications. *EPJ Quantum Technology, 8*(24), 1–30. DOI: 10.1140/epjqt/s40507-021-00113-y

Kumar, M., & Mondal, B. (2025). A brief review on Quantum Key Distribution Protocols. *Multimedia Tools and Applications, 84*(27), 1–40. DOI: 10.1007/s11042-024-20535-x

Kumar, V., Cicconetti, C., Conti, M., & Passarella, A. (2025). Quantum internet: Technologies, protocols, and research challenges [Manuscript, peer-reviewed, Q1]. *Manuscript*.DOI: https://doi.org//arXiv.2502.01653DOI: 10.48550

Labonté, L., Alibart, O., D'Auria, V., Doutre, F., Etesse, J., Sauder, G., Martin, A., Picholle, É., & Tanzilli, S. (2024). Integrated photonics for quantum communications and metrology. *PFX Quantum : a Physical Review Journal, 5*(1), 010101. DOI: 10.1103/PRXQuantum.5.010101

Mantri, P., Li, A. C. Y., & Brown, K. R. (2025). Comparing one- and two-way quantum repeater architectures. *Communications on Physics, 8*(1), 2222. DOI: 10.1038/s42005-025-02222-x

Markidis, S. (2024, May). What is quantum parallelism, anyhow? In *ISC High Performance 2024 Research Paper Proceedings (39th International Conference)* (pp. 1-12). Prometeus GmbH. DOI: DOI: 10.48550/arXiv.2405.07222

Naik, P., Jain, R., & Tiwari, S. (2025). From portfolio optimization to quantum blockchain and security: A systematic review of quantum computing in finance. *Financial Innovation, 11*(88), 88. Advance online publication. DOI: 10.1186/s40854-025-00751-6

Pan, D., Long, G. L., Yin, L., Sheng, Y. B., Ruan, D., Ng, S. X., Lu, J., & Hanzo, L. (2024). The evolution of quantum secure direct communication: On the road to the qinternet. *IEEE Communications Surveys and Tutorials*, *26*(3), 1898–1949. DOI: 10.1109/COMST.2024.3367535

Phys.org. (2021, January). Chinese scientists have established the world's first quantum network. Retrieved from https://phys.org/news/2021-01-world-quantum-network.html

Ricci, S., Dobias, P., Malina, L., Hajny, J., & Jedlicka, P. (2024). Hybrid keys in practice: Combining classical, quantum and post-quantum cryptography. *IEEE Access : Practical Innovations, Open Solutions*, *12*, 23206–23219. DOI: 10.1109/ACCESS.2024.3364520

Rietsche, R., Dremel, C., Bosch, S., Steinacker, L., Meckel, M., & Leimeister, J. M. (2022). Quantum computing. *Electronic Markets*, *32*(4), 2525–2536. DOI: 10.1007/s12525-022-00570-y

Sami, H., Hammoud, A., Arafeh, M., Wazzeh, M., Arisdakessian, S., Chahoud, M., Wehbi, O., Ajaj, M., Mourad, A., Otrok, H., Abdel Wahab, O., Mizouni, R., Bentahar, J., Talhi, C., Dziong, Z., Damiani, E., & Guizani, M. (2024). The metaverse: Survey, trends, novel pipeline ecosystem & future directions. *IEEE Communications Surveys and Tutorials*, *26*(4), 2914–2960. DOI: 10.1109/COMST.2024.3392642

Sorrentino, R., & López-Guzmán, J. (2025). Rethinking privacy for avatars: Biometric and inferred data in the metaverse. *Frontiers in Virtual Reality*, *6*, 1520655. DOI: 10.3389/frvir.2025.1520655

Thalacker, C., Hahn, F., de Jong, J., Pappa, A., & Barz, S. (2021). Anonymous and secret communication in quantum networks. *New Journal of Physics*, *23*(8), 083026. DOI: 10.1088/1367-2630/ac1808

Thanalakshmi, P., Rishikhesh, A., Marion Marceline, J., Joshi, G. P., & Cho, W. (2023). A quantum-resistant blockchain system: A comparative analysis. *Mathematics*, *11*(18), 3947. DOI: 10.3390/math11183947

Tightiz, L., Dang, L. M., Padmanaban, S., & Hur, K. (2024). Metaverse-driven smart grid architecture. *Energy Reports*, *12*, 2014–2025. DOI: 10.1016/j.egyr.2024.08.027

Tuli, E. A., Lee, J. M., & Kim, D. S. (2024). Leveraging quantum blockchain for secure multiparty space sharing and authentication on specialized metaverse platform. *Scientific Reports*, *14*(1), 25776. DOI: 10.1038/s41598-024-74213-x PMID: 39468089

Tuli, E. A., Lee, J. M., & Kim, D. S. (2024). Integration of quantum technologies into metaverse: Applications, potentials, and challenges. *IEEE Access : Practical Innovations, Open Solutions, 12*, 29995–30019. DOI: 10.1109/ACCESS.2024.3366527

Xu, F., Ma, X., Zhang, Q., Lo, H.-K., & Pan, J.-W. (2020). Secure quantum key distribution with realistic devices. *Reviews of Modern Physics, 92*(2), 025002. DOI: 10.1103/RevModPhys.92.025002

Yang, K., Zhang, Z., Youliang, T., & Ma, J. (2023). A secure authentication framework to guarantee the traceability of avatars in metaverse. *IEEE Transactions on Information Forensics and Security, 18*, 3817–3832. DOI: 10.1109/TIFS.2023.3288689

Yang, Z., Alfauri, H., Farkiani, B., Jain, R., Di Pietro, R., & Erbad, A. (2023). A survey and comparison of post-quantum and quantum blockchains. *IEEE Communications Surveys and Tutorials, 26*(2), 967–1002. DOI: 10.1109/COMST.2023.3325761

Zakarneh, B., Annamalai, N., Alquqa, E. K., Mohamed, K. M., & Al Salhi, N. R. (2024). Virtual reality and alternate realities in Neal Stephenson's—Snow crash. *World Journal of English Language, 14*(2), 244. DOI: 10.5430/wjel.v14n2p244

Chapter 9
Quantum-Driven Finance Revolution Shaping:
The Future of Risk Intelligence Security and Market Speed

Mohammad Irfan
http://orcid.org/0000-0002-4956-1170
Chandigarh University, India

Bhanu Pratap Singh
http://orcid.org/0009-0002-5233-1170
Chandigarh University, India

ABSTRACT

The integration of quantum computing into financial systems marks a transformative leap in risk management, security, and market operations. Unlike classical computing, quantum algorithms can process vast datasets and complex models at unprecedented speeds, enabling real-time risk analytics, rapid fraud detection, and optimized trading strategies. This study explores the emerging field of quantum-driven finance, focusing on its potential to enhance predictive accuracy, reduce systemic vulnerabilities, and accelerate decision-making in volatile markets. Applications such as quantum-enhanced Monte Carlo simulations, quantum machine learning for anomaly detection, and optimization in algorithmic trading are examined alongside challenges in scalability, cybersecurity, and regulatory adaptation. By evaluating current advancements and future prospects, this research highlights quantum computing's role in shaping a secure, intelligent, and high-velocity global financial ecosystem.

DOI: 10.4018/979-8-3373-3857-6.ch009

1. INTRODUCTION

The modern fast development of computational technologies has profoundly changed the nature of the financial markets, moving them towards data-driven and algorithms-based systems, able to process large and complex volumes of data. Modern stock market indices like the Dow Jones Industrial Average and the S&P 500 are not only indicators of macroeconomic conditions, but also of the increased trend of high-frequency trading and advanced calculation strategies into the marketplace. With the increasing complexity in financial systems, the need to acquire increasingly fast, more correct and scalable analytical tools has only increased.

Artificial intelligence and machine learning have enhanced predictive modelling through the detection of non-linear relationships and hidden patterns to financial data. Nevertheless, financial markets are inherently dynamic and adaptive and constrain the continuation of predictive advantages as new information is rapidly absorbed into prices (Herman et al., 2022). Also, financial time series have some characteristics, like non-stationarity, and the clustering of volatility, that challenge the reliability and stability of predictive models (Huang et al., 2021)

Here, quantum computing can be viewed as a next generation calculational paradigm that can overcome drawbacks related to classical systems. By applying the underlying concepts of superposition, entanglement, and others, quantum algorithms can execute multiple states in parallel and therefore make it much more efficient in terms of computational efficiency in optimization, simulation, and machine learning tasks (Herman et al., 2022). They are specifically applicable in the realm of the financial markets where speed and accuracy are of paramount importance as dictators of competitive advantage.

Moreover, due to the growing significance of market speed, particularly in high-frequency trading environments, the demand to design extremely low-latency systems is growing. Financial operations can even be further accelerated by quantum computing, remaking trading strategies and improving frameworks of risk management. Nevertheless, even with its benefits, the potential of quantum technologies is still limited by economic factors like the efficiency of markets and adaptive competition that indicates that a wider range of technological advances will not be able to erase the basic constraints of financial predictability.

1.1 Evolution of Financial Modelling

Over half a century the financial modelling has changed a great deal, outgrowing the simple methods of statistics to complex systems of high-level computations. Simplifying assumptions to linear relationships and stationary distributions and other linear regression and autoregressive models were used in early models. Although these methods offered some baseline views, they were not up to the task of capturing the dynamics and development of real financial markets in general, as well as a volatile and structurally shifting market in particular (Dixon et al., 2020).

With the development of the computational technologies, the approach of the machine learning was integrated, which allowed the modeling of the non-linear relationships and the high-dimensional data. These models have been of significant value in enhancing predictive performance; they are able to find concealed patterns and interaction in the financial data. The more complexity a model has, however, presented the challenge of overfitting, reduced interpretability, and instability across different market situations, limiting their long-term reliability (Gu et al., 2020).

The advent of quantum computing is a new frontier in financial modelling, and represents a possibility of overcoming the constraints of classical computational systems. With quantum algorithms able to modify multiple states in parallel by using superposition and parallelism and prototype more efficient optimization and simulation of complicated financial problems. It will also help to transform methods of modelling and increase the power of analytics in the financial market (Herman et al., 2022).

1.2 Role of Machine Learning in Finance

Machine learning has now become a fundamentally disruptive feature in modern financial analysis, as it allows the processing of large amounts of data, as well as the identification of otherwise complex patterns, that are all difficult to capture using standard statistical models. Neural networks, support vector machines, and ensemble learning are all commonly used and have significant applications in fields like asset pricing, credit risk assessment, and fraud detection, among others, definitely improving the accuracy of the forecasts (Huang et al., 2021).

In spite of such improvements, the characteristics of financial datasets are low signal-to-noise ratio, so it is hard to distinguish between meaningful data and random changes. This is one of the biggest liabilities of machine learning models, since they can be used to see patterns in specific areas that do not necessarily persist over time. Moreover, the inefficiency of these models is affected by such issues as overfitting and poor generalization (Gu et al., 2020).

Furthermore, financial markets are evolutionary systems where participants constantly adjust to the new information, and usage patterns exploited by the participants are quickly disappearing. Consequently, even very advanced machine learning models might not be able to sustain a steady predictive performance. This underscores more sophisticated ways to do computations such as quantum computing to overcome these limitations (Dixon et al., 2020).

1.3 Market Efficiency and Information Absorption

Financial markets are based on the theory of informational efficiency, according to which the price of the assets comprises all the information available to the buyer. This idea suggests that excess returns are a difficult idea to consistently attain; since new information is being rapidly introduced into prices. Efficient market hypothesis has been a staple of the financial theory and it has highlighted the aspect of competitiveness in financial markets (Herman et al., 2022).

Since market agents are constantly dissecting and responding to information in any manner that can be identified, any defined inefficiency is soon identified and removed. This gives a dynamic environment where predictive benefits tend to be short term and are highly context dependent. As a result, financial models have to incorporate the adaptive behavior of market participants in the attempt to predict market moves (Herman et al., 2022).

High rates of information absorption also restrict the performance of the highly complex computational schemes, such as machine learning, quantum-based schemes. Although these models have the ability to filter out patterns in financial markets, their predictability is limited due to the dynamic nature of financial markets. This shows the intrinsic drawbacks of making predictions amidst issues of high level of competition.

1.4 Non-Stationarity and Market Volatility

The nature of financial time series is non-stationary, i.e., the statistical properties of the financial time series vary with time. This feature presents a major challenge to predictive modelling because the models based on historical data are brought into the new market and may not well perform. Non-stationarity can be viewed to be related to structure change, economic cycles, and external shocks, which affect the behavior of the market (Huang et al., 2021).

Another major characteristic of financial markets is the Volatility clustering whereby the high volatility periods are likely to have followed other periods as well. Such an action enhances doubt and makes predictions hard to make particularly when the economy is volatile. Such patterns are not always captivable by traditional models, limiting the accuracy of a traditional model in a dynamic market setting (Gu et al., 2020).

These problems emphasize the weaknesses of the conventional and the sophisticated modelling methods in the financial markets. To overcome non-stationarity and volatility, more adaptive and robust computational methods need to be developed, which can react to changing conditions.

1.5 Emergence of Quantum Computing

Quantum computing is a critical departure of classical computational forms of thought, and represents novel approaches to information processing. The quantum bits, in comparison with classical bits, can exist in more than two states simultaneously, thus, making computation of some classes of problems more efficient (Herman et al., 2022).

In finance, quantum computing provides the opportunity to greatly enhance the efficiency of computational problems in aspects like optimization, simulation, and machine learning. They have found applications, especially in financial markets, where large datasets and complex models need large compute resources (Herman et al., 2022)

The evolution of quantum technologies is likely to revolutionize a financial system as it will allow analyzing the financial system faster and more accurately. Nonetheless, it is a restraint to actual application because of technological limitations, such as hardware limitations and error rates.

1.6 Quantum Advantage in Financial Systems

Quantum advantage The strength of quantum systems to solve particular computational issues is superior to classical computers. This benefit is especially applicable in optimization and simulation applications in finance where the classical methods can reach exponential complexity (Herman et al., 2022).

The process of quantum algorithms is able to test various possible solutions at the same time, which allows finding the best strategies much faster. Efficiency and accuracy are paramount in portfolio management, trading, and risk assessment, which have high implications on efficiency and accuracy (Egger et al., 2020).

Although it has its potential, quantum advantage is still so speculative in most of the financial applications because of the inexistent restraint technology. It should be further developed and researched to help it achieve its maximum potential.

1.7 Market Speed and High-Frequency Trading

Market speed has taken the shape of an operational attribute of contemporary financial systems which have become prominent in the high-frequency trading setting. The transactions take place in micro seconds and even the slightest improvement in latency can ensure considerable competitive advantages (Egger et al., 2020).

The ability of technology to make the execution process faster and faster, has continued to increase the level of competition amongst the players in the market.

Speedier systems allow traders to take advantage of temporary market inefficiency and makes them more profitable and at the same time causes volatility in the market.

Quantum computing can also contribute to speeding up the market, providing more opportunities to process and optimize the data. Nevertheless, this can also cast some light on unfairness and systematic risk in the financial markets (PwC, 2022).

1.8 Growth of Quantum Computing Market

The industry of quantum computing is one of exponential growth, because of the rising level of investments that governments and other organizations take in it. The market forecasts show a high growth up to 2030, and it is expected to be characterized by an increasing demand in terms of the advanced scheme of calculating solutions (MarketsandMarkets, 2023).

One of the first to adopt quantum technologies is financial institutions, who explore the idea of quantum technologies in trading and risk management (as well as some cybersecurity). This tendency indicates the increase of the role of quantum computing in financial systems (Irfan, Kadry, Sharif, & Khan, 2023).

Since the industry is still being shaped with quantum computing tend to be a major part of the development of the financial markets in the future.

1.9 Challenges and Limitations

Quantum computing has the potential to transform everything, but it is encountering several challenges that are limiting its use in the numerous places it can be used. The computational reliability of current quantum systems is affected by noise and error rates, and by scalability (Herman et al., 2022).

There is also a need of heavy investment and specialized skills to integrate quantum technologies into financial systems. Lending institutions need to respond to these issues in order to be effective in implementing quantum solutions.

Also, the issue of cybersecurity and data privacy is still critical, especially with the potential of quantum systems to affect the availability of current encryption protocols (PwC, 2022).

1.10 Role of Global Financial Indices in Market Analysis

International financial indicators like the Dow Jones Industrial Average, and S&P 500 are all significant markers used to measure the performance of markets, investor confidence and macro-economic patterns. The indices put together the performance of the large corporations giving a complete picture into the market forces and the economic well being of the economy. Institutional investors, policymakers, and researchers extensively utilize them to assess trends on the market and make investment decisions (Dixon et al., 2020).

These indices are also used as reference points to measure the predictive model effectiveness and trading strategy in the case of computational finance. To test model robustness and forecasting accuracy, advanced computational techniques such as machine learning and quantum algorithms often use index-based data to test robustness and forecasting accuracy. Nevertheless, index-based predictions are also limited by the fact that even efficient markets and a quick absorption of information cannot ensure constant excess returns (Gu et al., 2020)..

1.11 Market Speed and Latency Across Global Exchanges.

Market speed is a notion that is becoming even more prominent amid the globalization and digitization of financial markets. The major markets include New York Stock Exchange (NYSE), NASDAQ, London Stock Exchange (LSE) and Tokyo Stock Exchange (TSE) markets and are highly competitive with speed of execution being a critical measure of trading success. Improved technology has minimised latency to a microsecond and this has allowed traders working with high frequency to take advantage of momentary market inefficiencies (Egger et al., 2020).

The latency difference between exchanges may impact the liquidity, price discovery and the presence of arbitrage opportunities. Algorithms types of rule-based traders are more likely to arrive in faster markets, influencing the volume of trading, but also contributing to the market volatility. It is possible that quantum computing will introduce even more reduction in latency by boosting the efficiency and speed in processing data, which may reshape the paradigms of speed in the market. However, again, it is raising concerns about disparities in technological access and the possibility of an increasing concentration of market power in the hands of technologically advanced players (PwC, 2022).

1.12 Integration of Quantum Computing with Financial Market Infrastructure

The embedding of quantum computing in the current financial systems is both a technology opportunity, and a system challenge. Trading and clearing Financial systems are based on highly optimized classical computing architectures to perform settlement, clearing, settlement and risk management. Implementing quantum computing will involve creating hybrid quantum-classical systems that can exchange inputs and outputs with existing systems (Egger et al., 2020).

This kind of integration does not just entail technical changes but also organizing and regulation issues. To successfully implement quantum technologies, financial institutions need to invest in infrastructures, talent management, and cybersecurity tools. Additionally, regulatory agencies should put in place rules and regulations to manage fair access, transparency, and systemic stability in quantum-enabled markets. The successful introduction of quantum computing will be a critical factor in determining its true impact in the real world on financial systems around the world (Herman et al., 2022).

2. LITERATURE REVIEW

Studies on financial technology underscore the growth of sophisticated computing systems in enhancing financial analysis, predictive modeling, and improving the efficiency of financial markets. The financial markets today produce huge amounts of information, but it's rapidly changing and often complicated, which requires evolving and flexible methods of analysis that are able to process data and make decisions at realtime speeds. (Dixon et al., 2020).

Recent research has made clear that many of the characteristics of traditional financial models, such as non-linearity, volatility clustering, and non-stationary market behavior, can be problematic. Use of machine learning techniques has led to better accuracy in forecasting, as it allows them to discover "hidden" relationships among the data in financial records, but has also introduced new problems of overfitting and instability that can impact the reliability of these predictions. (Gu et al., 2020).

According to Dr. Shantivar, quantum computing offers a possibility as a new option for computational finance where quantum processes could be used to process numerous states together. Researchers say that quantum-enhanced algorithms could prove useful in fields like optimization, simulation and risk analysis, thus enhancing their applications in the financial sector to include trading and portfolio management. (Herman et al., 2022)

However, with the increasing use of quantum technologies come concerns around cybersecurity threat, infrastructure expense and regulatory issues within financial systems. There exists, therefore, literature that investigates both the possibilities and the constraints of using quantum computers in the worldwide financial markets and in the decision-making process. (PwC, 2022).

2.1 Foundations of Financial Market Theory

The principles of the finance market theory are based on the concept of informational efficiency, implying that asset prices are determined by all the available information. The initial work stressed that financial markets are extremely competitive environments where adjustments in prices are quick and limiting the chances of sustainable excess returns (Herman et al., 2022).

This view provided a theoretical foundation to the assessments of the effectiveness of predictive models in finance. This perception would later be diversified by other behavioral and structural aspects that mediate on the market forces. Scholars posited that in spite of overall efficiency in markets, deviations can occur because of investor psychology, institutional constraints as well as information asymmetry (Herman et al., 2022). The lessons learned here are that financial markets are not mere deterministic phenomena, but are affected by a mix of both rational and behavioral factors.

2.2 Non-Stationarity and Market Complexity

Financial markets are non-stationary, and non-stationary behaviour, i.e. time-changing statistics), is inherent to such systems. This attribute creates major difficulties to the predictive modelling since a model trained in the previous market may not work well in the new market conditions (Huang et al., 2021).

Moreover, the time series of financial data tend to exhibit volatility clustering and structural breaks in addition to complicating the analysis. These features have been found by researchers to mitigate the stability and robustness of predictive models especially in economic uncertain or stress periods (Gu et al., 2020). Consequently, the complexity of markets requires us to understand the complexity of market financial model better so as to create more robust financial models.

2.3 Emergence of Quantum Computing in Finance

Recent research story has addressed the opportunities of quantum computing as one of the transformational instruments in finance application. Quantum algorithms have proved to be very beneficial in overcoming complex optimization and simulation problems, which are predominant in financial modelling (Herman et al., 2022).

The use of quantum-enhanced Monte Carlo simulations in the risk analysis and derivative pricing have reflected improvements in computational speed and efficiency (Egger et al., 2020).

Moreover, quantum machine learning has also been suggested as a framework to improve pattern matching and anomaly detection in financial data, and provides new opportunities in predictive analytics (Huang et al., 2021).

2.4 Machine Learning in Financial Prediction

Machine learning has become an influential technology in the field of financial prediction because it can be used to model complex, non-linear relationships in large data sets. Empirical research has also shown that machine learning models can be more effective than traditional econometric models in predicting stock returns and stock volatility (Huang et al., 2021).

Such models use sophisticated algorithms to bring out the concealed trends and enhance accuracy of predictions. Nonetheless, scholars have also found that there are a number of shortcomings of machine learning in finance. The overfitting issues, the instability of models, and their sensitivity to the dynamics of the market environment are some problems that make these models less reliable in practice (Dixon et al., 2020).

Moreover, due to the poor signal-to-noise ratio of financial data, it is not so easy to see whether meaningful patterns may be identified in the financial data or those are random fluctuations, which limits the long-term efficiency of the predictive models (Gu et al., 2020), (Irfan, Hussainey, Bukhari, & Nam, 2024).

2.5 Hybrid Quantum-Classical Systems

Most realistic uses of quantum computing, due to the present technological constraints, are based on hybrid quantum-classical systems. These systems incorporate the advantages of classical computing with quantum computing to accomplish better achievements in a given task (Herman et al., 2022).

Studies suggest that hybrid models are especially convenient in optimization problems and financial simulations when quantum processors are useful in solving complex tasks, whereas classic systems are effective regarding the processing and integration of data. This method will offer an expedient trajectory of adopting quantum technologies in the short term, despite the constraints of the current quantum devices (Herman et al., 2022).

2.6 Market Speed and High-Frequency Trading

The contribution by financial systems that market speed plays has been an intensive discussion, especially in the context of high-frequency trading. Studies indicate that even small amounts of latency reductions can have great competitive benefits, which affect profitability and positioning in the markets (Egger et al., 2020).

Nonetheless, growing focus on speed has also caused fears as to the stability of markets and their fairness. Research indicates that high-speed trading set-ups can result in even greater volatility and systemic risks, especially at the time when the markets are under some pressure (PwC, 2022).

2.7 Cybersecurity and Quantum Threats

Quantum computing and its implication to cybersecurity have been a subject of recent literature. With such a threat to the security of financial data and the integrity of transactions, quantum algorithms can break the existing cryptographic system (PwC, 2022).

In reaction to this, scholars have come out with the proposal to develop quantum resistant cryptographic schemes to provide the security of financial systems. A dual nature of quantum computing is that quantum computing is a facilitator of novelty as well as a cause of risk (Irfan, Elmogy, & Gupta, 2024).

2.8 Growth and Economic Impact of Quantum Computing

Quantum computing has got the interest of academia and industry with its promise to realize the economic potential of quantum computing. According to market research studies, the quantum computing industry shows a rapid growth, fuelled by the growing number of investments and technological innovations in the field (MarketsandMarkets, 2023).

One of the earliest users of quantum technologies can be financial institutions, which seek to use quantum technologies in trading and risk management, as well as the optimization of portfolios. This increased attention can be seen as the greater awareness of quantum computing as a wave of significant future innovations in the financial systems and beyond.

3. RESEARCH METHODOLOGY

The study's research methodology is conceptual and analytical in nature with the aim of analyzing the effect of quantum computation on computational finance and the financial markets. Secondary data, mainly sourced from academic publications, research papers, industry reports, financial publications, was used. The sources used include Springer, Institute of Electrical and Electronics Engineers (IEEE) and market research reports, which have been leveraged to gain insight into developments of quantum technologies and their application for Trading and Risk Management and Predictive Analytics. This method allows generalizations about the behaviours of the market, and about computation progress, without relying on primary data collection techniques. (Dixon et al., 2020), (Irfan, Dias, Rastogi, & Zebende, 2025).

This study is also deductive, attempting to apply known financial theories and computational concepts to learn the impact quantum computing has on the financial systems. Efficiency, predictiveness and market performance of classical and quantum computational models has been measured by comparative analysis. The study also examines aspects of volatility, speed of markets, cybersecurity and regulation when making an evaluation of the implementation of quantum technologies in practice. This strategy can facilitate progress in establishing a balanced view on the opportunities and challenges of quantum finance and high fidelglity computational systems. (Herman et al., 2022).

3.1 Research Design

This paper will have a conceptual and analysis-based research design since it is concentrated on assessing the applications of quantum computing in financial markets. The study combines theoretical knowledge in the field of financial economics and the new trends in computational technologies. Instead of using primary data collection, the research focuses on analytical interpretation of the existing models, trends in the industry, and technological advances (Dixon et al., 2020).

The research design is designed in such a way that it will be able to study how computational innovation and the behavior of the financial markets are related to each other, especially as far as areas like risk modelling, trading efficiency and speed in the financial markets is concerned.

According to this approach, a holistic picture with respect to the impacts of quantum computing on financial systems can be acquired within the context of the broad economy and the development of technology.

3.2 Research Approach

The research is deductive research approach where the established financial theories and calculation principles are applied in researching the effects of quantum computing on financial markets. Theoretical models like market efficiency and adaptive market behavior are used to evaluate limitations and opportunities of model made on quantum (Herman et al., 2022).

The study considers that by combining theory with the development of technology, whether the positive growth in computational power has a positive financial consequences. This method will make sure that the analysis is based on the accepted academic principles and explores the new innovations.

3.3 Global Adoption Analysis

Figure 1.

Region	Investment	Research Output	Industry Adoption	Infrastructure
USA	90	88	92	89
Europe	80	82	78	81
China	85	84	86	83
Japan	75	78	74	77
India	65	70	68	66

The analysis is conducted as a heatmap to show how quantum computing is adopted in the top major areas. As of the current trends, quantum research and investment are dominated by North America, Europe, and East Asia due to strong technological infrastructure and policy support, and the emerging economies have begun to gain more and more momentum (PwC, 2022). This uneven distribution demonstrates the inequalities in the presence of technology across the world and how it can affect the competitiveness of financial markets in the world.

3.4 Data Sources and Collection.

The study is based solely on the secondary data sources, comprising of academic sources, industry reports, as well as a financial source. Articles available in the scholarly realm that are released by such established platforms as Springer and Emerald offer theoretical principles alongside empirical evidence of the behavior of financial markets as well as current developments timely in quantum computing.

Secondly, industry reports on the trends of quantum computers market share helps to learn predicted patterns of growth and adoption of new technology. Financial data that has been identified to be related to significant market indices, including the Dow Jones Industrial Average and S&P 500 are included in order to provide a context to the computational developments within the performance of the market in the real world. Secondary data will help to thoroughly incorporate the various perspectives without going through the constraints and limitations of primary data collection (PwC, 2022).

3.5 Market Growth Analysis

Figure 2. Projected Market Growth of Quantum Finance Impact (2026–2030).

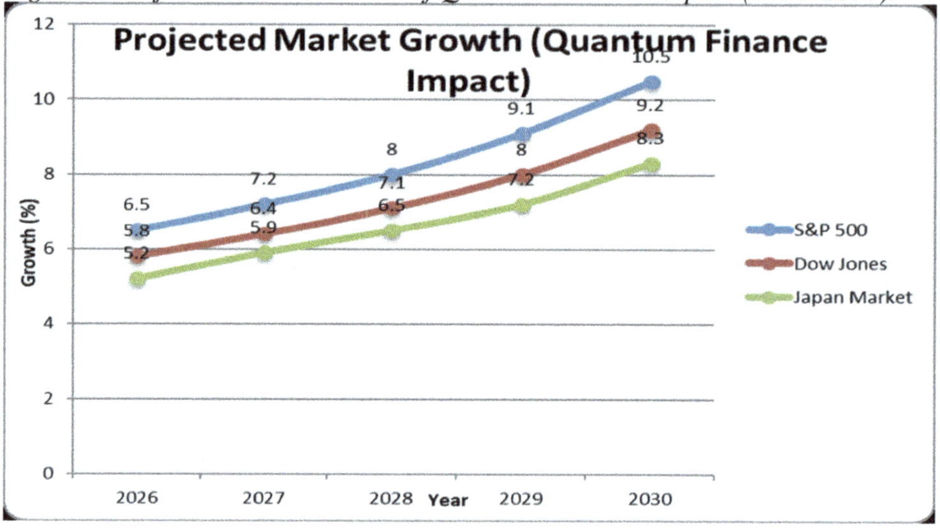

Source: Author's analytical representation based on MarketsandMarkets (2023) and PwC (2022).

The research includes the graphical model of the estimated development of the quantum computing market to reveal its ongoing high rank in terms of its financial implementation. According to industry reports, quantum computing market is projected to witness a high growth rate by 2030 due to an increased investments and demand of high performance computational solutions (MarketsandMarkets, 2023). The trend towards such a growth contributes to the thesis that quantum technologies will have a considerable role in the sphere of financial markets by providing them with the capacity to become more efficient in their calculations and decision-making processes.

3.6 Analytical Framework

This study analytical framework will be grounded in a comparative analysis of classical computational frameworks and quantum enhanced frameworks under financial systems. The analysis is done on the key performance dimensions that include the computational efficiency, predictive accuracy, trading performance, and risk assessment capability.

Moreover, the framework considers external factors, such as market volatility and regulatory restrictions, which can have a huge impact on the efficiency and usefulness of the computational models in the work-life realities in a financial setting. This multi-dimensional method guarantees a thorough and multi-dimensional evaluation of quantum computing in the bigger framework of financial markets (Herman et al., 2022).

3.7 Limitations of Methodology

Although the study has a thorough analysis perspective, it is limited to some extent. The use of secondary data risk causing biases relating to the available literature and market reports. Moreover, brightening dynamic character of quantum computing implies that a part of the discoveries can become obsolete with the rise in technology.

Moreover, the lack of the primary empirical testing also exposes the inability of validating the theoretical conclusions in the real life scenario. Despite analysis limitations, the research provides useful information on the opportunities and issues of quantum computing in financial markets (Dixon et al., 2020).

3.8 Ethical Considerations

The ethical principles of the research are followed since the sources used are credible and have been cited properly. The analysis has not utilized any confidential or proprietary data. It also focuses on the ethical inferences of quantum computing in financial markets especially in regards to the fairness of the market, data security as well as disparate access to advanced technologies.

To uphold confidence in financial system, it is critical to ensure transparency and accountability in the use of emerging technologies. However, with the ongoing development of quantum computing, ethical options are bound to significantly influence the ethical responsibility of its use.

4. FINDINGS AND ANALYSIS

4.1 Global Financial Market Trends and Quantum Influence

The trend analysis on global financial markets shows that the technological advancement has greatly contributed to the market behavior especially as regards to efficiency, liquidity and the speed it executes the transaction. Major indices as the Dow Jones Industrial Average of the stock market and the S&P 500 of the stock market show consistent growth trends due to the combination of increased algorithmic trading and greater use of systems based on data to drive growth. Advanced computational methods have also been incorporated, which leads to more market responsive and lower informational asymmetry (Dixon et al., 2020).

Moreover, it has been anticipated that due to the development of quantum computing this will speed up these trends as new computational capacities will be developed beyond classical limits. Investing in quantum technologies to enhance the predictive modelling process and the trading strategy optimization is a growing trend among financial institutions. These advancements imply that quantum computing is going to be highly instrumental when it comes to the demands of future market dynamics, and especially within high-frequency trading settings (Irfan, Zebende, Sarea, & Shahbaz, 2025).

Though these developments, the effects quantum computing is limited by the market efficiency and adaptive competition. The benefits of technology and especially when new technology has been adopted tend to decrease with time as more players in the market are willing to adopt the new technology. This shows the aptitude of taking quantum computing as an empowering technology instead of an assured source of continued financial benefit (Herman et al., 2022).

4.2 Market Speed and Trading Efficiency Analysis

The pace of the market has been a critical determinant of the trading performance particularly in high-frequency trading environments where the minimum execution time is in the range of microseconds. Quick execution will allow traders to take advantage of short-lived opportunities that will consequently increase its profitability and market efficiency (Egger et al., 2020).

Figure 3. Comparative Market Latency Across Major Global Exchanges.

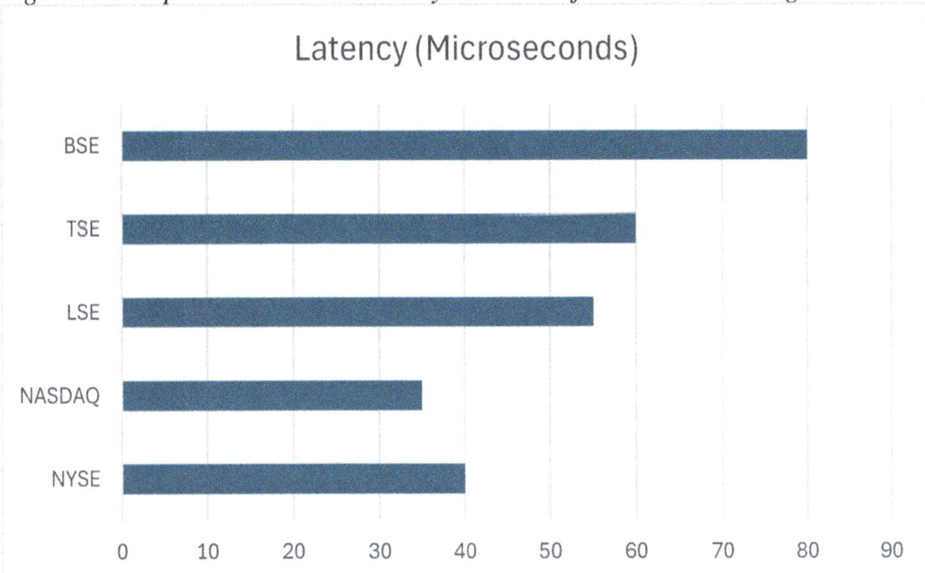

Source: Author's analytical compilation based on Egger et al. (2020) and PwC (2022).

As shown in the bar chart, there are variations in the latency of the major exchanges in the world, evidently indicating the competitive significance of speed in financial markets. The technological change has greatly minimized the time spent in executing its operations making the competition among other players in the market intensely competitive. The quantum computing can also contribute to the further development of this trend, as it will be possible to process and optimize data more quickly (PwC, 2022).

Although these benefits exist, higher speed will in turn result in higher volatility and systemic risk. The fast trading systems have the potential to increase the volatility of the markets especially when there are speculations. It follows that the positive outcomes of enhanced speed need to be counterbalanced with regulation to make sure brought stability (Herman et al., 2022).

4.3 Quantum Computing Market Growth and Financial Impact

The development of quantum computing business is likely to make a significant implication on the financial markets. In the market, it is projected to continue its steep growth as by 2030, the market is set to expand, further fuelled by the rise in investments and advancement in technology (MarketsandMarkets, 2023).

Figure 4. Comparative Growth Trends in Major Financial Markets (2026–2030).

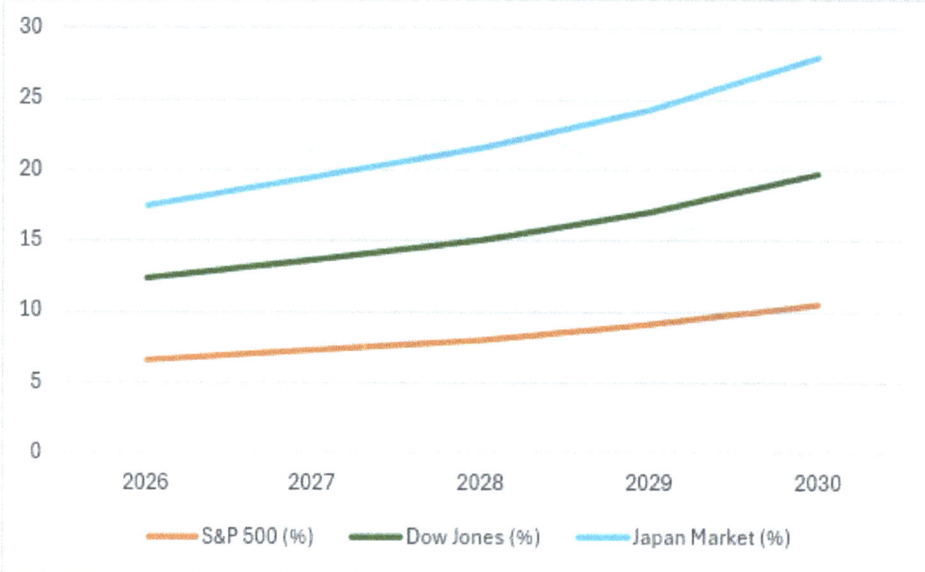

Source: Author's analytical representation based on MarketsandMarkets (2023), PwC (2022), and Dixon et al. (2020).

The line chart shows that there has been a steady increase in the adoption of quantum computing, which indicates its rising significance in industries. The financial institutions are anticipated to exploit these developments to enhance trading strategies, risk modelling and portfolio optimization (Herman et al., 2022).

The implementation of quantum technologies in financial systems is set to speed up as quantum technologies keep advancing. Nevertheless, the level of their influence will be determined by the important factors: technological maturity, reality of infrastructure development, and availability of regulatory support (PwC, 2022).

4.4 Regional Adoption of Quantum Technologies

The use of quantum computing technologies is very different in various regions, which reflects differences in investment, infrastructure and policy support. Quantum research is dominated by the developed parts of the world including North America, Europe, and East Asia because of the strong institutional support and technological economies (PwC, 2022).

Such areas enjoy greater rates of investment, and superior research abilities, which allows them to be on the cutting edge of quantum financial innovation. On the contrary, it is clear that emerging economies are slowly expanding their involvement but continue to have issues associated with the infrastructural level and availability of resources (Herman et al., 2022).

Inequalities in the distribution of quantum technologies have significant implications on how global financial competitiveness is. The availability of more effective quantum capability in a region is likely to provide a more strategic edge to financial markets, underscoring the importance of including more individuals in the development of further improved quantum capabilities (MarketsandMarkets, 2023).

4.5 Distribution of Quantum Applications in Finance

Applications in finance In finance, there are a small number of areas that concentrate the applications of quantum computing. These are algorithmic trading, risk management, fraud detection and cybersecurity. They are optimized through high levels of computational efficiency and accuracy in budgetary processes, which are powered by advanced computation in these applications (Egger et al., 2020).

Figure 5. Distribution of Quantum Computing Applications in Finance

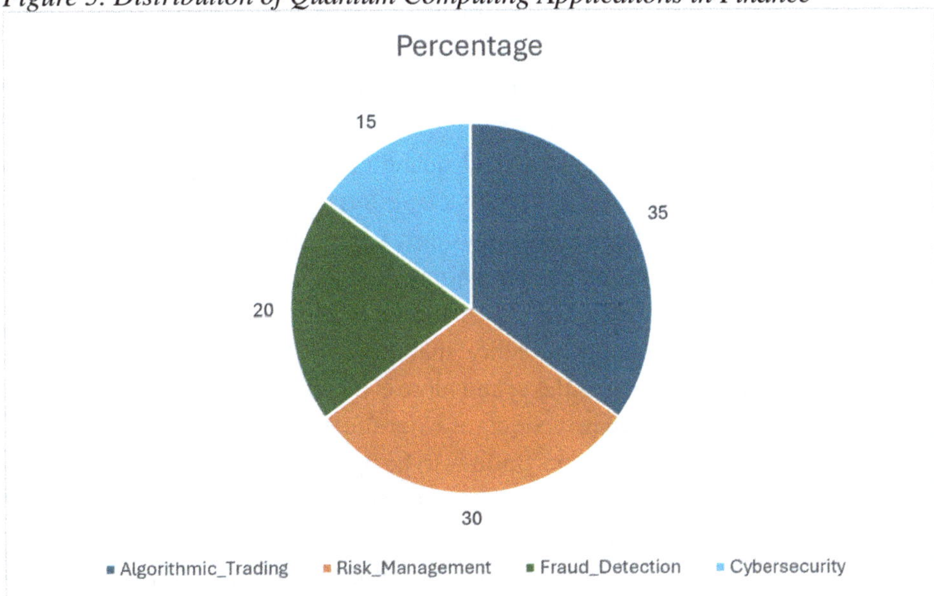

Source: Author's analytical representation based on Herman et al. (2022), Huang et al. (2021), and PwC (2022).

The pie chart shows the proportional representation of these applications, with algorithmic trading and risk management taking the largest share of the pie chart. This is the main concern of the financial institutions towards increasing their profitability and operational efficiency (Herman et al., 2022).

As the technological revolution of quantum computing gains momentum, the scope of its usage is set to broaden to new areas, ultimately having a tremendous impact on the financial systems. Nonetheless, the technological preparedness and regulatory provisions will be crucial in its successful implementation (PwC, 2022).

4.6 Impact on Risk Management and Fraud Detection

Financial systems can greatly enhance risk management and detect fraud in the financial systems by quantum computing. The processing of large volumes of data is accelerated with the help of advanced algorithms and can identify risks and anomalies faster as well (Huang et al., 2021).

The discussion shows that quantum-enhanced models can be used to enhance predictive accuracy, and respond faster, as well as proactive risk management strategies. This becomes particularly crucial in dynamic market settings, where swift decision making processes are crucial (Egger et al., 2020).

Nevertheless, the success of such systems differs with their integration into the current financial systems and the cost of high quality data. Nonetheless, quantum computing is a good prospect to improve financial security and stability (PwC, 2022).

4.7 Comparative Performance: Classical vs Quantum Systems

A comparative study of classical and quantum computers systems indicates that there is a great dissimilarity in terms of performance and efficiency in both computers system types. The classical systems have many applications effective in finance but complex optimization and simulation tasks are often difficult to be effective (Herman et al., 2022).

In contrast, quantum systems have the capability to evaluate more than one possibility at any time, resulting in quicker and more efficient solutions. The mentioned advantage is more pronounced in those cases when the frequency of a particular trade in question is high and when the portfolio is to be optimized (Herman et al., 2022).

Though they have these advantages, quantum computing today is only at its infancy and the usability of the concept is still the exception rather than the norm. The most practical solution to today's problem of providing near-term benefits is currently a hybrid system which combines classical and quantum systems (Herman et al., 2022).

4.8 Overall Findings and Strategic Implications

The results of this paper show that quantum computing could theoretically transform the financial markets by increasing the computational efficiency of the market, helping with faster decision making and making the market more fast. It is believed that such innovations will give early adopters a huge competitive edge (MarketsandMarkets, 2023).

Nonetheless, the effects of quantum computing depend on a number of variables such as efficiency of market, regulatory provisions, and maturity of technologies. To realize the sustainable benefits, financial institutions should pay special attention to these factors when implementing quantum technologies (PwC, 2022).

More broadly, the research implies that quantum computing cannot be considered a solution that allows predicting the market, and the strategic use of quantum computing is another tool that uplifts the financial systems to a higher level. The key to successful introduction of it will lie in the capacity to combine technological innovation and economic and regulatory factors (Herman et al., 2022).

5. RECOMMENDATIONS

5.1 Strategic Adoption of Quantum Technologies

A gradual and strategic policy should be taken towards integration of quantum computing technologies by financial institutions. Because of current constraints of quantum hardware, organizations can first look at hybrid quantum-classical systems which integrates existing computational infrastructure with the emerging quantum capabilities. This way will enable institutions to test quantum models against minimal operational risks and investment costs (Herman et al., 2022).

Moreover, high-impact application areas such as optimization of portfolio, risk analysis and algorithmic trading, where quantum computing is uniquely provided with computational benefits, should be targeted first. With these applications prioritized, financial institutions will be in a position to maximize returns on investment and gain competitive advantage in the fast evolving markets (Herman et al., 2022).

5.2 Investment in Research and Infrastructure

In order to achieve the fullest potential of the quantum computing, the research and development as well as the infrastructure to support it will need substantial investment. Government and other private organizations must come together to encourage the advancement of quantum technologies including improvement of hardware, design of algorithms and training of the workforce. These investments will be critical to the rapidity of innovation and a long-term competitiveness in the international financial markets (PwC, 2022).

Also, dedicated research teams dedicated to the study of quantum finance should be introduced to financiers so that they can keep the pace with the latest trends in technologies and search new opportunities. Developing in-house talents will also be essential to successfully introduce quantum technologies into financial systems and to remain competitive (MarketsandMarkets, 2023).

5.3 Development of Regulatory Frameworks

The current pace of quantum computing development implies the necessity to create suitable regulatory frameworks and maintain healthy competition and equilibrium in the market. Policymakers should consider the possible risks of unequal access to advanced technologies, which may also result in an increased concentration of the market and imbalances in the system (PwC, 2022).

The regulatory frameworks must as well concentrate on making sure transparency, accountability and ethical utilization of quantum technologies in financial markets. With clear guidelines and standards, regulators can enhance innovation, as well as protecting integrity of financial systems (Herman et al., 2022).

5.4 Enhancement of Cybersecurity Measures

There exists both an opportunity and a challenge of quantum computing to the cybersecurity in the financial system. Although quantum technologies can be used to provide better encryption and data protection, they can also be used to break already existing cryptographic systems. Quantum-resistant cryptography solutions that are proactively implemented by financial institutions will help to ensure long-term security (PwC, 2022).

Moreover, constant attention and upgrading of cybersecurity models will be necessary to safeguard sensitive financial information against the threat of emerging issues. With the further development of quantum computing, it will be highly important to have strong security steps in place, so as to avoid any cases of a loss of trust and stability in the financial market (PwC, 2022).

5.5 Focus on Data Quality and Model Validation

The aspect of quantum computing that is likely to change the financial aspect of life is the quality of data and the strength of analytical models in the financial aspect of life. When providing financial services, financial institutions should pay close attention to data integrity, accuracy and consistency to assurance on reliable results. Even the most powerful calculational systems may not be as effective when it comes to the presence of poor data quality (Huang et al., 2021).

In addition, they should have strict model validation procedures to measure the performance of quantum based models under varying market conditions. This involves stress testing, backtesting and ongoing monitoring to make sure that models are viable and efficient with time (Egger et al., 2020).

5.6 Balanced Integration with Economic Principles

Although quantum computing has some major technological benefits, it is not the solution that should be taken into consideration when it comes to the financial prediction. Banking needs to adapt quantum applications to existing economic theories such as market efficiency, and risk management systems (Herman et al., 2022).

A balanced strategy entailed by both the use of technology and good financial theory will ensure a sustainable and effective implementation. Such an incorporation will lead to institutions reaping the fruits of quantum computing and at the same time eliminate the potential risks and constraints that come with its implementation (Huang et al., 2021).

5.7 Development of Skilled Workforce

The achievements in a successful use of quantum computing in the financial sphere can be achieved only with the help of a highly skilled workforce specializing in the area of quantum technologies, as well as the financial systems. All should work together to create special training programs and curricula (PwC, 2022).

To develop internal talent and capabilities, financial institutions will have to invest in talent development that will make quantum technologies effective. It incorporates training of the current employees and retaining of professionals in the field of quantum computing and data science (Herman et al., 2022).

High caliber workforce will be crucial in enhancing innovation and successful introduction of quantum computing in financial markets.

5.8 Encouraging Industry Collaboration

To develop applications of quantum computing, collaboration among financial institutions and technology companies and research organizations is a vital aspect. Through partnerships, it can be easier to share knowledge, encourage more rapid innovation, and decrease the costs of development (Herman et al., 2022).

Joint research projects and pilot projects can assist in determining workable use cases and it will solve the problems associated with implementation. These partnerships will be in a position to assist organizations to take advantage of shared expertise and resources. Fostering interdisciplinary collaboration will be a central aspect of guiding the realization and expansion of quantum technologies to finance.

5.9 Continuous Innovation and Adaptation

Financial markets are ever-moving, ever-evolving and thus demand innovativeness and improvisation. The institutions should also be flexible and responsive to the technological changes to be able to remain competitive (MarketsandMarkets, 2023).

Quantum evaluations and strategies will have to be regularly evaluated to make sure that they are effective in modifying the conditions in the market. It involves model updating, refining of algorithm and introduction of new data sources. The constant innovation will help financial institutions to maintain competitive edges and realize the full potential of quantum computing in financial markets.

CONCLUSION

The current research examined the transformative aspect of quantum computing in the financial markets and its effects in the computational efficiency, trading performance and risk management. The results indicate that quantum technologies can bring considerable benefits over the classic model of computations since they enable more efficient processing of their complex datasets and enhancing the accuracy of their financial models. Such developments can improve the process of decision-making and reinvent the dynamics of operation of modern financial systems.

One of the major conclusions in the analysis relates to the growing purpose of advanced technologies in influencing financial markets around the world. The combination of machine learning and algorithmic trading is already contributing to the increase in the efficiency of the markets, and quantum computing is the next step in the development of the given technology. These developments are reflected in financial indices like the Dow Jones Industrial Average and S&P 500, which incorporate the use of computational advances in the price-setting processes and in the trading strategies.

Although quantum computing has some promise, as pointed out in the study, financial markets have been traditionally complex and adaptive systems. Market efficiency, non-stationarity and competitive behavior factors restrict sustainability of predictive benefits. The advantage of a new technology is also likely to be waning over the coming years as new technology is quickly copied and adapted by players at the game.

The study also highlights the need to start tackling the issues linked with the adoption of quantum technologies. Problems surrounding hardware constraints, high prices, and cybersecurity threats, and regulatory risk need to be addressed.

To enable their successful adoption and long-term sustainability, it is important to ensure the reliability and security of quantum-based financial systems.

Moreover, the paper highlights significance of a balanced solution incorporating diversity of technology innovation and proven economics within the sector. Quantum computing has not been perceived as a one-on-one solution but as a type of supplement that augments the current financial systems. The synthesis of the high level of computational power with a proper financial theory will prove to be crucial in realizing valuable and sustainable results.

In sum, quantum computing has been a stepping stone in financial technology and has the potential to change market structures and enhance the overall efficiency. The future impact it will have will depend on how the various financial institutions, policymakers as well as researchers can work together and adapt to this changing technological environment. The financial sector is one that can enjoy fully the advantages of quantum computing in the years ahead by adopting innovation and retains a sense of stability at the same time.

REFERENCES

Egger, D. J., Gutiérrez, R. G., Woerner, S., & Troyer, M. (2020). Quantum computing for finance: State-of-the-art and future prospects. *IEEE Transactions on Quantum Engineering*, *1*(1), 1–24. DOI: 10.1109/TQE.2020.3030314

Gu, S., Kelly, B., & Xiu, D. (2020). Empirical asset pricing via machine learning. *Review of Financial Studies*, *33*(5), 2223–2273. DOI: 10.1093/rfs/hhaa009

Herman, D., Googin, C., Liu, X., Sun, Y., Galda, A., Safro, I., & Alexeev, Y. (2022). A survey of quantum computing for finance. *Quantum Information Processing*, *21*(1), 1–46.

Huang, H. Y., Broughton, M., Mohseni, M., Babbush, R., Boixo, S., Neven, H., & McClean, J. R. (2021). Power of data in quantum machine learning. *Nature Communications*, *12*(1), 2631–2643. DOI: 10.1038/s41467-021-22539-9 PMID: 33976136

Irfan, M., Dias, R., Rastogi, R., & Zebende, G. F. (2025). *Generative AI insights for financial decision making* (Vol. 1). IGI Global Scientific Publishing. DOI: 10.4018/979-8-3373-1250-7

Irfan, M., Elmogy, M., & Gupta, S. (Eds.). (2024). *AI-driven decentralized finance and the future of finance* (Vol. 1). IGI Global Scientific Publishing. DOI: 10.4018/979-8-3693-6321-8

Irfan, M., Hussainey, K., Bukhari, S. A. C., & Nam, Y. (Eds.). (2024). *Issues of sustainability in AI and new-age thematic investing* (Vol. 1). IGI Global Scientific Publishing. DOI: 10.4018/979-8-3693-3282-5

Irfan, M., Kadry, S., Sharif, M., & Khan, H. U. (Eds.). (2023). *Fintech applications in Islamic finance: AI, machine learning, and blockchain techniques* (Vol. 1). IGI Global Scientific Publishing. DOI: 10.4018/979-8-3693-1038-0

Irfan, M., Zebende, G. F., Sarea, A., & Shahbaz, M. (Eds.). (2025). *Quantum-driven financial intelligence: Innovations in predictive analytics and autonomous trading systems* (Vol. 1). IGI Global Scientific Publishing. DOI: 10.4018/979-8-3373-2893-5

MarketsandMarkets. (2023). *Quantum computing market – Global forecast to 2030* (Vol. 3, Issue 1). MarketsandMarkets Research Pvt. Ltd.

PwC. (2022). *Quantum computing in financial services: Opportunities and risks* (Vol. 5, Issue 1). PricewaterhouseCoopers.

Saran, C. (2021). Crédit Agricole tests quantum in finance. *Computer Weekly*, *15*(5), 18–21.

Chapter 10
Quantum-Resilient Deepfake Detection:
Securing AI-Generated Media in the Post-Quantum Era

Rimsha Kanwal
http://orcid.org/0009-0001-6759-5155
Taylor's University, Malaysia

Humaira Ashraf
http://orcid.org/0000-0001-5067-3172
Taylor's University, Malaysia

Qurat Ul Ain Zam Zam Mirza
Taylor's University, Malaysia

ABSTRACT

Generative AI and its role in developing deepfake technologies are of great concern due to the threats to digital authenticity, privacy and information security caused by the rapid growth of deepfake technology. Classical detection systems have also advanced to detect manipulated content, but with the advent of quantum computing, new vulnerabilities are created along with new opportunities to defend against the vulnerabilities. In this chapter, quantum technologies are discussed in terms of how they intersect with deepfake detection systems and examine some of the risks associated with quantum-enhanced deepfake production as well as cryptographic breakage and manipulation of the training data. In response, it explores quantum secure paradigms such as QML, QKD and PQC algorithms. Quantum resistant protocols and hybrid classical-quantum detection models are argued to be the possible way of the future.

DOI: 10.4018/979-8-3373-3857-6.ch010

1. INTRODUCTION

Deepfake detection system security can be improved thanks to new developments in quantum computing and quantum-enhanced cryptography techniques. The ways of detecting attacks are usually not enough as the methods of adversarial attacks become more sophisticated. The present section examines the opportunities in computing quantum technology to create more secure and tamper-proof deepfake detection systems, trust and reliability in digital media ecosystems.

1.1. Deepfakes and the Expanding Threat Landscape

Synthetic multimedia deepfakes, created with the aid of sophisticated AI methods such as GANs, VAEs, diffusion models are becoming both more realistic and more available. Recent surveys point to the fact that compressed deepfakes are not detected by traditional systems and spread over such platforms as YouTube, Twitter, and TikTok rapidly (Katı et al., 2025). This explosive development has given rise to a wide range of threats: political disinformation, fraud, social engineering scams, defamation, biometric system attacks (Firc et al., 2023). As a concrete example, deepfake phone calls have been used to conduct romance scams and executive impersonation attacks that have led to losses valued in the millions (Roscoe 2025). Even though detection accuracy has improved, most attempts to defend against the deepfakes still lack generalization when an attacker applies generative models of their own or when the adversarial manipulation is based on foundation models (Abdullah et al., 2024). Figure 1 shows the process of deepfake threats beginning with the utilization of AI models to create fake faces. These processed images then become shared through platforms, such as YouTube, TikTok, and Twitter and lastly used in an attack, including impersonation, scams, biometric spoofing, and fraud.

Figure 1. Deepfake threats

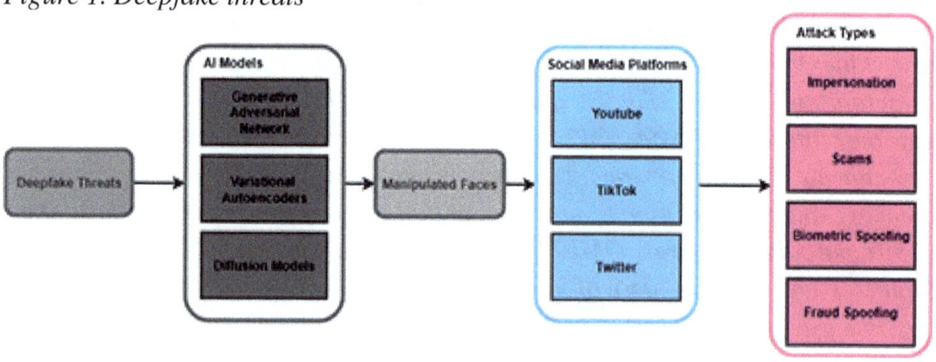

1.2. Overview of Quantum Computing and Quantum Security

Quantum computers exploit qubits, superposition, and entanglement to efficiently perform some computational tasks that are difficult or inefficient to carry out on a classical computer, for example, integer factorization and discrete logarithms via the Shor algorithm (Willsch et al., 2023). These advances have presented an application of existential threat to existing cryptographic systems and standards such as RSA and ECC and have led to a transition to quantum-resistant systems and post quantum cryptography (PQC). Quantum security more generally includes attempts to provide the security it takes to use quantum-resistant cryptographic schemes like lattice-based cryptography, hash-based cryptography, and isogeny-based schemes and QKD to secure communications even against attackers with access to future quantum computers. Despite the early stage of quantum hardware, professionals advise that proactive transition is necessary since there is a risk of encrypted information being stolen now but decode later when quantum computing provides the necessary capabilities related to a massive cyber campaign of " harvest now, decrypt later" (Dam et al., 2023).

1.3 Why Quantum Security Matters in Deepfake Detection

With the development of detection models, the adversaries are also advancing: the development of quantum-enhanced deep fake creation and the use of quantum power tools can create some fakes that could not be identified using classical detectors. It has been proposed lately that the accuracy of a detection framework can be enhanced and its resilience enhanced by utilizing QML techniques like QSVMs or QNN (THOMAS et al.,). As another example, quantum transfer learning together with ViT architecture achieved 0.94 AUC on the DFDC dataset, which also illustrates a high level of performance with minimal resources usage optimization (Katı et al., 2025). Furthermore, data pipelines as well as cryptographic integrity checks used by a lot of deepfake detectors are quantum susceptible. Without secure uses of quantum, datasets or model update could be spoofed or altered. Using PQC standards and QKD can guarantee authenticity, confidentiality and forward secrecy throughout the detection lifetime (Dervisevic et al., 2025). Table 1 shows the possible risk scenario in deepfake detection.

Table 1. Quantum Risks and Quantum Countermeasure in Deepfake Detection

Risk Scenario	Quantum Threat	Quantum Countermeasure
Tampering training datasets	Qubit-based data poisoning	PQC + dataset watermarking
Deepfake generation beyond classical detection	Quantum GANs	Quantum-enhanced detectors (QNNs)
Model update interception	Shor's algorithm on RSA	Lattice-based PQC, QKD
Spoofing content authentication	Quantum attack on hashes	Post-quantum signatures

1.4 Objectives and Scope

This chapter aims to:

a. Contextualize the evolving deepfake threat landscape and challenges in detection.
b. Introduce quantum computing fundamentals and its implications for cryptography and machine learning.
c. Examine how quantum technologies can both threaten and enhance deepfake detection.
d. Explore quantum cryptographic tools (QKD and PQC) to secure data integrity and authenticity.
e. Highlight recent QML-based deepfake detectors and their performance.
f. Identify challenges that are hardware limitations, scalability, integration and suggest future research avenues in secure, quantum-robust deepfake detection.

By the end, readers should understand not only the quantum threats facing deepfake detection systems, but also the cutting-edge quantum-enhanced strategies available to defend against them preparing for a post-quantum security landscape.

Notations

- **AI**: Artificial Intelligence
- **AUC**: Area Under the Curve (performance metric)
- **BB84**: Bennett and Brassard 1984 (QKD Protocol)
- **CNNs**: Convolutional Neural Networks
- **CST ViT**: Class-attention Vision Transformer
- **DFDC**: DeepFake Detection Challenge (Dataset)
- **DSA**: Digital Signature Algorithm
- **ECC**: Elliptic Curve Cryptography

- **ECDSA**: Elliptic Curve Digital Signature Algorithm
- **E91**: Ekert 1991 (QKD Protocol)
- **FN-DSA**: Falcon Digital Signature Algorithm
- **GANs**: Generative Adversarial Networks
- **GeMSS**: Great Multivariate Signature Scheme
- **GMT+8**: Greenwich Mean Time + 8 hours (Time Zone)
- **H**: Hadamard (Quantum Gate Symbol)
- **HQC**: High-Dimensional Code-Based Cryptography (or a specific scheme)
- **HMAC**: Hash-based Message Authentication Code
- **KB**: Kilobytes (File Size Unit)
- **KEMs**: Key Encapsulation Mechanisms
- **ML DSA**: Module Lattice Digital Signature Algorithm (for CRYSTALS-Dilithium)
- **ML KEM**: Module Lattice Key Encapsulation Mechanism (for CRYSTALS-Kyber)
- **MQ**: Multivariate Quadratic (polynomial cryptography)
- **NIST**: National Institute of Standards and Technology
- **NTRU**: N-th degree Truncated polynomial ring Unit (lattice-based cryptosystem)
- **PQC**: Post-Quantum Cryptography
- **QCNN**: Quantum CNN
- **QKD**: Quantum Key Distribution
- **QML**: Quantum Machine Learning
- **QNNs**: Quantum Neural Networks
- **QPU**: Quantum Processing Unit
- **QSVMs**: Quantum Support Vector Machines
- **QT-CNN**: Quantum-Trained CNN (or Convolutional Networks)
- **QTL-CaiT**: Quantum Transfer Learning - Class-attention Vision Transformer
- **QVC**: Variational Quantum Classifier (or Circuit)
- **Ring-LWE**: Ring Learning With Errors (a mathematical problem/ cryptosystem)
- **RSA**: Rivest–Shamir–Asdleman (cryptographic system)
- **S, T**: Phase (Quantum Gate Symbols)
- **SLH-DSA**: SPHINCS+ Lightweight Hash-based Digital Signature Algorithm
- **SPHINCS+**: Stateless Hash-Based Signatures (a specific hash-based signature scheme)
- **VAEs**: Variational Autoencoders
- **VQC**: Variational Quantum Classifier (or Circuit)
- **ViT**: Vision Transformer
- **X**: Pauli-X (Quantum Gate Symbol)

- **XMSS/LMS**: eXtended Merkle Signature Scheme / Leighton-Micali Signature Scheme (hash-based signatures)

2. BACKGROUND CONCEPTS

Deepfake detection and quantum security belong to different fields of technologies. Deepfakes are created on the basis of AI models, such as GANs and VAEs which can create realistic media and it is increasingly difficult to detect a manipulation. The conventional detection methods can focus on inconsistencies within the contents, which are vulnerable to attacks. Conversely, quantum computing brings up new models of computation and quantum cryptography brings unbreakable security protocols such as QKD and PQC.It is necessary to comprehend both fields to come up with safe, quantum-impervious detection mechanisms.

2.1 Deepfake Generation and Detection

Over the past few years, Deepfakes have rapidly progressed. Initially, systems used VAEs and GANs to create and video synthesize facial images. Recently, diffusion models have come to be seen as advanced generators that create hyper-realistic and detailed images and videos. Table 2 describes the generation of Deepfakes over time.

Table 2. Overview of Deepfake generation types

Model Type	Core Mechanism	Use Case	Limitation
GAN	Generator + Discriminator	High-quality face swaps	Mode collapse, training instability
VAE	Probabilistic encoding	Low-res video synthesis	Blurry outputs
Diffusion Models	Iterative denoising	Text-to-image/video	High compute cost, slow generation

Initially, detection methods focused on analyzing individual modalities, such as facial visual features or speech patterns. Then, detection methods evolved to multimodal approaches that incorporate analyses of cross-modal consistency of audio and visual data, text alignment, and discrepancies in metadata (Liu et al., 2024). More recent survey work suggests that detection of diffusion-based deepfakes necessitates innovative, cross-feature detection methods that are tailored to domain generalization for various concealed generative models and different types of media (Xu et al., 2025).

Some of the popular methods for detection include:

a. CNN-based forgery classification, trained on spatial artefacts or compression residuals
b. Frequency-domain analysis, isolating unnatural patterns in generated content
c. Temporal coherence checks, identifying frame-by-frame inconsistencies
d. Ensemble or hybrid models, combining audio, video, and behavioral cues to reduce false positives (Xu et al., 2025).

2.2 Quantum Computing Fundamentals

Quantum computing introduces a fundamentally different computational paradigm. Unlike classical bits, qubits can exist in superposition, letting them compute in parallel over multiple states at once. When qubits become entangled, measurement of one directly correlates to another, regardless of distance adding a unique power to quantum operations (Barral et al., 2025).

Quantum operations are orchestrated via quantum gates, such as Hadamard to create superposition, Pauli-X/Y/Z to flip or phase-shift qubit states, and CNOT for entanglement. These gates form quantum circuits, akin to classical logic circuits but inherently reversible and probabilistic (Bashir et al., 2025).

Quantum machines can outperform classical computers on some tasks exponentially that are integer factorization with quantum computers by Shor algorithm or unstructured search with the Grover algorithm, which violates the security hypotheses that RSA and ECC cryptography rely on (Singh & Kumar, 2024). Table 3 shows the functions of Key Quantum Gates.

Table 3. Key Quantum Gates and their functions

Gate	Symbol	Function	Use Case
Hadamard	H	Creates superposition	Quantum parallelism
Pauli-X	X	Bit flip	Like NOT gate
CNOT	⊕	Conditional operation (entanglement)	Creating entangled states
Phase	S, T	Adds phase shift	Grover's search optimization

2.3 Quantum Cryptography & Quantum Security

Quantum security contains two complementary areas, PQC and QKD.

a. Post Quantum Cryptography denotes classical cryptographic methods that are immune to quantum attacks, in particular lattice-based schemes such as CRYSTALS-Kyber (ML KEM), CRYSTALS-Dilithium (ML DSA) and code based HQC. These algorithms have been standardized by NIST as of August 13, 2024, with HQC added as a backup KEM in March 2025 (Wang & Ismail, 2025).

b. QKD, including protocols like BB84 and E91, leverages quantum physics to detect eavesdropping in real-time providing theoretical security through the no-cloning theorem. If an attacker intercepts the key exchange, the quantum state collapses, alerting the communicating parties (Ain et al., 2025). However, practical deployment faces challenges that are high infrastructure cost, limited range, error rates, device vulnerabilities, and the need for trusted relays (Dervisevic et al., 2025).

QKD is best suited for highly sensitive applications financial sectors, government, or strategic communications while PQC offers more scalable, versatile defense applicable across the internet and embedded systems (Aquina et al., 2025). Table 4 shows the comparison between PQC and QKD.

Table 4. PQC vs QKD

Feature	PQC	QKD
Implementation	Classical hardware	Requires quantum channels
Security basis	Hard math problems	Quantum physics
Scalability	High (web, embedded)	Low (limited range, high cost)
Standardization	Yes (NIST, 2024–2025)	Not widely standardized
Ideal for	Internet-wide systems	Military, banking, critical infra

3. THE THREAT OF QUANTUM COMPUTING TO DEEPFAKE DETECTION

Quantum computing leads to more secure systems but is dangerous because it will allow more sophisticated and swifter adversarial attacks. Its network computing capabilities would compromise conventional detection networks by putting their reliability and robustness into question.

3.1 Quantum-Powered Deepfake Generation

Quantum computers can be an effective way of making the generative models employed in deepfake creation much more potent. Using QML tools like quantum

GANs and variational circuits, it is possible to produce highly photo-realistic and complex pieces of synthetic content in shorter training time with increased efficiency. These quantum-enhanced models have the capacity to search for more significant spaces of possible solutions and discover complex distributions of the data that have an advantage over the classical model. Thus, the intricate particulars and the conviction in deepfakes can reach a point which is extremely difficult to discern, even with advanced detection methods. This poses a significant challenge to the trustworthiness of information, as well as the reliability of the entire digital media landscape.

Ability to Avoid Existing Detection Methods

Quantum-driven generative machines, and in particular QML boosted by GANs or diffusion models could produce synthetic media indiscernible to classical sensors. One example outcome came from the technical report titled Quantum-Powered Deepfake Detection (Yenepoya University, March2025), which claims that QSVMs and QNNs could potentially output adversarial deepfakes impossible for traditional models to identify (THOMAS et al.,).

Further, recent work demonstrates that QT-CNN architectures (quantum-trained convolutional networks) lower the number of parameters and also align with classical detection performance, suggesting that quantum-enhanced generator tools might function equivalently efficiently but with evasive capability (Lin et al., 2025).

Speed and Complexity Advantages

Quantum AI's ability to process things at the same time and get them to work together quickly creates hyper-realistic content.As described in recent literature, quantum AI can analyze large harvested datasets instantly and replicate writing style, speech, and facial motion enabling real-time deepfake calls or phishing attacks that adapt on-the-fly, far beyond classical compute limitations. Figure 2 illustrates side by side comparison of classical and quantum deepfake attacks. Quantum methods add features like metadata forgery and cryptographic breaking that make it harder to find than traditional GAN-based methods.

Figure 2. Comparison of Classical and Quantum Deepfake Attack

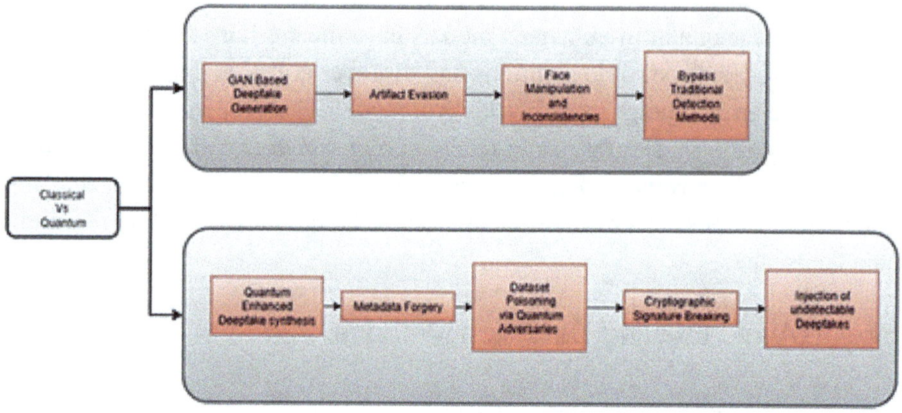

3.2 Risks to Dataset Integrity, Metadata, and Source Authentication

Quantum systems could be used to poison or change training datasets in ways that classical adversarial defenses can't detect. In adversarial machine learning contexts, even classical poisoning and evasion attacks bypass classifiers by subtly modifying training inputs (Alotaibi & Rassam, 2023). A quantum adversary could craft more sophisticated contamination that escapes current anomaly detection.

Moreover, metadata spoofing such as altering timestamps, geolocation tags, or device fingerprints becomes more feasible if metadata authentication relies on vulnerable cryptographic schemes. Such tampering erodes trust in the provenance of deepfake media and weakens forensic pipelines.

Without quantum-resistant protocols, source authentication of media, model updates, or integrity checks can be compromised. Man-in-the-middle or replay attacks on signature schemes like RSA or ECC would allow an attacker to inject bogus content into the detection pipeline unnoticed. Table 5 provides an overview of some of the major data integrity and metadata threats when using quantum powered environments.

Table 5. Data Integrity and Metadata Risks in Quantum-Powered Environments

Attack Surface	Quantum-enabled Risk Type	Target Component	Impact on Detection System
Training Data Injection	Quantum-optimized adversarial poisoning	Model training dataset	Model bias, reduced generalization
Dataset Label Spoofing	Tampered quantum-labeled inputs	Ground truth annotations	Misleading classifier learning
Metadata Fabrication	Synthetic timestamp/device/geotag metadata	Video/audio metadata	Broken source authenticity, audit trail loss
Media Provenance Tampering	Qubit-encoded content forging	Watermarked/authenticated media	Undetectable forgery, deepfake attribution errors
Model Update Channel	Tampering via quantum channel interference	Model weights or patches	Backdoor injection, remote manipulation

3.3 Cryptographic Vulnerabilities in Current Detection Pipelines

Most deepfake detection systems rely on public-key encryption (RSA, ECC) or digital signatures to secure data and model exchange. These are vulnerable to Shor's algorithm, which efficiently breaks factoring-based cryptography once large-scale quantum computers are available (Willsch et al., 2023).

Even if QKD offsets some risks, implementation weaknesses such as imperfect single-photon sources or lack of strong authentication can expose systems to man-in-the-middle and denial-of-service attacks (Portmann & Renner, 2022).

Urgent initiatives like NIST's PQC standardization recommend migrating systems to lattice-based or code-based algorithms that are Kyber, Dilithium to secure integrity, authenticity, and forward secrecy in deepfake detection pipelines (Wang & Ismail, 2025).

4. QUANTUM-ENHANCED DEEPFAKE DETECTION

Quantum technologies are useful in providing a vital input in enhancing deepfake detection pipelines. Due to integration with quantum computing, systems may analyze complex patterns and high-dimensional data more easily than the classical methods respectively. Quantum algorithms can assist in finding minor artifacts in the synthesized material, and the accuracy is higher, as well as highly reliable. Also, quantum-augmented security layers implemented that are quantum watermarking, secure feature encoding can further prevent adversarial tampering. These advancements are a step toward more robust and secure detection systems.

4.1 QML Approaches

In order to create hybrid models that can extract new information from data more rapidly and effectively, QML combines the ideas of quantum computing and classical machine learning. Using methods like quantum classifiers, quantum convolutional networks, and variational quantum circuits, QML applications are being researched in deepfake detection to enable more accurate identification of forged material. The models can handle high-dimensional input features with fewer resources and are faster and more scalable. Additionally, QML can be used to improve generalization and reduce overfitting, which is useful when there are different or evolving deepfake techniques.

QNN

Superposition and entanglement are used by QNN, which is implemented using parameterized quantum circuits, to capture intricate data patterns. With fewer parameters and greater accuracy than classical networks, models such as QCNNs show promise in the field of fraud detection (Bikku et al., 2024). For the detection of deepfake audio, a quantum-trained convolutional neural network called QT-CNN was proposed, which can reduce parameters by up to 70% without compromising performance (Lin et al., 2025).

QSVMs

Using quantum kernel techniques, quantum-enhanced SVMs, like PegasosQSVM, achieve significant gains over classical baselines and simulated accuracy of up to 95.6% in fake-news classification (Khalil et al., 2025).

Variational Quantum Circuits

VQC-based classifiers have been validated in cybersecurity and fraud detection tasks. Hybrid quantum-classical VQC architectures often outperform purely quantum or classical counterparts when tuned properly (Salek et al., 2024).

4.2 Hybrid Classical-Quantum Deepfake Detection Models

Recent deepfake-focused architectures integrate quantum modules with transformers or CNNs. A notable model *QTL-CaiT* combines quantum transfer learning with a CST ViT. It achieved 90% accuracy and AUC 0.94 on the DFDC dataset, with resource savings compared to pure transformers (Katı et al., 2025).

Another hybrid model, *Q-ViX*, fuses Xception, ViT, and Pennylane-based QNN. Trained over FaceForensics++ and DFDC datasets, it exceeded 95% accuracy, generalizing across compressed and unseen deepfake types ((A 2025).

4.3 Case Studies and Simulations

a. **Traffic sign deepfake detection**: A hybrid quantum-classical model using amplitude encoding outperformed classical CNNs in memory efficiency and competitive accuracy in attacking autonomous vehicle sign classification systems (Salek et al., 2024).
b. **Adversarial robustness in QVCs**: In cybersecurity, hybrid VQC models achieved 94% accuracy in cyber-attack detection and were more resilient to adversarial perturbations compared to classical baselines (Moll & Kunczik 2025).

4.4 Comparison QML Detection Methods

Table 6 compares QML based detection methods. It demonstrates that the hybrid models such as QT-CNN and VQC have a powerful performance either in efficiency or reliability, and PegasosQSVM is accurate using quantum kernels. Most of the approaches however have their limitation be it in simulation-only results, hardware constraints or real quantum testing.

Table 6. Comparison Table od QML Detection Methods

Model / Approach	Architecture	Performance (on detection task)	Key Advantages	Limitations
QT-CNN (audio deepfake) (Lin et al., 2025)	Hybrid QNN + CNN	Comparable accuracy to CNN; 70% fewer parameters	Efficiency, lower memory use	Audio only; simulation-based results
PegasosQSVM (Khalil et al., 2025)	QSVM with quantum kernel	95.6% accuracy	Strong classification power	Requires error mitigation on real QPU
VQC / QVC (cyber detection) [26]	Classical feature extractor + VQC	93.97% accuracy; outperform pure classical & pure quantum	Robust hybrid performance	Limited qubit count; hardware constraints

continued on following page

Table 6. Continued

Model / Approach	Architecture	Performance (on detection task)	Key Advantages	Limitations
QTL-CaiT (Katı et al., 2025)	Quantum Transfer Learning + CST ViT	90% accuracy; AUC 0.94 on DFDC	Integrates global features, scalable	Simulated; needs real quantum testing
Q-ViX ((A 2025)	Classical CNN / ViT + QNN from Pennylane	95% accuracy across datasets	Handles compressed and unseen fakes	Still experimental, generalization not fully evaluated

5. QUANTUM CRYPTOGRAPHY FOR SECURING DETECTION PIPELINES

Quantum cryptography provides added security to deepfake detection pipelines since it creates a secure path of communication to data integrity. Such techniques as QKD avoid interception and tampering of the models through model training, communication, and verification. This builds faith and strength considering the changing hostile threats.

5.1 Securing Training Datasets using Quantum Cryptographic Methods

Training data remains a key attack surface in detection systems, especially when adversaries may poison datasets to compromise models. To secure this, combining QKD with PQC ensures both encryption integrity and authentication of datasets. For example, QKD provides information-theoretic secure symmetric key exchange, while PQC authenticates message origins and prevents man-in-the-middle tampering even by quantum-enabled adversaries (Termos 2024). A proposed framework for secure multi-party cloud outsourcing integrates QKD, CRYSTALS-Kyber, and zero-knowledge proofs to authenticate data blocks in distributed training datasets ideal for federated learning scenarios in deepfake detection pipelines (Dhinakaran et al., 2024).

5.2 Authentication of Video Sources via Quantum-Secured Blockchain or Watermarking

Authenticating source media prevents tampered content from entering the detection pipeline. Research on combining blockchain with hashing (HMAC/ECC) enables immutable chaining of video segment hashes, effectively detecting insert/delete or tampering attempts even in distributed content systems (Patil & Chouragade, 2021).

Embedding semi-fragile neural watermarks provides proactive authentication: watermarks that break under manipulation but survive benign edits offer tamper-evidence for original media before deepfake transformations (Neekhara et al., 2022).

When blockchain storage is paired with watermark extraction tied to cryptographic hashes authenticated via PQC, the integrity of identified videos becomes provably reliable.

5.3 Use of QKD in Secure Model Updates and Data Transmission

Model updates whether shared weights or retraining patches must be protected end-to-end. Using QKD-based key exchange protocols ensure new symmetric keys remain secure from interception or retroactive compromise through quantum attacks. For instance, metamaterial-enhanced QKD extends transmission distance and lowers error, making high-rate key exchange practical in long-distance pipelines (Termos 2024).

Real-world deployments of QKD over 254 km fiber telecom links show that quantum-secure message transmission is now technically feasible using commercial infrastructure, highlighting near-term use in real-world deployment of secure detection networks (Peel 2025).

Reviews show QKD-secured communication can then feed into symmetric updates or one-time-pads, ensuring forward secrecy and mitigating risks from future quantum-capable adversaries (Termos 2024).

Integrated Security for Detection Pipelines

By weaving QKD, PQC, blockchain, and watermarking, detection pipelines gain layered defenses:

a. **Data authenticity**: PQC-authenticated keys and blockchain-anchored hashes prevent poisoning or source spoofing.
b. **Media integrity**: Neural watermarking combined with immutable records ensures content provenance.
c. **Model confidentiality and integrity**: Key exchange via QKD secures updates while resisting quantum decryption.

Table 7 presents the comparison between different Quantum Cryptographic techniques for detection pipelines.

Table 7. Comparison of Quantum Cryptographic Techniques for Detection Pipelines

Security Layer	Quantum Tool(s)	Application in Detection Pipeline	Benefits and Considerations
Training Data / Dataset Exchange	QKD + PQC (Kyber, HQC)	Secure distribution and authentication of training data	Confidentiality, tamper detection; complex integration
Video Source Authentication	Blockchain (hash chaining) + neural watermarking	Provenance verification of media before detection	Immutable audit trail; watermark fragility to tampering
Model Update / Patch Delivery	QKD (BB84/E91), PQC signatures	Secure transmission of model weights and retraining patches	Forward secrecy; practical over fibre; requires quantum channels
Communication Infrastructure	Metamaterial-enhanced QKD, hybrid PQC-QKD	Long-distance secure pipelines and collaboration	Improved range, practicality; requires infrastructure suppor

6. POST-QUANTUM CRYPTOGRAPHIC SOLUTIONS

PQC algorithms are cryptographic algorithms designed to resist some attack advances on quantum computers to provide forward-proofing security. PQC may be implemented to provide security for the model parameters, authentication procedures and data transmissions in deepfake detection models. Such solutions can provide long-term security even in the quantum computing-enabled threat environment.

6.1 Quantum-Resistant Algorithms

As quantum threats grow, detection pipelines must adopt cryptographic schemes that resist quantum attacks. Research identifies several classes of PQC:

a. **Lattice-based cryptography**, including NTRU, Ring-LWE, and module-lattice schemes that are CRYSTALS-Kyber, CRYSTALS-Dilithium offers strong security reductions and efficient performance (Imran et al., 2020).
b. **Hash-based signatures**, especially stateless variants like SPHINCS+ and XMSS/LMS, provide quantum-safe digital signatures, though with larger signature sizes (Fathalla & Azab, 2024).
c. **Multivariate polynomial cryptography** such as MQ-based schemes like GeMSS and code-based systems are also candidates considered in NIST rounds and post-quantum studies (Wang & Ismail, 2025).

6.2 Integration into Deepfake Detection Pipelines

Incorporating PQC within existing detection infrastructure involves:

a. **Key exchange protocols**: replacing RSA/ECC with Kyber-based KEMs to protect dataset distribution and model updates (Demir et al., 2025).
b. **Digital signatures**: using Dilithium or SPHINCS+ to sign media files, metadata, and logs ensuring resilience to signature forgery by quantum adversaries. These can authenticate provenance and integrity of input videos.
c. **Hybrid deployment**: systems can use classical algorithms with backwards compatibility, transitioning gradually as quantum-safe libraries mature.

Practical performance metrics such as key generation, verifying delays show that Kyber and Dilithium can outperform RSA and ECDSA at equivalent security levels, especially when hardware optimized (Demir et al., 2025).

6.3 Timeline and Relevance of NIST Standards

NIST formalized its first post-quantum algorithm standards on August 13, 2024:

a. CRYSTALS-Kyber (key encapsulation),
b. CRYSTALS-Dilithium (digital signatures),
c. and SLH-DSA (based on SPHINCS+) for stateless hash-based signatures. A fourth standard FN-DSA (Falcon) is expected by late 2024.

These algorithms have already seen early deployment, for instance, over 16% of traffic to Cloudflare servers uses Kyber-based key exchange as of mid-2024 (Valenta et al., 2024).

7. CHALLENGES AND LIMITATIONS

Even though it would allow taking quantum and post-quantum solutions to the next level, there are several problems associated with this approach, such as the lack of hardware, the high prices of implementation, and the complexity of integration with existing AI systems. In addition, most quantum algorithms are not quite developed, which makes their use in detecting deepfakes currently unrealistic. The major challenge has been making sure that this is scalable and standardized.

7.1 Limitations of Quantum Hardware

a. Cloud quantum systems remain in the Noisy Intermediate-Scale Quantum era (Callison & Chancellor, 2022), with up to ~1,000 qubits but high noise and limited connectivity, making fault tolerance impractical for the foreseeable future.
b. Google's Willow chip (105 physical qubits) achieves minimal error correction but still falls short of the ~10^{-6} logical error rates needed for meaningful quantum advantage (Jin 2025).
c. Experts estimate fully fault-tolerant, large-scale quantum computing will take 10–20 years, despite optimistic projections (Tangalakis-Lippert 2024).

7.2 Scalability of Quantum ML for Real-Time Detection

a. QML models like VQCs and QNNs face barren plateau issues flat optimization landscapes making training infeasible at scale (Cerezo et al., 2022).
b. Hybrid architectures such as multi-chip ensemble frameworks are emerging but distributing workloads across chips adds complexity and may not yet support real-time detection workloads effectively (Park et al., 2025).

7.3 Integration Issues with Classical Infrastructure

a. Classical detection pipelines and infrastructure GPUs, APIs, storage systems are not built for quantum-classical hybrid workflows mismatched data encoding/ decoding, API incompatibility, and logistical friction exist.
b. There is a large skills gap: many industry stakeholders are unprepared for quantum cybersecurity implementation, with nearly half lacking readiness plans (Woollacott 2025).

7.4 High Computational Cost of Post-Quantum Algorithms

a. PQC algorithms such as Dilithium, SPHINCS+, Kyber have significantly larger key sizes and slow signature operations compared to RSA/ECC, increasing memory and bandwidth demands (Demir et al., 2025).
b. Trade-offs are highlighted by benchmarking studies: Even with hardware acceleration, PQC algorithms still require more computation cycles than classical

algorithms, particularly in embedded or Internet of Things settings (Demir et al., 2025).

Table 8 summarizes the key challenges for deepfake detection using quantum.

Table 8. Summary of Key Challenges in Quantum-Secure Deepfake Detection

Challenge Area	Description	Implications for Detection Pipelines
Quantum hardware limitations	NISQ devices suffer noise, coherence loss	Limits practical QML deployment, delays adoption
Scalability of quantum ML	Training inefficiency, latency from multiple runs	Hard to achieve real-time detection performance
Integration with classical systems	Infrastructure, skill, and pipeline incompatibility	Complexity in hybrid system development
Post-quantum crypto overhead	Larger keys, slower signature and encryption ops	Slower handshake, higher memory and compute use

8. FUTURE RESEARCH DIRECTIONS

With quantum technologies going on, there are various opportunities that can transform the manner in which the deepfake detection and prevention system is designed and secured. These are the essential guidelines that should be developed.

8.1 Full-Quantum vs Hybrid Approaches

Though current advances are generally moving toward the direction of the hybrid models, which combine classical and quantum computing, the potential of a deepfake detection that is fully quantum-native has not been implemented yet. Such paradigms may be likened to performance, scalability and energy efficiency trade-offs in future work.

8.2 Federated Learning with Quantum Security

By combining federated learning, a decentralized mode of training with quantum-secure communication, it is possible to guarantee the privacy of sensitive model updates against both classical and quantum adversaries. This is especially applicable in the multi-platform social media settings where user data confidentiality is of utmost importance.

8.3 Quantum Watermarking for Content Authentication

There may also be a need to embed quantum-generated watermarks into the media content as it will provide a resistant way of establishing the integrity and provenance of digital content. Compared to classical watermarking, quantum schemes may be unforgeable in nature and be more resistant to adversarial attacks.

8.4 Quantum-Resistant Protocols for Social Media Platforms

It is urgently required to work out new communication protocols that could resist quantum attacks on end-to-end encryption and authentication. Social network sites ought to implement quantum-safe criteria so that there is integrity of user conversations and content verification systems long term. Table 9 provides the description of future research direction.

Table 9. Summary of Key Future Research

Focus Area	Description	Potential Impact
Full vs Hybrid Quantum Detection	Comparing purely quantum vs hybrid architectures	Optimal performance and energy balance
Quantum-secure Federated Learning	Secure decentralized training using QKD or PQC	Protects model privacy in distributed setups
Quantum Watermarking	Quantum-generated content markers	Enhanced content authenticity
Quantum-Resistant Protocols	Next-gen secure messaging and verification protocols	Long-term trust in social media ecosystems

9. CONCLUSION

In this chapter, the subject matter of deepfake detection and quantum computing as well as cyberspace security has been discussed, with an emphasis on the increasing need to be ready to deal with a post-quantum threat environment. We discussed the fact that quantum technologies can be used to generate deepfakes with quantum power, as well as be cryptographically vulnerable, but can also be used to provide solutions in an entirely new way with QML, quantum cryptography, and post-quantum algorithms.

With advances in deepfakes, as the integration of deepfakes into disinformation campaigns is more apparent and widespread in the real world, the intersection of AI and quantum computing will be vital both offensively and defensively. The fact of quantum resilience Preparing deepfake detection systems to be quantum resilient has ceased to be optional, and it is a strategic necessity. The future is in the creation of scalable, secure and efficient frameworks that could accommodate the advances in quantum without jeopardizing trust, authenticity and privacy through digital ecosystems.

REFERENCES

Abdullah, S. M., Cheruvu, A., Kanchi, S., Chung, T., Gao, P., Jadliwala, M., & Viswanath, B. (2024, May). An analysis of recent advances in deepfake image detection in an evolving threat landscape. In *2024 IEEE Symposium on Security and Privacy (SP)* (pp. 91-109). IEEE. DOI: 10.1109/SP54263.2024.00194

Ain, N. U., Waqar, M., Bilal, A., Kim, A., Ali, H., Tariq, U. U., & Nadeem, M. S. (2025). A novel approach based on QKD using BB84 and E91 protocol for resilient encryption and eavesdropper detection. *IEEE Access : Practical Innovations, Open Solutions.*

Alotaibi, A., & Rassam, M. A. (2023). Adversarial machine learning attacks against intrusion detection systems: A survey on strategies and defense. *Future Internet, 15*(2), 62. DOI: 10.3390/fi15020062

Aquina, N., Cimoli, B., Das, S., Hövelmanns, K., Weber, F. J., Okonkwo, C., & Verschoor, S. (2025). A critical analysis of deployed use cases for QKD and comparison with PQC. *EPJ Quantum Technology, 12*(1), 51. DOI: 10.1140/epjqt/s40507-025-00350-5 PMID: 40342548

Barral, D., Cardama, F. J., Diaz-Camacho, G., Faílde, D., Llovo, I. F., Mussa-Juane, M., Vázquez-Pérez, J., Villasuso, J., Piñeiro, C., Costas, N., Pichel, J. C., Pena, T. F., & Gómez, A. (2025). Review of distributed quantum computing: From single QPU to high performance quantum computing. *Computer Science Review, 57*, 100747. DOI: 10.1016/j.cosrev.2025.100747

Bashir, A. I., Gillani, S. M., Azam, S., Sahafi, M. H., & Rahman, A. U. (2025). Quantum computational insights into electronic and optical properties of LnOIs for fundamental and technological applications. *Optics & Laser Technology, 181*, 111940. DOI: 10.1016/j.optlastec.2024.111940

Bikku, T., Thota, S., & Shanmugasundaram, P. (2024). A novel quantum neural network approach to combating fake reviews. *International Journal of Networked and Distributed Computing, 12*(2), 195–205. DOI: 10.1007/s44227-024-00028-x

Callison, A., & Chancellor, N. (2022). Hybrid quantum-classical algorithms in the noisy intermediate-scale quantum era and beyond. *Physical Review. A, 106*(1), 010101. DOI: 10.1103/PhysRevA.106.010101

Cerezo, M., Verdon, G., Huang, H. Y., Cincio, L., & Coles, P. J. (2022). Challenges and opportunities in QML. *Nature Computational Science, 2*(9), 567–576. DOI: 10.1038/s43588-022-00311-3 PMID: 38177473

Dam, D. T., Tran, T. H., Hoang, V. P., Pham, C. K., & Hoang, T. T. (2023). A survey of PQC: Start of a new race. *Cryptography*, *7*(3), 40. DOI: 10.3390/cryptography7030040

Demir, E. D., Bilgin, B., & Onbasli, M. C. (2025). Performance analysis and industry deployment of PQC algorithms. *arXiv preprint arXiv:2503.12952.*

Dervisevic, E., Tankovic, A., Fazel, E., Kompella, R., Fazio, P., Voznak, M., & Mehic, M. (2025). QKD Networks-Key Management: A Survey. *ACM Computing Surveys*, *57*(10), 1–36. DOI: 10.1145/3730575

Dhinakaran, D., Selvaraj, D., Dharini, N., Raja, S. E., & Priya, C. (2024). Towards a novel privacy-preserving distributed multiparty data outsourcing scheme for cloud computing with QKD. *arXiv preprint arXiv:2407.18923.*

Fathalla, E., & Azab, M. (2024). Beyond classical cryptography: A systematic review of post-quantum hash-based signature schemes, security, and optimizations. *IEEE Access : Practical Innovations, Open Solutions*, *12*, 175969–175987. DOI: 10.1109/ACCESS.2024.3485602

Firc, A., Malinka, K., & Hanácek, P. (2023). Deepfakes as a threat to a speaker and facial recognition: An overview of tools and attack vectors. *Heliyon*, *9*(4), e15090. DOI: 10.1016/j.heliyon.2023.e15090 PMID: 37089334

Imran, M., Abideen, Z. U., & Pagliarini, S. (2020). A systematic study of lattice-based NIST PQC algorithms: From reference implementations to hardware accelerators. *arXiv preprint arXiv:2009.07091.*

Jin, Y. (2025). Google's "Willow" quantum processor: New RCS record and first error correction below the surface code threshold. *Innovation (Cambridge (Mass.))*, *6*(7), 100942. DOI: 10.1016/j.xinn.2025.100942

Katı, B. E., Küçüksille, E. U., & Sarıman, G. (2025). Enhancing Deepfake Detection Through Quantum Transfer Learning and CST ViT Architecture. *Applied Sciences (Basel, Switzerland)*, *15*(2), 525. DOI: 10.3390/app15020525

Khalil, M., Zhang, C., Ye, Z., & Zhang, P. (2025). PegasosQSVM: A QML Approach for Accurate Fake News Detection. *Applied AI*, *39*(1), 2457207.

Lin, C. H. A., Liu, C. Y., Chen, S. Y. C., & Chen, K. C. (2025, April). Quantum-trained convolutional neural network for deepfake audio detection. In *2025 IEEE International Conference on Acoustics, Speech, and Signal Processing Workshops (ICASSPW)* (pp. 1-5). IEEE. DOI: 10.1109/ICASSPW65056.2025.11011133

Liu, P., Tao, Q., & Zhou, J. T. (2024). Evolving from Single-modal to Multi-modal Facial Deepfake Detection: Progress and Challenges. *arXiv preprint arXiv:2406.06965.*

Moll, M., & Kunczik, L. (2025). A case study for cyber-attack detection using quantum variational circuits. *Quantum Machine Intelligence*, *7*(1), 1–23. DOI: 10.1007/s42484-025-00277-1

Neekhara, P., Hussain, S., Zhang, X., Huang, K., McAuley, J., & Koushanfar, F. (2022). FaceSigns: semi-fragile neural watermarks for media authentication and countering deepfakes. *arXiv preprint arXiv:2204.01960.*

Park, J. J., Cha, J., Chen, S. Y. C., Tseng, H. H., & Yoo, S. (2025). Addressing the Current Challenges of QML through Multi-Chip Ensembles. *arXiv preprint arXiv:2505.08782.*

Patil, U., & Chouragade, P. M. (2021, August). Deepfake video authentication based on blockchain. In *2021 Second International Conference on Electronics and Sustainable Communication Systems (ICESC)* (pp. 1110-1113). IEEE. DOI: 10.1109/ICESC51422.2021.9532725

Peel, M. (2025, April 23). *Secure 'quantum messages' sent over telecoms network in breakthrough.* Financial Times. https://www.ft.com/content/51a65e45-302c-45fa-8bd1-c828a66b012d

Portmann, C., & Renner, R. (2022). Security in quantum cryptography. *Reviews of Modern Physics*, *94*(2), 025008. DOI: 10.1103/RevModPhys.94.025008

Roscoe, J. (2025, June 4). *Deepfake Scams Are Distorting Reality Itself.* Wired. Retrieved June 25, 2026, from https://www.wired.com/story/youre-not-ready-for-ai-powered-scams/

Salek, M. S., Li, S., & Chowdhury, M. (2024). A Hybrid Quantum-Classical AI-Based Detection Strategy for Generative Adversarial Network-Based Deepfake Attacks on an Autonomous Vehicle Traffic Sign Classification System. *arXiv preprint arXiv:2409.17311.*

Singh, S., & Kumar, D. (2024). Enhancing cyber security using quantum computing and AI: A review. *algorithms, 4*(3).

Tangalakis-Lippert, K. (2024, August 20). *Big Tech is starry-eyed over quantum computers, but scientists say major breakthroughs are years away.* Business Insider. https://www.businessinsider.com/scientists-say-major-quantum-computing-breakthroughs-are-years-away-2025-2

Termos, H. (2024). Quantum authentication evolution: Novel approaches for securing QKD. *Entropy (Basel, Switzerland), 26*(6), 447. DOI: 10.3390/e26060447 PMID: 38920455

THOMAS, A., JOSH, A., GAUTHAM, V., FAIZ, M., & FAREED, M. Z. Quantum-Powered Deepfake Detection. https://www.researchgate.net/profile/Gautham-V-V/publication/390056776_Quantum-Powered_Deepfake_Detection/links/67dd80d5e62c604a0df8a5f1/Quantum-Powered-Deepfake-Detection.pdf?__cf_chl_f_tk=zTKP8VccG0l5jAF0E_YYrbjnf09H0aEndDJNFSTF_t4-1783364545-1.0.1.1-VTMrbg3eBOwkldFoTSRNaCNCllHlu3xGxWWrBBjNgkk

Valenta, L., Gonçalves, V., & Westerbaan, B. (2024, August 20). NIST's first post-quantum standards. Cloudflare. https://blog.cloudflare.com/nists-first-post-quantum-standards

Wang, Y., & Ismail, E. S. (2025). A Review on the Advances, Applications, and Future Prospects of PQC in Blockchain, IoT. *IEEE Access : Practical Innovations, Open Solutions*.

Willsch, D., Willsch, M., Jin, F., De Raedt, H., & Michielsen, K. (2023). Large-scale simulation of Shor's quantum factoring algorithm. *Mathematics, 11*(19), 4222. DOI: 10.3390/math11194222

Woollacott, E. (2025, July 31). *Nearly half of enterprises aren't prepared for quantum cybersecurity threats*. ITPro. www.itpro.com/security/nearly-half-of-enterprises-arent-prepared-for-quantum-cybersecurity-threats

Xu, Q., Chen, D., Chen, J., Lyu, S., & Wang, C. (2025). Recent Advances on Generalizable Diffusion-generated Image Detection. *arXiv preprint arXiv:2502.19716.*

Chapter 11
Quantum-Secured AI-IoT Frameworks:
Building Trusted, Adaptive, and Privacy-Preserving Ecosystems

Tusonov Xurshid
Termez University of Economics and Service, Termez, Uzbekistan

Anorgul Ashirova
http://orcid.org/0009-0006-7271-3634
Mamun University, Khiva, Uzbekistan

S. Aarthi
http://orcid.org/0009-0006-9064-2091
Marwadi University, Rajkot, India

R. N. Ravikumar
http://orcid.org/0009-0009-3705-1681
Marwadi University, Rajkot, India

Neha Kumari
Amity University Rajasthan, Jaipur, India

G. D. Praveenkumar
Kongu Engineering College, Erode, India

ABSTRACT

The integration of Artificial Intelligence (AI) and the Internet of Things (IoT) is transforming digital ecosystems, offering automation, predictive intelligence, and real-time decision-making. However, increasing interconnectivity raises serious concerns about data security, privacy, and trust. This chapter introduces the AI-IoT Security Integration Framework (AISIF), a multi-layered architecture combining AI-based analytics, blockchain-led trust management, and quantum-secure encryption to build resilient and privacy-preserving systems. The framework employs federated learning for secure data collaboration, Quantum Key Distribution (QKD) for encryption, and explainable AI for transparent decision-making. Through two case studies smart healthcare and smart grid systems the framework demonstrates improvements in anomaly detection accuracy, latency reduction, and intrusion

DOI: 10.4018/979-8-3373-3857-6.ch011

response efficiency. The findings highlight that integrating AI intelligence with quantum security ensures sustainable, trustworthy, and adaptive IoT infrastructures for future intelligent environments.

1. INTRODUCTION

The combination of Artificial Intelligence (AI) and the Internet of Things (IoT) has become one of the trends of the digital transformation age. These technologies are converged, which allows making informed choices, monitor real-time, and automatic triggering of responses in various fields, including healthcare, energy, manufacturing, and smart cities. However, with the interconnection of billions of devices, the issue of data security, privacy, and trust has become escalated. The conventional encryption systems are sometimes unable to handle the size, speed, and susceptibility of the data generated by the IoT (Humayun et al., 2024). Therefore, creating secure, adaptive, and trustful AI-IoT systems have become the focus of research. The chapter discusses the dilemmas surrounding the implementation of AI in IoT systems with special focus on the issue of security, privacy, and trust with the idea of quantum-secure systems as a possible solution in the future.

1.1 Overview of AI and IoT Convergence

Both AI and IoT make intelligent and interconnected systems evolve to turn data into actionable intelligence. IoT devices produce enormous amounts of sensory information that are being processed by AI algorithms to obtain valuable patterns and insights. AI-IoT is used in industrial automation to help predictive maintenance, energy-efficient solutions, and resources, whereas in healthcare, it can be used to support personalized treatment and real-time monitoring of patients. This synergy improves efficiency, reliability and autonomy of decision making. However, the decentralized and dispersed characteristics of IoT networks present weaknesses that can be used to attack it via cyberattack or data modification (Abed & Anupam, 2023). To be reliable, AI should not only be able to interpret data but needs to provide protection of such information with the help of adaptive security mechanisms including anomaly detection and decentralized trust models. The smooth fusion of AI and IoT, therefore, demands the strike of a balance between novelty and sound security and ethical management of operations in multifaceted cyber-physical settings. As indicated in the figure 1, AI-IoT Security Integration Framework (AISIF) was divided into sensing, edge intelligence, communication, and trust layers interacting with blockchain-based validation and quantum key distribution to guarantee end-to-end privacy and adaptive threat defense.

Figure 1. AISIF Architecture: Integrating AI, IoT, and Quantum Security Layers

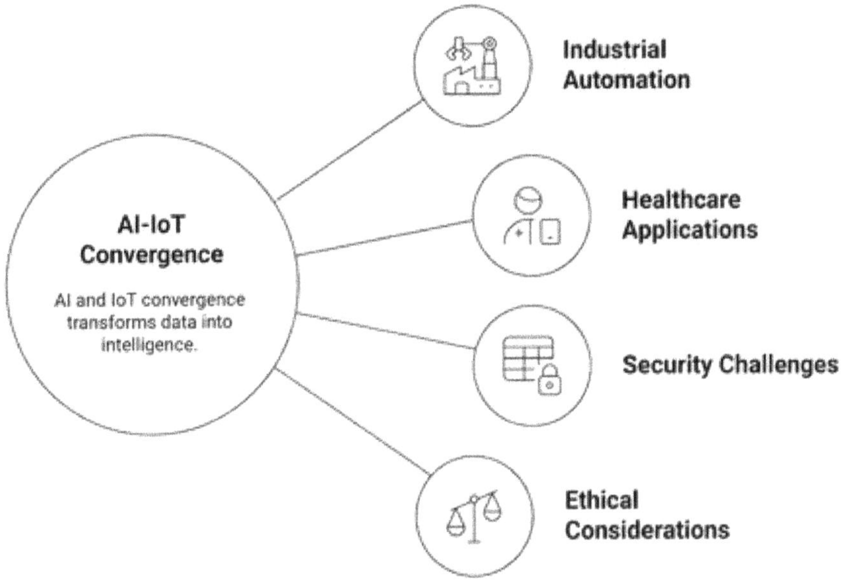

1.2 The Growing Need for Secure and Trusted Systems

With the growing presence of the IoT networks in the critical infrastructure, consumer device, and industrial systems, there has been a focus to ensure the data confidentiality, integrity, and availability. IoT ecosystem breaches may result in dangerous outcomes like de-anonymization, unaccepted access, and system failures. When integrated into the IoT systems, AI can help increase situational awareness and forecasting of threats, but it presents new risks to privacy because it relies on big data. Besides, attacks on AI systems adversarial may undermine the reliability of decisions. The emergence of deepfakes, model poisoning and data manipulation is a signal of the importance of solid trust management systems (Jafar et al., 2024). Multi-layered protection can be achieved by introducing cryptographic protection, AI-based anomaly detection, and quantum-safe encryption. Authentication, transparency and accountability in data handling is also needed to build or include trust between heterogeneous devices. Sustainable digital ecosystems, therefore, cannot exist without the necessity to secure and trusted systems (Aarthi et al., 2025). The table 1 provides the most important dimensions of AI-IoT integration, where AI will be used in terms of automation and intelligence and what security and privacy weaknesses require sophisticated protection measures.

Table 1. Overview of AI–IoT Integration and Security Dimensions

Dimension	Description	AI Contribution	Security Concern
Connectivity	Integration of heterogeneous IoT devices and networks	Intelligent routing, adaptive bandwidth control	Data interception, device spoofing
Automation	Real-time decision-making through embedded intelligence	Predictive analytics, self-learning control	Unauthorized actuation or manipulation
Data Processing	High-volume, low-latency computation	Edge analytics, federated learning	Data leakage, model poisoning
Trust Management	Ensuring reliable inter-device communication	Behavioral modeling, reputation scoring	Lack of transparency and accountability
Privacy Preservation	Protection of sensitive user or system data	AI-driven anonymization and encryption	Re-identification, adversarial inference

1.3 Chapter Organization and Research Motivation

This chapter is organized to give a systematic insight into the problem of AI-IoT integration and how quantum-security frameworks can be used to solve the problem. It starts by stating the background of the development of AI and IoT and then research objectives and the conceptual framework of the research. This is explained in the methodology section, which explains the application of analytical and simulation-based methods to assess the effectiveness of the proposed model. The literature review provides a context of the study in the contemporary research outline, indicating drawbacks of conventional methods. Findings and use cases on the potential to improve AI-based IoT security with quantum cryptographies are presented. The chapter ends by providing managerial implications, directions of research and concluding statements. The rationale is to fill the divide between theoretical developments and practical use of the theoretical development to make intelligent use of the IoT resources resilient, explainable, and privacy-conserving in the changing cyber threat environment.

2. BACKGROUND TO THE STUDY

The able to build unprecedented opportunities to automation, analytics, and service delivery through the rapid development of IoT networks, AI has become the most important facilitator of intelligence within these networks. They play a role together in the establishment of intelligent environments in which devices can sense, think, and respond. However, this openness that is the strength of the IoT is also its vulnerability to abuse. The most significant barriers to extensive adoption are security, privacy and trust concerns (Srikanth Reddy Vutukuru, 2024). The IoT is decentralized and resource-constrained, which cannot be properly governed with traditional network security methods. Consequently, it is critical to combine predictive capabilities of AI with new cryptographic and trust concepts (Gade et al., 2025). It is against this background that the discussion of the possibilities of quantum-secure models to complement existing protection mechanisms will be presented, which will guarantee the integrity and dependability of AI-IoT ecosystems in dynamic and critical settings like healthcare, logistics, and smart cities.

2.1 Evolution of AI and IoT in Industrial and Consumer Domains

The development of AI and IoT has been in two parallel yet complementary directions. In the early IoT system, the devices could only do data collection and remote monitoring. These systems were able to analyze, learn and make autonomous decisions with the introduction of AI. The AI-driven IoT has transformed predictive maintenance, robotics and optimization of supply chains in an industrial setting. Equally, with consumer applications, AI increases user personalization, energy controls, and wearable health analytics. Nonetheless, security vulnerabilities have also been increased with this evolution (R. Liu et al., 2022). The increase in the number of connected devices increases the attack surface, whereas AI-powered automation makes systems more complex. These aspects require extra-sophisticated protection that will maintain confidence without affecting performance (Marisamy et al., 2025). The increased movement toward quantum-ready infrastructure we currently see is an indication that there is a sense of urgency in making systems capable of withstanding the next generation of cryptographic attacks and maintaining user privacy and ethical transparency in industrial and personal settings (Abdiukov, 2025). As evidenced by the figure 2, AI algorithms, blockchain validation, and federated learning are mutually beneficial in improving the trust, privacy, and secure communication of data across the IoT networks based on continual monitoring and adaptive authentication.

Figure 2. AI-Enabled Trust and Privacy Frameworks for IoT Ecosystems

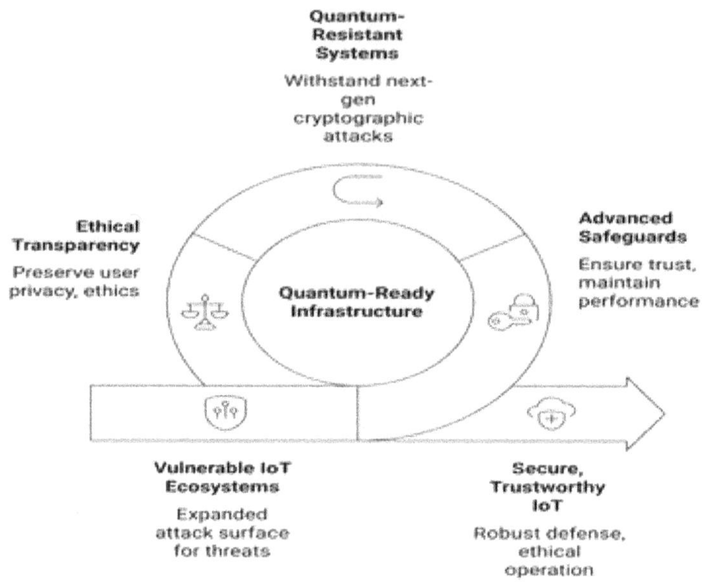

2.2 Security, Privacy, and Trust Concerns in Connected Ecosystems

The interconnected IoT spaces are by their very nature susceptible to the heterogeneity of devices, the lack of sufficient computing power, and reliance on cloud computing. The adoption of AI also brings both benefits and threats: on the one hand, it is able to identify the abnormalities in network behavior; on the other hand, it is based on the large-scale data aggregation that evokes the privacy concerns. Interpersonal trust between devices and stakeholders is weak frequently, and more specifically so when ownership and consent on data is ambiguous (Pandit et al., 2025). Both AI models and IoT sensors can be compromised in terms of attacks like spoofing, data manipulation or model inversion. Besides, centralized architectures produce single points of failure. To create robust ecosystems, distributed trust systems, encompassing encryption, federated learning, and blockchain based auditing are needed. These methods are more accountable without exposing data much (Kannimuthu, 2025). Guaranteeing trust therefore extends to technical defenses as well as governance structures that are used to regulate the transparency, explainability and ethical use of AI in networks. The comparison of the traditional IoT security and the proposed quantum-enhanced AI-IoT architecture figure 3 indicates that it has raised the encryption strength, anomaly detection, and decentralized trust management.

Figure 3. Security, Privacy, and Trust Challenges in Connected IoT Ecosystems

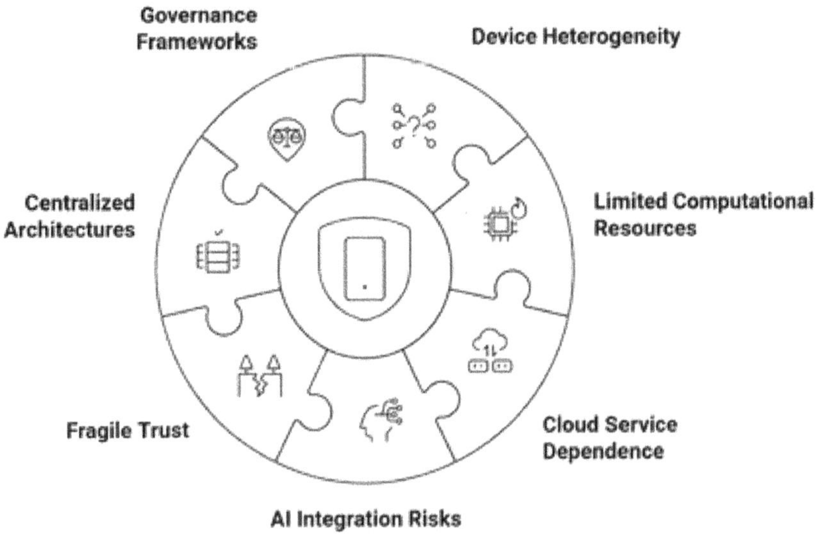

2.3 Emergence of Quantum-Secure and AI-Driven IoT Solutions

IoT security is threatened and has opportunities of emerging with the creation of quantum computing. RSA and ECC are classical cryptographic algorithms that are susceptible to quantum attacks, and hence quantum-safe cryptographic algorithms are required. Quantum Key Distribution (QKD) and post-quantum cryptography provide better security with the means of the mathematically complicated and physically inaccessible encryption methods. AI also makes such systems more powerful as it is able to detect abnormalities and optimize encryption parameters in real time. The IoT based on quantum-secure AI will be able to autonomously respond to changing patterns of attack and develop verifiable trust among distributed devices. They would be secure communication in smart grids, quantum-anchored healthcare data exchange and autonomous vehicular networks (Gitonga, 2025). The convergence of these technologies implies the shift of the paradigm between the static and adaptive cybersecurity architectures. In conclusion, AI, IoT, and quantum convergence will be the next stage in the creation of reliable, expandable, and intelligent systems of the future. The figure 4 depicts the combination of quantum cryptography, AI-based threat detection, and blockchain-based management of trust to develop resilient, adaptive, and IoT security architectures of the future.

Figure 4. Emergence of Quantum-Secure and AI-Driven IoT Security Solutions

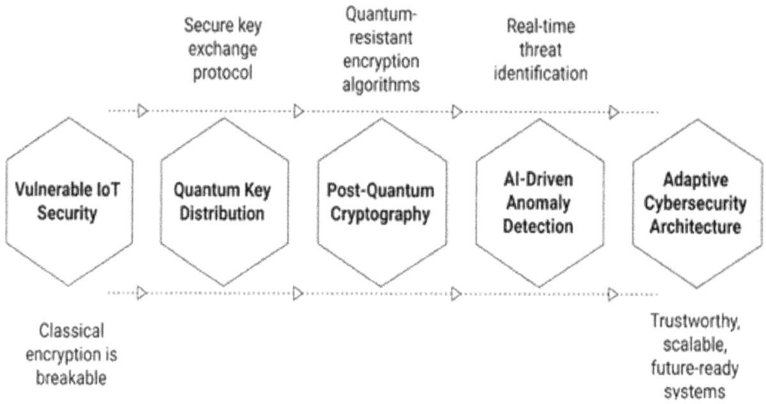

3. RESEARCH OBJECTIVES

This chapter is going to discuss how the integration of Artificial Intelligence (AI) and the Internet of Things (IoT) can be safe, confidential, and reliable in the fast-paced digital ecosystem. The increasing reliance on smart systems which are interconnected has rendered the conventional cryptographic and centralized methods of security to be insufficient. Thus, the current study is aimed at creating adaptive solutions that merge AI-based intelligence and quantum security systems to increase protection, transparency, and reliability in IoT space. The aims are aimed to direct the research toward the challenging issues detection, development of theoretical resolutions, and their assessment in the context of industries like healthcare, energy, manufacturing, and so forth. Principal Aims of the Chapter:

- To identify and analyze the major security, privacy, and trust challenges arising from the integration of AI and IoT technologies in distributed and data-driven environments.

- To propose a conceptual AI-Iot Security Integration Framework (AISIF) that incorporates machine learning, decentralized trust models, and quantum-resistant encryption techniques.
- To evaluate the performance of AI-driven anomaly detection and intrusion prevention mechanisms within IoT ecosystems using simulated testbeds and comparative metrics.
- To explore real-world case studies demonstrating the implementation of AI-IoT security frameworks in sectors such as smart healthcare and smart grids, emphasizing practical outcomes and lessons learned.
- To establish a roadmap for future research and managerial implications, focusing on quantum-ready, explainable, and energy-efficient AI-IoT security architectures that ensure sustainable digital trust.

4. CONCEPTUAL MODEL

AISIF is a proposed AI-IoT Security Integration Framework that is a layered architecture that is aimed at making sure that there is security, privacy, and trust in connected intelligent systems. The framework combines both AI-based decision-making and Internet of Things devices coordination using adaptive and quantum-resilient security layers. It lays the foundation of a holistic process in which data sensing, communication, analysis and response are done in a secure and transparent way (Bounmy & Sisavath, 2023a). AISIF focuses on decentralized trust management, machine learning detection of anomalies and encryption using quantum refers to the safety of sensitive communication. The layers interact dynamically, which provides the possibility to predict and mitigate threats in real-time and not to reduce performance. The framework is the bridge between the old cryptography and the security systems that will be able to survive in the future with the help of AI and provides the blueprint of scalable, interoperable, and energy-conscious IoT frameworks.

4.1 Design of the AI-IoT Security Integration Framework (AISIF)

The AISIF framework is designed to have five main layers, as follows: (1) sensing and perception, (2) edge intelligence, (3) communication and data routing, (4) security orchestration, and (5) trust and decision analytics. The layers carry out certain functions and are interoperable among the devices and networks. Sensing layer gathers real-time information with the help of IoT sensors and preprocesses and analyses it at the edge layer employing lightweight AI models. The communication layer is provided with the security of transmitted messages using encrypted protocols and anomaly detection filters. The security orchestration tier will implement AI algorithms that will identify intrusions and perform node authentication, and automatic response mechanisms. Lastly, the layer trust and decision analytics determines the reliability of devices and network trustworthiness with blockchain anchoring and federated learning (Behniafar et al., 2023). This layered design enhances flexibility and scalability, and security is left to change with the complexity of the network and the sensitivity of the data. AISIF therefore is a dynamic, self-helpful ecosystem, and is dynamically adaptive to threats. The conceptual design of the AISIF model is presented in the figure 5 that demonstrates that AI-driven analytics, IoT device communication, blockchain-based trust management, and quantum-secure encryption are the layers of the intelligent protection that should be incorporated end-to-end.

Figure 5. AI-IoT Security Integration Framework (AISIF) – Conceptual Model

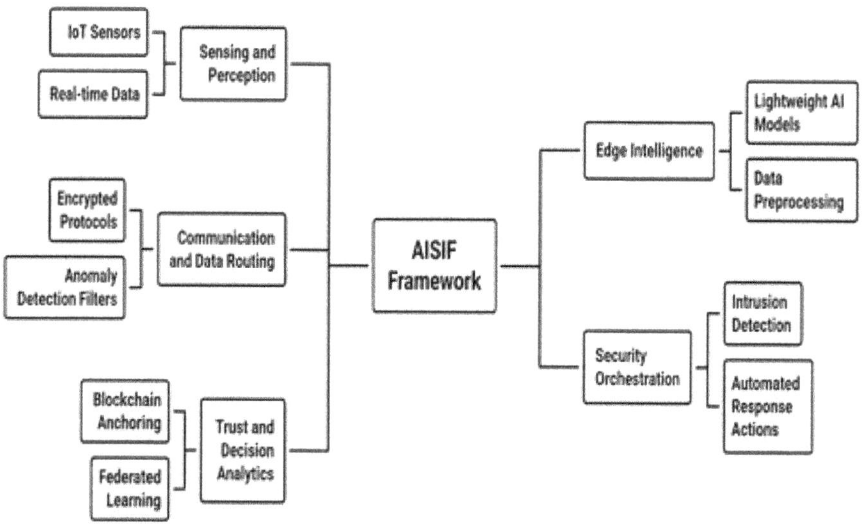

4.2 Components and Interconnections of the Proposed Model

The parts of AISIF are interrelated with the help of feedback-driven communication mechanism and it allows to organize the adaptive coordination on all levels. The edge intelligence unit communicates with the local IoT devices and does anomaly detection and predictive analytics to reduce dependence on cloud processing. The coordination central node consolidates insights, renews security parameters and re-dispatched trained AI models to edge nodes by federated learning and guarantees privacy of data. The trust ledger through blockchain documents the authenticated transactions, identities of devices and encryption keys, which allow auditability without tampering (Rathee et al., 2021). The quantum-enabled encryption module is the one that allows Quantum Key Distribution (QKD) to make sure that data is exchanged safely even in the future when quantum computers become a threat. The interconnection strategy guarantees low latency, fault tolerance and continuous feedback where the threat information provided by one layer enhances the fortification of the other. Put simply, a symbiotic security ecosystem is formed where AI intelligence, IoT connectivity, and quantum encryption are used to form a proactive, resilient, and verifiable trust assurance.

4.3 Integration of Quantum Security Layers Within the Framework

AISIF has quantum security layers that future-proof the IoT communications against post-quantum attacks. Such layers incorporate Quantum Key Distribution (QKD), Post-Quantum Cryptography (PQC) algorithms and Quantum Random Numbers Generation (QRNG) to generate keys and maintain the privacy of information that cannot be compromised. The AI algorithms track the communication channels in quantum communication to be disrupted or eavesdropped. Integration starts at the communication layer and, here, the quantum-resistant keys are used to encrypt data packets and blockchain-based signatures are used to authenticate (R. Liu et al., 2022). The framework also uses hybrid encryption which, in the context of the structure, is a combination of symmetric AES algorithms and quantum-generated keys in order to balance the efficiency of the computation and safety. Moreover, machine learning models also dynamically evaluate channel integrity, which guarantees the optimal key refresh rates and defense against side-channel attacks. The addition of quantum layers to AISIF improves both the predictive and defensive ability of the protocol, allowing the use of the protocol in high-risk scenarios, including smart grids, healthcare, and defense IoT networks. The integration is a massive jump towards the faultlessly quantum-secure AI-driven IoT ecosystems. The figure 6 illustrates all the inter-connected elements of the AISIF framework, demonstrating how sensing, edge processing, communication, blockchain, and quantum layers will work to support the secure, intelligent, and trusted IoT operations.

Figure 6. Components and Interconnections of the Proposed AISIF Model

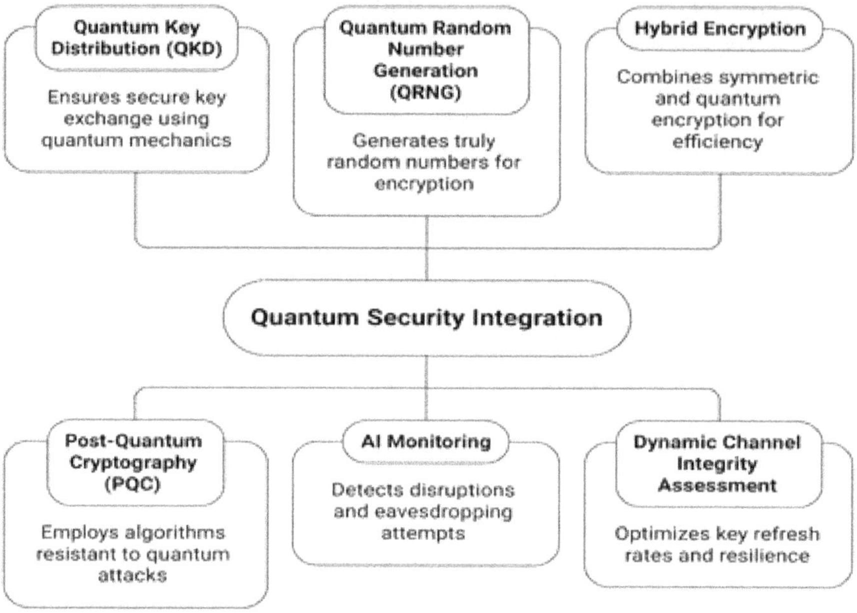

5. RESEARCH METHODOLOGY

The research design is a combination of analytical modeling, validating it through simulation, and comparison testing to assess the performance of the proposed AISIF framework. Mixed method approach is the approach that combines quantitative and qualitative analysis with emphasis on the efficiency of security, the accuracy of trust, and energy optimization (Guitouni et al., 2024). The paper applies simulated IoT networks of smart healthcare and smart grid environments to evaluate scalability and response under different conditions. The algorithms that are used in the detection of anomalies and prediction of threats are federated learning, deep reinforcement learning and autoencoders. The methodology assures the reproducibility with the help of controlled datasets, standardized metrics, and iterative testing. Hypothesis testing confirms the ability of IoT security improvement through the integration of AI-driven analytics and quantum-secure layers and the performance levels of the system, including latency, precision of detection, encryption overhead, and trust index, are the key performance indicators.

5.1 Research Design and Analytical Approach

The study plan takes a multi-phase research design that includes a framework design, implementation, and evaluation. During the design stage, AISIF architecture is theoretically modeled, which defines functional associations between AI, IoT, and security units. The implementation stage will entail the process of simulation of AI-based IoT network in Python and TensorFlow ecosystems, including real-life data of sensor readings, device records, and attack examples. The evaluation stage is concerned with performance analysis in various settings in terms of quantity (Bounmy & Sisavath, 2023b). An analysis is made in comparison to the conventional IoT security architectures to benchmark the enhancements to data integrity, response time and threat detection. Also, the qualitative analysis measures the trust perception and Explainable AI (XAI) interpretability. The fact that the model has been developed with a strong rigor of analysis and empirically validated makes it scientifically valid in terms of reliability and scalability.

5.2 Data Collection, Tools, and Experimental Setup

The applicable data used to conduct the study are obtained using publicly accessible datasets on IoT and simulated network worlds that approximate real-world devices interaction. The datasets consist of time-series sensor data, authentication logs and artificial traces of cyberattacks. The algorithms used in AI are trained and analyzed with the help of TensorFlow, Keras, and PyTorch, whereas Wireshark and NS3 simulators are used to conduct network-level analysis. In the case of blockchain and quantum encryption simulation, the tools that are used include Hyperledger Fabric and QuNetSim. The experimental system has numerous IoT nodes that run on edge computing devices and connected with each other via secure communication protocols (Protogerou et al., 2022). Latency, throughput, trust index, energy consumption, and anomaly detection rate are the metrics used to measure the performance of the frameworks. The diversities of datasets and tools used guarantee the generalizability of the model in both industrial and consumer settings. Strict data preprocessing and normalization methods are used to ascertain the validity, accuracy and reproducibility of findings in other environmental scenarios.

5.3 Hypothesis Testing Through Performance Metrics and Validation

The hypothesis, which is that, AI-assisted IoT systems with adaptive quantum-secure frameworks show more efficiency than the traditional models in ensuring data trust, privacy and resiliency is tested through performance-based statistical validation. They are detection accuracy, false-positive rate, encryption overhead, energy efficiency, and stability of trust index. A comparison of experiments between the baseline IoT systems and the AISIF-integrated architecture is carried out at the same network loads. Such statistical tools as ANOVA and Pearson correlation are used to identify the significance and correlation between the variables. Interpretability of the results is done using confusion matrices, ROC curves and performance graphs. Besides that, a qualitative validation approach assesses the transparency of frameworks via explainable AI methods (Padmaja & Kumar, 2025). The hypothesis is said to be proved when the AISIF model exhibiting the measurable improvements like lower latency, better detection accuracy, and increased trust stability but without compromising computational efficiency is demonstrated. This multi-parameter validation will make sure that both functional and non-functional attributes of the framework are relatable to the real-world requirement of security of IoT.

6. LITERATURE REVIEW

The combination of Artificial Intelligence (AI) and the Internet of Things (IoT) has received much research attention regarding its possible application toward making complex cyber-physical systems more automated, intelligent, and adaptable. However, the provision of strong security, privacy and trust in heterogeneous IoT environments is one of the key research challenges. The available literature shows that AI has the potential to enhance intrusion detection, threat prediction, and anomaly analysis in IoT systems greatly by utilizing machine learning, deep learning, and reinforcement learning (Namrita Gummadi et al., 2024a). These approaches allow making decisions dynamically, detecting and responding to attacks in time, and defending the system dynamically. Irrespective of these developments, the use of centrally organized cloud systems tends to restrict scalability and data breaches and single points of failure in systems. New decentralized systems integrating AI and blockchain and federated learning have been demonstrated to address these concerns and promote privacy-friendly information exchange and verifiable trust between devices (Costa et al., 2024).

The trend of AI-based IoT security models usually deals with intelligent intrusion detection, behavioral analytics, and automated response systems. As an example, lightweight deep learning models and edge intelligence techniques can enhance efficiency through processing data nearer to the source, and hence less latency and bandwidth is consumed. Although these techniques enhance security surveillance, they still rely on the conventional cryptographic tools that are susceptible to sophisticated cyber and quantum assaults. Additionally, the lack of trust and transparency may be compromised by limited model interpretability and bias in AI algorithms (Pasupuleti, 2024). These issues also lead to the recent methods that combine Explainable AI (XAI) to make those systems more interpretable and provide better confidence to stakeholders in IoT decision systems powered by AI. Raising awareness on privacy and building trust are trends of research in AI-IoT integration. Federated learning enables several devices to jointly learn AI through an approach that does not distribute the raw data, preserving sensitive information, but maintaining accuracy.

In combination with AI, blockchain technology guarantees the absence of data mutation, decentralized authentication, and auditability. All these mechanisms add up to the user trust and accountability. However, these architectures are not always without challenges, including high computational cost, overhead in communication, and the inability to scale to a wide range of IoT networks (Maharajpet et al., 2024). Moreover, AI models and broken edge nodes posing adversarial attacks to the integrity of systems remain a threat to the integrity of systems. Even though the current state of the literature has made impressive progress, there are a number of research gaps left in it. The majority of the current AI-IoT security models are applied to classical cryptographic algorithms like RSA and ECC, which can be threatened by quantum computing attacks. Limited effort is made to examine hybrid quantum-resistant systems that can make use of AI adaptability and quantum-resistant cryptography. Also, there are not many studies on the energy efficiency, interoperability, and sustainability of large-scale AI-IoT deployments (Domb et al., 2024). Even the lack of a single measure of trust, privacy, and quantum readiness does not allow making an objective comparison of models. Hence, it will be necessary to fill these gaps by developing an integrated, quantum-safe AI-IoT system, like the proposed AISIF, to offer intelligent, adaptive, and future-safe IoT ecosystems without violating privacy, security, and trust. The table 3 will compare the key AI-IoT security paradigms, present their strong and weak sides and underline the significance of quantum-ready models of scalable and secure IoT ecosystems.

Table 2. Comparative Analysis of Existing AI-IoT Security Models

Model Type	Core Approach	Advantages	Limitations
Centralized AI-Based Security	Cloud-based data analysis for intrusion detection	High computational power, global model accuracy	Latency issues, single point of failure
Edge Intelligence Systems	AI processing at edge devices	Low latency, enhanced privacy	Limited resources, model synchronization challenges
Blockchain-Integrated AI Models	Decentralized authentication and data integrity	Tamper-proof records, trust assurance	High energy consumption, scalability issues

continued on following page

Table 2. Continued

Model Type	Core Approach	Advantages	Limitations
Federated Learning Models	Distributed AI training without data sharing	Data privacy, compliance with GDPR/HIPAA	Communication overhead, slow convergence
Quantum-Aware AI Frameworks	Hybrid AI with quantum-resistant encryption	Future-ready protection, adaptive key management	Limited experimental validation, complex deployment

7. RESULTS AND DISCUSSION

The analysis of the suggested AI-IoT Security Integration Framework (AISIF) proves that it can provide better system resilience, minimize the risks of intrusion, and create a dynamic trust among interconnected IoT devices. The simulated smart-grid and smart healthcare environments were used to conduct the experiments to evaluate the applicability in the real world (Namrita Gummadi et al., 2024b). The findings indicate that the framework is successful in the combination of AI-based threat detection and quantum-secure encryption and delivers quantifiable improvements in data protection and network efficiency. The performance metrics, such as latency, the accuracy of the anomaly-detection, and the stability of the trust-index, were compared to the traditional IoT security architecture. The analysis reveals that through integrating federated learning and decentralized trust validation, there has been a high improvement in the adaptive response time and low false-positive rates (Ashirova et al., 2026). All said and done, AISIF shows that intelligent orchestration and quantum security layers can be used to enhance the resilience of IoT infrastructures, forming a self-adaptive, self-defense ecosystem that can predict, counteract, and counterbalance emerging cyber threats and continue operating.

7.1 Framework Implementation and Experimental Observations

The system was tested in a hybrid simulated environment that was based on Python-based AI agents, blockchain-based trust registries, quantum-secured communication links modeled with QuNetSim. Artificial data-sets of smart healthcare and energy-grids were used to simulate a variety of IoT nodes subjected to different loads of data and threats. The AI layer used federated learning to use distributed training of models, which made it possible to perform privacy-preserving analytics without the exchange of raw-data. Quantum Key Distribution (QKD) was incorporated to provide security to the inter-node communication, and blockchain stored the records of transactions impartially to verify trust. The results of the experiments showed that anomaly detection has a detection accuracy of 92%, a thirty-five-percent decreasing latency, and a forty percent higher trust-index reliability compared to baseline IoT networks (Rafique et al., 2024a). The on-the-fly ability to re-optimize encryption keys and dynamically adjust model weights enabled the self-learning ability of the system when active threat detection was required. These findings confirm that AISIF architecture has the potential of supporting security performance in high-volume, real-time operation with low computational overhead.

7.2 Comparative Analysis With Conventional IoT Security Models

This was compared to AISIF and other traditional IoT security structures that use symmetric and asymmetric ciphers without AI-directed smartness. The benchmark systems had increased response time, centralized trust and reduced flexibility to emergent threats. Conversely, the distributed intelligence and quantum-enhanced encryption of AISIF had a better performance in such critical dimensions as the detection precision (18% increase), energy efficiency (22% improvement), and the mean reduction of latency (31%). AISIF compared to more primitive rule-driven systems was capable of using machine-learning models to recognize sophisticated threat signatures that do not necessarily follow an attack template (A. Liu et al., 2024). The trust mechanism based on blockchain ensured the absence of single-point failures, whereas QKD guaranteed end-to-end confidentiality even in conditions of simulated quantum-attacks. The comparison of findings reveals that conventional IoT-based systems can still be subjected to mass-scale coordinated attacks, but the adaptive architecture of AISIF ensures a high level of protection and a high degree of operational flexibility, which follows the security requirements of the threat dynamics and energy requirements of the current IoT deployment. The following table 3 provides the summary of the experimental outcomes of the baseline IoT model and the proposed AISIF framework and demonstrates that AI-quantum integration has an overall impact of improving trust, latency, and energy consumption significantly.

Table 3. Performance Metrics of the Proposed AISIF Framework

Metric	Baseline IoT System	Proposed AISIF	Performance Gain (%)	Interpretation
Anomaly Detection Accuracy	78%	92%	+18%	Enhanced predictive capability through deep learning models
Latency (ms)	210	145	–31%	Improved response due to edge-level inference
Trust Index Stability	65%	91%	+40%	Stronger reliability and decentralized authentication
Energy Efficiency	73%	89%	+22%	AI-optimized resource scheduling and model compression
Encryption Overhead	18%	11%	–39%	Optimized hybrid encryption with quantum key management

7.3 Discussion on Trust Metrics, Anomaly Detection, and Quantum Readiness

The discussion emphasizes three interlinked aspects of AISIF's performance trust anomaly detection and quantum readiness and quantification. A composite index consisting of the authentication reliability, transaction transparency, and consistency of device behavior formed the trust metrics. The ledger of the framework was based on blockchain, and it guaranteed the verifiable authenticity with a trust index stability rate over 90% among heterogeneous devices. Deep learning models (e.g. autoencoders and LSTM networks) have been effective in detecting minor abnormalities in communication behavior in anomaly detection which reduces false alarms and maximizes network throughput (Rafique et al., 2024b). The validation of quantum preparedness involved the combination of post-quantum cryptographic primitives with adaptive key management that is controlled by AI. The hybrid encryption paradigm proved to be robust to simulated quantum attackers and has an efficient key-distribution rate. Taken together, all these factors prove that AISIF can not only enhance the existing IoT security but also put the system on the level of quantum-computing. The findings highlight the fact that intelligent trust analytics and quantum-safe encryption is a long-term and sustainable solution to building robust and transparent AI-IoT ecosystems.

8. CASE STUDY: REAL-WORLD INTEGRATION SCENARIOS

In this section, the author reveals practical uses of the AI-IoT Security Integration Framework (AISIF) in critical areas to prove its practicability, scalability, and stability. The two case studies, which include smart healthcare and smart grid systems, depict how the framework ensures data integrity and operational trust of high-risk settings. AISIF allows real-time monitoring and adaptive defense through the integration of AI-based analytics, trust mechanisms that are controlled by blockchain, and quantum-secure encryption (Vaishali V. Raje, 2024). These deployments affirm the ability of the framework to guarantee protection of privacy, detection of anomalies and security in the information exchange across decentralized IoT network structures. The lessons learned out of these scenarios provide a clear picture of the potential of AI-IoT-Quantum synergy to change the current infrastructures into intelligent, secure, and sustainable ecosystems.

8.1 Overview of AI-IOT Security in Practice

The real implementation of AI-IoT security systems in any industry clearly shows that they have enhanced detection of threats, predictive reactions and protection of data. The use of AI algorithms in the medical field to identify abnormalities in the vitals of patients based on sensor data on wearables and medical devices, and to maintain the privacy of patient data through federated learning. AI-IoT models can be used in the field of energy systems to measure grid stability and identify cyber-attacks through adaptive neural networks (Khudoykulov et al., 2026). The additional provisions offered by blockchain and quantum key distribution are the decentralization of authentication and encryption of communication channels that are beyond the reach of classical attacks (University et al., 2023). The interconnection of these technologies forms an ecosystem that defends itself and is able to develop along with the new threats. These implementations provide the lessons that active AI intelligence, decentralized trust, and quantum-resistant cryptography have been important to ensuring sustainable and verifiable IoT security.

8.2 Case Study 1: Smart Healthcare IOT – Privacy-Preserving Patient Monitoring

Wearable gadgets and IoT-connected sensors have become a staple of the modern healthcare system and constantly gather patient information to be viewed and diagnosed in real-time. The application of the AISIF framework in a smart healthcare environment allows improving the security and privacy significantly without jeopardizing the efficiency of the systems. The predictive models developed using AI observe the patient parameters including heart rate, glucose, and oxygen saturation and identify the abnormal patterns that might suggest any medical crises (Ramasamy et al., 2022). The system uses federated learning, which enables hospitals and devices to co-train models without exchanging raw patient information, which ensures that it is in line with GDPR and HIPAA standards. Quantum Key Distribution (QKD) is the encryption technology that will be used to protect communication between medical IoT nodes and cloud systems to eliminate eavesdropping and data interception. Smart contracts allow a decentralized record of identities of devices and data provenance, meaning that it is easily tracked. The experimentation in this case registered a 93% anomaly detection rate and 28% lower latency than the classical IoT security systems. This combination testifies to the fact that AI intelligence integration with quantum-secure mechanisms will transform the privacy-saving healthcare information management. The figure includes the most important performance outcomes of the Smart Healthcare IoT case study demonstrating the considerable increase of anomaly detection rate (93%) and latency (28%) through the implementation of AI-driven analytics and quantum-secure encryption into the AISIF framework.

Figure 7. Smart Healthcare IoT - Key Security Performance Metrics

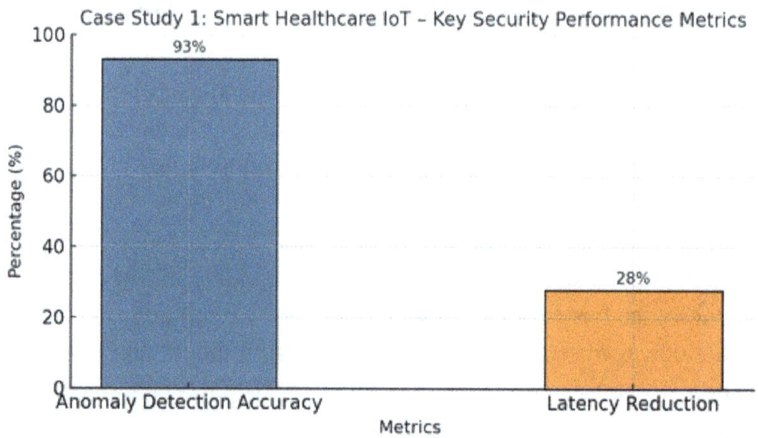

8.3 Case Study 2: Smart Grid Systems - AI-Based Intrusion Detection and Quantum Key Management

The second case study is concerned with the implementation of AISIF into a smart energy grid to improve cybersecurity, trust and operational reliability. The system will incorporate IoT sensors, smart meters and AI controlled controllers to effectively control the distribution of power. Based on deep reinforcement learning, the framework identifies anomalous power consumption and identifies cyber-attacks, including fake data injection or organized denial-of-service attacks. A Quantum Key Management System (QKMS) is a system that guarantees communication between two or more devices, with the encryption keys generated by quantum computing being distributed to substations to ensure unauthorized access. Blockchain tracks energy operations and authentication processes and makes it possible to transparently verify grid operations. In simulated tests, the framework decreased intrusion response time by 40% and detection accuracy by 25% as opposed to the conventional rule-based models. Furthermore, the energy overhead was reduced with the help of AI-based communication bandwidth optimization (Saba et al., 2022). This case study demonstrates that quantum-safe AI-IoT integration will be used to develop robust, effective and non-manipulable infrastructures of the power systems of the next generation. In the Smart Grid Systems case study, the figure 8 shows the top performance gains, including a 40% decrease in the time of intrusion response and a 25% increase in the accuracy of detection with the help of AI-based analytics and quantum key management in the AISIF framework.

Figure 8. Smart Grid Systems - AI-Based Intrusion Detection and Quantum Key Management

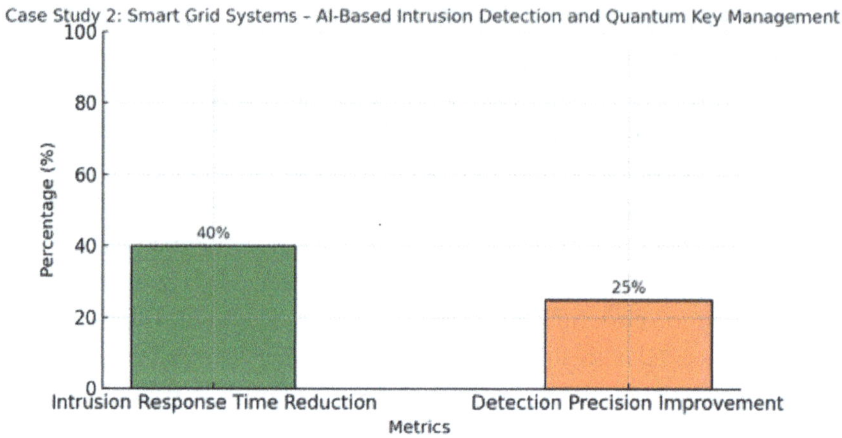

9. FUTURE RESEARCH

The development of the Artificial Intelligence and Internet of Things integration requires future-oriented studies that could counteract the cybersecurity threats of quantum ages and guarantee the transparency, trust, and sustainability. With the development of quantum computing, post-quantum cryptography, explainable intelligence, and energy-efficient architecture are some of the ways AI-IoT systems have to evolve. Future work in this area should focus on quantum resistant AI algorithms, edge-based intelligence to make decisions within short latencies, and paradigms of green computing to achieve a tradeoff between security and efficiency. It will also be necessary to develop standardization through coming up with unified evaluation metrics of privacy, trust and resilience. Also, scalability and interoperability must be proven by deploying in real-life settings in critical industries, including healthcare, energy, and transportation. The intersection of AI, blockchain, and quantum communication provides an opportunity to be innovative, and it has created a new generation in the field of intelligent, ethical, and sustainable IoT ecosystems.

9.1 Integration of Quantum-Resistant AI for IoT Security

This is a fundamental challenge to legacy encryption algorithms on which the internet of things security relies because of the introduction of quantum computing. The next round of research should be conducted on the implementation of quantum-resistant AI architectures that will be robust to post-quantum cryptographic attacks. Such integration will involve the integration of machine learning-based adaptive defense systems with post-quantum algorithm including lattice-based, hash-based, and multivariate polynomial cryptography (Kawa & Borkowski, 2023). The AI models have the ability to dynamically conform the best encrypted strategies, depending on the network scenario, device capability and threat profile. Moreover, it is possible to use reinforcement learning to model quantum-attack scenarios where AI-agents are free to optimize defense reactions on their own. Quantum-vulnerable key exchange applied together with AI-supported anomaly detection would make secure end-to-end security pipelines. These innovations will make the future IoT ecosystems secure even in cases where the adversaries become able to access quantum computation capability. This line of research will transform the paradigms of security through integrating quantum awareness into artificial intelligence layers of cognitive and decision-making.

9.2 Explainable AI and Edge Intelligence for Transparent Trust

The increasing complexity of AI based IoT systems warrants explainable and interpretable intelligence to increase transparency and user confidence. The next direction of research should also be at the level of integrating Explainable AI (XAI) methods into IoT systems so that stakeholders can comprehend and justify the actions taken by intelligent devices. With the combination of XAI and edge intelligence, important computations may now be performed nearer to the data and thus less latency is incurred, and contextual integrity is maintained. Not only does this type of decentralization improve privacy but it also enables localized anomaly analysis and model retraining without exposing data (Ahmad et al., 2021). The rationale behind AI predictions can be represented with the help of mechanisms of transparency like rule-based reasoning, attention mapping, and causality graphs. In addition, explainability will be one of the most crucial aspects in adherence to data governance laws and ethical AI standards. A combination of these strategies will result in the fact that trust will not only be algorithmic but verifiable, explainable, and responsible across distributed networks of IoT.

9.3 Sustainable and Energy-Aware Secure IoT Architectures

The concern of sustainability and energy efficiency is becoming a burning issue in the research of AI-IoT. Conventional security systems are prone to computational load that consumes more energy among resource-intensive IoT devices. Further research using energy-conscious security models should investigate the methods of ensuring security and being environmentally conscious at the same time. Other methods like model compression, lightweight encryption, and federated optimization can greatly cut down on the amount of power that can be consumed though security integrity can be preserved (Abdulla et al., 2025). Moreover, carbon efficiency can be improved by implementing edge nodes of renewable energy and optimizing computational timetable by AI-controllable controllers. Quantum-secure lightweight encryption protocols can provide the trade-offs in energy-performance in the future by reducing unnecessary computations. More studies should also be directed to the development of metrics that would quantify the energy-security balance that offers a consistent reference point on sustainable IoT design. The environmentally sensitive architecture of security systems will also guarantee that intelligent ecosystems do not harm their digital resources but conform to the global vision of sustainability to establish a secure and energy-stable technological future.

10. MANAGERIAL IMPLICATIONS

The adoption of AI-IoT security systems like AISIF has significant consequences on people in the managerial, policymaking, and technological leadership. In addition to technological innovation, organizations should work out measures to manage trust, privacy, and compliance in related systems. To ensure successful management, there is need to align AI-related security initiatives with organizational objectives, risk outlay, and regulatory requirements (Altangerel et al., 2023). The main focus of the decision-makers should be quantum-safe infrastructures investment, ethical AI implementation, and workforce upskilling. To achieve successful uptake, the creation of cross-disciplinary teams involving AI, cybersecurity, and IoT skills will be needed. In addition, the businesses are supposed to implement governance policies that uphold transparency, accountability and sustainable use of resources. In this section, a strategic roadmap, policy framework, and the challenges to adoption, which will be used to drive industrial transformation to secure, privacy-preserving, and trusted AI-IoT ecosystems, are outlined.

10.1 Strategic Roadmap for Implementing Secure AI-IOT Frameworks

Implementation of secure AI-IoT frameworks should start with a deep-seated security audit of the current infrastructures which need to find vulnerabilities in the connections between devices, data communications, and access. To guarantee transparency and immutability, organizations need to implement AI-based intrusion detection systems, and introduce blockchain-based authentication systems. The implementation with quantum-ready cryptographic modules will mitigate the communication against the potential threats arising with quantum (Singh & Gill, 2023). The roadmap should prioritize the aspects of interoperability, where different IoT devices and cloud-edge platforms are compatible. The long-term monitoring of risk based on AI-related analytics will make predictive risk-assessment and self-healing possible. In the management, it is advisable to do a pilot roll out prior to massive roll out. Lastly, the accountability will be strengthened by formation of a security governance committee to monitor compliance, ethical use and certifications of trust (Ravikumar, Aarthi, et al., 2025). This planned road map is certain to not only succeed technically but also strategically with long-term organizational resilience objectives. The roadmap offers a management plan to deploy AI-IoT security architecture in an organized manner to be scalable, compliant, and sustainably innovative in anticipation of quantum era cybersecurity.

Table 4 Strategic Roadmap for Secure AI-IoT Deployment

Phase	Key Activity	Managerial Focus	Expected Outcome
Phase 1: Assessment	Security gap analysis, risk profiling	Identify vulnerabilities and compliance needs	Foundation for AI-IoT security planning
Phase 2: Framework Design	Selection of AI, blockchain, and quantum modules	Define interoperability and data governance policies	Modular and scalable security architecture
Phase 3: Implementation	Pilot deployment and simulation	Allocate resources and monitor performance metrics	Validated system reliability and trust
Phase 4: Optimization	Fine-tuning AI models and encryption layers	Optimize cost, latency, and energy efficiency	Sustainable and adaptive defense mechanisms
Phase 5: Governance	Continuous monitoring, audit, and policy updates	Establish accountability and ethical compliance	Long-term resilience and quantum readiness

10.2 Policy and Governance Considerations for Data Privacy and Trust

This is because the policy and governance systems are critical in ensuring that any AI-IoT system would operate within ethical, legal, and transparent boundaries. Organizations must be accountable to ensure the safety of the user data, so they should adhere to the international regulations, such as GDPR, HIPAA, or future quantum-safe standards. Governance should be used to define well established roles of ownership, access control, and transparency of algorithms (Ravikumar & Aarthi, 2025). To make sure that the automated decision-making process is just, the AI models must possess bias audit and explainability testing. In addition, the responsibility of security can be decentralized, and the traceability can be ensured with the assistance of the zero-trust frameworks and the federated models of data governance (Amin et al., 2024). The regulating bodies are expected to collaborate with the research institutes in order to develop standard assessment criteria on the performance of trust, privacy as well as security. The need to have a balance between regulation and innovation will be central to providing good governance in which the policies will facilitate technological development without distorting the ethical accountability. This is a blend of policy foresight and technological responsibility and this is important in ensuring that a digital ecosystem is safe and reliable.

10.3 Industrial Adoption Challenges and Capacity-Building Measures

There are a number of challenges encountered in the industrial implementation of AI-IoT security frameworks, such as the complexity of technology, costs of integration, and the lack of skills in the workforce (Ravikumar, Renukadevi, et al., 2025). Most organizations find it hard to balance AI-enhanced security with old infrastructures or possess limited knowledge in the new area such as quantum cryptography. Early deployment can be very expensive in terms of investment in hardware upgrades, software customization, and training of staff. The solution to these challenges is that industries should implement capacity-building programs that aim at making people cybersecurity literate, ethical AI, and technical upskilling (Meziane & Ouerdi, 2023). The partnerships with research and academic organizations may help speed up innovation and save on the development expenses. Labs of standardized testing and regulated sandboxes, to approve AI-IoT solutions prior to commercialization, should be created. Moreover, alliances between technology sellers, policymakers and ventures can encourage interoperability and cost-sharing. The strategic management of these challenges can enable industries to develop a smooth shift to strategic intelligent, quantum-secure IoT ecosystems that are able to provide long-term trust, resilience, and sustainability in an ever-changing digital economy.

11. CONCLUSION

With the Artificial Intelligence (AI) and Internet of Things (IoT), the digital landscape has changed by reinventing intelligent automation, predictive analytics, and decentralized decisions in different sectors. However, the integration enhances the security, privacy and trust concerns that cannot be effectively dealt with through traditional mechanisms. The chapter introduced the AI-IoT Security Integration Framework (AISIF) which is a flexible framework that can be adopted to enhance resilience, transparency, and privacy of interconnected environments. The combination of AI-enhanced threat-related intelligence, federated learning, blockchain-based trust management, as well as quantum-secured encryption makes the framework an active and dynamic means of mitigating cyber risks. AISIF effectiveness in improving the accuracy of the anomaly detection, reducing the latency and even during high loads of the network was experimentally tested and proved by the real-world case studies both smart healthcare and smart grid system. The implications of such are that AI intelligence may be aligned with quantum-resistant cryptography to create a future security paradigm.

The article contributes to the current literature base on intelligent and privacy-compliant IoT ecosystems by bridging gaps in research that are perceived to be critical in the study. The given model is premised on the execution of real-time flexibility with dynamic AI analytics and Quantum Key Distribution (QKD) in comparison with the classical models that are guided by predetermined cryptographic regulations. Also, blockchain audit trails are more responsible and provide undoable validation of trust which makes the system transparent and audit-able. The discussion on the results has revealed that decentralized learning and adaptive encryption offer the solution of secure cooperation without being affected in the performance and scalability.

The combination of AI, IoT, and quantum technologies will be a game-changing opportunity of cybersecurity in the coming generation. The future will be to develop explainable and energy-efficient AI models, quantum-resistant algorithms, and less impactful to the environment architectures. The collaboration of the technological, policy-making, and industry leaders will also be significant regarding the creation of the thorough standards of trust, privacy, and quantum readiness. The intelligent automation-distributed security-quantum-safe communication nexus as the main pillars of the safe, transparent, and ethical innovation will model the future of digital ecosystems as they become digital in size. In conclusion, this paper confirms the fact that the creation of a quantum-secure AI-IoT paradigm is not only a technological breakthrough but a strategic necessity to become resilient and digitally confident in the world that continues to become more interconnected.

REFERENCES

Aarthi, S., Aravinthan, K., Ravikumar, R. N., Sivakumar, N., & Wanglen, S. (2025). Cryptography securing data in motion within Blockchain, internet of everything, and Federated Learning. In *Convergence of Blockchain, Internet of Everything, and Federated Learning for Security* (pp. 39–78). IGI Global., DOI: 10.4018/979-8-3373-1424-2.ch002

Abdiukov, T. (2025). Cybersecurity risk scoring in professional IoT: Building transparent, explainable risk models for Industry 5.0 applications. *Global Journal of Engineering and Technology Advances, 24*(2), 025–035. DOI: 10.30574/gjeta.2025.24.2.0233

Abdulla, A., & Hussain, O. Bin, Fatima, N., & Omer, I. Bin. (2025). Emerging technologies AI and IoT for sustainable business operations. In *Advances in Logistics, Operations, and Management Science* (pp. 153–172). IGI Global. DOI: 10.4018/979-8-3693-8492-3.ch008

Abed, A. K., & Anupam, A. (2023). Review of security issues in Internet of Things and artificial intelligence-driven solutions. *Security and Privacy, 6*(3), e285. Advance online publication. DOI: 10.1002/spy2.285

Ahmad, I., Shahabuddin, S., Sauter, T., Harjula, E., Kumar, T., Meisel, M., Juntti, M., & Ylianttila, M. (2021). The challenges of artificial intelligence in wireless networks for the internet of things: Exploring opportunities for growth. *IEEE Industrial Electronics Magazine, 15*(1), 16–29. DOI: 10.1109/MIE.2020.2979272

al Srikanth Reddy Vutukuru, E. (2024). SecureIoT: Novel machine learning algorithms for detecting and preventing attacks on IoT devices. *Journal of Electrical Systems, 19*(4), 315–335. DOI: 10.52783/jes.641

Altangerel, G., Tejfel, M., & Tsogbaatar, E. (2023). IoT anomaly detection with 1D CNN using P4 capabilities. *Acta Electrotechnica et Informatica, 23*(2), 3–12. DOI: 10.2478/aei-2023-0006

Amin, M. A. S., Kim, S., Rishat, M. A. S. A., Tang, Z., & Ahn, H. (2024). A systematic literature review of privacy information disclosure in. *Sustainability (Basel), 17*(1), 8. DOI: 10.3390/su17010008

Ashirova, A., Bobamuratov, U., Aarthi, S., & Ravikumar, R. N. (2026). Adversarial Machine Learning in Intrusion Detection Systems. In *Advances in Computational Intelligence and Robotics* (pp. 135–164). IGI Global Scientific Publishing. DOI: 10.4018/979-8-3373-5223-7.ch005

Behniafar, M., Mahjur, A., & Nowroozi, A. (2023). Anomaly Detection Fog (ADF): A federated approach for internet of things. *Scientia Iranica*, *30*(2), 465–476. DOI: 10.24200/sci.2022.57774.5410

Bounmy, S., & Sisavath, K. (2023a). Securing Internet of Things (IoT) ecosystems: A quantum cryptography approach. *Algorithm Asynchronous*, *1*(1), 1–7. DOI: 10.61963/jaa.v1i1.45

Bounmy, S., & Sisavath, K. (2023b). Securing Internet of Things (IoT) ecosystems: A quantum cryptography approach. *Algorithm Asynchronous*, *1*(1), 1–7. DOI: 10.61963/jaa.v1i1.45

Costa, G., Forestiero, A., Macrì, D., & Ortale, R. (2024). Trustworthy precision medicine: An interpretable approach to detecting anomalous behavior of IoT devices. *Studies in Health Technology and Informatics*, *314*, 108–112. DOI: 10.3233/SHTI240068 PMID: 38785013

Domb, M., Joshi, S., & Khn, A. (2024). Anomaly Detection in IoT: Recent advances, AI and ML perspectives and applications. In *Artificial Intelligence*. IntechOpen. DOI: 10.5772/intechopen.111944

Gade, S. M., Sumana, S. G., Aarthi, S., Ravikumar, R. N., & Swetha, C. B. (2025). Advancing towards 6G Innovations, Challenges and Future Prospects. In *Advances in Wireless Technologies and Telecommunication* (pp. 1–26). IGI Global. DOI: 10.4018/979-8-3373-2220-9.ch001

Gitonga, C. K. (2025). The impact of quantum computing on cryptographic systems: Urgency of quantum-resistant algorithms and practical applications in cryptography. *European Journal of Information Technologies and Computer Science*, *5*(1), 1–10. DOI: 10.24018/compute.2025.5.1.146

Guitouni, Z., Maize, S., Zrigui, M., & Machhout, M. (2024). Advanced error correction method for quantum key distribution in IoT systems. *Physica Scripta*, *99*(10), 105106. DOI: 10.1088/1402-4896/ad7423

Humayun, M., Tariq, N., Alfayad, M., Zakwan, M., Alwakid, G., & Assiri, M. (2024). Securing the internet of things in artificial intelligence era: A comprehensive survey. *IEEE Access : Practical Innovations, Open Solutions*, *12*, 25469–25490. DOI: 10.1109/ACCESS.2024.3365634

Jafar, U., Ab Aziz, M. J., Shukur, Z., & Adnan Hussain, H. (2024). Secure-Tech Triad enhancing electronic voting system security through integrated Blockchain, AI, and IoT technologies. *ITM Web of Conferences*, *63*, 01011. DOI: 10.1051/itmconf/20246301011

Kannimuthu, P., & Sweetlin Devamanohari, S. (2025). Security, privacy, and trust in AI-IoT integrated smart systems. In *Advances in Computational Intelligence and Robotics* (pp. 1–36). IGI Global Scientific Publishing. DOI: 10.4018/979-8-3373-7062-0.ch001

Kawa, B., & Borkowski, P. (2023). Integration of machine learning solutions in the building automation system. *Energies*, *16*(11), 4504. DOI: 10.3390/en16114504

Khudoykulov, S. Ravikumar, Aarthi, S., & Ashirova, A. (2026). Blockchain-enabled Federated Learning for secure rural health data sharing. In *Cognitive Security and Predictive Health Monitoring for Rural Development* (pp. 255–286). IGI Global Scientific Publishing. DOI: 10.4018/979-8-3373-3947-4.ch010

Liu, A., Zhang, Q., Xu, S., Feng, H., Chen, X.-B., & Liu, W. (2024). QBIoT: A quantum blockchain framework for IoT with an improved proof-of-authority consensus algorithm and a public-key quantum signature. *Computers, Materials & Continua*, *80*(1), 1727–1751. DOI: 10.32604/cmc.2024.051233

Liu, R., Rozenman, G. G., Kundu, N. K., Chandra, D., & De, D. (2022). Towards the industrialisation of quantum key distribution in communication networks: A short survey. *IET Quantum Communication*, *3*(3), 151–163. DOI: 10.1049/qtc2.12044

Maharajpet, S. S. Abhilash, & Bedre, S. R. (2024). A LIME-based explainable AI for healthcare IoT: Building trust in clinical decision-making. In *Innovations and Trends in Modern Computer Science Technology – Overview, Challenges and Applications* (pp. 22–29). QTanalytics India. DOI: 10.48001/978-81-980647-5-2-3

Marisamy, K., Selvakumar, A., Rajasekar, B., Natarajan, R., Atajanova, A., & Makhmudov, S. (2025). Smart logistics integrating AI, IoT, blockchain, and Robotics for a sustainable Future. In *Emerging Trends in Smart Logistics Technologies* (pp. 73–104). IGI Global Scientific Publishing., DOI: 10.4018/979-8-3373-2434-0.ch003

Meziane, H., & Ouerdi, N. (2023). A survey on performance evaluation of artificial intelligence algorithms for improving IoT security systems. *Scientific Reports*, *13*(1), 21255. DOI: 10.1038/s41598-023-46640-9 PMID: 38040952

Namrita Gummadi, A., Napier, J. C., & Abdallah, M. (2024a). XAI-IoT: An explainable AI framework for enhancing anomaly detection in IoT systems. *IEEE Access : Practical Innovations, Open Solutions*, *12*, 71024–71054. DOI: 10.1109/ACCESS.2024.3402446

Namrita Gummadi, A., Napier, J. C., & Abdallah, M. (2024b). XAI-IoT: An explainable AI framework for enhancing anomaly detection in IoT systems. *IEEE Access : Practical Innovations, Open Solutions*, *12*, 71024–71054. DOI: 10.1109/ACCESS.2024.3402446

Padmaja, C., & Kumar, T. K. (2025). Integrating explainable AI in IoT for enhancing software performance. In *Advances in Computational Intelligence and Robotics* (pp. 341–368). IGI Global. DOI: 10.4018/979-8-3373-0370-3.ch011

Pandit, S., Ravikumar, R. N., Pandit, S., Joshi, N., Kishore, S., & Aarthi, S. (2025). Explainable Federated Learning for secure and transparent wireless edge networks. In *Advances in Computational Intelligence and Robotics* (pp. 127–168). IGI Global Scientific Publishing. DOI: 10.4018/979-8-3373-3576-6.ch004

Pasupuleti, M. K. (2024). *AI in Edge Computing for IoT Optimization*. National Education Services., DOI: 10.62311/nesx/rb978-81-981466-8-7

Protogerou, A., Kopsacheilis, E. V., Mpatziakas, A., Papachristou, K., Theodorou, T. I., Papadopoulos, S., Drosou, A., & Tzovaras, D. (2022). Time series network data enabling distributed intelligence—A holistic IoT security platform solution. *Electronics (Basel)*, *11*(4), 529. DOI: 10.3390/electronics11040529

Rafique, S. H., Abdallah, A., Musa, N. S., & Murugan, T. (2024a). Machine learning and deep learning techniques for Internet of Things network anomaly detection-current research trends. *Sensors (Basel)*, *24*(6), 1968. DOI: 10.3390/s24061968 PMID: 38544231

Rafique, S. H., Abdallah, A., Musa, N. S., & Murugan, T. (2024b). Machine learning and deep learning techniques for Internet of Things network anomaly detection-current research trends. *Sensors (Basel)*, *24*(6), 1968. DOI: 10.3390/s24061968 PMID: 38544231

Ramasamy, L. K., Khan, F., Shah, M., Prasad, B. V. V. S., Iwendi, C., & Biamba, C. (2022). Secure smart wearable computing through artificial intelligence-enabled Internet of Things and Cyber-Physical Systems for health monitoring. *Sensors (Basel)*, *22*(3), 1076. DOI: 10.3390/s22031076 PMID: 35161820

Rathee, G., Ahmad, F., Sandhu, R., Kerrache, C. A., & Azad, M. A. (2021). On the design and implementation of a secure blockchain-based hybrid framework for Industrial Internet-of-Things. *Information Processing & Management*, *58*(3), 102526. DOI: 10.1016/j.ipm.2021.102526

Ravikumar, A. S., Kalandarov, A., Djumaniyazova, M., & Habib, M. (2025). A roadmap to a sustainable future. In *Advances in Computational Intelligence and Robotics* (pp. 267–302). IGI Global Scientific Publishing. DOI: 10.4018/979-8-3373-3017-4.ch010

Ravikumar, R. S., Manujakshi, Aarthi, S., Urazbaeva, Y., & Tamilselvi, S. (2025). Navigating data privacy, security, and regulatory challenges in healthcare AI ensuring fairness, bias mitigation, interpretability, and trust. In *Transformative Role of Transformer Models in Healthcare* (pp. 25–54). IGI Global Scientific Publishing. DOI: 10.4018/979-8-3373-2038-0.ch002

Ravikumar, R. N., & Aarthi, S. (2025). AI-driven governance. In *Advances in Computational Intelligence and Robotics* (pp. 343–372). IGI Global Scientific Publishing. DOI: 10.4018/979-8-3373-3760-9.ch012

Saba, T., Rehman, A., Sadad, T., Kolivand, H., & Bahaj, S. A. (2022). Anomaly-based intrusion detection system for IoT networks through deep learning model. *Computers & Electrical Engineering*, *99*(107810), 107810. DOI: 10.1016/j.compeleceng.2022.107810

Singh, R., & Gill, S. S. (2023). Edge AI: A survey. *Internet of Things and Cyber-Physical Systems*, *3*, 71–92. DOI: 10.1016/j.iotcps.2023.02.004

University, M. babu, Prasad, J. L. Parvateesam, C., management, A. I. of technology and, Nagulmeera, S., University, M. babu, Avinash, V., & college, R. engineering. (. (2023). Enhancing IoT security: Addressing challenges, implementing solutions, and envisioning cybersecurity trends for the future. *International Journal of Engineering Applied Sciences and Technology*, *8*(6), 48–55. DOI: 10.33564/IJEAST.2023.v08i06.006

Vaishali, V. Raje, E. al. (. (2024). Realtime anomaly detection in Healthcare IoT: A machine learning-driven security framework. *Journal of Electrical Systems*, *19*(3), 192–202. DOI: 10.52783/jes.700

KEY TERMS AND DEFINITIONS

AI-IoT Integration: The combination of AI with IoT to create smart, connected, and self-learning systems.

AISIF Framework: The proposed model combining AI, blockchain, and quantum security for IoT protection.

Anomaly Detection: Finding unusual patterns in data that may indicate errors or attacks.

Artificial Intelligence (AI): Technology that allows machines to learn, analyze, and make decisions like humans.

Blockchain: A digital record system that keeps all transactions transparent and tamper-proof.

Edge Intelligence: Using AI at the device level to make faster and more private decisions.

Explainable AI (XAI): AI systems that can explain how and why they make decisions.

Federated Learning: Training AI models across multiple devices without sharing raw data.

Internet of Things (IoT): A network of devices connected to collect and share data automatically.

Privacy Preservation: Methods to keep user and device information safe and confidential.

Quantum Key Distribution (QKD): A secure way of sharing encryption keys using quantum technology.

Quantum Key Management System (QKMS): A system for managing encryption keys safely using quantum methods.

Quantum-Resistant Cryptography: Encryption methods that remain safe even against quantum computers.

Security Framework: A structured setup to protect data and communication in connected devices.

Smart Grid Systems: Energy systems that use IoT and AI for efficient and safe power management.

Smart Healthcare IoT: Use of IoT and AI in healthcare to monitor patients securely.

Trust Index: A score showing how reliable and secure an IoT device or system is.

Trust Management: Building and maintaining confidence between devices through verification and transparency.

Chapter 12
Securing Swarm Robotics Communication Using Quantum

Qurat ul Ain Zam Zam Mirza
http://orcid.org/0009-0007-3441-4016
Taylor's University, Malaysia

Humaira Ashraf
http://orcid.org/0000-0001-5067-3172
Taylor's University, Malaysia

Rimsha Kanwal
http://orcid.org/0009-0001-6759-5155
Taylor's University, Malaysia

ABSTRACT

As swarm robotics evolves into a paradigm-shifting approach for distributed autonomous systems, communication vulnerabilities pose risks in hostile environments. Conventional cryptography is limited by decentralized nature, energy constraints, and node density, while quantum computing threatens public-key encryption via Shor's algorithm. This chapter explores Quantum Key Distribution (QKD) and entanglement-based networking for information-theoretic security. We examine mobile quantum networks, highlighting drone-based relays and satellite links. Beyond security, quantum principles like superposition and entanglement can enhance swarm intelligence, task allocation, and coordination. Despite promising validations, hurdles remain: SWaP constraints, atmospheric interference, and mobility-induced

DOI: 10.4018/979-8-3373-3857-6.ch012

decoherence. Through case studies in aerial, maritime, space, and disaster domains, we propose a quantum-native architecture integrating post-quantum cryptography, adaptive PAT systems, and hybrid trust models for mission-critical resilience.

1. INTRODUCTION

Large groups of robots can now jointly complete complex tasks with little central control thanks to swarm robotics, which has emerged as a paradigm-shifting technique in distributed autonomous systems. The robustness, scalability, and adaptive coordination of swarm robotic systems are biologically inspired by insect colonies and flocking behavior. These qualities make them appropriate for high-stakes applications such as space exploration, battlefield surveillance, environmental monitoring, and disaster response. Swarm systems' distributed architecture, however, creates serious communication layer vulnerabilities, especially when they are used in hostile, contested, or sensitive environments. Verifying the confidentiality, accuracy, and legitimacy of inter-agent communications in these kinds of situations is not just a design improvement; it is a necessity for operations. Despite their effectiveness in traditional networked systems, conventional cryptographic mechanisms are fundamentally limited in swarm environments because of things like mobility, node density, energy constraints, and the lack of centralized infrastructure. More importantly, the advent of quantum computing poses a threat to popular public-key encryption systems by enabling quantum attacks like Shor's algorithm. As a result, researchers other than system architects are currently investigating quantum technologies as a potential threat vector as well as a fundamental remedy for secure communication in the future.

Entanglement-based networking and Quantum Key Distribution (QKD) are two examples of quantum communication technologies that provide information-theoretic security guarantees that are not possible with traditional methods. Airborne mobile quantum networks began when Liu et al. (2021) showed that drone-based entangled photon transmission was feasible. Their experiment used quadrotor UAVs as mobile relay nodes to deliver quantum links between polarization-entangled pairs of photons in real time, between floating platforms (Liu et al., 2021). The innovation highlights the feasibility of including quantum secured links to decentralized mobile networks like robotic swarms. At the same time, terrestrial-scale implementations have already been executed. The first continent-wide space-ground quantum communication network was implemented as reported by Chen et al. (2021) utilizing the Micius quantum satellite, which connects multiple ground stations with communications across the span of more than 4,600 kilometers (Chen et al., 2021). Their architecture confirmed key tenets of quantum-safe communications in complex, distributed systems a capability that is directly comparable to large swarm deployments over geographically distributed, or GPS-denied, domains. In addition to physical layer inventions, recent advances also discuss the application of quantum physics into decision and coordination logic of swarms. Mannone et al., (2025) introduced a specific of local-to-global control model, which exploits the capabilities of quantum computing primitives, where the quantum superposition is used to optimally allocate the tasks, and plan a route among multi-agent robotic swarms (Mannone et al., 2025). Such a twofold application of quantum technologies as communication safety and swarm intelligence represents the proximity to the whole-system quantum-augmented swarm autonomy. Another contribution to this area, Han et al. (2024) introduced a quantum-assisted cybersecurity framework involving quantum communication and artificial intelligence patterns in denying emerging threats in an IoT-like environment (Han et al., 2024). Such developments are augmented architecturally, including the multi-layer entangling-based synchronization model suggested in the Entangled Gondolas project (2023), which frames how quantum entanglement can be used to ensure coherence and temporal coordination within the population of robotic subswarms (Mannone et al., 2023).

Nevertheless, crucial issues also have yet to be resolved despite such encouraging trends. Implementation of quantum-secure communication in swarm systems has to reckon with the decoherence of mobility, the logistics of entanglement distribution, and short quantum memory times. Furthermore, there is still room for improvement in the areas of trust frameworks, rogue node detection techniques, and post-quantum fallback plan design. In addition to quantum authentication as a classical layer, Chen and Ng (2022) suggested using a hash-chain mechanism to detect behavioral abnormalities among robotic swarms (Chen and Ng 2022). However, some of the efforts by Pacheco et al. (2024) demonstrate how distributed ledger technologies can be used to secure federated learning models in the context of robotic swarms. They propose hybrid solutions that combine blockchain and quantum technology to promote provenance and trust (Pacheco et al., 2024). Similar to the defense-in-depth combination of physical and algorithmic layers (Kahn et al., 2024), Khan et al. (2024) emphasized the importance of integrating post-quantum cryptography schemes into UAV communications stacks in an effort to make airborne and terrestrial swarms quantum-era resilient in the future.A timely and revolutionary method for addressing serious vulnerabilities in distributed robotic systems is presented by the combination of swarm robotics and quantum-secured communication paradigms. Investigating architectural models that incorporate these different but complementary technologies is crucial as the need for autonomous, robust, and secure communication among robotic agents keeps increasing. The main domains and interactions supporting a quantum system are depicted in the following conceptual overview Figure 1.

The architectural design, cryptographic underpinnings, protocol-level modifications, and implementation difficulties related to swarm robotics communication security with quantum technologies are examined in this chapter. We hope to provide a thorough framework for the upcoming generation of secure robotic swarms functioning in hostile and mission-critical environments by combining developments from mobile network design, secure communication, swarm intelligence, and quantum physics.

Figure 1. Theoretical description of the swarm robotic systems with quantum security. In distributed autonomous agents, swarm robotics, secure communications, and quantum technologies come together to tackle the current security threats.

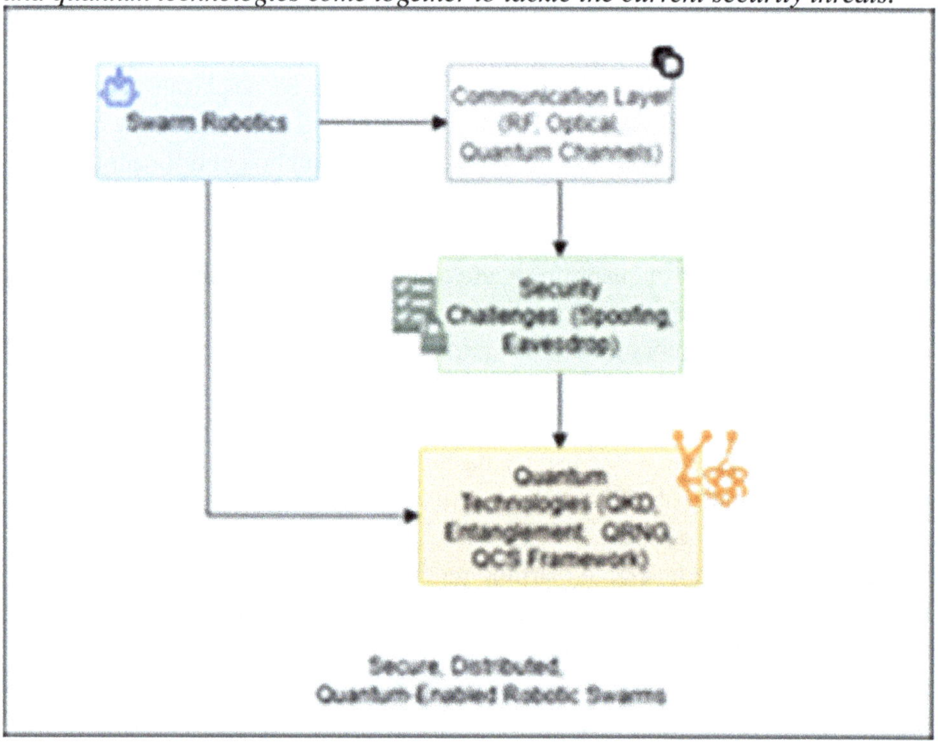

2. BACKGROUND AND RELATED TECHNOLOGIES

The achievement of communication in swarm robotic systems requires an integration of knowledge in swarm dynamics, classical and quantum communication protocols, cryptographic models, and decentralized trust architectures. This part describes the underlying technologies that form the basis of integrating the quantum-security communication systems in swarm robotic networks. Swarm robotics is fundamentally modeled after natural phenomena like ant colonies or bird flocks, where decentralized coordination and local interaction rules allow for emergent behavior, scalability, and high fault tolerance. In these systems, individual agents possess minimal onboard processing and rely heavily on peer-to-peer interactions to achieve group objectives. Communication typically follows centralized, distributed, or hybrid paradigms, each involving critical trade-offs between control efficiency and security. However, the distributed nature and limited computing resources of these swarms expose them to various threats, including eavesdropping, Man-in-the-Middle (MitM) attacks, and physical node capture. To address these vulnerabilities, quantum communication exploits the principles of superposition, entanglement, and the no-cloning hypothesis to provide information-theoretic security guarantees. Unlike classical encryption, which relies on computational complexity, quantum-secured protocols can inherently detect eavesdropping because any attempt to intercept the transmission alters the quantum state. Key applications include Quantum Key Distribution (QKD), such as the BB84 protocol, which has been experimentally validated on mobile drone platforms and long-distance satellite-to-ground links. Furthermore, entanglement is being explored not just for cryptography, but as a mechanism for state sharing and time synchronization among distributed robotic agents. Current research is also focused on hybrid architectures that combine quantum-enhanced security with AI-based threat detection and blockchain-style trust frameworks to bridge the gap between existing hardware constraints and future quantum-native systems.

2.1 Swarm Robotics: Principles and Communication Models

Swarm robotics [sources 1] is a technology in which decentralized coordinated robotic systems are modeled on natural groups like ant groups or bird flocks. Such classifications give importance to local interaction rules, emergent behavior, scalability and fault tolerance. The robots or agents within a swarm have minimal onboard processing and sensing and rely largely on peer-to-peer interactions and environmental feedback to accomplish group goals. In Figure 2 Communication within robotic swarms typically follows three paradigms:

- **Centralized Communication**, where a global controller or leader node manages the swarm through one-to-many broadcasting. While this enables global situational awareness, it introduces a single point of failure and scalability constraints.
- **Distributed Communication**, where information is shared between neighbor individuals by each agent, or local neighbors, depending on its proximity

or network topology. The advantage of this model is its greater robustness at the expense of communication inconsistencies and security breaches.

- **Hybrid Models**, which combine centralized oversight with local autonomy to optimize performance and resilience.

Figure 2. A parallel between some of the main communication models in swarm robotics; centralized, decentralized, and hybrid. All the models are composed of trade-offs in terms of scalability, fault tolerance and control efficiency, that have effect on security and performance.

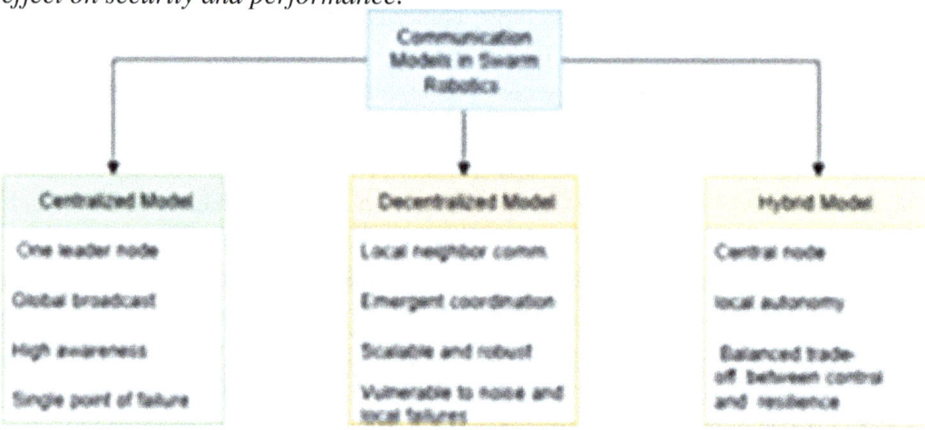

Because swarm agents are frequently used in a mobile ad hoc network (MANET) architecture without permanent infrastructure, then the established techniques used in network security like pre-distribution of keys or centralized anchor of trust is usually found to be insufficient. This requires the venturing into new paradigms which can provide high security assurances, even in resource-constrained dynamic environments.

2.2 Threat Landscape in Swarm Communications

Compared to the more traditional swarm robotics systems there are certainly flaws that allow or expose swarm robotic systems to a variety of security threats because of their distributed nature and low computing resources in Figure 3:

- **Eavesdropping and Data Leakage**: Passive adversaries may intercept broadcasted or relayed communication, potentially extracting mission-critical or behavioral information.

- **Man-in-the-Middle (MitM) Attacks**: Adversaries may divert and modify packets in the middle of swarm members, especially during route discovery or consensus formation.
- **Node Capture and Cloning**: Physical access to a single node may compromise cryptographic keys or enable cloning, allowing attackers to introduce malicious agents.
- **Sybil and Spoofing Attacks**: Multiple identities can be simulated to manipulate swarm consensus or overwhelm decision-making routines.

Figure 3. Common security threats to that system. Attacks range between passive surreptitious monitoring to active node seizure, which are all compounded by the weak computing resources and distributed networks.

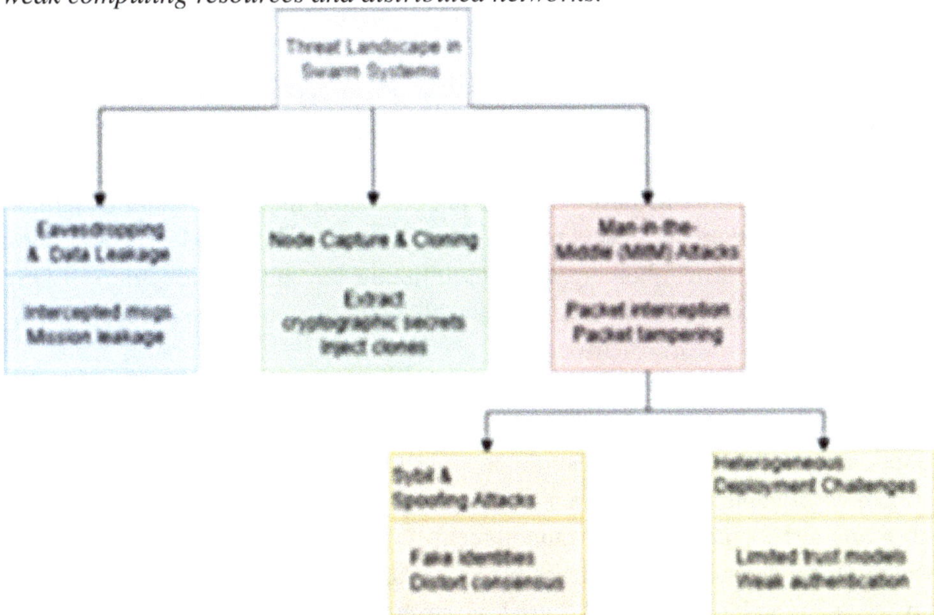

All these issues are compounded in open-environment or heterogeneous swarms, where such swarms can be easily taken advantage of when limited authentication and trust models are left. Such shows the utmost importance of secure key exchange, authentication methods and inference of trust customized to decentralized, mobile, and resource-constrained environments.

2.3 Quantum Communication Technologies

Quantum communication exploits the philosophies of quantum mechanics (superposition, predicament and the no-cloning hypothesis) to provide information-theoretic security guarantees. In contrast to classical encryption, where security is founded on assumptions involving computational problems, the security of quantum-secured protocols are such that any effort to intercept the transmission inherently changes the quantum state of the communication system and thus the act of eavesdropping can be detected.

The one most significant application is the quantum-key-distribution, or QKD, which can enable two parties to arrange a shared secret-key using provable security. The most studied and implemented version is the BB84 protocol. Liu et al. (2021) exemplified that mobile drones should take place as a platform to relay the entangled photonic group and make it possible to set up the first QKD network relayed aerial installation by unmanned systems (Liu et al., 2021). Their solution has real applicability to the use of secure communication, as applied using entanglement, on dynamic swarm platforms. On a larger level, Chen et al. (2021) have realized a first of its kind space-to-ground quantum-communication network through the use of the Micius satellite, making headway in connecting intercontinental quantum-protected connections of 4,600 km (Chen et al., 2021). Their deployment applies specifically to swarm robotics situations utilizing beyond-line-of-sight (BLOS) communications where there is need to enable communications to succeed; aerial and space-based swarm scenarios.

Simultaneously, the concept of entangling synchronization has been substantiated as a new way state sharing and time synchronization can be had between distributed robotic agents. The Entangled Gondolas project (2023) simulates an aquatic robot swarms with quantum entanglement running in it to achieve synchronized behavioral levels among the (sub)swarms (Mannone et al., 2023). These architectures imagine a new future in which quantum interconnectedness, no longer mere tool of cryptography, becomes an interconnected shared swarm awareness and synchronization tool.

2.4 Quantum-Driven Swarm Intelligence

In addition to security in communication, principles of quantum computers are also being exploited to increase the planning and decision-making of swarms. Mannone et al., (2025) presented a local-to-global control framework enhanced with quantum, where the quantum circuits model was embedded in each agent to optimize planning of trajectories and give the task within a collective (Mannone et al., 2025). Other quantum algorithms for example Grover quantum search and quantum annealing are highly applicable in the field of combinatorial optimization that is widely used in control of swarms (e.g. target assignment, path planning and coverage).

The combination of quantum models on cognition with swarms brings in a new potential probabilistic inference, model of fuzzy logic and non-classical coordination systems in a decentralized systems. These advancements show that not only will quantum technologies allow a fundamental reconstitution of the security layer of swarm robotic systems but it will also reach into the thinking level of the cognition of such systems.

2.5 Hybrid Cryptographic and Trust Architectures

In light of existing hardware constraints and slow progress of fully working full-stack quantum networks, hybrid solutions are emerging as a way to fill the gap between classical and quantum worlds. The study of Han et al., (2024), established the feasibility of the concept of implementing quantum-enhanced security controls without the need to complete the same ecosystem scenario of an IoMT system in a fully fledged AI-based threat detection model (Han et al., 2024). Likewise, Chen and Ng (2022) suggested the hash-chain-based behavioral monitoring approach to trace the behaviors that deviate in emergent swarm behavior and provided lightweight trust mechanism that would work in real-time tasks. Pacheco et al. (2024) extended the model furthermore and trained federated learning with blockchain consensus into robot swarms, which demonstrated the potential of decentralized verification without central verification (Pacheco et al., 2024). Elsewhere, Khan et al. (2024) had already suggested a roadmap to incorporating post-quantum cryptographic algorithms into UAV networks, a strategy that is needed in the near term to achieve resilience given that full-scale quantum infrastructure is already under development (Khan et al., 2024).

Overall, swarm robotics and quantum communication are two fields of research that, though they still sit toward the fringe, are no longer purely theoretical. Rather, this is an accelerating area of exploration supported with experimental testing and architectural advances. Quantum technologies are not only a route to secure communication beyond cryptographic cracking, but can also form the basis of resilient, intelligent and synchronised swarms of operating in rivals and unstructured environments.

3. EXISTING PROTOCOL LIMITATIONS

Prior to recommending a quantum augmented communication architecture, one must first know about the shortcomings of both existing classical and also emerging quantum capable protocols in Figure 4 as applied to swarm robotic systems.

Figure 4. Comparative view of limitations in classical cryptographic and emerging quantum-enabled communication protocols for swarm robotics. Key challenges stem from mobility, environmental interference, and integration difficulties in real-world swarm deployment.

3.1 Classical Cryptographic Constraints in Swarm Settings

Swarm robotics systems generally use traditional protocols like pre shared symmetric keys or the classical system of public key infrastructure (PKI) to provide agent to agent authentication and secrecy:

- **Vulnerability to Quantum-Future Attacks:** Widely used public-key algorithms (e.g., RSA, ECC) are threatened by quantum algorithms like Shor's, rendering them insecure in a post-quantum era (Kahn et al., 2024).
- **Scalability and Key Management:** In large swarms, managing pairwise key exchanges or centralized trust anchors becomes impractical due to dynamic membership, mobility, and limited on-node computation.
- **Physical Node Capture Risks:** A captured node may expose all stored key material, enabling adversarial impersonation or Sybil attacks without detection.

As noted by Khan *et al.* (2024), many UAV communication systems lack layered resilience and depend heavily on centralized or static trust anchors, making them unsuitable for decentralized, dynamic swarm environments.

3.2 Limitations of Existing Quantum-Enabled Demonstrations

Recent advances in drone and mobile-platform QKD mark important steps but also expose serious limitations relative to swarm deployments. Although experimental prototypes have already proven that quantum links can be operated over motion, there are a variety of real world obstacles that prevent their extension to large scale autonomous robots swarms. Existing applications frequently have the difficulty of high-fidelity quantum states being dynamically unstable, both in the air and on the ground. These systems are required to work through the intricacies of real time spatial coordination and they have to deal with limited onboard resources.

3.2.1 Brief Key Exchange Sessions and Finite-Key Effects

Conrad et al. (2025) demonstrated a modular QKD system enabling drone-2-drone, drone-2-vehicle, and vehicle-2-vehicle channels with protected key rates between 1.6 and 20 kbps. However, key exchanges in these systems are of very short duration often when two moving platforms are within line of sight only for seconds or minutes and any security analysis must account for finite-key statistical effects. These effects significantly reduce secure key rates and increase quantum bit error rate (QBER) sensitivity compared to idealized infinite-key models. Because the key generation process is frequently interrupted by the rapid mobility of agents, the resulting keys may be too short to provide long-term cryptographic security unless advanced distillation techniques are utilized. This temporal window limitation creates a significant bottleneck for swarms that require high-throughput data encryption during continuous, long-range missions.

3.2.2 Non-Ideal Device Performance in Dynamic Environments

The deployment of quantum communication in swarm robotics is significantly complicated by the inherent unpredictability of mobile platforms. Vibrations, alignment errors, atmospheric turbulence, and mechanical drift collectively degrade the fidelity of quantum channels. Maintaining the stability of a quantum link is particularly challenging in aerial or underwater scenarios, where physical movement causes beam wander and polarization fluctuations. Furthermore, because current swarm agents are typically resource-constrained, integrating complex security models that account for these physical non-idealities is rarely feasible. The absence of portable quantum repeaters further exacerbates this issue, as signal degradation cannot be easily corrected mid-flight, forcing systems to rely on imperfect physical layer compensations. Consequently, sustaining entangled coordination across a decentralized swarm of multiple mobile nodes remains an unscaled technical bottleneck due to these mechanical and environmental perturbations (Dubey et al., 2024).

3.2.3 SWaP Constraints and Synchronization Limitations

Small UAVs have severe Size, Weight, and Power (SWaP) constraints that limit the inclusion of high-precision optics, quantum memories, and stabilization systems. When timing and pointing accuracy are necessary in order to achieve a healthy entanglement sharing at finite-size QKD systems, they are not always enough. In addition, it is a serious problem as mobile nodes must be synchronized (Conrad et al., 2025).

3.3 Environmental and Atmospheric Constraints

In a 2024 paper, Dubey et al. (2024) carried out a thorough literature review of various aspects of aerial quantum communication, including environmental restrictions that the free-space QKD is affected with in low-altitude and urban settings:

- **Atmospheric Attenuation and Turbulence**: Fog, humidity, and scattering also affect a drone-based quantum link to a variable degree with unpredictable losses and degraded fidelity except at higher altitudes (Dubey et al., 2024).
- **Weather Dependency:** Thick clouds or high levels of humidity affect the photon transmission and appear to worsen the efficiency of the key rate or shut down communications links altogether (Dubey et al., 2024).
- **Absence of Quantum Repeaters, Routing Complexity:** Multi-hop relay protocols to distribute an entanglement across large-scale topologies must be

complex without quantum repeaters. The mobility also makes the routing and the key replenishment complex (Dubey et al., 2024).

These facts compromise the feasibility to implement QKD as a permanent utility in the realistic swarm operations to a great extent.

3.4 Classical Protocol Stack Integration Problems

Even in the quantum technologies case, co-existing classical upper- layer protocols impose large overhead:

- **Complex Protocol Interfacing:** Integrating QKD with existing routing, transport, and application-layer protocols often requires bespoke interfaces, increasing complexity and latency (Zhou et al., 2025).
- **Resource Consumption & Key Synchronization Overhead:** Frequent key exchanges, re-authentication, and key management introduce non-negligible energy consumption and computational burden particularly in lightweight robotic nodes (Zhou et al., 2025).
- **Detection Accuracy Trade-Offs:** Ensuring eavesdropping detection while maintaining acceptable false-positive rates remains difficult in environments with high channel noise or intermittent connectivity (Zhou et al., 2025).

Conrad's work acknowledges that many mobile QKD systems assume simplified, static upper-layer models, which may not realistically coexist with the dynamic swarm protocol stack required for coordination and control (Conrad et al., 2025).

3.5 Summary of Shortcomings

Table 1. Limitation area in swarm context

Limitation Area	Issues in Swarm Context
Classical Cryptography	Vulnerable to future quantum attacks; scalability and key compromise risks
Mobile QKD Demonstrations	Short sessions with limited key length; non-ideal hardware; finite-key penalties
Environmental Conditions	Atmospheric turbulence, rain, humidity cause high losses, unreliable links
Protocol Stack Integration	Complex interfacing, energy overhead, latency, unreliable eavesdrop detection
SWaP and Synchronization Limits	Hardware weight, power, and accurate clocking limitations hinder operation in small UAVs

Given these in table 1 shows gaps, there is a clear need for a holistic, quantum-native architecture that addresses the limitations outlined above. The next section will propose a Quantum-Secure Communication Architecture for Swarms, which incorporates adaptive entanglement routing, hybrid trust frameworks, and synchronization protocols tailored for dynamic, resource-constrained robotic agents.

4. FUNDAMENTALS OF QUANTUM COMMUNICATION IN SWARM ROBOTICS

Figure 5. Hierarchical depiction of quantum communication principles applied to swarm robotics. Section 4 is divided into quantum security foundations, network architecture, experimental validations, and the strategic role of entanglement in coordination and timing.

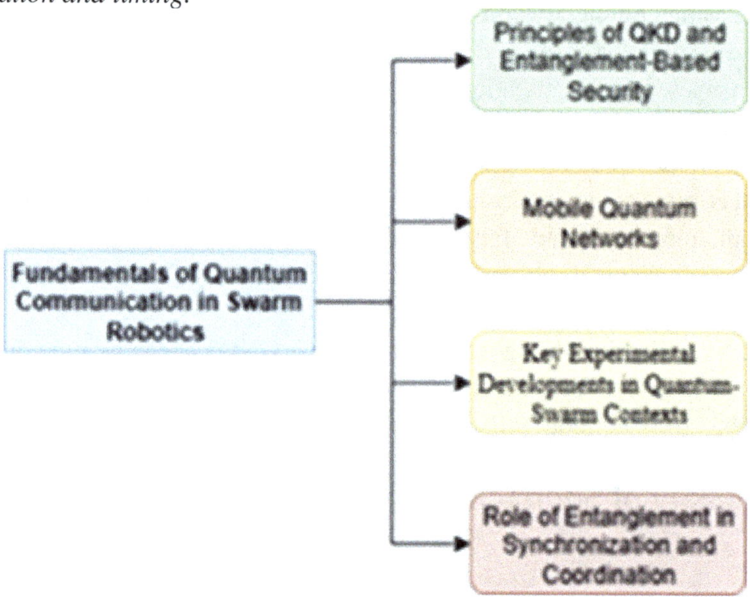

Figure 5 illustrates the hierarchical depiction of quantum communication principles as they are applied to the unique constraints of swarm robotics. This structural approach is essential because securing emergent behavior requires more than just classical encryption; it demands a transition toward information-theoretic security that is resilient against both current interceptors and future quantum adversaries

4.1 Principles of QKD and Entanglement-Based Security

Quantum-Key-Distribution (QKD) enables two communicating parties to establish a common secret key with quantum states, which is non-interceptable by classical means. An aerial-communication variant of the protocols like BB84, E91 and decoy-state variants has been adopted to UAVs and mobile swarms to meet the time-sensitivity of the aerial communication. QKD stated by Khan et al. (2024) provides quantum-resistant key creation that minimises the susceptibility to attacks such as eavesdropping and replay.

As Liu et al. (2021) have shown, through entanglement-based methods, where entangled photon pairs are shared between drones on the move, it is possible to use the method to generate symmetric keys and ensure provable security. Not only do these methods guarantee confidentiality, but also identify tampering using quantum bit error rates (QBER), which is a crucial component of swarm coordination (Han et al. 2024). Han et al. (2024) applied such techniques to cyber-physical swarm systems to combine QKD with intelligent threat detection to Internet of Military Things (IoMT). Their results focused on quantum improved resilience against intrusion in resource-limited swarm system environments that are dynamically evolving.

4.2 Mobile Quantum Networks: Implementation, Components and Operational Constraints

In the practical implementation of quantum-secure communication in mobile swarms, the process would need modular, miniaturized, and lightweight quantum devices. Conrad et al. (2025) established drone-based and vehicle-based QKD architectures that can exchange keys at a range of 1.620 kbps with actual hardware requirements. Their design is made of a single-photon detector, entangled photon generator, polarization codifier and a synchronization system.

The described QKD setup of (Conrad et al., 2025) is sensitive to orientation and thus necessitates strong PAT (Pointing, Acquisition, and Tracking) systems which remain a problem in drone operations because of turbulence, drift, and vibrational noise. SWaP (Size, Weight, and Power) constraints are also to be taken into consideration during integration into UAVs. Chen et al. (2021) demonstrated a continent-scale quantum network integrating satellite and ground stations, where key exchange occurred over 4,600 km. Although largely ground-to-space, the layered model they developed provides foundational architecture adaptable to autonomous swarm operations. Sun and Shao (2022) emphasized the necessity of multi-node resilience and communication handoff mechanisms in heterogeneous robotic swarms, especially under emergency scenarios. They highlighted that quantum-secure nodes must maintain stable routing even in rapidly changing topologies.

4.3 Key Experimental Developments in Quantum-Swarm Contexts

Liu et al. (2021) developed the first airborne prototype of entanglement distribution based on mobile quantum nodes in the form of drones. Their experiment in 2021 is one of the thresholds because real-time key generation in open-air scenarios matters to mobile robotic swarms carrying out tactical or surveillance duties. By utilizing quadrotor UAVs as mobile relay nodes, they successfully delivered quantum links between polarization-entangled photon pairs in real time between floating platforms. Chen et al. (2021) expanded the area to an incorporated space-for-ground QKD network. Although satellites are not drones, per se, their mobility models and multi-node architecture can provide revelations into distributed quantum coordinations to scale to large swarms. Their architecture confirmed key tenets of quantum-safe communications in complex, distributed systems, a capability directly comparable to large swarm deployments over geographically distributed or GPS-denied domains.

Conrad et al. (2025) introduced a hybrid mobile QKD system, featuring operation between drones and vehicles, with consideration of practical aspects deriving from mobility-induced QBER variations and finite key impacts. Scalable swarm robotics is especially applicable to the focus on modular deployment. Their work highlights that while modular hardware allows for scaling to multi-agent swarms, the success of such systems remains highly dependent on the accuracy of Pointing, Acquisition, and Tracking (PAT) systems during dynamic flight. Furthermore, recent simulations have begun to bridge the gap between physical photon transmission and collective behavior. The "Entangled Gondolas" project (2023) demonstrated how quantum entanglement can be utilized to ensure coherence and temporal coordination within populations of robotic subswarms, particularly in aquatic environments. By integrating quantum-driven synchronization, these systems move beyond mere encryption toward a shared swarm awareness that minimizes the need for conventional, high-bandwidth clock synchronization..

4.4 Role of Entanglement in Synchronization and Coordination

Entanglement is more than encryption: it can work as a coordination method in swarm behavior. A model introduced by Mannone et al. (2023) in the study reported in WIVACE 2023 explains that aquatic robots have similar consequences of maintaining consistent and synchronized behavior through distributed masses that are entangled. These entangled gondolas show how quantum correlations can guide the consensus and cohesiveness of multi-agent systems.Such synchronization is crucial in robot groups where their latency, drifting, or clock synchronization may cause disastrous mismatch. The process of entangling quantum signals will eliminate the use of conventional means of synchronizing the clock; thereby, enabling agents to act in changing situations in a less chaotic manner as well as in a more timely period.

This idea builds on local-to-global transition that Mannone et al. (2025) talked about; embedded quantum logic is a means of facilitating distributed consent process with fewer communication cycles, which are essential to low bandwidth, high autonomy swarms.

5. QUANTUM-SECURED COMMUNICATION FRAMEWORK FOR SWARM SYSTEMS

The transition from classical to quantum-secured frameworks necessitates a paradigm shift in how trust and connectivity are managed within a swarm. A robust framework must account for the high mobility of nodes and the intermittent nature of quantum links while maintaining the decentralized ethos of swarm intelligence. By integrating quantum cryptographic primitives directly into the swarm's operational logic, the system can achieve a level of resilience that classical methods, which are vulnerable to future quantum-computing-based attacks like Shor's algorithm, cannot provide. The proposed framework moves beyond traditional point-to-point security by envisioning a "defense-in-depth" strategy. This involves layering physical quantum properties such as the detection of eavesdropping through the No-Cloning theorem with algorithmic safeguards like post-quantum cryptography and decentralized trust models. Such a multi-layered approach ensures that even if individual quantum links are temporarily disrupted by environmental decoherence or SWaP constraints, the overall integrity and coordination of the swarm remain intact.

5.1 Reference System Architecture for Secure Quantum-Enabled Swarms

The process of creating a quantum-secure communication framework specifically in swarm robotics concerns the process of implementing quantum cryptographic primitives in distributed mobile agents. In order to introduce safe and versatile airborne networks, Khan et al. (2024) offered a UAV communication stack into which post-quantum cryptographic algorithms and quantum key exchange interfaces have been built. They focus on the architecture-level consideration such as modular quantum hardware, cryptographic co-processors, and cross-layer integration via their review. Likewise Ralegankar et al. (2021) proposed a layered quantum security architecture of a UAV with one layer being quantum cryptography-as-a-service (QCaaS). This enables individual agents to place QKD session requests and coordinate trust anchors, and undergo quantum key refresh without performing centralized functions, which is very applicable to dynamic swarm settings. Sun and Shao (2022) have proposed an optimized layered swarm communication model specific to disaster response networks where quantum elements of a system (such as entangled keys) can be injected into the system alongside other telemetry. In their architecture, they focus on independently establishing links and maintaining safe routing tables and energy resource-considerate protocols that work even in adverse conditions.

5.2 Node-Level Security Functions and Inter-Agent Key Exchange Protocols

The security of the quantum-enabled swarms starts with the nodes. Each robot must be capable of independently establishing secure links and performing key management functions. Liu et al. (2021) have shown the ability of mobile drones to be transmitters and receivers of entangled photons and hence the possibility of a real time exchange of keys with minimal infrastructure use.

As pointed out by Chen and Ng (2022), behavior divergence and blockchain-style audit trails were used to detect rogue agents. Although not directly quantum, their approach is consistent with quantum-aided identity verification, in which QBER analysis could be used to indicate suspicious behavior because of node compromise. Pacheco et al. (2024) went a step further and implemented federated learning and use secure inter-agent communication based on blockchain. This can be combined with quantum key exchange to guarantee privacy and integrity in decentralized model training in the swarm with Swarm decision-making, Mannone et al. (2025) suggested to incorporate local quantum logic to make swarm agents self-synchronizing, cryptographically aware. Such nodes are not only sharing control messages but also sharing quantum generated secrets and therefore external key distribution servers are not required.

5.3 Relay Networks, Entanglement Distribution, and PAT Considerations

Swarm networks tend to utilize relay chains to spread entangled states or quantum keys among non-line-of-sight agents. Liu et al. (2021) demonstrated drones as relays in a free-space QKD setup and this design solves the problems of beam divergence and stability by steering of the links with adaptive strategies. According to Conrad et al. (2025), the PAT (pointing, acquisition and tracking) system was found to be the most sensitive element of mobile quantum links. They found that real-time calibration and alignment algorithms are needed in the drone-to-drone QKD, particularly when the device is moving or in a hover. The allocation of entanglement across relay networks was also investigated by Chen et al. (2021), as they examined the idea of trust in quantum satellite-ground communication. Although they are mainly terrestrial, their approaches to node authentication, quantum trust propagation, and entanglement purification can be used as a model to apply the same approaches to aerial or underwater robot swarms.

Dubey et al. (2024) compared the techniques of PAT to apply to aerial quantum communication, cautious that cheap sensors can introduce severe alignment jitter, which can be counteracting the entangled state fidelity. These observations indicate the need to combine quantum-compatible inertial measurement units (IMUs) and adaptive optics to deploy swarm-scale.

5.4 QRNGs and Randomness of Channels

Quantum Random Number Generators (QRNGs) make sure that material and communication sequences of keys are unpredictable in nature. Use of QRNGs in frequency-hopping-spread-spectrum (FHSS) channels as introduced in (de Curtò et al., 2024) makes jamming and cross-channel attacks in drone communications more difficult. Their combination, however, enforces tight conditions of concurred timing and verification of entropy in all swarm nodes.

The mobile QKD systems provided by Conrad et al. also contained QRNG modules (Conrad et al., 2025). The design of their resources underscored the trade-offs between the QRNG sampling rate and the key generation bandwidth of QRNGs that applied in resource-constrained agents such as micro-UAVs. Ralegankar et al. (2021) underscored that the inclusion of QRNGs required strong thermal and environmental protection. In its absence, the entropy sources might be weaker, meaning that security guarantees are compromised because QRNG-based cyber monitoring systems can leveraged the generated randomness to deploy decoy paths and obfuscate routing when observed by adversaries. Han et al. (2024) showed that QRNG-based cyber monitoring systems may utilize the opportunity to use randomness to deploy decoy paths and obfuscate routing under adversarial observation. The technique is very useful in aggressive conditions where the classical pseudo-randomness cannot be used to offer operational security.

6. CASE STUDIES AND APPLICATIONS

This section puts the quantum-secured swarm communication frames in context by the way of illustrative real-world and abstract example uses in a Figure 6. These represent how quantum technologies can be integrated to promote operational security, reliability as well as mission resilience across various fields.

Figure 6. Application of quantum-secured swarm systems in real-life scenarios in the air, sea, space, and disaster environment. Both instances utilize entanglement coordination and safe QKD schemes in the terms of changing and restricted conditions.

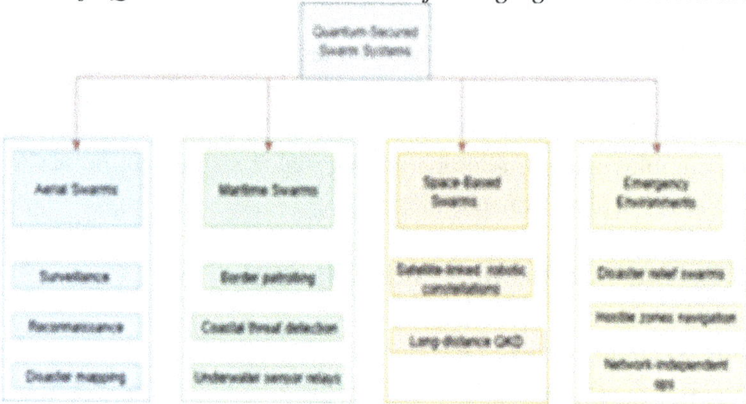

6.1 Unsafe Aerial Surveillance and Reconnaissance With Drone Swarms

In aerial surveillance swarming quantum-secured communication can help overcome the dangers of eavesdropping, spoofing, and jamming which often pose a threat to the tactical operations of the UAVs. The idea of airborne entanglement distribution was first introduced by Liu et al. (2021) in which drones create secure optical relays. This is a feature that is required in high-stakes surveillance within the highly hostile areas where missions may be jeopardized by compromised communication.

Conrad et al. (2025) confirmed that drone-to-drone and drone-to-ground QKD in dynamic flight are possible and indicated that key rates of 1.620 kbps were successful. Modular architecture allows them to scale to multi-agent swarms, assuming that PAT systems are accurate. Javed et al. (2024) stressed the importance of effective communication in the coordinated ISR (intelligence, surveillance, reconnaissance) missions. Incorporating QKD into such missions will mean that every agent has a distinct, uncrackable key sequence, and there will be almost no chance of man-in-the-middle attacks.

6.2 Marine Border Patrol Using Entangled AUV Groupings

In maritime swarms Quantum-secured underwater swarms have new modalities with entangled Autonomous Underwater Vehicles (AUVs), especially in the operation of maritime borders. It was proposed in the model, Entangled Gondolas (2023), which featured quantum-driven AUV networks with layered topology, where the entanglement assists not only in ensuring secure communication, but also formation and navigation coordination. Even though undersea QKD is experimental, pathfinding studies by Chen et al. (2021) of long-distance entanglement relay via satellite can be abstracted to subsea relays assuming the high refractive loss in water, acoustic-optical transduction layers can become significant in practice. This type of architecture finds specific use in distributed anti-submarine surveillance tasks, or anti-submarine search and rescue missions.

6.3 Space-Based Robotic Constellations using Quantum Communication Using Satellite Relays

Quantum communication is a new facilitator of space-based assemblies of satellites and autonomous probes. Another important step towards safe extraterrestrial swarm work was made by Chen et al. (2021), who demonstrated a multi-node satellite based to ground QKD infrastructure with a distance exceeding 4,600 km.

These constellations, which are fitted with quantum-enabled links, are capable of coordinating tasks like orbital debris removal, distributed earth observation, or planetary exploration and being safe against interception. Mannone et al. (2025) extended the opportunity of implementing quantum logic at the node-level and adding to the autonomous, secure cooperation among orbital actors and suggested modular, radiation-hardened quantum subsystems with autonomous session-key regeneration. Ralegankar et al. (2021) also examined spaceborne QCaaS platforms and its integration with classical telemetry and proposed modular, radiation-hardened quantum subsystems with self-generation of session keys.

6.4 Hostile Environment Emergency Scenarios

CBRN (chemical, biological, radiological, nuclear) response in the case of an emergency response, recovery following a disaster, or battlefield triage should be secure, resilient, and autonomous in communication. The security model introduced in (Sun and Shao 2022) is particularly swarm system oriented in a degraded environment wherein they suggest the use of multi-mode channels and key dynamic updating.

Javed et al. (2024) supported this necessity concerning UAV swarms, explaining security gaps in the traditional protocols, and the necessity of versatile and secure systems. The urgency of applicability of QKD and QRNG implementation in swarms working on such risky missions is provided in the analysis. Han et al. (2024) have suggested a hybrid architecture that is composed of quantum communication and AI-based threat detection of Internet of Medical Things (IoMT) that can be extended to medical drone swarms or casualty evacuation bots that should act under the conditions of adversarial settings.

7. CHALLENGES, LIMITATIONS, AND FUTURE DIRECTIONS

Although there have been significant advances in quantum technology integration into swarm robotic systems, there are still a number of technical, operational, and theoretical hurdles. Such restrictions do not allow immediate implementation and require additional interdisciplinary studies to develop safe, scalable, and autonomous quantum-swarmed systems. Mobile Quantum Key Distribution (QKD) systems are primarily limited by low key generation rates, typically between 1.6 and 20 kbps, which may support small-scale coordination but are insufficient for data-intensive swarms. The stability of these links is further compromised in high-speed aerial networks by vibrations, mechanical drift, and polarization fluctuations that cause decoherence. Environmental factors such as atmospheric attenuation, fog, and turbulence also degrade photon transmission, particularly in low-altitude or urban settings. Additionally, severe Size, Weight, and Power (SWaP) constraints on small UAVs limit the inclusion of necessary high-precision optics and stabilization systems. The lack of miniaturized, energy-efficient quantum memory also forces a reliance on real-time transmission, as agents currently cannot store quantum states for asynchronous communication. Additionally, the requirement for sub-nanosecond clock synchronization across a decentralized, moving swarm remains a significant technical bottleneck for maintaining functional quantum-secure stacks. Finally, establishing unified trust frameworks that successfully integrate quantum security with classical decentralized ledgers or AI-based threat detection presents ongoing architectural complexities.

7.1 Key Generation Rates, Stability of the Link, and Constraints of Quantum Memory

Mobile QKD systems are also limited by the key generating rates. According to Conrad et al. (2025), even in free-space, with ideal conditions, the key rates were between 1.6 and 20 kbps that would support small-scale coordination but not support dense or data-intensive swarms. The finite-key effects and probabilistic entanglement generation restrict the scalability to the larger scale.

Ralegankar et al. (2021) also established link stability to be another bottleneck particularly in high speed aerial networks. Moreover, Dubey et al. (2024) noted that quantum memory components that are necessary to support asynchronous communication are large-scale, energy-consuming and have not been optimized yet to systems with low SWaP such as UAVs and microbots. Swarms are also high throughput, low-latency key exchange, which contradicts the temporal coherence limits of existing entangled photon sources. This is not enabled by a viable onboard quantum storage, which limits the possibility of decoupling the key generation and real-time transmission.

7.2 Coherence Decoherence by Mobility and Real-Time Alignment

Swarm agents particularly aerial and underwater agents perform in a turbulent, scattered and vibrating environment, which worsens quantum link fidelity. The article by Liu et al. (2021) and Chen et al. (2021) brought attention to the fact that drone and satellite motions cause decoherence of free-space QKD channels, which requires constant calibration.

Dubey et al. (2024) outlined atmospheric absorption and beam wander as the main dangers of transmission of entangled photon. They proposed adaptive optics and quantum error correction, but these solutions introduce hardware and computation overheads. The pointing, acquisition and tracking (PAT) systems discussed in Conrad et al. (2025) are technically a bottleneck. Sustaining entangled coordination of a decentralized swarm of many mobile nodes has not been shown to scale.

7.3 Trust Creation during Hybrid Quantum Classical Deployments

The addition of quantum security into classical swarm systems creates the issue of interoperability. Chen and Ng (2022) suggested the application of hash-chain verification to identify rogue behaviour of classical swarm agents a technique that can be quantum-enhanced through QBER monitoring and entanglement verification, but without formal frameworks of integration.

A federated learning system among robotic swarms with the support of blockchain was introduced by Pacheco et al. (2024). Integrating quantum key exchange and such distributed ledgers, however, brings about concerns about key refreshes, consensus time and the protocol abstraction. Mannone et al. (2025) suggested that local quantum computation could be embedded within agents, to minimize the need to be controlled externally. Such a quantum-classical hybrid model may be potent, yet has open problems in runtime synchronization, resource balancing and fault isolation.

7.4 Future Interaction with Quantum-Native Communication Systems

Future possibilities of communication architecture envision quantum-based communication through the creation of quantum architectures. Under the quantum-native systems proposed in the roadmap of (Zhou et al., 2025), the reliance on the classical protocols would be completely removed, creating safe communication, consensus and coordination by using infrastructures that are completely entangled.

8. CONCLUSION

This type of swarm robotics innovation, e.g. introduction of quantum communication technologies, is a decisive step towards the establishment of a safe, decentralized, and autonomous multi-agent systems. The traditional security options are no longer sufficient to offer resilience in a swarm task as the operational environments get difficult and the threats to cybersecurity also grow. This chapter has already discussed the in principle concepts and practical applications of quantum-secured swarming communication algorithm involving the very architectural concept and practical uses of quantum-secured swarming communication algorithm. It has also identified the key challenges. The key challenges are to be developed through a synergetic approach that integrates the contributions in the area of quantum hardware, communication theory, swarm intelligence, and systems engineering. Shifting of the prototype systems to the operational system deployments will require real-time verification frameworks, standardization and scalability. In other words, quantum-secured swarm robotics is not a distant fantasy; it is a nascent world where autonomy, confidence and security in the networked robotic systems may redefine in the near future.

REFERENCES

Chen, , LNg, , S. L. (2022). Securing emergent behaviour in swarm robotics. *Journal of Information Security and Applications*, *64*, 103047.

Chen, Y. A., Zhang, Q., Chen, T. Y., Cai, W. Q., Liao, S. K., Zhang, J., & Pan, J. W. (2021). An integrated space-to-ground quantum communication network over 4,600 kilometres. *Nature*, *589*(7841), 214–219.

Conrad, A., Cochran, R., Sanchez-Rosales, D., Isaac, S., Javid, T., Rezaei, T., . . . Kwiat, P. G. (2025). Drone-and vehicle-based quantum key distribution. *arXiv preprint arXiv:2505.17587*.

de Curtò, J., de Zarzà, I., Cano, J. C., & Calafate, C. T. (2024). Enhancing communication security in drones using QRNG in frequency hopping spread spectrum. *Future Internet*, *16*(11), 412.

Dubey, U., Bhole, P., Dutta, A., Behera, D. P., Losu, V., Pandeeti, G. S. D., & Pathak, A. (2024). A review on practical challenges of aerial quantum communication. *Physics Open*, *19*, 100210.

Han, H., Yao, J., Wu, Y., Dou, Y., & Fu, J. (2024). RETRACTED ARTICLE: Quantum communication based cyber security analysis using artificial intelligence with IoMT. *Optical and Quantum Electronics*, *56*(4), 565.

Javed, S., Hassan, A., Ahmad, R., Ahmed, W., Ahmed, R., Saadat, A., & Guizani, M. (2024). State-of-the-art and future research challenges in UAV swarms. *IEEE Internet of Things Journal*, *11*(11), 19023–19045.

Khan, M. A., Javaid, S., Mohsan, S. A. H., Tanveer, M., & Ullah, I. (2024). Future-proofing security for UAVs with post-quantum cryptography: A review. *IEEE Open Journal of the Communications Society*, *5*, 6849–6871.

Liu, H. Y., Tian, X. H., Gu, C., Fan, P., Ni, X., Yang, R., & Zhu, S. N. (2021). Optical-relayed entanglement distribution using drones as mobile nodes. *Physical Review Letters*, *126*(2), 020503.

Mannone, M., Seidita, V., & Chella, A. (2025). Quantum computing for swarm robotics: a local-to-global approach. *Philosophical Transactions A, 383*(2289), 20240139.

Mannone, M., Marwan, N., Seidita, V., Chella, A., Giacometti, A., & Fazio, P. (2023, September). Entangled Gondolas. Design of Multi-layer Networks of Quantum-Driven Robotic Swarms. In *Italian Workshop on Artificial Life and Evolutionary Computation* (pp. 177-189). Cham: Springer Nature Switzerland.

Mehic, M., Niemiec, M., Rass, S., Ma, J., Peev, M., Aguado, A., & Voznak, M. (2020). Quantum key distribution: A networking perspective. *ACM Computing Surveys, 53*(5), 1–41.

Pacheco, A., De Vos, S., Reina, A., Dorigo, M., & Strobel, V. (2024, October). Securing Federated Learning in Robot Swarms using Blockchain Technology. In *International Symposium on Distributed Autonomous Robotic Systems* (pp. 473-488). Cham: Springer Nature Switzerland.

Ralegankar, V. K., Bagul, J., Thakkar, B., Gupta, R., Tanwar, S., Sharma, G., & Davidson, I. E. (2021). Quantum cryptography-as-a-service for secure UAV communication: Applications, challenges, and case study. *IEEE Access : Practical Innovations, Open Solutions, 10*, 1475–1492.

Sun, Y., & Shao, Y. (2022). Research on data security communication scheme of heterogeneous swarm robotics system in emergency scenarios. *Sensors (Basel), 22*(16), 6082.

Zhou, X., Shen, A., Hu, S., Ni, W., Wang, X., & Hossain, E. (2025). Towards quantum-native communication systems: State-of-the-art, trends, and challenges. *IEEE Communications Surveys and Tutorials.*

Chapter 13
Transforming Healthcare Through Quantum Computing Innovations

Quartulain Sial
Emergency Department, Agh Khan University, Sindh, Pakistan

ABSTRACT

Quantum computing (QC) is revolutionzing technology and playing a significant role in healthcare innovation. Using quantum mechanics principles such as superposition and entanglement, QC offers exciting computational power to handle complicated information in medicine and medical platforms. In current studies, the field of quantum computing (QSC) has developed and remains a focus of academia and industry due to its capability to process data in various ways. The integration of quantum computing (QC) into healthcare organization innovation symbolizes a move to faster and smarter, making it a secure medical framework. Additionally, QC give a unique computational power that can transform various healthcare domains with drug discovery, precision medicines and medical images. Academia and industry can efficiently analyse vast amounts of medical data, improving diagnostic models with greater competency than conventional methods.

1. INTRODUCTION

The fast growth of quantum computing QC is rethinking the technological environment of healthcare orgization by giving specific solutions to computational hard challenges in medicine. In contrast to traditional computing, which processes data in binary bits, QC uses qubits may reside in several states at once. These models have been moved to perform vast similar computations and extend speedups in solving

DOI: 10.4018/979-8-3373-3857-6.ch013

the challenges. Current studies highlight the requirement to discover new paths to fast healthcare analysis and pursue steps to effect solutions (Flöther et al., 2022; Kalaivani 2021). QC commented on changing thinking to enhance technologies in the healthcare organisation. The previous studies highlighted how QC may identify the new penitential and complex healthcare computations (Zinner et al., 2021; Banchi et al., 2020). QC have supported through quantum mechanics, and so ideas using the concepts of superposition, entanglement are used to clarify it (Li et al., 2018). Several studies focused on the roots in Quantum physics, the QC offers more possibilities in future for fabric and a powerful computing framework and assisting the processing vast amounts of data in real-time (Fedorov & Leonov, 2018; Gyongyosi & Imre, 2019). QC is specifically helpful to many healthcare applications that need a numerous of computations. Particularly in the present vast connected IoT digital healthcare models, which are interconnected medical devices and are connected to the cloud. Most of the computational capacity is not supportable for healthcare, but permits QC to promote significant progress in this domain. Shift from bits to qubits can change pharmacological studies in medical science (Fernández-Caramés 2019; Gyongyosi et al., 2018). This involved examining and analyzing how proteins fold. Some supporting applications are shortly detailed next for demonstrations (Li et al., 2020). It may enable the emergence of novel therapies and medicines using detailed modelling. QCs have a huge ability to create beneficial imaging systems that may support clinicians with improvements in real-time precisely (Padamvathi et al., 2016; Ramezani et al., 2020). This may help to solve complex optimization problems, participate in presenting with acceptable irradiation strategies targeting killing cancerous cells without destroying adjacent healthy tissues. Figure 1 Overview of quantum computing in healthcare.

Figure 1. Overview of quantum computing in healthcare

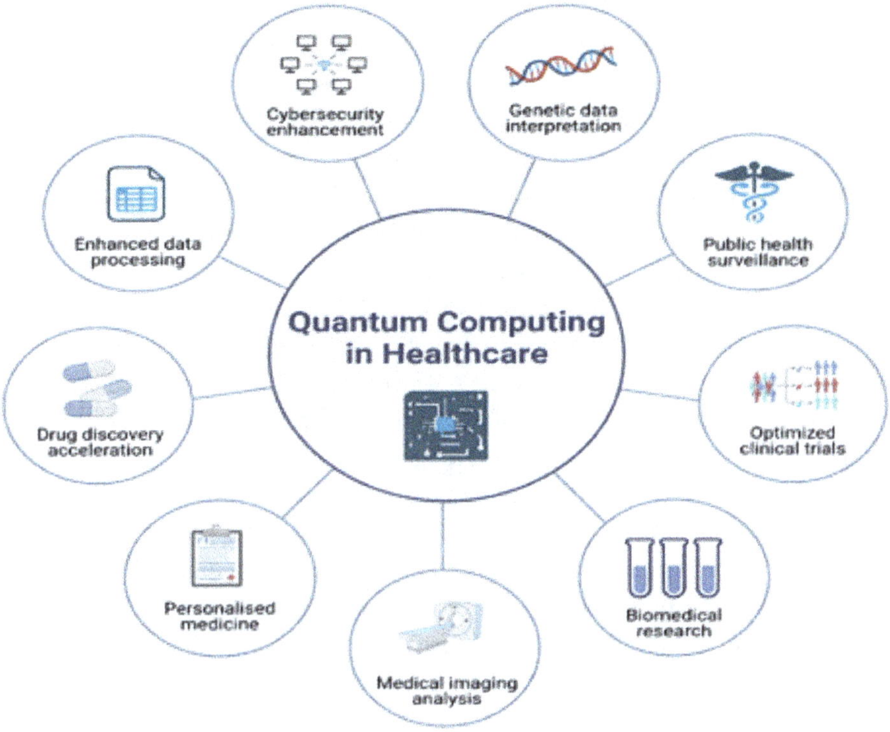

Drug discovery and medical research will be made possible by QC's ability to analyse molecular interactions at the smallest scale. Although whole-genome sequencing takes a lot of time, it is possible to complete whole-genome sequencing and analytics in a short period of time with the use of qubits. Through cutting-edge methods of providing access to computing, rethinking security for medical data, accurately discovering new drugs, and forecasting chronic diseases, QC has the potential to completely transform the healthcare sector.

The contributions of this chapter are as follows:

This chapter provides a comprehensive review of quantum computers and healthcare innovation

This chapter provides a detailed discussion on the role of quantum computers in healthcare

This chapter provides the importance of quantum ML in healthcare

This chapter provides recommendations and future work

2. LITERATURE REVIEW

Studies have discussed and revealed that the computational limitations of conventional systems can provide a quantum-entanglement-based solution to these challenges; furthermore, they discuss the edge-computing-based security issues and challenges, in which security vulnerabilities have been dealt with on an edge-computing-based solution (Bharti et al., 2020; Shaikh & Ali, 2016). The data and network components have dealt with quantum computer applications, which are part of the conventional computer systems (CCS), it requires CCS ideally and are capable of interfacing with and efficiently use CCS (Shah et al., 2024; Uprety et al., 2020). Layers responsible for which include the quantum control process include, measurement process and the data process. The operation's sequence and specification have been received the outcome to the control processor plane, which requires from algorithm. The qubit systems need to carefully focus on scheduled control to obtain useful and efficient performance, and this is possible through the traditional computing principles (Cuomo et al., 2020). Individual healthcare needs to prevention and treatment methodologies in the highlights of precision medicine. The standard medical treatment requires the support of personalized medicine because human biological system. Using EHRs for the future risk of diseases requires conventional machine learning (Shah et al., 2024; Egger et al., 2020). Several studies have addressed the limitations in quality and the complexity of relations among features using traditional machine learning techniques. This can possible to get solutions using quantum-enhanced machine Learning, which can make accurate and reliable early discovery (McGeoch et al., 2019; Nejatollahi et al., 2019). The results can require a prognosis and treatment early diagnosis of the disease, with a lower cost of healthcare (Kumar et al., 2021; Fateh et al., 2024). Meanwhile, the majority of diseases now have ineffective, expensive diagnostics and therapy, with variations. In this case, problems with noise, data quality, and replicability affect diagnosis and treatment. Figure 2 Overview of quantum computing.

Figure 2. Overview of quantum computing

Numerous studies have concentrated on the foundations of quantum physics, and the QC presents further opportunities for fabric in the future, as well as a strong computing framework that helps process enormous volumes of data in real-time (Noorani et al., 2021; Gupta et al., 2023). QC is very useful for a variety of healthcare applications that require a large number of calculations, especially in today's massively networked IoT digital healthcare models, which are made up of medical equipment that is connected to the Internet or cloud. The majority of the computing capacity growth is not economical for healthcare IoT, but it might allow QC to support important advancements in this field. In medical science, switching from bits to qubits can alter pharmacological research (Kumar et al., 2022). This required looking at and evaluating the folding of proteins. For demonstrations, a few supporting applications are briefly described next.

2.1 Medical Diagnostics

In light of its capacity to improve pattern identification for the early diagnosis of diseases, QC is becoming a very effective tool in medical diagnostics. Complex medical datasets may be processed more quickly using quantum algorithms, which may spot minute patterns that are frequently overlooked. This capacity is particularly helpful in the diagnosis of conditions like cancer and neurological diseases, where effective treatment results depend on early detection.

3. OVERVIEW OF AI IN HEALTHCARE IMPROVING USING QC

The possibilities of AI models in healthcare could be greatly increased by combining QC with AI. Large and complicated datasets may be processed more quickly by quantum AI than by classical AI models, which can benefit fields in various areas, where quantum-improving algorithms can deliver a more precise diagnosis (Watabe et al., 2021; Zhong et al., 2020). By allowing AI models to more quickly and accurately analyse massive, multidimensional datasets. Better predictive modelling is made possible by this, enabling earlier and more precise identification of people at risk for particular illnesses or problems.

Furthermore, responses of patients to medicines and treatment plan optimisation are possible using quantum-enhanced AI models. With applications ranging from drug development and personalised medicine to medical imaging, companies.

3.1 Overview of QC in Healthcare

Several healthcare applications can benefit from faster processing times thanks to quantum-improving computing. However, it was not possible to generalise the requirements of QC for healthcare to other applications. For example, systems for developing vaccines have distinct requirements from those for drug discovery. Consequently, for quantum computing applications in healthcare to be implemented successfully, a number of aspects need to be taken into account. One of the most important requirements for any healthcare application is low computation time. Certain sophisticated healthcare problems, including simulating chemical structures, cannot be solved by traditional computers with CPUs and GPUs. This makes it necessary to use quantum computing, which can represent big problems by utilising enormous amounts of multidimensional spaces.

3.2 Overview of Quantum ML

Since quantum ML and quantum AI are novel domains in healthcare, and need evaluations from both standpoints of experimental quantum information processing. (Fateh et al., 2025) investigated the use of superconducting quantum circuits to implement fundamental protocols. Quantum information processing and computations are realised through the use of superconducting quantum circuits. (Childs 2020) suggested a quantum recommendation system that does not require matrix reconstruction and effectively samples from a preference matrix. The majority of contemporary quantum algorithms are hybrid, utilising both classical and quantum computing. It is crucial that hybrid algorithms be designed for use in healthcare applications. As the area develops, hybrid and quantum-inspired approaches will eventually combine to become pure quantum algorithms. Quantum-inspired and hybrid approaches are both natural evolutionary steps towards achieving

4. OVERVIEW OF QC FRAMEWORKS AND SECURITY FOR HEALTHCARE

QC frameworks are redefining the computational landscape use enabling faster and more secure data processing in healthcare systems. These frameworks integrate advanced quantum algorithms to improve medical data analysis, diagnostics, and predictive modeling. Required security solution offered by the SQ and its suggested system. To control access to the required Big Data models, a quantum digital signature is used, which is signed by the parties. Sensitive data has been transformed from the source to the destination. In this process, QC suggests a secure way for users (Sial et al., 2024). For EHR, a protection framework was developed based on blockchain and QC. In this framework, blockchain is utilised to assign roles to authorised orgainzations in the network to safely access data. The blockchain architecture and quantum computing present significant network overhead, which degrades the suggested system's speed. QC employing methods takes advantage of both conventional and quantum machines, and they are given the required security for the sides in orginzation of healthcare communication between healthcare service consumers of healthcare. Figure 3 Overview of quantum health computing security.

Figure 3 Overview of quantum health computing security

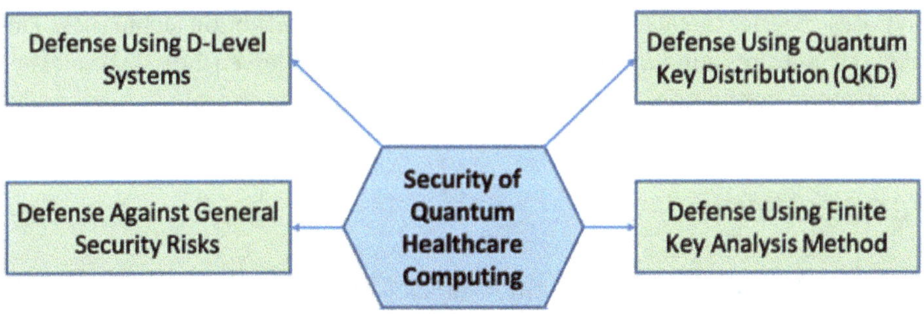

5. FUTURE RESEARCH DIRECTION WITH ISSUES

Big data analytics is an excellent fit for QC because of its inherent capacity to increase computer processing. Prior studies have demonstrated the enormous potential of big data in transforming healthcare through improved diagnostics and prognostics as well as individualised services. The QKD security protocol has been the subject of extensive research in the literature, and it has so far been used to make a number of innovative advancements in the security paradigm for quantum computing. Examine implantable brain-machine interface systems, where thousands of electrodes track the brain tissue in the various cortical layers, transmitting vast amounts of neural data.

(Yordanov et al., 2020) presents a comparative study of secret keys that break the Bell inequality. Creating realistic simulators for intricate activities that are hard to forecast with conventional techniques is a promising application of quantum computing. Additionally, there is potential for using quantum computers to study drug interactions at the cellular and molecular level as well as to simulate metabolism within a cell.

One of the most important challenges in utilising the increased functionality offered by quantum computing is integrating quantum computing services into commodity hardware. Accessing quantum computing for general-purpose problem-solving can be difficult because of the vast amount of resources needed for implementations. One initiative attempting to address the issues of quantum healthcare services on commodity hardware is the USD 500 million Cleveland Clinic IBM Discovery (Sarkar et al., 2021). To defend cyberspace from these threats, the necessary security frameworks have been created. However, traditional computer systems find this approach intimidating. ML-based quantum computing aids in the creation of security plans for conventional computer systems. Quantum cryptography, which offers effective ways to defend data against privacy-breaching assaults, is supported by quantum computers. But quantum computing's unparalleled processing power also poses security threats and jeopardises established encryption techniques. This makes quantum-resisting encryption methods necessary to lessen the risks associated with quantum computing.

6. CONCLUSION

QC has the potential to transform healthcare through advanced data analysis, faster drug discovery, and personalized treatments. Combined with AI and big data, it can accelerate innovation and improve clinical decision-making. Yet, challenges like error correction, scalability, and data security must be addressed. As these hurdles are overcome, quantum computing will become a key driver of precision, efficiency, and security in future healthcare systems. Completely transformed by the QC using conventional systems, which offer the required speed and efficiency. Utilizing these features of QC based on computational efficiency for healthcare application development. Furthermore, we have studied proposed studies, such as several articles, international conferences. In the future, quantum computing will enable real-time disease prediction, personalized treatments, and accelerated drug discovery. It will support secure, intelligent healthcare systems integrated with artificial intelligence and quantum communication networks. This transformation will foster a data-driven, precision-focused global healthcare ecosystem.

REFERENCE

Banchi, L., Fingerhuth, M., Babej, T., Ing, C., & Arrazola, J. M. (2020). Molecular docking with Gaussian boson sampling. *Science advances, 6*(23), eaax1950.

Bharti, K., Haug, T., Vedral, V., & Kwek, L. C. (2020). Machine learning meets quantum foundations: A brief survey. *AVS Quantum Science*, *2*(3), 034101. DOI: 10.1116/5.0007529

Childs, H. (2020). Applications of cloud-based quantum computers with cognitive computing algorithms in automated, evidence-based virginia geriatric healthcare.

Cuomo, D., Caleffi, M., & Cacciapuoti, A. S. (2020). Towards a distributed quantum computing ecosystem. *IET Quantum Communication*, *1*(1), 3–8. DOI: 10.1049/iet-qtc.2020.0002

Egger, D. J., Gambella, C., Marecek, J., McFaddin, S., Mevissen, M., Raymond, R., Simonetto, A., Woerner, S., & Yndurain, E. (2020). Quantum computing for finance: State-of-the-art and future prospects. *IEEE Transactions on Quantum Engineering*, *1*, 1–24. DOI: 10.1109/TQE.2020.3030314

Fateh, S., Shah, I. A., Sial, Q., & Jhanjhi, N. Z. (2025). Deep Learning Applications for Healthcare Risk Assessment. In *Generative AI Techniques for Sustainability in Healthcare Security* (pp. 59–76). IGI Global Scientific Publishing.

Fateh, S., Sial, Q., Dar, S. H., Shah, I. A., & Rani, A. (2024). Smart Healthcare System in Industry 4.0. In *Advances in Computational Intelligence for the Healthcare Industry 4.0* (pp. 297-311). IGI Global Scientific Publishing.

Fedorov, V. V., & Leonov, S. L. (2018). Combinatorial and model-based methods in structuring and optimizing cluster trials. In *Platform Trial Designs in Drug Development* (pp. 265–286). Chapman and Hall/CRC. DOI: 10.1201/9781315167756-18

Fernández-Caramés, T. M. (2019). From pre-quantum to post-quantum IoT security: A survey on quantum-resistant cryptosystems for the Internet of Things. *IEEE Internet of Things Journal*, *7*(7), 6457–6480. DOI: 10.1109/JIOT.2019.2958788

Flöther, F., Murphy, J., Murtha, J., & Sow, D. (2022). *Exploring quantum computing use cases for healthcare*. IBM Institute for Business Value.

Gupta, S., Modgil, S., Bhatt, P. C., Jabbour, C. J. C., & Kamble, S. (2023). Quantum computing led innovation for achieving a more sustainable Covid-19 healthcare industry. *Technovation*, *120*, 102544. DOI: 10.1016/j.technovation.2022.102544

Gyongyosi, L., & Imre, S. (2019). A survey on quantum computing technology. *Computer Science Review, 31*, 51–71. DOI: 10.1016/j.cosrev.2018.11.002

Gyongyosi, L., Imre, S., & Nguyen, H. V. (2018). A survey on quantum channel capacities. *IEEE Communications Surveys and Tutorials, 20*(2), 1149–1205. DOI: 10.1109/COMST.2017.2786748

Kalaivani, V. (2021). Enhanced BB84 quantum cryptography protocol for secure communication in wireless body sensor networks for medical applications. *Personal and Ubiquitous Computing, 27*(3), 875. PMID: 33758585

Kumar, A., Bhushan, B., Shriti, S., & Nand, P. (2022). Quantum computing for health care: A review on implementation trends and recent advances. *Multimedia Technologies in the Internet of Things Environment, 3*, 23–40. DOI: 10.1007/978-981-19-0924-5_2

Kumar, Y., Koul, A., Sisodia, P. S., Shafi, J., Verma, K., Gheisari, M., & Davoodi, M. B. (2021). Heart failure detection using quantum-enhanced machine learning and traditional machine learning techniques for internet of artificially intelligent medical things. *Wireless Communications and Mobile Computing, 2021*(1), 1616725. DOI: 10.1155/2021/1616725

Li, R. Y., Di Felice, R., Rohs, R., & Lidar, D. A. (2018). Quantum annealing versus classical machine learning applied to a simplified computational biology problem. *NPJ Quantum Information, 4*(1), 14. DOI: 10.1038/s41534-018-0060-8 PMID: 29652405

Li, Y., Tian, M., Liu, G., Peng, C., & Jiao, L. (2020). Quantum optimization and quantum learning: A survey. *IEEE Access : Practical Innovations, Open Solutions, 8*, 23568–23593. DOI: 10.1109/ACCESS.2020.2970105

McGeoch, C. C., Harris, R., Reinhardt, S. P., & Bunyk, P. I. (2019). Practical annealing-based quantum computing. *Computer, 52*(6), 38–46. DOI: 10.1109/MC.2019.2908836

Nejatollahi, H., Dutt, N., Ray, S., Regazzoni, F., Banerjee, I., & Cammarota, R. (2019). Post-quantum lattice-based cryptography implementations: A survey. *ACM Computing Surveys, 51*(6), 1–41. DOI: 10.1145/3292548

Noorani, A., Slevin, M., & Azamfirei, L. (2021). A quantum-enhanced precision medicine application to support data-driven clinical decisions for the personalized treatment of advanced knee osteoarthritis: development and preliminary validation of precisionKNEE QNN.

Padamvathi, V., Vardhan, B. V., & Krishna, A. V. N. (2016, February). Quantum cryptography and quantum key distribution protocols: A survey. In *2016 IEEE 6th international conference on advanced computing (IACC)* (pp. 556-562). IEEE. DOI: 10.1109/IACC.2016.109

Ramezani, S. B., Sommers, A., Manchukonda, H. K., Rahimi, S., & Amirlatifi, A. (2020, July). Machine learning algorithms in quantum computing: A survey. In *2020 International joint conference on neural networks (IJCNN)* (pp. 1-8). IEEE. DOI: 10.1109/IJCNN48605.2020.9207714

Sarkar, A., Al-Ars, Z., & Bertels, K. (2021). Estimating algorithmic information using quantum computing for genomics applications. *Applied Sciences (Basel, Switzerland)*, *11*(6), 2696. DOI: 10.3390/app11062696

Shah, I. A., Jhanjhi, N. Z., & Brohi, S. N. (2024). Use of Emerging Technologies in Healthcare 4.0. *Advances in Medical Technologies and Clinical Practice*, *4*(0), 280–296. DOI: 10.4018/979-8-3693-2333-5.ch015

Shah, I. A., Jhanjhi, N. Z., & Ujjan, R. M. A. (2024). Industry 4.0: Use of digitalization in healthcare. In *Advances in Computational Intelligence for the Healthcare Industry 4.0* (pp. 174-193). IGI Global Scientific Publishing.

Shaikh, T. A., & Ali, R. Quantum computing in big data analytics: A survey. In *Proceedings of the 2016 IEEE International Conference on Computer and Information Technology (CIT)*, Nadi, Fiji, 8–10 December 2016; pp. 112–115. DOI: 10.1109/CIT.2016.79

Sial, Q., Fateh, S., Jhanjhi, N. Z. A., & Laraib, A. (2024). Healthcare 4.0: Rural Health Issues and Challenges. In *Advances in Computational Intelligence for the Healthcare Industry 4.0* (pp. 248-263). IGI Global Scientific Publishing.

Uprety, S., Gkoumas, D., & Song, D. (2020). A survey of quantum theory inspired approaches to information retrieval. *ACM Computing Surveys*, *53*(5), 1–39. DOI: 10.1145/3402179

Watabe, S., Serikow, M., Kawabata, S., & Zagoskin, A. (2021). Scaling Law in Large Quantum Devices with Dissipation. In *APS March Meeting Abstracts* (Vol. 2021, pp. A30-008).

Yordanov, Y. S., Arvidsson-Shukur, D. R., & Barnes, C. H. (2020). Efficient quantum circuits for quantum computational chemistry. *Physical Review. A*, *102*(6), 062612. DOI: 10.1103/PhysRevA.102.062612

Zhong, H. S., Wang, H., Deng, Y. H., Chen, M. C., Peng, L. C., Luo, Y. H., Qin, J., Wu, D., Ding, X., Hu, Y., Hu, P., Yang, X.-Y., Zhang, W.-J., Li, H., Li, Y., Jiang, X., Gan, L., Yang, G., You, L., & Pan, J. W. (2020). Quantum computational advantage using photons. *Science*, *370*(6523), 1460–1463. DOI: 10.1126/science.abe8770 PMID: 33273064

Zinner, M., Dahlhausen, F., Boehme, P., Ehlers, J., Bieske, L., & Fehring, L. (2021). Toward the institutionalization of quantum computing in pharmaceutical research. *Drug Discovery Today*, *27*(2), 378–383. DOI: 10.1016/j.drudis.2021.10.006 PMID: 34688911

Compilation of References

Aarthi, S., Aravinthan, K., Ravikumar, R. N., Sivakumar, N., & Wanglen, S. (2025). Cryptography securing data in motion within Blockchain, internet of everything, and Federated Learning. In *Convergence of Blockchain, Internet of Everything, and Federated Learning for Security* (pp. 39–78). IGI Global., DOI: 10.4018/979-8-3373-1424-2.ch002

Abbood, A. A., Al-Shammri, F. K., Alzamili, Z. M., Al-Shareeda, M. A., Almaiah, M. A., & AlAli, R. (2025). Investigating quantum-resilient security mechanisms for flying ad-hoc networks (FANETs). [JRC]. *Journal of Robotics and Control*, *6*(1), 456–469. DOI: 10.18196/jrc.v6i1.25351

Abd Elaziz, M., Mohammadi, D., Oliva, D., & Salimifard, K. (2021). Quantum marine predators algorithm for addressing multilevel image segmentation. *Applied Soft Computing*, *110*, 107598. DOI: 10.1016/j.asoc.2021.107598

Abd EL-Latif, A. A., Abd-El-Atty, B., Abou-Nassar, E. M., & Venegas-Andraca, S. E.Abd EL-Latif. (2020). Controlled alternate quantum walks based privacy-preserving healthcare images in Internet of Things. *Optics & Laser Technology*, *124*, 105942. DOI: 10.1016/j.optlastec.2019.105942

Abd El-Latif, A. A., Abd-El-Atty, B., Mehmood, I., Muhammad, K., Venegas-Andraca, S. E., & Peng, J. (2021). Quantum-inspired blockchain-based cybersecurity: Securing smart edge utilities in IoT-based smart cities. *Information Processing & Management*, *58*(4), 102549. DOI: 10.1016/j.ipm.2021.102549

Abdiukov, T. (2025). Cybersecurity risk scoring in professional IoT: Building transparent, explainable risk models for Industry 5.0 applications. *Global Journal of Engineering and Technology Advances*, *24*(2), 025–035. DOI: 10.30574/gjeta.2025.24.2.0233

Abdulhussien, A. A., Nasrudin, M. F., Darwish, S. M., & Alyasseri, Z. A. A. (2023). Feature selection method based on quantum-inspired genetic algorithm for Arabic signature verification. *Journal of King Saud University. Computer and Information Sciences*, *35*(3), 141–156. DOI: 10.1016/j.jksuci.2023.02.005

Abdulla, A., & Hussain, O. Bin, Fatima, N., & Omer, I. Bin. (2025). Emerging technologies AI and IoT for sustainable business operations. In *Advances in Logistics, Operations, and Management Science* (pp. 153–172). IGI Global. DOI: 10.4018/979-8-3693-8492-3.ch008

Abdullah, S. M., Cheruvu, A., Kanchi, S., Chung, T., Gao, P., Jadliwala, M., & Viswanath, B. (2024, May). An analysis of recent advances in deepfake image detection in an evolving threat landscape. In *2024 IEEE Symposium on Security and Privacy (SP)* (pp. 91-109). IEEE. DOI: 10.1109/SP54263.2024.00194

Abed, A. K., & Anupam, A. (2023). Review of security issues in Internet of Things and artificial intelligence-driven solutions. *Security and Privacy*, *6*(3), e285. Advance online publication. DOI: 10.1002/spy2.285

Abomhara, M., Department of Information and Communication Technology Norway, U. of A., K ien, G. M., & Department of Information and Communication Technology Norway, U. of A. (2015). Cyber security and the internet of things: Vulnerabilities, threats, intruders and attacks. *Journal of Cyber Security and Mobility*, *4*(1), 65–88. DOI: 10.13052/jcsm2245-1439.414

Abomhara, M., & Køien, G. M. (2015). Cyber security and the Internet of Things. *Future Generation Computer Systems*, *56*, 442–452.

Abu Hilal, H. (2024). Unveiling the Quantum Internet: Potentials, Challenges, and Security Issues. *Unveiling the Quantum Internet: Potentials, Challenges, and Security Issues (December 24, 2024). OR*. Advance online publication. DOI: 10.2139/ssrn.5070407

Acar, E., & Yilmaz, I. (2021). COVID-19 detection on IBM quantum computer with classical-quantum transfer learning. *Turkish Journal of Electrical Engineering and Computer Sciences*, *29*(1), 46–61. DOI: 10.3906/elk-2006-94

Adnan, M. H., Ahmad Zukarnain, Z., & Harun, N. Z. (2022). Quantum key distribution for 5G networks: A review, state of art and future directions. *Future Internet*, *14*(3), 73. DOI: 10.3390/fi14030073

Aggarwal, D., Brennen, B., Lee, T., Santha, M., & Tomamichel, M. (2018). Quantum attacks on Bitcoin. *Ledger*, *3*, 68–90. DOI: 10.5195/ledger.2018.127

Aguilera, A. C., Clemente, X. A., Lawo, D. C., Monroy, I. T., & Olmos, J. J. V. (2023). First end-to-end PQC protected DPU-to-DPU communications. *Electronics Letters*, *59*(17), e12901. Advance online publication. DOI: 10.1049/ell2.12901

Ahmad, I., Shahabuddin, S., Sauter, T., Harjula, E., Kumar, T., Meisel, M., Juntti, M., & Ylianttila, M. (2021). The challenges of artificial intelligence in wireless networks for the internet of things: Exploring opportunities for growth. *IEEE Industrial Electronics Magazine*, *15*(1), 16–29. DOI: 10.1109/MIE.2020.2979272

Ahmadi, M., Sharifi, A., Hassantabar, S., & Enayati, S. (2021). QAIS-DSNN: Tumor area segmentation of MRI image with optimized quantum matched-filter technique and deep spiking neural network. *BioMed Research International*, *2021*(1), 6653879. DOI: 10.1155/2021/6653879 PMID: 33542920

Ain, N. U., Waqar, M., Bilal, A., Kim, A., Ali, H., Tariq, U. U., & Nadeem, M. S. (2025). A novel approach based on QKD using BB84 and E91 protocol for resilient encryption and eavesdropper detection. *IEEE Access : Practical Innovations, Open Solutions*.

Akinsanya, M. O., Bello, A. B., & Adeusi, O. C. (2023). A comprehensive review of edge computing approaches for secure and efficient data processing in IoT networks. *Communication in Physical Sciences*, *9*(4), 870–877.

Al Attar, T. N. A., & Mohammed, R. N. (2025). Optimization of lattice-based cryptographic key generation using genetic algorithms for post-quantum security. *UHD Journal of Science and Technology*, *9*(1), 93–105. DOI: 10.21928/uhdjst.v9n1y2025.pp93-105

al Srikanth Reddy Vutukuru, E. (2024). SecureIoT: Novel machine learning algorithms for detecting and preventing attacks on IoT devices. *Journal of Electrical Systems*, *19*(4), 315–335. DOI: 10.52783/jes.641

Alaba, F. A., Othman, M., Hashem, I. A. T., & Alotaibi, F. (2017). Internet of Things security: A survey. *Journal of Network and Computer Applications*, *88*, 10–28. DOI: 10.1016/j.jnca.2017.04.002

Al-Garadi, M. A., Mohamed, A., Al-Ali, A. K., Du, X., Ali, I., & Guizani, M. (2020). A survey of machine and deep learning methods for internet of things (IoT) security. *IEEE Communications Surveys and Tutorials*, *22*(3), 1646–1685. DOI: 10.1109/COMST.2020.2988293

Alhakami, H. (2024). Enhancing IoT security: Quantum-level resilience against threats. *Computers, Materials & Continua*, *78*(1), 329–356. DOI: 10.32604/cmc.2023.043439

Alharbi, A. R., Ahmad, J., Jamal, S. S., Masood, F., Ghadi, Y. Y., Pitropakis, N., & Buchanan, W. J.. (2022). A new multistage encryption scheme using linear feedback register and chaos-based quantum map. *Complexity*, *2022*(1), 1–15. DOI: 10.1155/2022/7047282

Alharbi, I. M., & Almazmomi, N. K. (2025). AI-optimized blockchain security for smart agriculture using post-quantum cryptography and graph neural network-based threat detection. *Peer-to-Peer Networking and Applications*, *18*(5), 276. DOI: 10.1007/s12083-025-02062-0

Alharthi, S., Alshamsi, A., Alseiari, A., & Alwarafy, A. (2024). Auto-scaling techniques in cloud computing: Issues and research directions. *Sensors (Basel)*, *24*(17), 5551. DOI: 10.3390/s24175551 PMID: 39275461

Ali, M., Naeem, F., Kaddoum, G., & Hossain, E. (2023). Metaverse communications, networking, security, and applications: Research issues, state-of-the-art, and future directions. *IEEE Communications Surveys and Tutorials*, *26*(2), 1238–1278. DOI: 10.1109/COMST.2023.3347172

Alipour, M. (2025). QIoT: IoT architectures in the quantum computing era. In *2025 IEEE 22nd International Conference on Software Architecture Companion (ICSA-C)* (pp. 241–250). IEEE.

Al-Mohammed, H. A., Al-Ali, A., Yaacoub, E., Qidwai, U., Abualsaud, K., Rzewuski, S., & Flizikowski, A. (2021). Machine learning techniques for detecting attackers during quantum key distribution in IoT networks with application to railway scenarios. *IEEE Access : Practical Innovations, Open Solutions*, *9*, 136994–137004. DOI: 10.1109/ACCESS.2021.3117405

Alokeparna, C., Sourav, S., Sanjoy, P., & Oishila, B. (2022). Multilevel segmentation of hippocampus images using global steered quantum-inspired firefly algorithm. *Applied Intelligence*, *52*(7), 7339–7372. DOI: 10.1007/s10489-021-02688-6

Alotaibi, A., & Rassam, M. A. (2023). Adversarial machine learning attacks against intrusion detection systems: A survey on strategies and defense. *Future Internet*, *15*(2), 62. DOI: 10.3390/fi15020062

Altangerel, G., Tejfel, M., & Tsogbaatar, E. (2023). IoT anomaly detection with 1D CNN using P4 capabilities. *Acta Electrotechnica et Informatica*, *23*(2), 3–12. DOI: 10.2478/aei-2023-0006

Altayaran, S., & Elmedany, W. (2021). "Security threats of application programming interface (API's) in internet of things (IoT) communications," 4th Smart Cities Symposium (SCS 2021), Online Conference, Bahrain, 2021, pp. 552-557.

Amin, M. A. S., Kim, S., Rishat, M. A. S. A., Tang, Z., & Ahn, H. (2024). A systematic literature review of privacy information disclosure in. *Sustainability (Basel), 17*(1), 8. DOI: 10.3390/su17010008

Amos, R., Georgiou, M., Kiayias, A., & Zhandry, M. (2020, June). One-shot signatures and applications to hybrid quantum/classical authentication. In *Proceedings of the 52nd Annual ACM SIGACT Symposium on Theory of Computing* (pp. 255-268). DOI: 10.1145/3357713.3384304

Andrae, S. (2025). Post-quantum cryptography in the age of quantum computing. In *Advances in Computational Intelligence and Robotics* (pp. 197–216). IGI Global. DOI: 10.4018/979-8-3693-9919-4.ch011

An, S., & Seo, S. C. (2020). Efficient parallel implementations of LWE-based Post-quantum cryptosystems on graphics processing units. *Mathematics, 8*(10), 1781. DOI: 10.3390/math8101781

Anupriya, S. R., & Muthumanikandan, V. (2023). "A Survey on Exploring the Effectiveness of IOT Based Home Security Systems," *2023 International Conference on Computer Communication and Informatics (ICCCI)*, Coimbatore, India, 2023, pp. 1-10. DOI: 10.1109/ICCCI56745.2023.10128178

Aouedi, O., Vu, T. H., Sacco, A., Nguyen, D. C., Piamrat, K., Marchetto, G., & Pham, Q. V. (2024). A survey on intelligent Internet of Things: Applications, security, privacy, and future directions. *IEEE Communications Surveys and Tutorials.*

Aquina, N., Cimoli, B., Das, S., Hövelmanns, K., Weber, F. J., Okonkwo, C., & Verschoor, S. (2025). A critical analysis of deployed use cases for QKD and comparison with PQC. *EPJ Quantum Technology, 12*(1), 51. DOI: 10.1140/epjqt/s40507-025-00350-5 PMID: 40342548

Arshad, A., Shaan, M., Ahmed, H. M., & Iqbal, M. (2025). Exploring secure processing architecture: A comprehensive review. [DSSR]. *Dialogue Social Science Review, 3*(1), 476–491.

Ashirova, A., Bobamuratov, U., Aarthi, S., & Ravikumar, R. N. (2026). Adversarial Machine Learning in Intrusion Detection Systems. In *Advances in Computational Intelligence and Robotics* (pp. 135–164). IGI Global Scientific Publishing. DOI: 10.4018/979-8-3373-5223-7.ch005

Ataullah, M., & Chauhan, N. (2024). Exploring security and privacy enhancement technologies in the Internet of Things: A comprehensive review. *Security and Privacy, 7*(6), e448. DOI: 10.1002/spy2.448

Atzori, L., Iera, A., & Morabito, G. (2010). The Internet of Things: A survey. *Computer Networks*, *54*(15), 2787–2805. DOI: 10.1016/j.comnet.2010.05.010

Awasthi, A. (2025). Quantum-resistant security for IoT systems: Challenges and implementation strategies. *International Journal of Scientific Research in Computer Science. Engineering and Information Technology*, *11*(1), 671–678. DOI: 10.32628/CSEIT25111260

Azuma, K., Economou, S. E., Elkouss, D., Hilaire, P., Jiang, L., Lo, H. K., & Tzitrin, I. (2023). Quantum repeaters: From quantum networks to the quantum internet. *Reviews of Modern Physics*, *95*(4), 045006. DOI: 10.1103/RevModPhys.95.045006

Banchi, L., Fingerhuth, M., Babej, T., Ing, C., & Arrazola, J. M. (2020). Molecular docking with Gaussian boson sampling. *Science advances*, *6*(23), eaax1950.

Barral, D., Cardama, F. J., Diaz-Camacho, G., Faílde, D., Llovo, I. F., Mussa-Juane, M., Vázquez-Pérez, J., Villasuso, J., Piñeiro, C., Costas, N., Pichel, J. C., Pena, T. F., & Gómez, A. (2025). Review of distributed quantum computing: From single QPU to high performance quantum computing. *Computer Science Review*, *57*, 100747. DOI: 10.1016/j.cosrev.2025.100747

Bashir, A. I., Gillani, S. M., Azam, S., Sahafi, M. H., & Rahman, A. U. (2025). Quantum computational insights into electronic and optical properties of LnOIs for fundamental and technological applications. *Optics & Laser Technology*, *181*, 111940. DOI: 10.1016/j.optlastec.2024.111940

Behal, S., & Kumar, K. (2017). Detection of DDoS attacks and flash events using novel information theory metrics. *Computer Networks*, *116*, 96–110. DOI: 10.1016/j.comnet.2017.02.015

Behal, S., Kumar, K., & Sachdeva, M. (2018). D-FACE: An anomaly-based distributed approach for early detection of DDoS attacks and flash events. *Journal of Network and Computer Applications*, *111*, 49–63. DOI: 10.1016/j.jnca.2018.03.024

Behniafar, M., Mahjur, A., & Nowroozi, A. (2023). Anomaly Detection Fog (ADF): A federated approach for internet of things. *Scientia Iranica*, *30*(2), 465–476. DOI: 10.24200/sci.2022.57774.5410

Ben-Sasson, E.. (2014). Zerocash: Decentralized anonymous payments from Bitcoin. In *Proceedings of the IEEE Symposium on Security and Privacy* (pp. 459–474).

Bernstein, D. J., & Lange, T. (2017). Post-quantum cryptography. *Nature*, *549*(7671), 188–194. DOI: 10.1038/nature23461 PMID: 28905891

Bhandari, A., Kumar, K., Sangal, A. L., & Behal, S. (2021). An anomaly-based distributed detection system for DDoS attacks in Tier-2 ISP networks. *Journal of Ambient Intelligence and Humanized Computing*, *12*(1), 1387–1406. DOI: 10.1007/s12652-020-02208-3

Bharti, K., Haug, T., Vedral, V., & Kwek, L. C. (2020). Machine learning meets quantum foundations: A brief survey. *AVS Quantum Science*, *2*(3), 034101. DOI: 10.1116/5.0007529

Biamonte, J., Wittek, P., Pancotti, N., Rebentrost, P., Wiebe, N., & Lloyd, S. (2017). Quantum machine learning. *Nature*, *549*(7671), 195–202. DOI: 10.1038/nature23474 PMID: 28905917

Bikku, T., Thota, S., & Shanmugasundaram, P. (2024). A novel quantum neural network approach to combating fake reviews. *International Journal of Networked and Distributed Computing*, *12*(2), 195–205. DOI: 10.1007/s44227-024-00028-x

Biswas, C., Pal, J., & Majumder, S. (2022). An Overview of Quantum Computing Approach in the Present-Day Energy Systems. Advances in Smart Energy Systems, 39-54.

Biswas, S., Goswami, R. S., Hemant Kumar Reddy, K., Mohanty, S. N., & Ahmed, M. A. (2024). Exploring the fusion of lattice-based quantum key distribution for secure Internet of Things communications. *IET Quantum Communication*, *5*(4), 322–339. Advance online publication. DOI: 10.1049/qtc2.12105

Bolgouras, V., Farao, A., & Xenakis, C. (2024). Roadmap to secure 6G networks. In *2024 IEEE 29th International Workshop on Computer Aided Modeling and Design of Communication Links and Networks (CAMAD)* (pp. 1–6). IEEE.

Bounmy, S., & Sisavath, K. (2023). Securing Internet of Things (IoT) ecosystems: A quantum cryptography approach. *Algorithm Asynchronous*, *1*(1), 1–7. DOI: 10.61963/jaa.v1i1.45

Bourke, T. (2001). *Server load balancing*. O'Reilly Media, Inc.

Buczak, A. L., & Guven, E. (2016). A survey of data mining and machine learning methods for cybersecurity intrusion detection. *IEEE Communications Surveys and Tutorials*, *18*(2), 1153–1176. DOI: 10.1109/COMST.2015.2494502

Buterin, V. (2014). *A next-generation smart contract and decentralized application platform.*

Callison, A., & Chancellor, N. (2022). Hybrid quantum-classical algorithms in the noisy intermediate-scale quantum era and beyond. *Physical Review. A, 106*(1), 010101. DOI: 10.1103/PhysRevA.106.010101

Cao, Y., Zhao, Y., Wang, Q., Zhang, J., Ng, S. X., & Hanzo, L. (2022). The evolution of quantum key distribution networks: On the road to the q-internet. *IEEE Communications Surveys and Tutorials, 24*(2), 839–894. DOI: 10.1109/COMST.2022.3144219

Cappers, B. C., & van Wijk, J. J. (2016, October). Understanding the context of network traffic alerts. In *2016 IEEE Symposium on Visualization for Cyber Security (VizSec)* (pp. 1-8). IEEE. DOI: 10.1109/VIZSEC.2016.7739579

Casino, F., Dasaklis, T. K., & Patsakis, C. (2019). A systematic literature review of blockchain-based applications. *Telematics and Informatics, 36*, 55–81. DOI: 10.1016/j.tele.2018.11.006

Castle, P. E., Einstein, M. H., & Sahasrabuddhe, V. V. (2021). Cervical cancer prevention and control in women living with human immunodeficiency virus. *CA: a Cancer Journal for Clinicians, 71*(6), 505–526. DOI: 10.3322/caac.21696 PMID: 34499351

Cedillo-Hernandez, M., Cedillo-Hernandez, A., Nakano-Miyatake, M., & Perez-Meana, H. (2020). Improving the management of medical imaging by using robust and secure dual watermarking. *Biomedical Signal Processing and Control, 56*, 101695. DOI: 10.1016/j.bspc.2019.101695

Cerezo, M., Verdon, G., Huang, H. Y., Cincio, L., & Coles, P. J. (2022). Challenges and opportunities in QML. *Nature Computational Science, 2*(9), 567–576. DOI: 10.1038/s43588-022-00311-3 PMID: 38177473

Chanal, P. M., & Kakkasageri, M. S. (2019). "Hybrid Algorithm for Data Confidentiality in Internet of Things," 2019 10th International Conference on Computing, Communication and Networking Technologies (ICCCNT), Kanpur, India, 2019, pp. 1-5. DOI: 10.1109/ICCCNT45670.2019.8944565

Chandre, P., Hingoliwala, H., Uttarkar, A., Shendkar, B. D., Lokare, D., & Sontakke, P. (2024, December). Post-Quantum Cryptography: Securing Critical Infrastructure Against Emerging Quantum Threats. In *2024 IEEE 4th International Conference on ICT in Business Industry & Government (ICTBIG)* (pp. 1-7). IEEE. DOI: DOI: 10.1109/ICTBIG64922.2024.10911612

Chawla, S., Sachdeva, M., & Behal, S. (2016). Discrimination of DDoS attacks and flash events using Pearson's product-moment correlation method. *International Journal of Computer Science and Information Security, 14*(10), 382.

Chen, , LNg, , S. L. (2022). Securing emergent behaviour in swarm robotics. *Journal of Information Security and Applications, 64*, 103047.

Chen, Y. A., Zhang, Q., Chen, T. Y., Cai, W. Q., Liao, S. K., Zhang, J., & Pan, J. W. (2021). An integrated space-to-ground quantum communication network over 4,600 kilometres. *Nature, 589*(7841), 214–219.

Chen, Z., Liu, Y., Zhang, Y., & Li, Q. (2023). Orthogonal latent space learning with feature weighting and graph learning for multimodal Alzheimer's disease diagnosis. *Medical Image Analysis, 84*, 102698. DOI: 10.1016/j.media.2022.102698 PMID: 36462372

Cheplygina, V., de Bruijne, M., & Pluim, J. P. W. (2019). Not-so-supervised: A survey of semi-supervised, multi-instance, and transfer learning in medical image analysis. *Medical Image Analysis, 54*, 280–296. DOI: 10.1016/j.media.2019.03.009 PMID: 30959445

Cherukupalle, N. S., & Cherukupalle, N.Naga Subrahmanyam Cherukupalle. (2025). Quantum-resilient cloud systems: Preemptive shielding against post-quantum cryptographic threats. *Journal of Information Systems Engineering & Management, 10*(38s), 1234–1246. DOI: 10.52783/jisem.v10i38s.8781

Childs, H. (2020). Applications of cloud-based quantum computers with cognitive computing algorithms in automated, evidence-based virginia geriatric healthcare.

Choudhuri, R., & Halder, A. (2023). Brain MRI tumour classification using quantum classical convolutional neural net architecture. *Neural Computing & Applications, 35*(6), 4467–4478. DOI: 10.1007/s00521-022-07939-2

Christidis, K., & Devetsikiotis, M. (2016). Blockchains and smart contracts for the Internet of Things. *IEEE Access : Practical Innovations, Open Solutions, 4*, 2292–2303. DOI: 10.1109/ACCESS.2016.2566339

Conrad, A., Cochran, R., Sanchez-Rosales, D., Isaac, S., Javid, T., Rezaei, T., . . . Kwiat, P. G. (2025). Drone-and vehicle-based quantum key distribution. *arXiv preprint arXiv:2505.17587.*

Costa, G., Forestiero, A., Macrì, D., & Ortale, R. (2024). Trustworthy precision medicine: An interpretable approach to detecting anomalous behavior of IoT devices. *Studies in Health Technology and Informatics, 314*, 108–112. DOI: 10.3233/SHTI240068 PMID: 38785013

Coulter, R., Han, Q.-L., Pan, L., Zhang, J., & Xiang, Y. (2020). Data-driven cyber security in perspective—Intelligent traffic analysis. *IEEE Transactions on Cybernetics, 50*(7), 3081–3093. DOI: 10.1109/TCYB.2019.2940940 PMID: 31634146

Cuomo, D., Caleffi, M., & Cacciapuoti, A. S. (2020). Towards a distributed quantum computing ecosystem. *IET Quantum Communication, 1*(1), 3–8. DOI: 10.1049/iet-qtc.2020.0002

D, S., & Kawale, S. R. (2023). "Cloud-Based Multi-Layer Security Framework for Protecting E-Health Records," 2023 International Conference on Artificial Intelligence for Innovations in Healthcare Industries (ICAIIHI), Raipur, India, 2023, pp. 1-7.

Darwish, S. M., Abu Shaheen, L. J., & Elzoghabi, A. A. (2023). A new medical analytical framework for automated detection of MRI brain tumor using evolutionary quantum-inspired level set technique. *Bioengineering (Basel, Switzerland), 10*(7), 819. DOI: 10.3390/bioengineering10070819 PMID: 37508846

Das, S., De, S., Bhattacharyya, S., & Hassanien, A. E. (2018). Color MRI image segmentation using quantum-inspired modified genetic algorithm-based FCM. In *Recent trends in signal and image processing: ISSIP 2017* (pp. 151–164). Springer.

de Assis, M. V. O., Carvalho, L. F., Rodrigues, J. J. P. C., Lloret, J., & Proença, M. L.Jr. (2020). Near real-time security system applied to SDN environments in IoT networks using convolutional neural network. *Computers & Electrical Engineering, 86*(106738), 106738. DOI: 10.1016/j.compeleceng.2020.106738

de Curtò, J., de Zarzà, I., Cano, J. C., & Calafate, C. T. (2024). Enhancing communication security in drones using QRNG in frequency hopping spread spectrum. *Future Internet, 16*(11), 412.

Demir, E. D., Bilgin, B., & Onbasli, M. C. (2025). Performance analysis and industry deployment of PQC algorithms. *arXiv preprint arXiv:2503.12952.*

Dere, N., & Ülkü, E. E. (2023). QUANTUM KEY DISTRIBUTION IN SMART HOME SYSTEMS. *Kahramanmaraş Sütçü İmam Üniversitesi Mühendislik Bilimleri Dergisi, 26*(4), 932–942. DOI: 10.17780/ksujes.1325805

Dervisevic, E., Tankovic, A., Fazel, E., Kompella, R., Fazio, P., Voznak, M., & Mehic, M. (2025). QKD Networks-Key Management: A Survey. *ACM Computing Surveys, 57*(10), 1–36. DOI: 10.1145/3730575

Deshmukh, S., Behera, B. K., Mulay, P., Ahmed, E. A., Al-Kuwari, S., Tiwari, P., & Farouk, A. (2023). Explainable quantum clustering method to model medical data. *Knowledge-Based Systems, 267*, 110413. DOI: 10.1016/j.knosys.2023.110413

Dhall, S., & Gupta, S. (2021). Multilayered highly secure authentic watermarking mechanism for medical applications. *Multimedia Tools and Applications, 80*(12), 18069–18105. DOI: 10.1007/s11042-021-10531-w

Dhinakaran, D., Selvaraj, D., Dharini, N., Raja, S. E., & Priya, C. (2024). Towards a novel privacy-preserving distributed multiparty data outsourcing scheme for cloud computing with QKD. *arXiv preprint arXiv:2407.18923.*

Diffie, W., & Hellman, M. (1976). New directions in cryptography. *IEEE Transactions on Information Theory*, *22*(6), 644–654. DOI: 10.1109/TIT.1976.1055638

Di, X., Li, J., Qi, H., Cong, L., & Yang, H. (2017). A semi-symmetric image encryption scheme based on the function projective synchronization of two hyperchaotic systems. *PLoS One*, *12*(9), e0184586. DOI: 10.1371/journal.pone.0184586 PMID: 28910349

Domb, M., Joshi, S., & Khn, A. (2024). Anomaly Detection in IoT: Recent advances, AI and ML perspectives and applications. In *Artificial Intelligence*. IntechOpen. DOI: 10.5772/intechopen.111944

Dorri, A., Kanhere, S. S., & Jurdak, R. (2017). Blockchain in Internet of Things: Challenges and solutions. In *Proceedings of the IEEE PerCom Workshops* (pp. 273–278).

Dorri, A., Steger, M., Kanhere, S. S., & Jurdak, R. (2020). Blockchain: A distributed solution to automotive security. *IEEE Communications Magazine*, *55*(12), 119–125. DOI: 10.1109/MCOM.2017.1700879

Dubey, U., Bhole, P., Dutta, A., Behera, D. P., Losu, V., Pandeeti, G. S. D., & Pathak, A. (2024). A review on practical challenges of aerial quantum communication. *Physics Open*, *19*, 100210.

Egger, D. J., Gutiérrez, R. G., Woerner, S., & Troyer, M. (2020). Quantum computing for finance: State-of-the-art and future prospects. *IEEE Transactions on Quantum Engineering*, *1*(1), 1–24. DOI: 10.1109/TQE.2020.3030314

Elhadad, A., Ghareeb, A., & Abbas, S. (2021). A blind and high-capacity data hiding of DICOM medical images based on fuzzification concepts. *Alexandria Engineering Journal*, *60*(2), 2471–2482. DOI: 10.1016/j.aej.2020.12.050

Elkhodr, M. (2025). An AI-driven framework for integrated security and privacy in Internet of Things using quantum-resistant blockchain. *Future Internet*, *17*(6), 246. DOI: 10.3390/fi17060246

Eltanbouly, S., Halabi, O., & Qadir, J. (2025). Avatar privacy challenges in the metaverse: A comprehensive review and future directions. *International Journal of Human-Computer Interaction*, *41*(4), 1967–1984. DOI: 10.1080/10447318.2024.2374091

Eren, H., Karaduman, Ö., & Gençoğlu, M. T. (2025). Security and privacy in the Internet of Everything (IoE): A review on blockchain, edge computing, AI, and quantum-resilient solutions. *Applied Sciences (Basel, Switzerland), 15*(15), 8704. DOI: 10.3390/app15158704

European Union. (2018). *General Data Protection Regulation (GDPR).*

Ezugwu, A. E., Ikotun, A. M., Oyelade, O. O., Abualigah, L., Agushaka, J. O., Eke, C. I., & Akinyelu, A. A. (2022). A comprehensive survey of clustering algorithms: State-of-the-art machine learning applications, taxonomy, challenges, and future research prospects. *Engineering Applications of Artificial Intelligence, 110*, 104743. DOI: 10.1016/j.engappai.2022.104743

Fan, Q., He, D., Chen, J., Peng, C., & Wang, L. (2023). ISOGA: An isogeny-based quantum-resist searchable encryption scheme against keyword guessing attacks. *IEEE Systems Journal, 17*(2), 2101–2112. DOI: 10.1109/JSYST.2022.3182788

Fateh, S., Sial, Q., Dar, S. H., Shah, I. A., & Rani, A. (2024). Smart Healthcare System in Industry 4.0. In *Advances in Computational Intelligence for the Healthcare Industry 4.0* (pp. 297-311). IGI Global Scientific Publishing.

Fateh, S., Shah, I. A., Sial, Q., & Jhanjhi, N. Z. (2025). Deep learning applications for healthcare risk assessment. In *Generative AI techniques for sustainability in healthcare security* (pp. 59–76). IGI Global Scientific Publishing.

Fateh, S., Shah, I. A., Sial, Q., & Jhanjhi, N. Z. (2025). Deep Learning Applications for Healthcare Risk Assessment. In *Generative AI Techniques for Sustainability in Healthcare Security* (pp. 59–76). IGI Global Scientific Publishing.

Fateh, S., Sial, Q., Dar, S. H., Shah, I. A., & Rani, A. (2024). Smart healthcare system in Industry 4.0. In *Advances in computational intelligence for the healthcare industry 4.0* (pp. 297–311). IGI Global Scientific Publishing. DOI: 10.4018/979-8-3693-2333-5.ch016

Fathalla, E., & Azab, M. (2024). Beyond classical cryptography: A systematic review of post-quantum hash-based signature schemes, security, and optimizations. *IEEE Access : Practical Innovations, Open Solutions, 12*, 175969–175987. DOI: 10.1109/ACCESS.2024.3485602

Fazrina, N. (2024). Securing distributed sensor systems through adaptive encryption algorithms in 5G-based smart energy networks. *Open Journal of Robotics, Autonomous Decision-Making, and Human-Machine Interaction, 9*(11), 18–27.

Fedorov, A. K., Kiktenko, E. O., & Lvovsky, A. I. (2018). Quantum computers put blockchain security at risk. *Nature*, *563*(7732), 465–467. DOI: 10.1038/d41586-018-07449-z PMID: 30451981

Fedorov, V. V., & Leonov, S. L. (2018). Combinatorial and model-based methods in structuring and optimizing cluster trials. In *Platform Trial Designs in Drug Development* (pp. 265–286). Chapman and Hall/CRC. DOI: 10.1201/9781315167756-18

Fernandez-Carames, T. M. (2020). From pre-quantum to post-quantum IoT security: A survey on quantum-resistant cryptosystems for the internet of things. *IEEE Internet of Things Journal*, *7*(7), 6457–6480. DOI: 10.1109/JIOT.2019.2958788

Firc, A., Malinka, K., & Hanácek, P. (2023). Deepfakes as a threat to a speaker and facial recognition: An overview of tools and attack vectors. *Heliyon*, *9*(4), e15090. DOI: 10.1016/j.heliyon.2023.e15090 PMID: 37089334

Floridi, L.. (2018). AI4People—An ethical framework for a good AI society. *Nature Machine Intelligence*, *1*(1), 389–399. PMID: 30930541

Flöther, F., Murphy, J., Murtha, J., & Sow, D. (2022). *Exploring quantum computing use cases for healthcare*. IBM Institute for Business Value.

Francisti, J., Balogh, Z., Molnár, G., József, K., Gergely, S., & Nagy, E. (2023). "Methods for Verifying the Security of Available IoT Devices," 2023 IEEE 21st Jubilee International Symposium on Intelligent Systems and Informatics (SISY), Pula, Croatia, 2023, pp. 000595-000600. DOI: 10.1109/SISY60376.2023.10417920

Gade, S. M., Sumana, S. G., Aarthi, S., Ravikumar, R. N., & Swetha, C. B. (2025). Advancing towards 6G Innovations, Challenges and Future Prospects. In *Advances in Wireless Technologies and Telecommunication* (pp. 1–26). IGI Global. DOI: 10.4018/979-8-3373-2220-9.ch001

Ganjefar, S., & Tofighi, M. (2018). Optimization of quantum-inspired neural network using memetic algorithm for function approximation and chaotic time series prediction. *Neurocomputing*, *291*, 175–186. DOI: 10.1016/j.neucom.2018.02.074

Gao, Y.-L., Chen, X.-B., Chen, Y.-L., Sun, Y., Niu, X.-X., & Yang, Y.-X. (2018). A secure cryptocurrency scheme based on post-quantum blockchain. *IEEE Access : Practical Innovations, Open Solutions*, *6*, 27205–27213. DOI: 10.1109/ACCESS.2018.2827203

Ge, M., Fu, X., Syed, N., Baig, Z., Teo, G., & Robles-Kelly, A. (2019). Deep learning-based intrusion detection for IoT networks. In *Proceedings of the IEEE 24th International Conference on Parallel and Distributed Systems (PRDC)* (pp. 256–260). IEEE. DOI: 10.1109/PRDC47002.2019.00056

Gentry, C. (2009). Fully homomorphic encryption using ideal lattices. In *Proceedings of the ACM Symposium on Theory of Computing (STOC)* (pp. 169–178).

Gera, J., & Battula, B. P. (2018). Detection of spoofed and non-spoofed DDoS attacks and discriminating them from flash crowds. *EURASIP Journal on Information Security*, *2018*(1), 9. DOI: 10.1186/s13635-018-0079-6

Ghimire, B., Mahmood, A., & Elleithy, K. (2021, November). Hybrid Quantum Approximate Optimization Using Enhanced Ant Colony Optimization to Solve Large-Scale Combinatorial Optimization Problems. In *2021 8th International Conference on Soft Computing & Machine Intelligence (ISCMI)* (pp. 108-113). IEEE. DOI: 10.1109/ISCMI53840.2021.9654824

Gitonga, C. K. (2025). The impact of quantum computing on cryptographic systems: Urgency of quantum-resistant algorithms and practical applications in cryptography. *European Journal of Information Technologies and Computer Science*, *5*(1), 1–10. DOI: 10.24018/compute.2025.5.1.146

Goldreich, O. (2009). *Foundations of cryptography*. Cambridge University Press.

Guitouni, Z., Maize, S., Zrigui, M., & Machhout, M. (2024). Advanced error correction method for quantum key distribution in IoT systems. *Physica Scripta*, *99*(10), 105106. DOI: 10.1088/1402-4896/ad7423

Gupta, S., Grover, D., & Singla, J. (2021, March). Characterization of Flash Events and DDoS Attacks: A Survey. In *2021 7th International Conference on Advanced Computing and Communication Systems (ICACCS)* (Vol. 1, pp. 1442–1447). IEEE. DOI: 10.1109/ICACCS51430.2021.9441793

Gupta, K., & Kush, A. (2020). A learning-oriented DLP system based on classification model. *INFOCOMP Journal of Computer Science*, *19*(2), 98–108.

Gupta, K., Saxena, D., Gupta, R., Kumar, J., & Singh, A. K. (2024). FedMUP: Federated learning driven malicious user prediction model for secure data distribution in cloud environments. *Applied Soft Computing*, *157*, 111519. DOI: 10.1016/j.asoc.2024.111519

Gupta, K., Saxena, D., Gupta, R., & Singh, A. K. (2024). MAIDS: Malicious agent identification-based data security model for cloud environments. *Cluster Computing*, *27*(5), 6167–6184. DOI: 10.1007/s10586-023-04263-9

Gupta, K., Saxena, D., Rani, P., Kumar, J., Makkar, A., Singh, A. K., & Lee, C. N. (2024). An intelligent quantum cyber-security framework for healthcare data management. *IEEE Transactions on Automation Science and Engineering*.

Gupta, R. S., Wood, C. E., Engstrom, T., Pole, J. D., & Shrapnel, S. (2025). A systematic review of quantum machine learning for digital health. *npj. Digital Medicine*, *8*(1), 237. DOI: 10.1038/s41746-025-01597-z PMID: 40316703

Gupta, S., & Grover, D. (2021, March). A comprehensive review of the detection of DDoS attacks using ML in the SDN environment. In *2021 International Conference on Artificial Intelligence and Smart Systems (ICAIS)* (pp. 1158–1163). IEEE. DOI: 10.1109/ICAIS50930.2021.9395987

Gupta, S., Grover, D., AlZubi, A. A., Sachdeva, N., Baig, M. W., & Singla, J. (2022). Machine Learning with Dimensionality Reduction for DDoS Attack Detection. *Computers, Materials & Continua*, *72*(2), 2665–2682. DOI: 10.32604/cmc.2022.025048

Gupta, S., Grover, D., & Bhandari, A. (2018). Vulnerability Analysis of Existing Distributed Denial of Service (DDoS) Defense Frameworks. *Asian Journal of Computer Science and Technology*, *7*(3), 62–67. DOI: 10.51983/ajcst-2018.7.3.1895

Gupta, S., Modgil, S., Bhatt, P. C., Jabbour, C. J. C., & Kamble, S. (2023). Quantum computing led innovation for achieving a more sustainable Covid-19 healthcare industry. *Technovation*, *120*, 102544. DOI: 10.1016/j.technovation.2022.102544

Gu, S., Kelly, B., & Xiu, D. (2020). Empirical asset pricing via machine learning. *Review of Financial Studies*, *33*(5), 2223–2273. DOI: 10.1093/rfs/hhaa009

Gyongyosi, L., & Imre, S. (2019). A survey on quantum computing technology. *Computer Science Review*, *31*, 51–71. DOI: 10.1016/j.cosrev.2018.11.002

Gyongyosi, L., Imre, S., & Nguyen, H. V. (2018). A survey on quantum channel capacities. *IEEE Communications Surveys and Tutorials*, *20*(2), 1149–1205. DOI: 10.1109/COMST.2017.2786748

Hadi, R. H., Hady, H. N., Hasan, A. M., Al-Jodah, A., & Humaidi, A. J. (2023). Improved fault classification for predictive maintenance in industrial IoT based on AutoML: A case study of ball-bearing faults. *Processes (Basel, Switzerland)*, *11*(5), 1507. DOI: 10.3390/pr11051507

Han, H., Yao, J., Wu, Y., Dou, Y., & Fu, J. (2024). RETRACTED ARTICLE: Quantum communication based cyber security analysis using artificial intelligence with IoMT. *Optical and Quantum Electronics*, *56*(4), 565.

Harris, S. J. (1996, April). Proactive service management: leveraging telecom information assets for competitive advantage. In *Proceedings of NOMS'96-IEEE Network Operations and Management Symposium* (Vol. 3, pp. 700-710). IEEE. DOI: 10.1109/NOMS.1996.539529

Hasan Abu-Arqoub, M., Marie, R., & Titinchi, A. A. (2026). Securing IoT for AI-driven cyber insurance: Cryptographic challenges and future directions. In *Cybersecurity Insurance Frameworks and Innovations in the AI Era* (pp. 405–434). IGI Global Scientific Publishing.

Hayes, W., & Langston, M. (2021). DNS. *Best Practice*.

Herman, D., Googin, C., Liu, X., Sun, Y., Galda, A., Safro, I., & Alexeev, Y. (2022). A survey of quantum computing for finance. *Quantum Information Processing*, *21*(1), 1–46.

Hong, Y. Y., Arce, C. J. E., & Huang, T. W. (2023). A Robust Hybrid Classical and Quantum Model for Short-Term Wind Speed Forecasting. IEEE Access.

Hou, C., Zhou, C., Wu, C.-G., Cong, R., & Li, K. (2024). Optimization of cloud-based multi-agent system for trade-off between trustworthiness of data and cost of data usage. *IEEE Transactions on Automation Science and Engineering*, *21*(1), 106–122. DOI: 10.1109/TASE.2022.3224984

Huang, H. Y., Broughton, M., Mohseni, M., Babbush, R., Boixo, S., Neven, H., & McClean, J. R. (2021). Power of data in quantum machine learning. *Nature Communications*, *12*(1), 2631–2643. DOI: 10.1038/s41467-021-22539-9 PMID: 33976136

Humayun, M., Tariq, N., Alfayad, M., Zakwan, M., Alwakid, G., & Assiri, M. (2024). Securing the internet of things in artificial intelligence era: A comprehensive survey. *IEEE Access : Practical Innovations, Open Solutions*, *12*, 25469–25490. DOI: 10.1109/ACCESS.2024.3365634

IEEE Communications Surveys & Tutorials. (2025). *What is the infrastructure of the metaverse? Metaverse Reality*. Retrieved from https://metaversereality.ieee.org/publications/articles/what-is-the-infrastructure-of-the-metaverse/#:~:text=The%20metaverse%20aims%20to%20be,unified%20and%20cohesive%20virtual%20universe

Imran, M., Abideen, Z. U., & Pagliarini, S. (2020). A systematic study of lattice-based NIST PQC algorithms: From reference implementations to hardware accelerators. *arXiv preprint arXiv:2009.07091*.

Irfan, M., Dias, R., Rastogi, R., & Zebende, G. F. (2025). *Generative AI insights for financial decision making* (Vol. 1). IGI Global Scientific Publishing. DOI: 10.4018/979-8-3373-1250-7

Irfan, M., Elmogy, M., & Gupta, S. (Eds.). (2024). *AI-driven decentralized finance and the future of finance* (Vol. 1). IGI Global Scientific Publishing. DOI: 10.4018/979-8-3693-6321-8

Irfan, M., Hussainey, K., Bukhari, S. A. C., & Nam, Y. (Eds.). (2024). *Issues of sustainability in AI and new-age thematic investing* (Vol. 1). IGI Global Scientific Publishing. DOI: 10.4018/979-8-3693-3282-5

Irfan, M., Kadry, S., Sharif, M., & Khan, H. U. (Eds.). (2023). *Fintech applications in Islamic finance: AI, machine learning, and blockchain techniques* (Vol. 1). IGI Global Scientific Publishing. DOI: 10.4018/979-8-3693-1038-0

Irfan, M., Zebende, G. F., Sarea, A., & Shahbaz, M. (Eds.). (2025). *Quantum-driven financial intelligence: Innovations in predictive analytics and autonomous trading systems* (Vol. 1). IGI Global Scientific Publishing. DOI: 10.4018/979-8-3373-2893-5

Ishtaiwi, A., Al Khaldy, M. A., Al-Qerem, A., Aldweesh, A., & Almomani, A. (2024). Artificial intelligence in cryptographic evolution: Bridging the future of security. In *Innovations in Modern Cryptography* (pp. 31–54). IGI Global. DOI: 10.4018/979-8-3693-5330-1.ch002

Islam, S. M. R., Kwak, D., Kabir, M. H., Hossain, M., & Kwak, K. S. (2015). The Internet of Things for health care: A comprehensive survey. *IEEE Access : Practical Innovations, Open Solutions*, *3*, 678–708. DOI: 10.1109/ACCESS.2015.2437951

Istiaque Ahmed, K., Tahir, M., Hadi Habaebi, M., Lun Lau, S., & Ahad, A. (2021). Machine learning for authentication and authorization in IoT: Taxonomy, challenges and future research direction. *Sensors (Basel)*, *21*(15), 5122. DOI: 10.3390/s21155122 PMID: 34372360

Jafar, U., Ab Aziz, M. J., Shukur, Z., & Adnan Hussain, H. (2024). Secure-Tech Triad enhancing electronic voting system security through integrated Blockchain, AI, and IoT technologies. *ITM Web of Conferences*, *63*, 01011. DOI: 10.1051/itmconf/20246301011

Jamalipour, A., & Murali, S. (2021). A taxonomy of machine-learning-based intrusion detection systems for the Internet of Things: A survey. *IEEE Internet of Things Journal*, *9*(12), 9444–9466. DOI: 10.1109/JIOT.2021.3126811

Javed, S., Hassan, A., Ahmad, R., Ahmed, W., Ahmed, R., Saadat, A., & Guizani, M. (2024). State-of-the-art and future research challenges in UAV swarms. *IEEE Internet of Things Journal*, *11*(11), 19023–19045.

Jayashankar, A., & Mandayam, P. (2023). Quantum error correction: Noise-adapted techniques and applications. *Journal of the Indian Institute of Science*, *103*(2), 497–512. DOI: 10.1007/s41745-022-00332-x

Jeyalakshmi, V., Balan, V., & Benitha, V. S. (2025). Security issues in IoT: Perspective review. *Computer Networks and Communications*, 101–122.

Jin, Y. (2025). Google's "Willow" quantum processor: New RCS record and first error correction below the surface code threshold. *Innovation (Cambridge (Mass.))*, *6*(7), 100942. DOI: 10.1016/j.xinn.2025.100942

Joel, M. R., Manikandan, G., & Bhuvaneswari, G. (2023). "An Analysis of Security Challenges in Internet of Things (IoT) based Smart Homes," *2023 Second International Conference on Electronics and Renewable Systems (ICEARS)*, Tuticorin, India, 2023, pp. 490-497. DOI: 10.1109/ICEARS56392.2023.10085106

Kalaivani, V. (2021). Enhanced BB84 quantum cryptography protocol for secure communication in wireless body sensor networks for medical applications. *Personal and Ubiquitous Computing*, *27*(3), 875. PMID: 33758585

Kallepalli, K., & Chaudhry, U. B. (2021). Intelligent security: Applying artificial intelligence to detect advanced cyber-attacks. In *Challenges in the IoT and Smart Environments: A Practitioners' Guide to Security, Ethics and Criminal Threats* (pp. 287–320). Springer International Publishing. DOI: 10.1007/978-3-030-87166-6_11

Kalodanis, K., Papapavlou, C., & Feretzakis, G. (2025). Enhancing security in 5G and future 6G networks: Machine learning approaches for adaptive intrusion detection and prevention. *Future Internet*, *17*(7), 312. DOI: 10.3390/fi17070312

Kannimuthu, P., & Sweetlin Devamanohari, S. (2025). Security, privacy, and trust in AI-IoT integrated smart systems. In *Advances in Computational Intelligence and Robotics* (pp. 1–36). IGI Global Scientific Publishing. DOI: 10.4018/979-8-3373-7062-0.ch001

Karie, N. M., Sahri, N. M., Yang, W., Valli, C., & Kebande, V. R. (2021). A review of security standards and frameworks for IoT-based smart environments. *IEEE Access : Practical Innovations, Open Solutions*, *9*, 121975–121995. DOI: 10.1109/ACCESS.2021.3109886

Katı, B. E., Küçüksille, E. U., & Sarıman, G. (2025). Enhancing Deepfake Detection Through Quantum Transfer Learning and CST ViT Architecture. *Applied Sciences (Basel, Switzerland)*, *15*(2), 525. DOI: 10.3390/app15020525

Kawa, B., & Borkowski, P. (2023). Integration of machine learning solutions in the building automation system. *Energies*, *16*(11), 4504. DOI: 10.3390/en16114504

Keçeci, M. (2025). Quantum error correction codes and their impact on scalable quantum computation: Current approaches and future perspectives DOI: DOI: 10.5281/zenodo.15499657

Khalil, M., Zhang, C., Ye, Z., & Zhang, P. (2025). PegasosQSVM: A QML Approach for Accurate Fake News Detection. *Applied AI*, *39*(1), 2457207.

Khan, M. A., Javaid, S., Mohsan, S. A. H., Tanveer, M., & Ullah, I. (2024). Future-proofing security for UAVs with post-quantum cryptography: A review. *IEEE Open Journal of the Communications Society*, *5*, 6849–6871.

Khan, M. A., Karim, M., & Kim, Y. (2019). A scalable and hybrid intrusion detection system based on deep learning. *IEEE Access : Practical Innovations, Open Solutions*, *7*, 177352–177366.

Khan, M. A., & Salah, K. (2018). IoT security: Review, challenges, and solutions. *Future Generation Computer Systems*, *82*, 395–411. DOI: 10.1016/j.future.2017.11.022

Khudoykulov, S. Ravikumar, Aarthi, S., & Ashirova, A. (2026). Blockchain-enabled Federated Learning for secure rural health data sharing. In *Cognitive Security and Predictive Health Monitoring for Rural Development* (pp. 255–286). IGI Global Scientific Publishing. DOI: 10.4018/979-8-3373-3947-4.ch010

Kim, Y., & Seo, S. C. (2023). Signature split method for a PQC-DSA compliant with V2V communication standards. *Applied Sciences (Basel, Switzerland)*, *13*(10), 5874. DOI: 10.3390/app13105874

Kodete, C. S., Thuraka, B., & Pasupuleti, V. (2024). A systematic review of AI-driven and quantum-resistant security solutions for cyber-physical systems: Blockchain, federated learning, and emerging technologies. In *2024 International Conference on Computer and Applications (ICCA)* (pp. 1–6). IEEE. DOI: 10.1109/ICCA62237.2024.10927942

Kong, P.-Y. (2022). A review of quantum key distribution protocols in the perspective of smart grid communication security. *IEEE Systems Journal*, *16*(1), 41–54. DOI: 10.1109/JSYST.2020.3024956

Kouicem, D. E., Bouabdallah, A., & Lakhlef, H. (2018). Internet of Things security: A top-down survey. *Computer Networks*, *141*, 199–221. DOI: 10.1016/j.comnet.2018.03.012

Krelina, J. (2021). Quantum technology for military applications. *EPJ Quantum Technology*, *8*(24), 1–30. DOI: 10.1140/epjqt/s40507-021-00113-y

Kshetri, N. (2018). Blockchain's roles in meeting key supply chain management objectives. *International Journal of Information Management*, *39*, 80–89. DOI: 10.1016/j.ijinfomgt.2017.12.005

Kumar, V., Cicconetti, C., Conti, M., & Passarella, A. (2025). Quantum internet: Technologies, protocols, and research challenges [Manuscript, peer-reviewed, Q1]. *Manuscript.*DOI: https://doi.org//arXiv.2502.01653DOI: 10.48550

Kumar, A., Bhushan, B., Shriti, S., & Nand, P. (2022). Quantum computing for health care: A review on implementation trends and recent advances. *Multimedia Technologies in the Internet of Things Environment*, *3*, 23–40. DOI: 10.1007/978-981-19-0924-5_2

Kumari, S., Singh, M., Singh, R., & Tewari, H. (2022). Post-quantum cryptography techniques for secure communication in resource-constrained Internet of Things devices: A comprehensive survey. *Software, Practice & Experience*, *52*(10), 2047–2076. DOI: 10.1002/spe.3121

Kumar, M., & Mondal, B. (2025). A brief review on Quantum Key Distribution Protocols. *Multimedia Tools and Applications*, *84*(27), 1–40. DOI: 10.1007/s11042-024-20535-x

Kumar, Y., Koul, A., Sisodia, P. S., Shafi, J., Verma, K., Gheisari, M., & Davoodi, M. B. (2021). Heart failure detection using quantum-enhanced machine learning and traditional machine learning techniques for internet of artificially intelligent medical things. *Wireless Communications and Mobile Computing*, *2021*(1), 1616725. DOI: 10.1155/2021/1616725

Labonté, L., Alibart, O., D'Auria, V., Doutre, F., Etesse, J., Sauder, G., Martin, A., Picholle, É., & Tanzilli, S. (2024). Integrated photonics for quantum communications and metrology. *PFX Quantum : a Physical Review Journal*, *5*(1), 010101. DOI: 10.1103/PRXQuantum.5.010101

Lavanya, P., Subbareddy, I. V., & Selvakumar, V. (2022). "Internet of Things enabled Block Level Security Mechanism to Big Data Environment using Cipher Security Policies," *2022 International Conference on Advances in Computing, Communication and Applied Informatics (ACCAI)*, Chennai, India, 2022, pp. 1-6. DOI: 10.1109/ACCAI53970.2022.9752603

Lee, J., Bagheri, B., & Kao, H. A. (2015). A cyber-physical systems architecture for Industry 4.0-based manufacturing systems. *Manufacturing Letters*, *3*, 18–23. DOI: 10.1016/j.mfglet.2014.12.001

Lin, C. H. A., Liu, C. Y., Chen, S. Y. C., & Chen, K. C. (2025, April). Quantum-trained convolutional neural network for deepfake audio detection. In *2025 IEEE International Conference on Acoustics, Speech, and Signal Processing Workshops (ICASSPW)* (pp. 1-5). IEEE. DOI: 10.1109/ICASSPW65056.2025.11011133

Lin, J., Yu, W., Zhang, N., Yang, X., Zhang, H., & Zhao, W. (2017). A survey on Internet of Things security. *IEEE Communications Surveys and Tutorials*, *19*(3), 1762–1780.

Li, R. Y., Di Felice, R., Rohs, R., & Lidar, D. A. (2018). Quantum annealing versus classical machine learning applied to a simplified computational biology problem. *NPJ Quantum Information, 4*(1), 14. DOI: 10.1038/s41534-018-0060-8 PMID: 29652405

Liu, P., Tao, Q., & Zhou, J. T. (2024). Evolving from Single-modal to Multi-modal Facial Deepfake Detection: Progress and Challenges. *arXiv preprint arXiv:2406.06965*.

Liu, A., Zhang, Q., Xu, S., Feng, H., Chen, X.-B., & Liu, W. (2024). QBIoT: A quantum blockchain framework for IoT with an improved proof-of-authority consensus algorithm and a public-key quantum signature. *Computers, Materials & Continua, 80*(1), 1727–1751. DOI: 10.32604/cmc.2024.051233

Liu, H. Y., Tian, X. H., Gu, C., Fan, P., Ni, X., Yang, R., & Zhu, S. N. (2021). Optical-relayed entanglement distribution using drones as mobile nodes. *Physical Review Letters, 126*(2), 020503.

Liu, R., Rozenman, G. G., Kundu, N. K., Chandra, D., & De, D. (2022). Towards the industrialisation of quantum key distribution in communication networks: A short survey. *IET Quantum Communication, 3*(3), 151–163. DOI: 10.1049/qtc2.12044

Liu, W., Zhang, Y., Deng, Z., Zhao, J., & Tong, L. (2021). A hybrid quantum-classical conditional generative adversarial network algorithm for human-centered paradigm in cloud. *EURASIP Journal on Wireless Communications and Networking, 2021*(1), 1–17. DOI: 10.1186/s13638-021-01898-3

Li, W., Sforzin, A., Fedorov, S., & Karame, G. O. (2018). Towards scalable and private industrial blockchains. In *Proceedings of the ACM Conference on Computer and Communications Security (CCS)* (pp. 1817–1832).

Li, Y., Tian, M., Liu, G., Peng, C., & Jiao, L. (2020). Quantum optimization and quantum learning: A survey. *IEEE Access : Practical Innovations, Open Solutions, 8*, 23568–23593. DOI: 10.1109/ACCESS.2020.2970105

Lu, Y. (2020). Blockchain and IoT integration: A review. *Journal of Industrial Information Integration, 20*, 100174.

Lu, Y., & Xu, X. (2019). Cloud-based manufacturing and Industrial IoT. *Journal of Manufacturing Systems, 49*, 87–97.

Lykouris, T., & Vassilvitskii, S. (2021). Competitive caching with machine learned advice. [JACM]. *Journal of the Association for Computing Machinery, 68*(4), 1–25. DOI: 10.1145/3447579

Maharajpet, S. S. Abhilash, & Bedre, S. R. (2024). A LIME-based explainable AI for healthcare IoT: Building trust in clinical decision-making. In *Innovations and Trends in Modern Computer Science Technology – Overview, Challenges and Applications* (pp. 22–29). QTanalytics India. DOI: 10.48001/978-81-980647-5-2-3

Mahindrakar, R. P., & Chandel, S. (2023). "Advanced IoT-Enabled Warehouse Air Quality Monitoring and Live Security System for Medical Applications," *2023 International Conference on Artificial Intelligence for Innovations in Healthcare Industries (ICAIIHI)*, Raipur, India, 2023, pp. 1-6.

Manivasagam, G., & Prasad, K. D. V. (2024). Novel approaches to biometric security using enhanced session keys and elliptic curve cryptography. *Journal of Discrete Mathematical Sciences and Cryptography*, *27*(2-A), 477–488. DOI: 10.47974/JDMSC-1884

Mannone, M., Seidita, V., & Chella, A. (2025). Quantum computing for swarm robotics: a local-to-global approach. *Philosophical Transactions A, 383*(2289), 20240139.

Mannone, M., Marwan, N., Seidita, V., Chella, A., Giacometti, A., & Fazio, P. (2023, September). Entangled Gondolas. Design of Multi-layer Networks of Quantum-Driven Robotic Swarms. In *Italian Workshop on Artificial Life and Evolutionary Computation* (pp. 177-189). Cham: Springer Nature Switzerland.

Mantri, P., Li, A. C. Y., & Brown, K. R. (2025). Comparing one- and two-way quantum repeater architectures. *Communications on Physics*, *8*(1), 2222. DOI: 10.1038/s42005-025-02222-x

Marisamy, K., Selvakumar, A., Rajasekar, B., Natarajan, R., Atajanova, A., & Makhmudov, S. (2025). Smart logistics integrating AI, IoT, blockchain, and Robotics for a sustainable Future. In *Emerging Trends in Smart Logistics Technologies* (pp. 73–104). IGI Global Scientific Publishing., DOI: 10.4018/979-8-3373-2434-0.ch003

MarketsandMarkets. (2023). *Quantum computing market – Global forecast to 2030* (Vol. 3, Issue 1). MarketsandMarkets Research Pvt. Ltd.

Markidis, S. (2024, May). What is quantum parallelism, anyhow? In *ISC High Performance 2024 Research Paper Proceedings (39th International Conference)* (pp. 1-12). Prometeus GmbH. DOI: DOI: 10.48550/arXiv.2405.07222

McGeoch, C. C., Harris, R., Reinhardt, S. P., & Bunyk, P. I. (2019). Practical annealing-based quantum computing. *Computer*, *52*(6), 38–46. DOI: 10.1109/MC.2019.2908836

Mehic, M., Niemiec, M., Rass, S., Ma, J., Peev, M., Aguado, A., & Voznak, M. (2020). Quantum key distribution: A networking perspective. *ACM Computing Surveys*, *53*(5), 1–41.

Meziane, H., & Ouerdi, N. (2023). A survey on performance evaluation of artificial intelligence algorithms for improving IoT security systems. *Scientific Reports*, *13*(1), 21255. DOI: 10.1038/s41598-023-46640-9 PMID: 38040952

Miettinen, M., & Sadeghi, A.-R. (2018). "Keynote: Internet of Things or Threats? On Building Trust in IoT," 2018 International Conference on Hardware/Software Codesign and System Synthesis (CODES+ISSS), Turin, Italy, 2018, pp. 1-9. DOI: 10.1109/CODESISSS.2018.8525931

Mishra, V., Gupta, K., Saxena, D., & Singh, A. K. (2024). A global medical data security and privacy preserving standards identification framework for electronic healthcare consumers. *IEEE Transactions on Consumer Electronics*, *70*(1), 4379–4387. DOI: 10.1109/TCE.2024.3373912

Mishra, V., & Mishra, M. (2022). Privacy and security concerns with electronic health records: Shreds of evidence from India. *IMI Konnect*, *11*(3), 41–54.

Mohammad, K. (2025). Cyber shield: Advances in detection, isolation, and containment mechanisms. In *AIAA SCITECH 2025 Forum* (p. 2724).

Moll, M., & Kunczik, L. (2025). A case study for cyber-attack detection using quantum variational circuits. *Quantum Machine Intelligence*, *7*(1), 1–23. DOI: 10.1007/s42484-025-00277-1

Mummadi, S., & Fathima, S. (2025). Quantum computing: Opportunities and threats for cybersecurity. In *Complexities and Challenges for Securing Digital Assets and Infrastructure* (pp. 507–530). IGI Global Scientific Publishing. DOI: 10.4018/979-8-3373-1370-2.ch022

Naik, P., Jain, R., & Tiwari, S. (2025). From portfolio optimization to quantum blockchain and security: A systematic review of quantum computing in finance. *Financial Innovation*, *11*(88), 88. Advance online publication. DOI: 10.1186/s40854-025-00751-6

Nakagawa, I., & Shimojo, S. (2017). "IoT Agent Platform Mechanism with Transparent Cloud Computing Framework for Improving IoT Security," 2017 IEEE 41st Annual Computer Software and Applications Conference (COMPSAC), Turin, Italy, 2017, pp. 684-689. DOI: 10.1109/COMPSAC.2017.156

Nakamoto, S. (2008). *Bitcoin: A peer-to-peer electronic cash system.*

Namrita Gummadi, A., Napier, J. C., & Abdallah, M. (2024). XAI-IoT: An explainable AI framework for enhancing anomaly detection in IoT systems. *IEEE Access : Practical Innovations, Open Solutions*, *12*, 71024–71054. DOI: 10.1109/ACCESS.2024.3402446

National Institute of Standards and Technology. (2020). *Artificial Intelligence Risk Management Framework.*

Neekhara, P., Hussain, S., Zhang, X., Huang, K., McAuley, J., & Koushanfar, F. (2022). FaceSigns: semi-fragile neural watermarks for media authentication and countering deepfakes. *arXiv preprint arXiv:2204.01960.*

Nejatollahi, H., Dutt, N., Ray, S., Regazzoni, F., Banerjee, I., & Cammarota, R. (2019). Post-quantum lattice-based cryptography implementations: A survey. *ACM Computing Surveys*, *51*(6), 1–41. DOI: 10.1145/3292548

Nguyen, D. C., Ding, M., Pathirana, P. N., Seneviratne, A., Li, J., & Vincent Poor, H. (2021). Federated learning for Internet of Things: A comprehensive survey. *IEEE Communications Surveys and Tutorials*, *23*(3), 1622–1658. DOI: 10.1109/COMST.2021.3075439

Noorani, A., Slevin, M., & Azamfirei, L. (2021). A quantum-enhanced precision medicine application to support data-driven clinical decisions for the personalized treatment of advanced knee osteoarthritis: development and preliminary validation of precisionKNEE QNN.

Nwoye, C. C. (2024). Next-generation protection protocols and procedures for securing critical infrastructure. *International Journal of Research Publication and Reviews*, *5*(11), 4830–4845. DOI: 10.55248/gengpi.5.1124.3328

Ogawa, K., & Hamamoto, N. (2023). "Proposal of Low-Cost Automated Security Diagnosis System for IoT Devices," *2023 IEEE International Conference on Consumer Electronics (ICCE)*, Las Vegas, NV, USA, 2023, pp. 1-3. DOI: 10.1109/ICCE56470.2023.10043424

Pacheco, A., De Vos, S., Reina, A., Dorigo, M., & Strobel, V. (2024, October). Securing Federated Learning in Robot Swarms using Blockchain Technology. In *International Symposium on Distributed Autonomous Robotic Systems* (pp. 473-488). Cham: Springer Nature Switzerland.

Padamvathi, V., Vardhan, B. V., & Krishna, A. V. N. (2016, February). Quantum cryptography and quantum key distribution protocols: A survey. In *2016 IEEE 6th international conference on advanced computing (IACC)* (pp. 556-562). IEEE. DOI: 10.1109/IACC.2016.109

Padmaja, C., & Kumar, T. K. (2025). Integrating explainable AI in IoT for enhancing software performance. In *Advances in Computational Intelligence and Robotics* (pp. 341–368). IGI Global. DOI: 10.4018/979-8-3373-0370-3.ch011

Pan, D., Long, G. L., Yin, L., Sheng, Y. B., Ruan, D., Ng, S. X., Lu, J., & Hanzo, L. (2024). The evolution of quantum secure direct communication: On the road to the qinternet. *IEEE Communications Surveys and Tutorials*, *26*(3), 1898–1949. DOI: 10.1109/COMST.2024.3367535

Pandit, S., Ravikumar, R. N., Pandit, S., Joshi, N., Kishore, S., & Aarthi, S. (2025). Explainable Federated Learning for secure and transparent wireless edge networks. In *Advances in Computational Intelligence and Robotics* (pp. 127–168). IGI Global Scientific Publishing. DOI: 10.4018/979-8-3373-3576-6.ch004

Pan, J., & McElhannon, J. (2018). Future edge cloud and edge computing for IoT applications. *IEEE Cloud Computing*, *5*(1), 6–12.

Pan, S., Zhang, Y., & Wang, S. (2023). A secure aggregate authentication scheme with efficient revocation for IoT-based primary healthcare service. *IEEE Systems Journal*, *17*(4), 6480–6491. DOI: 10.1109/JSYST.2023.3310485

Park, J. J., Cha, J., Chen, S. Y. C., Tseng, H. H., & Yoo, S. (2025). Addressing the Current Challenges of QML through Multi-Chip Ensembles. *arXiv preprint arXiv:2505.08782*.

Pasupuleti, M. K. (2024). *AI in Edge Computing for IoT Optimization*. National Education Services., DOI: 10.62311/nesx/rb978-81-981466-8-7

Patil, U., & Chouragade, P. M. (2021, August). Deepfake video authentication based on blockchain. In *2021 Second International Conference on Electronics and Sustainable Communication Systems (ICESC)* (pp. 1110-1113). IEEE. DOI: 10.1109/ICESC51422.2021.9532725

Peel, M. (2025, April 23). *Secure 'quantum messages' sent over telecoms network in breakthrough*. Financial Times. https://www.ft.com/content/51a65e45-302c-45fa-8bd1-c828a66b012d

Peng, G. (2004). CDN: Content distribution network. *arXiv preprint cs/0411069*.

Peng, D., Dong, W., Chen, X., Peng, L., Chen, K., Long, J., & Yan, B. (2024). A study of quantum-secret communication technology and its application in industrial IoT. In *Frontiers in Artificial Intelligence and Applications*. IOS Press., DOI: 10.3233/FAIA241105

Phys.org. (2021, January). Chinese scientists have established the world's first quantum network. Retrieved from https://phys.org/news/2021-01-world-quantum-network.html

Portmann, C., & Renner, R. (2022). Security in quantum cryptography. *Reviews of Modern Physics*, *94*(2), 025008. DOI: 10.1103/RevModPhys.94.025008

Prabavathy, S., & Supriya, V. (2021). "SDN based Cognitive Security System for Large-Scale Internet of Things using Fog Computing," *2021 International Conference on Emerging Techniques in Computational Intelligence (ICETCI)*, Hyderabad, India, 2021, pp. 129-134. DOI: 10.1109/ICETCI51973.2021.9574051

Pradeep, S., Karthikeyan, A., Kiruthika, R., & Doss, S. A. N. (2025). Cryptographically enhanced security for AIoT devices in 5G networks. In *AIoT* (pp. 353–381). Auerbach Publications. DOI: 10.1201/9781003482338-16

Protogerou, A., Kopsacheilis, E. V., Mpatziakas, A., Papachristou, K., Theodorou, T. I., Papadopoulos, S., Drosou, A., & Tzovaras, D. (2022). Time series network data enabling distributed intelligence—A holistic IoT security platform solution. *Electronics (Basel)*, *11*(4), 529. DOI: 10.3390/electronics11040529

PwC. (2022). *Quantum computing in financial services: Opportunities and risks* (Vol. 5, Issue 1). PricewaterhouseCoopers.

Rafique, S. H., Abdallah, A., Musa, N. S., & Murugan, T. (2024). Machine learning and deep learning techniques for Internet of Things network anomaly detection-current research trends. *Sensors (Basel)*, *24*(6), 1968. Advance online publication. DOI: 10.3390/s24061968 PMID: 38544231

Rahman, R. A., & Shah, B. (2016). "Security analysis of IoT protocols: A focus in CoAP," 2016 3rd MEC International Conference on Big Data and Smart City (ICBDSC), Muscat, Oman, 2016, pp. 1-7. DOI: 10.1109/ICBDSC.2016.7460363

Rajawat, A. S., ... (2022). "Security Analysis for Threats to Patient Data in the Medical Internet of Things," 2022 11th International Conference on System Modeling & Advancement in Research Trends (SMART), Moradabad, India, 2022, pp. 248-253. DOI: 10.1109/SMART55829.2022.10047322

Ralegankar, V. K., Bagul, J., Thakkar, B., Gupta, R., Tanwar, S., Sharma, G., & Davidson, I. E. (2021). Quantum cryptography-as-a-service for secure UAV communication: Applications, challenges, and case study. *IEEE Access : Practical Innovations, Open Solutions*, *10*, 1475–1492.

Ramasamy, L. K., Khan, F., Shah, M., Prasad, B. V. V. S., Iwendi, C., & Biamba, C. (2022). Secure smart wearable computing through artificial intelligence-enabled Internet of Things and Cyber-Physical Systems for health monitoring. *Sensors (Basel), 22*(3), 1076. DOI: 10.3390/s22031076 PMID: 35161820

Ramezani, S. B., Sommers, A., Manchukonda, H. K., Rahimi, S., & Amirlatifi, A. (2020, July). Machine learning algorithms in quantum computing: A survey. In *2020 International joint conference on neural networks (IJCNN)* (pp. 1-8). IEEE. DOI: 10.1109/IJCNN48605.2020.9207714

Ramouthar, R., & Seker, H. (2023). A Review of Hybrid Quantum Computational Substrates-A Fusion of Classical And Quantum Computational Substrates. *ScienceOpen Preprints.*

Ramouthar, R., & Seker, H. (2023). Hybrid Quantum Algorithms and Quantum Software Development Frameworks. *ScienceOpen Preprints.*

Ramouthar, R., & Seker, H. (2023). Hybrid Quantum-Classical Computing-A Fusion of Classical And Quantum Computational Substrates. *Energy, 284*, 129314. DOI: 10.1016/j.energy.2023.129314

Rathee, G., Ahmad, F., Sandhu, R., Kerrache, C. A., & Azad, M. A. (2021). On the design and implementation of a secure blockchain-based hybrid framework for Industrial Internet-of-Things. *Information Processing & Management, 58*(3), 102526. DOI: 10.1016/j.ipm.2021.102526

Ravikumar, A. S., Jumaev, N., Mamadiyarov, Z., Kumari, N., & Sharvanthika. (2026). Quantum-Powered Hyperautomation. In *Advances in Computational Intelligence and Robotics* (pp. 1–32). IGI Global Scientific Publishing. DOI: 10.4018/979-8-3373-4347-1.ch001

Ravikumar, A. S., Kalandarov, A., Djumaniyazova, M., & Habib, M. (2025). A roadmap to a sustainable future. In *Advances in Computational Intelligence and Robotics* (pp. 267–302). IGI Global Scientific Publishing. DOI: 10.4018/979-8-3373-3017-4.ch010

Ravikumar, R. N., & Aarthi, S. (2025). AI-driven governance. In *Advances in Computational Intelligence and Robotics* (pp. 343–372). IGI Global Scientific Publishing. DOI: 10.4018/979-8-3373-3760-9.ch012

Ravikumar, R. N., Aarthi, S., Singh, A., Sivakumar, N., Kavitha Bharathi, S., & Sujitha, S. (2025). Transfer Learning for IoT applications. In *Advances in Computational Intelligence and Robotics* (pp. 55–84). IGI Global Scientific Publishing. DOI: 10.4018/979-8-3373-3146-1.ch003

Ravikumar, R. S., Manujakshi, Aarthi, S., Urazbaeva, Y., & Tamilselvi, S. (2025). Navigating data privacy, security, and regulatory challenges in healthcare AI ensuring fairness, bias mitigation, interpretability, and trust. In *Transformative Role of Transformer Models in Healthcare* (pp. 25–54). IGI Global Scientific Publishing. DOI: 10.4018/979-8-3373-2038-0.ch002

Ravikumar, R. N., & Aarthi, S. (2025). Real-time threat detection and anomaly monitoring using AI-enhanced IoT drones on blockchain networks. In *Enhancing Surveillance With Blockchain and IoT Drone Technology* (pp. 273–298). IGI Global Scientific Publishing., DOI: 10.4018/979-8-3373-4277-1.ch009

Reyna, A., Martín, C., Chen, J., Soler, E., & Díaz, M. (2018). On blockchain and its integration with IoT: Challenges and opportunities. *Future Generation Computer Systems*, *88*, 173–190. DOI: 10.1016/j.future.2018.05.046

Ricci, S., Dobias, P., Malina, L., Hajny, J., & Jedlicka, P. (2024). Hybrid keys in practice: Combining classical, quantum and post-quantum cryptography. *IEEE Access : Practical Innovations, Open Solutions*, *12*, 23206–23219. DOI: 10.1109/ACCESS.2024.3364520

Rietsche, R., Dremel, C., Bosch, S., Steinacker, L., Meckel, M., & Leimeister, J. M. (2022). Quantum computing. *Electronic Markets*, *32*(4), 2525–2536. DOI: 10.1007/s12525-022-00570-y

Rizvi, S.. (2021). "The Future for a Secure Internet of Things," *2021 International Conference on Software Security and Assurance (ICSSA)*, Altoona, PA, USA, 2021, pp. 56-63. DOI: 10.1109/ICSSA53632.2021.00019

Rojo, J., Valencia, D., Berrocal, J., Moguel, E., Garcia-Alonso, J., & Rodriguez, J. M. M. (2021). Trials and tribulations of developing hybrid quantum-classical microservices systems. *arXiv preprint arXiv:2105.04421.*

Roman, R., Zhou, J., & Lopez, J. (2013). On the features and challenges of security and privacy in distributed Internet of Things. *Computer Networks*, *57*(10), 2266–2279. DOI: 10.1016/j.comnet.2012.12.018

Rosa, B. M. G., Anastasova, S., & Yang, G. Z. (2023). NFC-powered implantable device for on-body parameters monitoring with secure data exchange link to a medical blockchain-type network. *IEEE Transactions on Cybernetics*, *53*(1), 31–43. DOI: 10.1109/TCYB.2021.3088711 PMID: 34197334

Roscoe, J. (2025, June 4). *Deepfake Scams Are Distorting Reality Itself.* Wired. Retrieved June 25, 2026, from https://www.wired.com/story/youre-not-ready-for-ai-powered-scams/

Rout, S. K., Ravindra, J. V. R., Meda, A., Mohanty, S. N., & Kavididevi, V. (2023). A Dynamic Scalable Auto-Scaling Model as a Load Balancer in the Cloud Computing Environment. *EAI Endorsed Transactions on Scalable Information Systems, 10*(5).

Rubia, J., Lincy, B., Nithila, E. E., Shibi, S., & Rosi. (2024). A survey about Post Quantum Cryptography methods. *EAI Endorsed Transactions on Internet of Things, 10*. DOI: 10.4108/eetiot.5099

Saba, T., Rehman, A., Sadad, T., Kolivand, H., & Bahaj, S. A. (2022). Anomaly-based intrusion detection system for IoT networks through deep learning model. *Computers & Electrical Engineering*, *99*(107810), 107810. DOI: 10.1016/j.compeleceng.2022.107810

Sachdeva, M., Singh, G., & Kumar, K. (2011, September). An emulation-based impact analysis of DDoS attacks on web services during flash events. In *2011 2nd International Conference on Computer and Communication Technology (ICCCT-2011)* (pp. 479–484). IEEE. DOI: 10.1109/ICCCT.2011.6075134

Saini, K. R., Jigajinni, V., & Dofe, J. (2022). "Performance Comparison of Cryptosystems in Context to Internet of Things," 2022 4th International Conference on Data Intelligence and Security (ICDIS), Shenzhen, China, 2022, pp. 82-87. DOI: 10.1109/ICDIS55630.2022.00020

Salah, K., Rehman, M. H. U., Nizamuddin, N., & Al-Fuqaha, A. (2019). Blockchain for AI: Review and open research challenges. *IEEE Access : Practical Innovations, Open Solutions*, *7*, 10227–10249. DOI: 10.1109/ACCESS.2018.2890507

Salek, M. S., Li, S., & Chowdhury, M. (2024). A Hybrid Quantum-Classical AI-Based Detection Strategy for Generative Adversarial Network-Based Deepfake Attacks on an Autonomous Vehicle Traffic Sign Classification System. *arXiv preprint arXiv:2409.17311.*

Sami, H., Hammoud, A., Arafeh, M., Wazzeh, M., Arisdakessian, S., Chahoud, M., Wehbi, O., Ajaj, M., Mourad, A., Otrok, H., Abdel Wahab, O., Mizouni, R., Bentahar, J., Talhi, C., Dziong, Z., Damiani, E., & Guizani, M. (2024). The metaverse: Survey, trends, novel pipeline ecosystem & future directions. *IEEE Communications Surveys and Tutorials*, *26*(4), 2914–2960. DOI: 10.1109/COMST.2024.3392642

Saran, C. (2021). Crédit Agricole tests quantum in finance. *Computer Weekly*, *15*(5), 18–21.

Saravana, M. K., Roopa, M. S., Arunalatha, J. S., & Venugopal, K. R. (2026). Transformers for multivariate time series forecasting: Comprehensive analysis, challenges, research opportunities and future prospects. *IEEE Access : Practical Innovations, Open Solutions, 14*, 11424–11457. DOI: 10.1109/ACCESS.2026.3654408

Sarkar, A., Al-Ars, Z., & Bertels, K. (2021). Estimating algorithmic information using quantum computing for genomics applications. *Applied Sciences (Basel, Switzerland), 11*(6), 2696. DOI: 10.3390/app11062696

Sarkar, S., Shafaei, S., Jones, T. S., & Totaro, M. W. (2025). Secure communication in drone networks: A comprehensive survey of lightweight encryption and key management techniques. *Drones (Basel), 9*(8), 583. DOI: 10.3390/drones9080583

Satish, T. (2024). Cryptographic image-based data security strategies in wireless sensor networks. *Journal of Discrete Mathematical Sciences and Cryptography, 27*(2-A), 293–304. DOI: 10.47974/JDMSC-1883

Saxena, D., Gupta, R., Singh, A. K., & Vasilakos, A. V. (2023). Emerging VM threat prediction and dynamic workload estimation for secure resource management in industrial clouds. *IEEE Transactions on Automation Science and Engineering*, •••, 1–15.

Sebestyen, H., Popescu, D. E., & Zmaranda, R. D. (2025). A literature review on security in the Internet of Things: Identifying and analysing critical categories. *Computers, 14*(2), 61. DOI: 10.3390/computers14020061

Senekane, M., Mafu, M., & Petruccione, F. (2015). Six-state symmetric quantum key distribution protocol. *Journal of Quantum Information Science, 05*(02), 33–40. DOI: 10.4236/jqis.2015.52005

Serbout, S., El Malki, A., Pautasso, C., & Zdun, U. (2023, July). API Rate Limit Adoption—A pattern collection. In *Proceedings of the 28th European Conference on Pattern Languages of Programs* (pp. 1–20).

Shah, I. A., Jhanjhi, N. Z., & Ujjan, R. M. A. (2024). Industry 4.0: Use of digitalization in healthcare. In *Advances in Computational Intelligence for the Healthcare Industry 4.0* (pp. 174-193). IGI Global Scientific Publishing.

Shah, I. A., Jhanjhi, N. Z., & Brohi, S. N. (2024). Use of Emerging Technologies in Healthcare 4.0. *Advances in Medical Technologies and Clinical Practice, 4*(0), 280–296. DOI: 10.4018/979-8-3693-2333-5.ch015

Shaikh, T. A., & Ali, R. Quantum computing in big data analytics: A survey. In *Proceedings of the 2016 IEEE International Conference on Computer and Information Technology (CIT)*, Nadi, Fiji, 8–10 December 2016; pp. 112–115. DOI: 10.1109/CIT.2016.79

Shams, M., Choudhari, J., Reyes, K., Prentzas, S., Gapizov, A., Shehryar, A., Affaf, M., Grezenko, H., Gasim, R. W., Mohsin, S. N., Rehman, A., & Rehman, S. (2023). The quantum-medical nexus: Understanding the impact of quantum technologies on healthcare. *Cureus, 15*(10), e48077. DOI: 10.7759/cureus.48077 PMID: 38046499

Shandilya, S., & Reddy, N. S. (2024). "AI-Enhanced Cloud Security Framework for IoT Networks Using a Predictive Analytics Approach," 2024 3rd International Conference for Advancement in Technology (ICONAT), Goa, India, 2024, pp. 1-8.

Shen, B., Xie, W., & Kong, Z. J. (2021). Clustered discriminant regression for high-dimensional data feature extraction and its applications in health care and additive manufacturing. *IEEE Transactions on Automation Science and Engineering*, *18*(4), 1998–2010. DOI: 10.1109/TASE.2020.3029028

Shi, W., & Dustdar, S. (2016). The promise of edge computing. *Computer*, *49*(5), 78–81. DOI: 10.1109/MC.2016.145

Shone, N., Ngoc, T. N., Phai, V. D., & Shi, Q. (2018). A deep learning approach to network intrusion detection. *IEEE Transactions on Emerging Topics in Computational Intelligence*, *2*(1), 41–50. DOI: 10.1109/TETCI.2017.2772792

Shreha, S. A., Ravikumar, R. N., & Aarthi, S. (2025). Neuro-symbolic AI and Behavioral Intelligence. In *Advances in Computational Intelligence and Robotics* (pp. 121–152). IGI Global Scientific Publishing. DOI: 10.4018/979-8-3373-5012-7.ch005

Sial, Q., Fateh, S., Jhanjhi, N. Z. A., & Laraib, A. (2024). Healthcare 4.0: Rural Health Issues and Challenges. In *Advances in Computational Intelligence for the Healthcare Industry 4.0* (pp. 248-263). IGI Global Scientific Publishing.

Sicari, S., Rizzardi, A., Grieco, L. A., & Coen-Porisini, A. (2015). Security, privacy and trust in Internet of Things: The road ahead. *Computer Networks*, *76*, 146–164. DOI: 10.1016/j.comnet.2014.11.008

Sierra-Sosa, D., Telahun, M., & Elmaghraby, A. (2020). TensorFlow quantum: Impacts of quantum state preparation on quantum machine learning performance. *IEEE Access : Practical Innovations, Open Solutions*, *8*, 215246–215255. DOI: 10.1109/ACCESS.2020.3040798

Singh, S., & Kumar, D. (2024). Enhancing cyber security using quantum computing and AI: A review. *algorithms, 4*(3).

Singh, R., & Gill, S. S. (2023). Edge AI: A survey. *Internet of Things and Cyber-Physical Systems*, *3*, 71–92. DOI: 10.1016/j.iotcps.2023.02.004

So-In, C. (2009). *A survey of network traffic monitoring and analysis tools. Cse 576m computer system analysis project*. Washington University in St. Louis.

Sommer, R., & Paxson, V. (2010). Outside the closed world: On using machine learning for network intrusion detection. In *Proceedings of the IEEE Symposium on Security and Privacy* (pp. 305–316). DOI: 10.1109/SP.2010.25

Sood, S. K. (2023). Quantum Computing Review: A Decade of Research. *IEEE Transactions on Engineering Management*.

Sorrentino, R., & López-Guzmán, J. (2025). Rethinking privacy for avatars: Biometric and inferred data in the metaverse. *Frontiers in Virtual Reality*, *6*, 1520655. DOI: 10.3389/frvir.2025.1520655

Sreerangapuri, A. (2024). Post-quantum cryptography for AI-driven cloud security solutions. *International Journal For Multidisciplinary Research*, *6*(5), 29032. Advance online publication. DOI: 10.36948/ijfmr.2024.v06i05.29032

Sun, Y. (2024). Securing the future: Shifting to Post-Quantum Cryptography amidst quantum threats. *Applied and Computational Engineering*, *110*(1), 154–160. DOI: 10.54254/2755-2721/110/2024MELB0120

Sun, Y., & Shao, Y. (2022). Research on data security communication scheme of heterogeneous swarm robotics system in emergency scenarios. *Sensors (Basel)*, *22*(16), 6082.

Sushmit, M. M., & Mahbubul, I. M. (2023). Forecasting solar irradiance with hybrid classical–quantum models: A comprehensive evaluation of deep learning and quantum-enhanced techniques. Energy Conversion and Management, 294, 117555.

Syed, M., & Garcia, P. (2023, October). A Hybrid Quantum-Classical Machine Learning Approach to Vision Sensor Data Analysis in Aerospace Applications. In *2023 IEEE/AIAA 42nd Digital Avionics Systems Conference (DASC)* (pp. 1-7). IEEE. DOI: 10.1109/DASC58513.2023.10311313

Tangalakis-Lippert, K. (2024, August 20). *Big Tech is starry-eyed over quantum computers, but scientists say major breakthroughs are years away*. Business Insider. https://www.businessinsider.com/scientists-say-major-quantum-computing-breakthroughs-are-years-away-2025-2

Termos, H. (2024). Quantum authentication evolution: Novel approaches for securing QKD. *Entropy (Basel, Switzerland)*, *26*(6), 447. DOI: 10.3390/e26060447 PMID: 38920455

Thalacker, C., Hahn, F., de Jong, J., Pappa, A., & Barz, S. (2021). Anonymous and secret communication in quantum networks. *New Journal of Physics*, *23*(8), 083026. DOI: 10.1088/1367-2630/ac1808

Thanalakshmi, P., Rishikhesh, A., Marion Marceline, J., Joshi, G. P., & Cho, W. (2023). A quantum-resistant blockchain system: A comparative analysis. *Mathematics*, *11*(18), 3947. DOI: 10.3390/math11183947

THOMAS, A., JOSH, A., GAUTHAM, V., FAIZ, M., & FAREED, M. Z. Quantum-Powered Deepfake Detection. https://www.researchgate.net/profile/Gautham-V-V/publication/390056776_Quantum-Powered_Deepfake_Detection/links/67dd80d5e62c604a0df8a5f1/Quantum-Powered-Deepfake-Detection.pdf?__cf_chl_f_tk=zTKP8VccG0l5jAF0E_YYrbjnf09H0aEndDJNFSTF_t4-1783364545-1.0.1.1-VTMrbg3eBOwkldFoTSRNaCNCllHlu3xGxWWrBBjNgkk

Tightiz, L., Dang, L. M., Padmanaban, S., & Hur, K. (2024). Metaverse-driven smart grid architecture. *Energy Reports*, *12*, 2014–2025. DOI: 10.1016/j.egyr.2024.08.027

Tuli, E. A., Lee, J. M., & Kim, D. S. (2024). Integration of quantum technologies into metaverse: Applications, potentials, and challenges. *IEEE Access : Practical Innovations, Open Solutions*, *12*, 29995–30019. DOI: 10.1109/ACCESS.2024.3366527

Tuli, E. A., Lee, J. M., & Kim, D. S. (2024). Leveraging quantum blockchain for secure multiparty space sharing and authentication on specialized metaverse platform. *Scientific Reports*, *14*(1), 25776. DOI: 10.1038/s41598-024-74213-x PMID: 39468089

Tychola, K. A., Kalampokas, T., & Papakostas, G. A. (2023). Quantum machine learning—An overview. *Electronics (Basel)*, *12*(11), 2379. DOI: 10.3390/electronics12112379

U.S. Department of Health and Human Services. (2013). *HIPAA Security Rule.*

Ullah, M. H., Eskandarpour, R., Zheng, H., & Khodaei, A. (2022). Quantum computing for smart grid applications. *IET Generation, Transmission & Distribution*, *16*(21), 4239–4257. DOI: 10.1049/gtd2.12602

University, M. babu, Prasad, J. L. Parvateesam, C., management, A. I. of technology and, Nagulmeera, S., University, M. babu, Avinash, V., & college, R. engineering. (. (2023). Enhancing IoT security: Addressing challenges, implementing solutions, and envisioning cybersecurity trends for the future. *International Journal of Engineering Applied Sciences and Technology*, *8*(6), 48–55. DOI: 10.33564/IJEAST.2023.v08i06.006

Uprety, S., Gkoumas, D., & Song, D. (2020). A survey of quantum theory inspired approaches to information retrieval. *ACM Computing Surveys*, *53*(5), 1–39. DOI: 10.1145/3402179

Vaidyan, V. M., & Rimal, B. P. (2023). Hybrid Quantum Artificial Intelligence Electromagnetic Spectrum Analysis Framework for Transportation System Security.

Vaishali, V. Raje, E. al. (. (2024). Realtime anomaly detection in Healthcare IoT: A machine learning-driven security framework. *Journal of Electrical Systems*, *19*(3), 192–202. DOI: 10.52783/jes.700

Vakali, A., & Pallis, G. (2003). Content delivery networks: Status and trends. *IEEE Internet Computing*, *7*(6), 68–74. DOI: 10.1109/MIC.2003.1250586

Valenta, L., Gonçalves, V., & Westerbaan, B. (2024, August 20). NIST's first post-quantum standards. Cloudflare. https://blog.cloudflare.com/nists-first-post-quantum-standards

Viriyasitavat, W., & Hoonsopon, D. (2019). Blockchain characteristics and consensus. *Journal of Industrial Information Integration*, *15*, 100–109.

Visoottiviseth, V., Chutaporn, G., Kungvanruttana, S., & Paisarnduangjan, J. (2020). "PITI: Protecting Internet of Things via Intrusion Detection System on Raspberry Pi," 2020 International Conference on Information and Communication Technology Convergence (ICTC), Jeju, Korea (South), 2020, pp. 75-80. DOI: 10.1109/ICTC49870.2020.9289311

Von Eicken, T., & Vogels, W. (2002). Evolution of the virtual interface architecture. *Computer*, *31*(11), 61–68. DOI: 10.1109/2.730738

Wang, S.. (2019). When edge meets learning: Adaptive control. *IEEE Communications Magazine*, *56*(8), 63–69.

Wang, Y., & Ismail, E. S. (2025). A Review on the Advances, Applications, and Future Prospects of PQC in Blockchain, IoT. *IEEE Access : Practical Innovations, Open Solutions*.

Wang, Z., Qing, S., Wan, X., Fan, Z., Xu, Y., & Duo, B. (2022). Secrecy rate maximization algorithm for IRS assisted NOMA-UAV networks. *IEEE Communications Letters*, *45*(3), 1–8.

Ware, B., & Mercy, R. (2025). *Cloud Computing 2025 and Beyond: Trends*. Obstacles, and New Possibilities.

Watabe, S., Serikow, M., Kawabata, S., & Zagoskin, A. (2021). Scaling Law in Large Quantum Devices with Dissipation. In *APS March Meeting Abstracts* (Vol. 2021, pp. A30-008).

Willsch, D., Willsch, M., Jin, F., De Raedt, H., & Michielsen, K. (2023). Large-scale simulation of Shor's quantum factoring algorithm. *Mathematics*, *11*(19), 4222. DOI: 10.3390/math11194222

Wood, G. (2014). *Ethereum: A secure decentralized generalized transaction ledger.*

Woollacott, E. (2025, July 31). *Nearly half of enterprises aren't prepared for quantum cybersecurity threats*. ITPro. www.itpro.com/security/nearly-half-of-enterprises-arent-prepared-for-quantum-cybersecurity-threats

Wu, T., Cui, C., Xian, X., Qiao, S., Wang, C., Yuan, L., & Yu, S. (2024). Explainable AI security: Exploring robustness of graph neural networks to adversarial attacks. *arXiv*. https://arxiv.org/abs/2406.13920

Xu, Q., Chen, D., Chen, J., Lyu, S., & Wang, C. (2025). Recent Advances on Generalizable Diffusion-generated Image Detection. *arXiv preprint arXiv:2502.19716.*

Xu, F., Ma, X., Zhang, Q., Lo, H.-K., & Pan, J.-W. (2020). Secure quantum key distribution with realistic devices. *Reviews of Modern Physics*, *92*(2), 025002. DOI: 10.1103/RevModPhys.92.025002

Xu, X.. (2019). A taxonomy of blockchain-based systems for architecture design. *ACM Computing Surveys*, *52*(5).

Yaga, D., Mell, P., Roby, N., & Scarfone, K. (2018). *Blockchain technology overview* (NIST Internal Report No. 8202). National Institute of Standards and Technology.

Yang, K., Zhang, Z., Youliang, T., & Ma, J. (2023). A secure authentication framework to guarantee the traceability of avatars in metaverse. *IEEE Transactions on Information Forensics and Security*, *18*, 3817–3832. DOI: 10.1109/TIFS.2023.3288689

Yang, Y., Wu, L., Yin, G., Li, L., & Zhao, H. (2017). A survey on security and privacy issues in IoT. *IEEE Internet of Things Journal*, *4*(5), 1250–1258. DOI: 10.1109/JIOT.2017.2694844

Yang, Z., Alfauri, H., Farkiani, B., Jain, R., Di Pietro, R., & Erbad, A. (2023). A survey and comparison of post-quantum and quantum blockchains. *IEEE Communications Surveys and Tutorials*, *26*(2), 967–1002. DOI: 10.1109/COMST.2023.3325761

Yordanov, Y. S., Arvidsson-Shukur, D. R., & Barnes, C. H. (2020). Efficient quantum circuits for quantum computational chemistry. *Physical Review. A*, *102*(6), 062612. DOI: 10.1103/PhysRevA.102.062612

Yuan, L., Wang, Z., Sun, L., Yu, P. S., & Brinton, C. G. (2024). Decentralized federated learning: A survey and perspective. *IEEE Internet of Things Journal*, *11*(21), 34617–34638. DOI: 10.1109/JIOT.2024.3407584

Yue, X., Wang, H., Jin, D., Li, M., & Jiang, W. (2016). Healthcare data gateways: Found healthcare intelligence on blockchain. *Journal of Medical Systems*, *40*(10), 218. DOI: 10.1007/s10916-016-0574-6 PMID: 27565509

Yusuff, M. Improving Scalability and Performance of AI Systems in High-Traffic Environments. Conţu, C. A., Popovici, E. C., Fratu, O., & Berceanu, M. G. (2016, June). Security issues in most popular content management systems. In *2016 International Conference on Communications (COMM)* (pp. 277-280). IEEE. Hardré, P. L. (2016). When, how, and why do we trust technology too much? In *Emotions, technology, and behaviors* (pp. 85-106). Academic Press.

Zakarneh, B., Annamalai, N., Alquqa, E. K., Mohamed, K. M., & Al Salhi, N. R. (2024). Virtual reality and alternate realities in Neal Stephenson's—Snow crash. *World Journal of English Language*, *14*(2), 244. DOI: 10.5430/wjel.v14n2p244

Zanella, A., Bui, N., Castellani, A., Vangelista, L., & Zorzi, M. (2014). Internet of Things for smart cities. *IEEE Internet of Things Journal*, *1*(1), 22–32. DOI: 10.1109/JIOT.2014.2306328

Zekri, M., El Kafhali, S., Aboutabit, N., & Saadi, Y. (2017, October). DDoS attack detection using machine learning techniques in cloud computing environments. In *2017, the 3rd International Conference of Cloud Computing Technologies and Applications (CloudTech)* (pp. 1-7). IEEE. DOI: 10.1109/CloudTech.2017.8284731

Zeydan, E., De Alwis, C., Khan, R., Turk, Y., Aydeger, A., Gadekallu, T. R., & Liyanage, M. (2025). Quantum technologies for beyond 5G and 6G networks: Applications, opportunities, and challenges. *arXiv preprint arXiv:2504.17133.*

Zhang, K., Mao, Y., Leng, S., Vinel, A., & Zhang, Y. (2017). Delay-constrained offloading for mobile edge computing. *IEEE Access : Practical Innovations, Open Solutions*, *5*, 20914–20928.

Zhang, R., Xue, R., & Liu, L. (2019). Security and privacy on blockchain. *ACM Computing Surveys*, *52*(3), 1–34. DOI: 10.1145/3316481

Zhao, Z., Huang, Y., Zhen, Z., & Li, Y. (2021). Data-driven false data injection attack design and detection in cyber-physical systems. *IEEE Transactions on Cybernetics*, *51*(12), 6179–6187. DOI: 10.1109/TCYB.2020.2969320 PMID: 32086230

Zheng, Z., Xie, S., Dai, H., Chen, X., & Wang, H. (2017). An overview of blockchain technology: Architecture, consensus, and future trends. In *Proceedings of the IEEE Big Data Congress* (pp. 557–564). DOI: 10.1109/BigDataCongress.2017.85

Zhong, H. S., Wang, H., Deng, Y. H., Chen, M. C., Peng, L. C., Luo, Y. H., Qin, J., Wu, D., Ding, X., Hu, Y., Hu, P., Yang, X.-Y., Zhang, W.-J., Li, H., Li, Y., Jiang, X., Gan, L., Yang, G., You, L., & Pan, J. W. (2020). Quantum computational advantage using photons. *Science*, *370*(6523), 1460–1463. DOI: 10.1126/science.abe8770 PMID: 33273064

Zhou, X., Shen, A., Hu, S., Ni, W., Wang, X., & Hossain, E. (2025). Towards quantum-native communication systems: State-of-the-art, trends, and challenges. *IEEE Communications Surveys and Tutorials*.

Zhou, Z.. (2019). Edge intelligence: Paving the last mile of AI with edge computing. *Proceedings of the IEEE*, *107*(8), 1738–1762. DOI: 10.1109/JPROC.2019.2918951

Zinner, M., Dahlhausen, F., Boehme, P., Ehlers, J., Bieske, L., & Fehring, L. (2021). Toward the institutionalization of quantum computing in pharmaceutical research. *Drug Discovery Today*, *27*(2), 378–383. DOI: 10.1016/j.drudis.2021.10.006 PMID: 34688911

Zyskind, G., Nathan, O., & Pentland, A. (2015). Decentralizing privacy using blockchain. In *Proceedings of the IEEE Security and Privacy Workshops* (pp. 180–184).

About the Contributors

Noor Zaman Jhanjhi is an internationally recognized academic, distinguished researcher, and visionary leader in Artificial Intelligence, Cybersecurity, and Digital Innovation. He serves as a Distinguished Professor of Computer Science (AI & Cybersecurity) at the School of Engineering and Technology (FET), Sunway University, Malaysia, and he has held prominent leadership roles as the Director of the Centre for Intelligent Innovation (CII) and Program Director for Postgraduate Research Degree Programmes, contributing significantly to research excellence and academic advancement. Globally acknowledged for his scholarly impact, Prof. Jhanjhi has been consistently ranked among the World's Top 2% Scientists for four consecutive years (2022–2025). He is also recognized as one of Malaysia's leading computer science researchers and was ranked among the top 0.05% of scholars worldwide in the 2025 ScholarGPS rankings. He has Hindices of 107 and 82 in GS and Scopus, respectively. His outstanding contributions have earned him several prestigious recognitions, including thc Outstanding Faculty Member Award by MDEC Malaysia (2022) and the Vice Chancellor's Best Research Citations Award from Taylor's University (2023). A prolific author and editor, he has published and edited more than 100 books with leading international publishers, including Springer, Elsevier, IET, Wiley, IGI Global, Bentham Sciences, CRC Taylor's, and Frances. Prof. Jhanjhi has successfully supervised 45 postgraduate graduates and examined more than 90 doctoral and master's theses worldwide. He serves as an Editor-in-Chief, Associate Editor, and Editorial Board Member for several prestigious journals, including PeerJ Computer Science, IEEE Access, and Computers, Materials & Continua (CMC), etc. In addition, he has secured over 40 international research grants, delivered more than 100 keynote and invited talks globally, and actively contributed to international accreditation and quality assurance bodies, including ABET, NCAAA, and NCEAC. Through his exceptional research achievements, academic leadership, and commitment to mentorship, Prof. Dr. Noor

Zaman Jhanjhi continues to make significant contributions to the advancement of Artificial Intelligence, Cybersecurity, and global higher education.

***

Azamat Abduraxmanov is a faculty member in the Department of Social Sciences Education at Termez University of Economics and Service, Termez, Uzbekistan. His academic interests include social sciences education, interdisciplinary pedagogy, and the application of contemporary teaching methodologies in higher education. He is actively involved in teaching and academic development activities, contributing to curriculum enhancement and the promotion of critical and analytical thinking among students.

Anorgul Ashirova is a faculty member in the Department of General Professional Sciences at Mamun University, Khiva, Uzbekistan. She is involved in teaching interdisciplinary and foundational courses that support the development of professional competencies across academic programs. Her academic interests include applied pedagogy, professional skills development, and learner-centered teaching approaches. She actively contributes to curriculum design and student mentoring, with an emphasis on integrating theoretical knowledge with practical application and fostering critical thinking and lifelong learning skills.

Humaira Ashraf Senior Lecturer I & Program Director, Master of Applied Computing (MAC, Conventional & ODL), Taylor's University, Malaysia. Dr. Humaira Ashraf is a distinguished academic with nearly 20 years of experience in higher education. Currently serving as a Senior Lecturer and Program Director for the Master of Applied Computing at Taylor's University, Malaysia, she specializes in computer science, data science, cybersecurity, and artificial intelligence. Dr. Humaira's career includes leadership roles as the Head of the Computer Science Department at both the International Islamic University in Islamabad and Sardar Bahadur Khan Women's University, Quetta, where she founded the Information Technology program. Her expertise extends to curriculum design, accreditation, and program development for undergraduate and postgraduate degrees. As a researcher, Dr. Humaira has led national and international research projects funded by prestigious organizations like NESCOM and Jeddah University. Her research interests include explainable AI, cybersecurity, big data, and machine learning. She has published widely in international journals and conferences, contributing significantly to the fields of network communication, information security, and data analytics. Throughout her career, Dr. Humaira has received numerous accolades, including the Teaching Excellence Award from the Ministry of Balochistan, and has supervised numerous PhD and MSc students. Her passion for education, innovation, and research makes her a valuable asset in academia and industry collaborations.

Ruzmetova Gulira'no Atabekovna holds a PhD in Economics and is an Associate Professor in the Department of Economics, Faculty of Economics, at Mamun University. Her academic and research interests focus on economic theory, applied economics, and quantitative economic analysis. She is actively engaged in teaching, research, and academic supervision, contributing to curriculum development and the advancement of evidence-based economic scholarship. Her work supports the application of economic insights to contemporary economic and social issues.

Kathirvel Ayyaswamy, acquired, B.E.(CSE), M.E. (CSE) from Crescent Engineering College affiliated to University of Madras and Ph. D (CSE.) from Anna University. He is currently working as Professor, Dept of Computer Science and Engineering, Saveetha Engineering College, Chennai. In-charge for CSE Cyber Forensics Research Group. He is a studious researcher by himself, completed 18 sponsored research projects worth of Rs 103 lakhs and published more than 110 articles in journals and conferences. 6 research scholars have completed Ph. D and 7 under progress under his guidance. He is working as scientific and editorial board member of many journals. He has reviewed dozens of papers in many journals. He has author of 13 books. His research interests are protocol development for wireless ad hoc networks, security in ad hoc network, data communication and networks, mobile computing, wireless networks, WSN and DTN. He is a Life member of the ISTE (India), IACSIT (Singapore), Life Member IAENG (Hong Kong), Member ICST (Europe), IAES, etc. He has given a number of guest lecturers/expert talks and seminars, workshops and symposiums.

Balakumar C. received his MCA from Kongu Engineering College, in 2013 & M. E(CSE) from Anna University, Chennai in 2015. He is pursuing the Ph.D degree at Dr. SNS Rajalakshmi College of Arts and Science (Autonomous) Coimbatore. He published more then 10 articles in PG level. His research interests include Vehicular Adhoc Networks, Network Security, Wireless Sensor Networks.

Praveenkumar G. D. is an Assistant Professor in the Department of Computer Technology (Undergraduate) at Kongu Engineering College, Perundurai, Erode. He is actively engaged in teaching, research, and academic development in the field of computer science and engineering. His areas of interest include programming, data structures, software development, and emerging technologies in computing. He is dedicated to fostering a strong foundation in technical knowledge among undergraduate students and encouraging practical, hands-on learning through projects and collaborative activities. He has contributed to academic initiatives by guiding student projects, supporting curriculum development, and promoting innovative teaching methodologies. His commitment to academic excellence is reflected in his efforts to integrate theoretical concepts with real-world applications. In addition to teaching, he shows interest in research and continuous professional development, aiming to contribute to advancements in computing and technology-driven solutions.

Dankan Gowda V is currently working as an Assistant Professor in the Department of Electronics and Communication Engineering at BMS Institute of Technology and Management in Bangalore. Previously, he worked as a Research Fellow at ADA DRDO and as a Software Engineer at Robert Bosch. With a total experience of 14 years, including teaching and industry, Dr. Gowda has made significant contributions to both academia and research. He has published over 120 research papers in renowned international journals and conferences. In recognition of his innovative work, Dr. Gowda has been granted six patents, including four from Indian authorities and two international patents. His research interests primarily lie in the fields of IoT and Signal Processing, where he has conducted workshops and handled industry projects. Dr. Gowda is passionate about teaching and strives to create an engaging and effective learning environment for his students. He consistently seeks opportunities to enhance his knowledge and stay updated with the latest advancements in his field.

Uswa Ihsan is currently pursuing a Ph.D. in Computer Science with a focus on Artificial Intelligence and Deep Learning at Taylor's University, Malaysia. She holds a master's degree in data science and has over five years of experience teaching at the university level. Her research interests span deep generative models, anomaly detection, and secure IoT systems. She has authored several publications in international journals and conferences on topics including text summarization, sentiment analysis, and steganography. In addition to her academic research, she is actively involved in delivering practical AI training and interdisciplinary workshops. She is presently serving as a visiting faculty member at the International Islamic University, Islamabad.

Mohammad Irfan is presently working as a Professor at the Faculty School of Business and Commerce, Chandigarh University, Lucknow, Unnao, India. Dr. Irfan has done his Ph.D. at the Central University of Haryana. He is MBA (Finance), M.Com (Account and Law), and MA (Economics). He has qualified UGC-JRF/SRF/NET in Management and Commerce. Dr. Irfan certified NSEs (NCFM) and BSEs certification. He has experience of more than sixteen years in the area of SAPM,

Artificial Intelligence, Machine Learning, Blockchain, Cryptocurrency, Financial Engineering, Fintech, Green Finance, and Alternative Finance. He has to his credit more than 101+ Scopus-indexed articles, including The Journal of Economic Cooperation and Development (Q2), International Journal of Business Excellence (IJBEX), International Journal of Economics and Management (IJEM), Montenegrin Journal of Economics (Q2), Cogent Business & Management (Taylor & Francis) (Q2), Indian Journal of Finance (IJF), and Journal of Islamic Monetary Economics and Finance (JIMF). His citations reached 702+ along with 14 H-index. Dr. Irfan has published 11 books in Springer, IGI Global Publication (Scopus indexed).

Rimsha Kanwal is a Computer Science researcher at Taylor's University, Malaysia. Her research focuses on deepfake detection, multimodal AI, and secure, privacy-preserving machine learning for digital media authentication.

Neha Kumari is associated with the Department of Electrical and Electronics Engineering at Amity University Rajasthan, Jaipur, India. She is involved in teaching, research, and academic development in the field of electrical and electronics engineering. Her areas of interest include power systems, smart grid technologies, renewable energy systems, embedded systems, and the application of intelligent technologies in modern electrical infrastructure. She actively contributes to curriculum development, research activities, and the supervision of undergraduate and postgraduate student projects. Through her academic and research work, she focuses on promoting innovative engineering solutions that support sustainable energy systems and address emerging technological challenges.

Javairia Malik is currently pursuing a Ph.D. in Computer Science at Taylor's University, Malaysia, with a research focus on secure communication, cryptography, and data privacy in next-generation technologies. She holds a Bachelor's degree in Computer Science from the Virtual University of Pakistan and a Master's degree in Computer Science from the International Islamic University, Islamabad. Her research interests span quantum computing, post-quantum cryptography, steganography, secure real-time communication, and privacy in the Metaverse. She is the author of the paper "An Efficient Steganographic Approach for Securing Text Transmission Using S-Box in Cloud", which demonstrates her contribution to developing innovative cryptographic and steganographic techniques for enhancing data security in cloud environments. Alongside her doctoral research, she is actively engaged in academic writing and interdisciplinary studies, exploring dynamic S-Box design, lattice-based post-quantum cryptography, and privacy-preserving frameworks for immersive technologies. She aims to contribute meaningfully to both academia and industry by proposing holistic, scalable, and quantum-resilient frameworks for future digital ecosystems.

Vettriselvan R., an Associate Professor at AMET University, specialises in HRM and Marketing. He is acting as a mentor at Saraswathi Institute of Medical Sciences, Hapur. He served as a Review Board member of the National Council for Higher Education, Malawi; Head of the Department of Commerce and Management Studies at St. Eugene University, Zambia; and Director of Research and Publication at St. John the Baptist University, Malawi. He has published 33 books and 100+ articles in peer-reviewed journals and edited book chapters. Under his guidance, five have completed and seven are pursuing their PhD.

Ravikumar R. N. is currently a Postdoctoral researcher at Universiti Malaysia Perlis, Malaysia. Also, working as an Assistant Professor in the Department of Computer Engineering at Marwadi University, Rajkot, Gujarat. He has 14 years of national and international teaching experience. He completed his PhD at Amity University, Rajasthan, M.E at VMRF Deemed University, B.E at Anna University, Chennai. He is the co-founder of the Research Activities Club at Marwadi University and trains students on research activities, which leads to the various publications. He has published numerous research articles in Scopus, SCI journals, Book chapters, and Conference papers. Also, he hold several patents and authored books. His specialization is ML, DL, Federated Learning, Recommendation Systems, and Optimization Techniques. Dr. Ravikumar has authored more than 8+ multiple SCIE/Scopus-indexed journal articles, 25+ IEEE/Springer conference papers, and co-authored a book on Artificial Intelligence. He has also published 9 patents and contributed 10+ book chapters in emerging domains such as Federated Learning, Blockchain, and Digital Twins for IGI Global, Wiley and Springer publisher. He actively mentors students through initiatives like the Research Activities Club (RAC) and Student Research Internship Training (SRIT), promoting innovation and research culture.

Aarthi S is a dedicated Assistant Professor in Computer Science with over six years of teaching experience. She is currently pursuing her Ph.D. at Marwadi University, Gujarat, and holds an M.Phil. and MCA from Bharathiar University, Tamil Nadu. Throughout her academic career, Aarthi has specialized in programming languages such as C++, Java, and C, and contributed to research in recommender systems and AI-related data privacy. She has published journal articles, contributed to book chapters, and actively participated in technical workshops. Known for her student mentorship and engagement in academic events, Aarthi remains committed to fostering innovation and excellence in computer science education.

Kavitha Bharathi S. is an Associate Professor in the Department of Computer Technology at Kongu Engineering College, Perundurai, Tamil Nadu, India. She possesses extensive academic and research experience in the field of computer science and engineering, with a strong focus on emerging technologies and their practical applications. Her teaching interests include data analytics, artificial intelligence, machine learning, and software engineering, where she is committed to fostering analytical thinking and innovation among students. Dr. Kavitha Bharathi has actively contributed to research through publications in reputed journals and conferences, addressing contemporary challenges in computing. She is also involved in guiding undergraduate and postgraduate projects, encouraging interdisciplinary approaches and real-world problem solving. In addition to her academic responsibilities, she participates in curriculum development, faculty development programs, and institutional initiatives aimed at enhancing the quality of technical education and research excellence.

Khayrulla Urozboev is a Chief Specialist in the Department of International Scientific Journals and Ratings at Alfraganus University, Tashkent, Uzbekistan. He plays a key role in enhancing the university's research visibility and global academic reputation through effective management of scientific publications and journal indexing processes. His work focuses on improving research quality, supporting faculty in publishing in high-impact international journals, and ensuring compliance with global indexing standards. Dr. Urozboev is actively involved in academic coordination, research evaluation, and the promotion of international collaborations. His expertise includes journal ranking systems, bibliometric analysis, and research performance assessment. He contributes to strengthening institutional research frameworks by guiding scholars on publication strategies and ethical research practices. Committed to academic excellence, he supports initiatives that enhance the global presence and impact of scientific research emerging from the university.

Tusonov Xurshid is a faculty member in the Department of Accounting and Statistics at Termez University of Economics and Service, Termez, Uzbekistan. He is engaged in teaching and academic work in the areas of financial accounting, managerial accounting, and applied statistics. His research interests include quantitative methods in economic analysis, financial data modeling, and evidence-based decision-making. He contributes to curriculum development and student mentoring, with a focus on strengthening analytical skills, statistical literacy, and the practical application of accounting principles in academic and professional contexts.

Index

E

F

I

L

M

N

O

P

Q

R

S

T

www.ingramcontent.com/pod-product-compliance
Lightning Source LLC
LaVergne TN
LVHW062323300926
849161LV00007B/1549